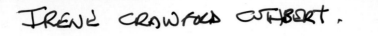
IRENE CRAWFORD CUTHBERT.

GREENWOOD
G U I D E S

First published in 2000 by Greenwood Guides,
12 Avalon Rd, London SW6 2EX, UK.

Eleventh edition

Copyright (c) June 2012 Greenwood Guides Ltd

Simon Greenwood has asserted his right to be identified as the author of this work.

ISBN 978-0-9551160-2-5

Printed in China through Colorcraft Ltd., Hong Kong.

THE GREENWOOD GUIDE TO
SOUTH AFRICA
hand-picked accommodation

Including Swaziland, Lesotho and Tuli in Botswana

eleventh edition

www.greenwoodguides.com

Acknowledgements

Series Editor: Simon Greenwood

Writing collaboration and inspections: Victoria Young, Roxanne Lautenbach, Mike Munro.
Map data provided by Collins Bartholomew Ltd.

Production, DTP and Design: Tory Gordon-Harris and Jo Ekin

Printing: through Colorcraft Ltd, Hong Kong

UK Distribution: Quiller Publishing Ltd

Front cover main photo courtesy Woodbury Lodge (entry 173).
Front cover bottom photos from left to right courtesy Kersefontein (entry 43), Plumtree Cottage (entry 78), The Bush House (entry 249), Enjo Nature Farm (entry 55) and Kersefontein (entry 43).
Back cover photos left to right: Boesmanskop (entry 152), Vrede Manor (entry 31) and Red Stone Hills (entry 153).

Cover design and digital manipulation by Tory Gordon-Harris.

Title page image: Boesmanskop, entry number 152

Province intro images: Botswana, Eastern Cape, Gauteng, KwaZulu Natal, Mpumalanga, Northern Cape, Soweto, Swaziland and Western Cape by Ollie Smallwood; Limpopo, Northwest Province and Free State by Roxanne Lautenbach.

The Team

Simon Greenwood

Mike Munro

Victoria Young

Roxanne Lautenbach

Contents

Introduction

Maps

WESTERN CAPE

Cape Town	1-41
West Coast	42-48
Cederberg	49-55
Cape Winelands	56-91
Overberg	92-112
Garden Route	113-147
Klein Karoo	148-157
Karoo	158-162

EASTERN CAPE — 163-187

KWAZULU NATAL — 188-228

FREE STATE — 229-232

LESOTHO — 233

NORTHERN CAPE — 234-241

GAUTENG — 242-244
Soweto — 245-247

NORTH-WEST PROVINCE — 248-250

MPUMALANGA — 251-262

SWAZILAND — 263

LIMPOPO — 264-267

TULI (BOTSWANA) — 268

Indexes by Town Name, House Name
and by Activities

Symbols
and what they mean

No credit cards accepted.

Meals can be provided, often by prior arrangement.

Rooms all have TVs.

Wild game can be seen.

Wireless Internet access.

Children are welcome without proviso.

Working farm.

Off-street car parking.

Access only for wheelchairs.

Full wheelchair facilities.

Swimming available in pool, sea, dam or river.

No smoking inside the buildings.

Good hiking or walking direct from the house.

Introduction

Welcome to the Greenwood Guide to South Africa, edition 11!

This edition represents business as usual for GG with some inspiring new places to sample. The overall standard just gets higher each year. I hope that you have a fantastic holiday and that you find the Greenwood Guide an indispensable and trustworthy help in finding wonderful places to stay.

The GG Approach

I receive a great deal of mail from travellers, which I encourage. It gives us a good idea of how our choices are being received out there in the field. And since we live or die on the happiometer of our travellers, i.e. you, then this information is vital. Our aim is to choose places that more-than-just pass muster. We will always be judged by the worst, not the best, of our choices. Which is right and meet.

We have made genuine human hospitality our common denominator rather than the sterile but safe judgement of a place's worth according to its facilities. We do not therefore distribute stars or tiaras. A place is either right for the guide or it isn't. Beyond that each traveller will need to look at location, rates and exactly what sort of place it is and make their own decisions.

First and foremost we assess the people running the accommodation and choose only those for whom looking after others, whether they be friends, family or paying guests, is a natural pleasure. Taste, furnishings, facilities, views, food, beds, bathrooms… all these things are important too, but only if they are provided by friendly, caring hosts.

Thank you for choosing our guide. We do put in an enormous amount of effort each year, revisiting each place each edition, weeding out places that have lost their energy - as often happens in the world of accommodation - and sounding out all the new great, good and ordinary places that open each year. The standard rises continually in South Africa and this does mean that new places emerge at the top and old places drop off the bottom too. We seriously recommend therefore that you make sure that this is a latest edition of the guide. It is published annually in June.

As I always say, we would be delighted to hear from you when you get back from your travels. One request though: emails (to simon@ greenwoodguides.com) are definitely preferable to letters or faxes.

The GG Website

www.greenwoodguides.com

Much is happening on our website these days. It is well worth a visit, even if you prefer having the book in hand for convenience when actually on the road.

MAPS

We should have transferred to Google maps by the time we go to print so you can pinpoint exactly the location of each place to stay.

CURRENT SPECIAL OFFERS

We now publish a monthly list of specials being offered by GG places. These change every month and are grouped by geographical area or by theme (places that specialise in cooking, or rock art, or self-catering, or being child-friendly etc). Go to the website and click on the 'SA specials' button and you will be able to take advantage if you happen to be booking your trip and your itinerary coincides with what's being offered.

BLOG OF UPCOMING EVENTS

We have a continually updating and highly eclectic blog of upcoming events written by Mark Bland, called An Ear to the Rail. Here are some wildly different recent items so you have an idea of what it's all about:
* A steam train ride.
* A tour of the under-city tunnels in Cape Town.
* A rickshaw ride round Durban
* The Darling Music Experience.
* A re-enactment of the Battle of Isandlwana.
* The Clarens beer fest.
* The Outeniqua farmers' market.
* The rugby world sevens tournament.
* The Ficksburg cherry fest.
* The Tokai Forest 15km fun run.
* Apricot picking at De Krans
Etc etc. Check out An Ear to the Rail at www.greenwoodguides.com.

RESTAURANT OF THE MONTH

Mark (who is a budding chef himself) also picks one or two restaurants each month that he is particularly keen on.

Some info on travelling with this book in South Africa

ARRIVAL

Make sure that you have two clear pages left in your passport. I am told that they are very strict about this and it would be a crazy way to be refused entry.

DRIVING
There is nowhere in South Africa that would make a 4-wheel drive a necessity.

CAR HIRE
Make sure that you have considered the amount of daily mileage your car hire company gives you. 100km or even 200km a day is virtually nothing and the final cost can be far higher than you estimated. Try and work out roughly what distances you will be covering and ask for the correct daily allowance. Or ask for unlimited mileage. There is usually a surcharge for taking your car across the border from SA into other countries.
N.B. Also make sure you are insured to drive the car on dirt roads.

We highly recommend Comet Car Rental, owned and run by Dave Halley and Cathy Heyburgh, on 021-386-2411 or info@cometcar.co.za. They are very friendly and helpful and we use them ourselves. Airport pick-ups and drop-offs are no problem. They have offices in Cape Town, Johannesburg, Durban and Port Elizabeth and are small enough to offer a friendly and efficient service where you are not just an unknown number. Dave and Cathy are also very experienced with over 20 years in the car rental industry and offer a professional service with no hidden costs like most of their larger competitors.

Also they are offering all GG travellers a discount of 10% on their car hire. Just mention that you are travelling with the Greenwood Guide if you decide to use Comet.

MOBILE/CELL PHONES
Airports all have shops that provide mobile phones. They are invaluable and we recommend that you get one. You can buy a cheap handset or just rent one for the duration of your stay and then pay for calls as you go with recharge cards.

TELEPHONE NUMBERS
The numbers printed for entries in SA in the book are all from within South Africa. To call South Africa from the UK dial 0027 then drop the 0 from the local code. To call the UK from South Africa you now dial 0044 - it used to be 0944 but this changed recently.
Another change is when dialling a local number you now always have to dial the full number including the area code.

TORTOISES
Look out for tortoises. They are slow, but seem to spend a lot of time, completely against the tide of advice put forward for their benefit, crossing roads.

TIPS on TIPPING
• In restaurants we tend to give 15%.
• At a petrol station my policy is to give no tip for just filling up, 3 rand for cleaning the windows, and 5 rand for cleaning the windows and checking oil and water. If you really don't want the attendant to clean your windows you need to make this a statement when you ask for the petrol… or they will often do it anyway.

• At a guest-house I would typically give R30 per person staying for up to two nights. If you are staying longer than two nights then you might feel like adding more. If there is obviously one maid to whom the tip will go then give it to her direct. If there are many staff members who will be sharing the tip then give it to your host.

* Tipping game rangers at game lodges: often these highly-qualified people are the main reason why you have such a great stay at a particular lodge. I suggest around R100 per guest per day depending on the quality of service you receive.

THE GARDEN ROUTE

Many people imagine, not unreasonably, that the Garden Route is a bit like a wine route where you can go from garden to garden, smelling roses and admiring pergolas and rockeries. Not so. The Garden Route is so named for its lushness and greenery. The area is covered in forests and rivers, which spill into the sea. And, although many people there surely do have lovely gardens, the name is a little misleading. A fantastic area for walking though.

TIME OF YEAR

I got in a bit of a tangle in the first edition trying neatly to package up what is really quite complicated. So I will limit myself to one observation. It seems to me that most Europeans come to South Africa in January, February and March to avoid their own miserable weather and write taunting postcards home from a sunny Cape.

However, the very best time of year to visit the Northern Cape, Mpumalanga, Limpopo, North West Province, KwaZulu Natal and the Karoo, i.e. the whole country except the southern Cape, is from May to October. The air is dry and warm, game viewing is at its best and there are fewer tourists keeping the prices higher.

PAY FOR ENTRY

We could not afford to research and publish this guide in the way we do without the financial support of those we feature. Each place that we have chosen has paid an entry fee for which we make no apology. It has not influenced our decision-making about who is right or wrong for the guide and we turn down many more than we accept. The proof of this is in the proverbial pudding. Use the book and see for yourself. It is also impossible for us to write up a place that we are not enthusiastic about.

THE MAPS SECTION

The maps at the front of the book are designed to show you where in the country each place is positioned and should not be used as a road map. There are many minor and dirt roads missing and we recommend that you buy a proper companion road atlas. Each place is flagged with a number that corresponds to the entry number below each entry.

Some have complained that it is hard to find detailed road maps of South Africa in the UK, so I suggest you buy one at the airport when you arrive in SA. Or try Stanfords in London on Long Acre in Covent Garden, 020-7836-1321.

CANCELLATION
Most places have some form of cancellation charge. Do make sure that you are aware what this is if you book in advance. Owners need to protect themselves against no-shows and will often demand a deposit for advance booking.

PRICES
The prices quoted are per person sharing per night, unless specifically stated otherwise. Every now and then complications have meant we quote the full room rate. Single rates are also given.

We have usually put in a range within which the actual price will fall. This may be because of fluctuating prices at different times of year, but also we have tried to predict the anticipated rise in prices over the book's shelf life. Obviously we cannot know what will happen to the value of the rand and prices might fall outside the quoted range.

Most game lodges quote an all-in package including meals and game activities.

Although South Africa has become substantially more expensive since the first edition of this guide came out 11 years ago, it is still great value on the whole. The value-for-money increases significantly the more off-the-beaten-track you wander.

CHILDREN
We have only given the child-friendly symbol to those places that are unconditionally accepting of the little fellows. This does not necessarily mean that if there is no symbol children are barred. But it may mean chatting with your hosts about their ages, their temperaments and how suitable a time and place it will be. Most owners are concerned about how their other guests will take to kids running wild when they are trying to relax on a long-anticipated holiday... from their own children. Places that are fully child-friendly are listed in the activities index at the back of the book.

DISCLAIMER
We make no claims to god-like objectivity in assessing what is or is not special about the places we feature. They are there because we like them. Our opinions and tastes are mortal and ours alone. We have done our utmost to get the facts right, but apologize for any mistakes that may have slipped through the net. Some things change which are outside our control: people sell up, prices increase, exchange rates fluctuate, unfortunate extensions are added, marriages break up and even acts of God can rain down destruction. We would be grateful to be told about any errors or changes, however great or small. We can make these edits at any time on the web version of this book.

DON'T TRY AND DO TOO MUCH. PLEASE.
It is the most common way to spoil your own holiday. South Africa is a huge country and you cannot expect to see too much of it on one trip. Don't over-extend yourself. Stay everywhere for at least two nights and make sure that you aren't spending your hard-earned holiday fiddling with the radio and admiring the dashboard of your hire car.

PLEASE WRITE TO US

My email address is simon@greenwoodguides.com for all comments. Although we visit each place each edition many of the places featured here are small, personal and owner-run. This means that their enjoyability depends largely on the happiness, health and energy of the hosts. This can evaporate in double-quick time for any number of reasons and standards plummet before we have had a chance to re-evaluate the place. So we are also very grateful to travellers who keep us up to date with how things are going. We are always most concerned to hear that the hosting has been inattentive.

THANKS

So that's about it for another year. My great thanks this year go to Victoria (Young) and Roxanne (Lautenbach) for all their efforts in researching and updating this 11th edition of the guide. Also my thanks to Emily Bate who stepped in to help out with a couple of late applicants in KwaZulu Natal. And to Mike Munro who wears so many hats in the GG colours. And to Mark Bland for his excellent work on the blogs. And finally to Richard Albion who works tirelessly on the website and all other matters technical that keep the good ship GG under sail!

I hope that this book will be seen as the main reason why you enjoyed your holiday as much as you did. Please feel free to write to me with praise or criticism for individual places that you visit at simon@greenwoodguides.com. And, once again, it really is worth having a look at www.greenwoodguides. com before you set off. Have a fantastic trip whether it is a major 4-week extravaganza or just a weekend break.

Simon.

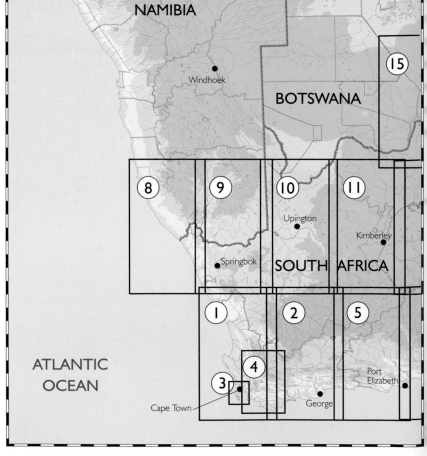

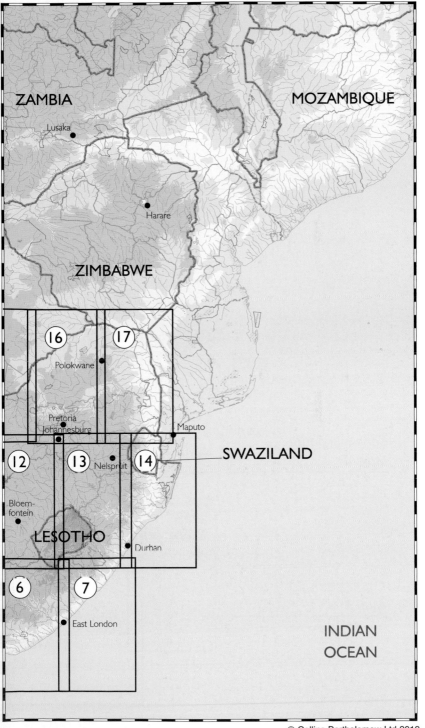

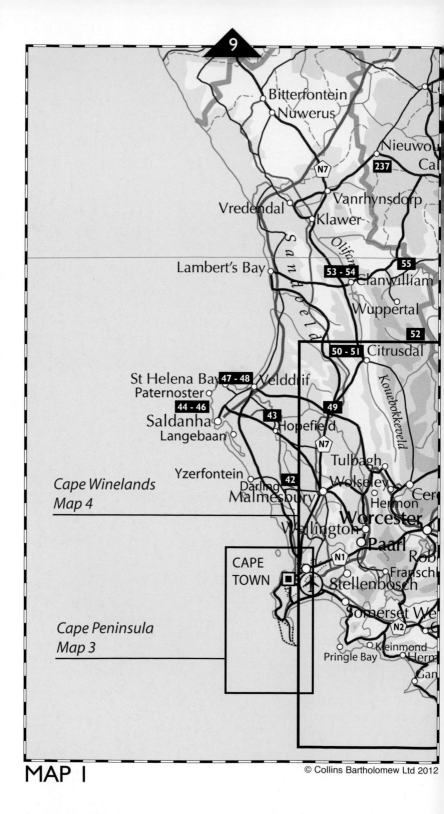

9

Bitterfontein
Nuwerus

Nieuwou
237   Ca

N7

Vredendal   Vanrhynsdorp
              Klawer

Lambert's Bay   53 - 54   55
                          Clanwilliam

                          Wuppertal

                          52

                    50 - 51   Citrusdal

St Helena Bay   47 - 48   Velddrif
Paternoster
              44 - 46   43
Saldanha   49
Langebaan   Hopefield
                          N7
                          Tulbagh

Yzerfontein   Wolseley
Cape Winelands   42   Cer
Map 4   Darling   Hermon
          Malmesbury
                          Worcester
              Wellington
                          Paarl   Rob
CAPE   Fransch
TOWN   N1
              Stellenbosch

                          Somerset We
Cape Peninsula   N2
Map 3
                    Kleinmond
              Pringle Bay   Herm
                          Gan

MAP I   © Collins Bartholomew Ltd 2012

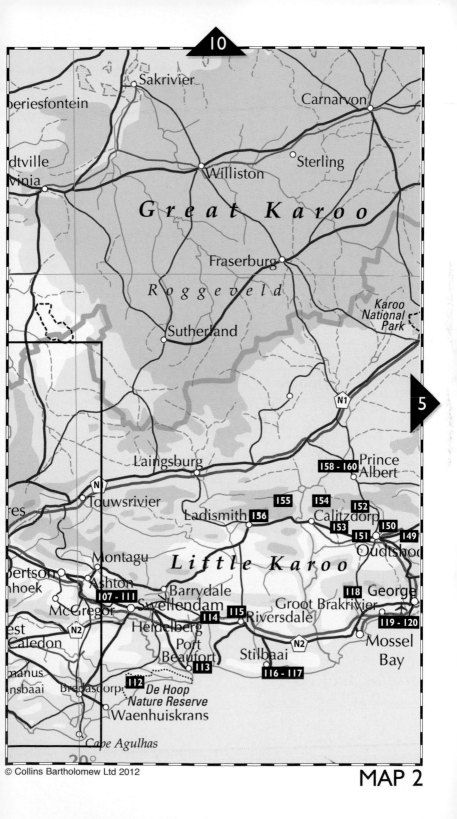

5

Sakrivier

Carnarvon

beriesfontein

Sterling

dtville
vinia

Williston

G r e a t   K a r o o

Fraserburg

R o g g e v e l d

Karoo
National
Park

Sutherland

Laingsburg

Prince
Albert

158 - 160

N

155

154

Touwsrivier

Ladismith 156

152

res

153

150

151

149

Montagu

L i t t l e   K a r o o

Oudtsho

bertson
hoek

Ashton

Barrydale

118 George

107 - 111

Swellendam

Groot Brakrivier

McGregor

114

115

Riversdale

119 - 120

Heidelberg

est
Caledon

N2

Port
Beaufort

Stilbaai

N2

Mossel
Bay

manus
nsbaai

Bredasdorp

113

116 - 117

112

De Hoop
Nature Reserve
Waenhuiskrans

Cape Agulhas

20°

MAP 2

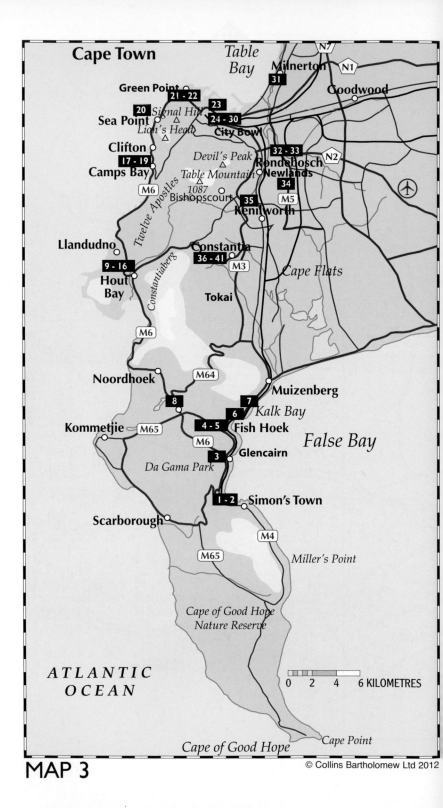

MAP 3

© Collins Bartholomew Ltd 2012

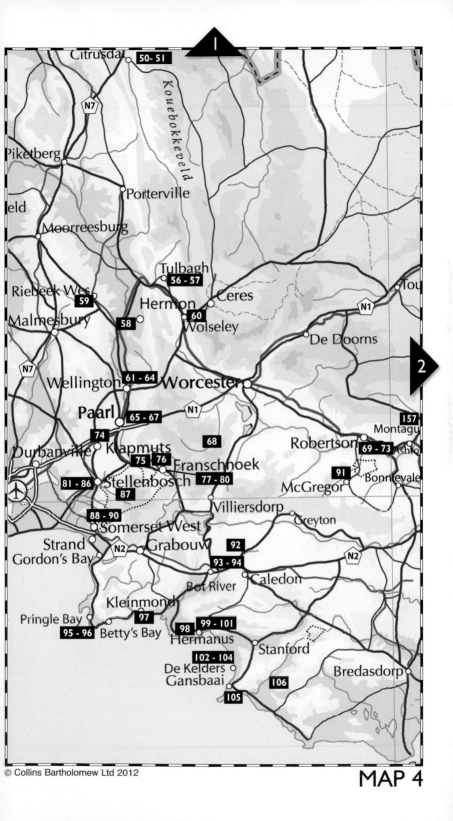

MAP 4

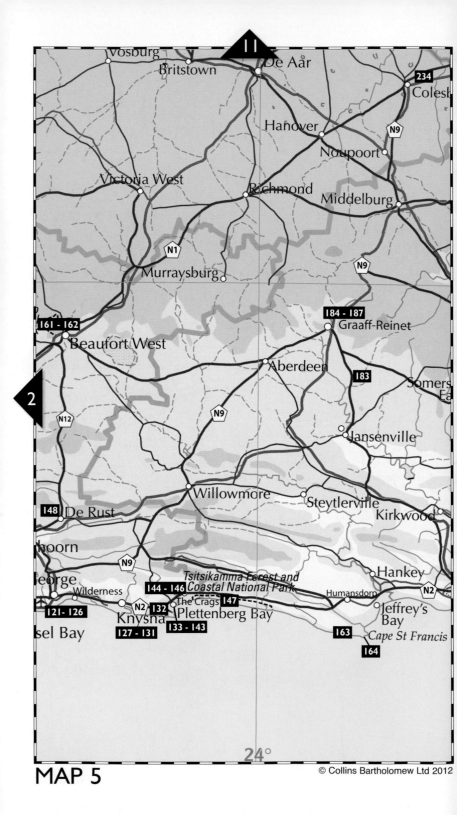

MAP 5

© Collins Bartholomew Ltd 2012

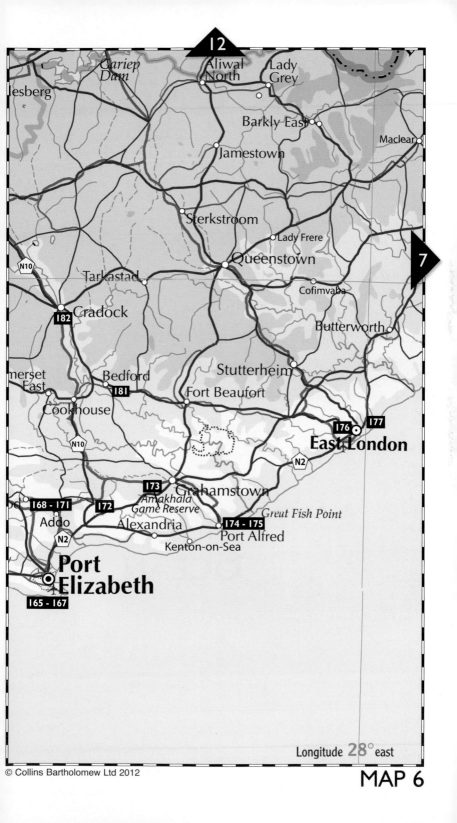

MAP 6

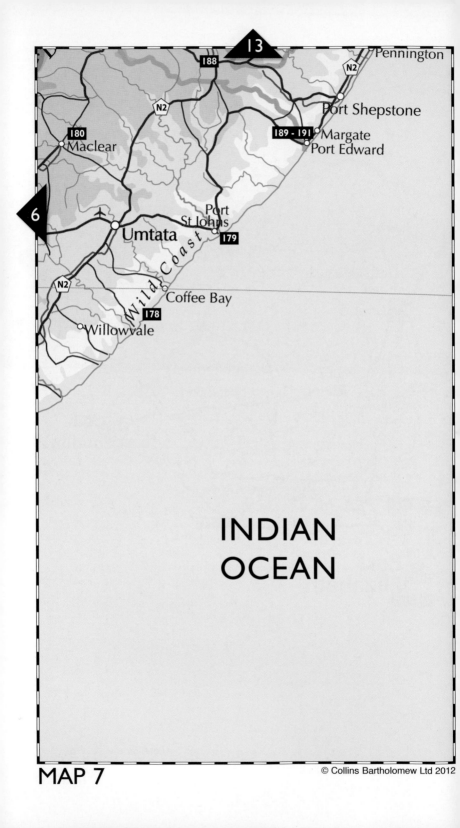

INDIAN
OCEAN

MAP 7

© Collins Bartholomew Ltd 2012

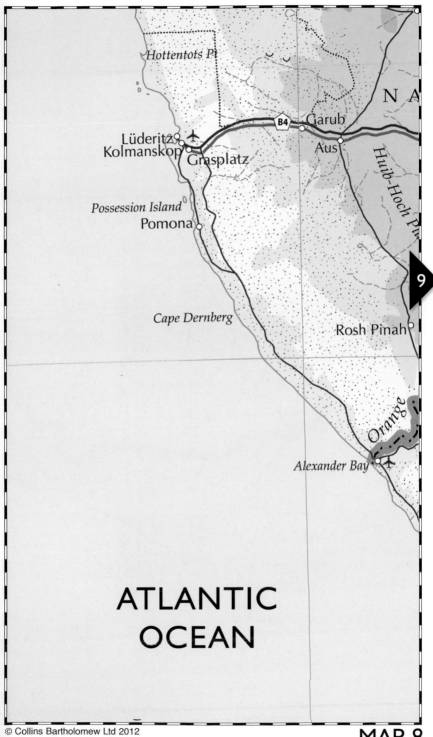

Hottentots Pt

N A

Lüderitz
Kolmanskop
Grasplatz
B4 Garub
Aus
Huib-Hoch Pl

Possession Island
Pomona

9

Cape Dernberg

Rosh Pinah

Orange

Alexander Bay

ATLANTIC
OCEAN

MAP 8

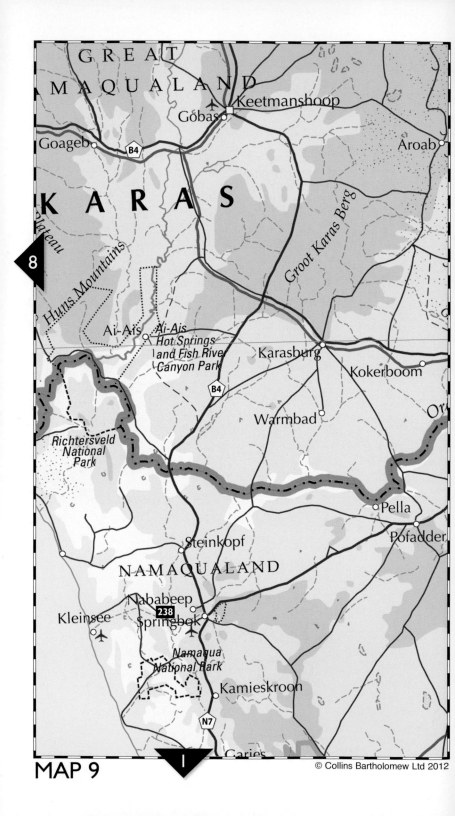

GREAT

MAQUALAND

Keetmanshoop

Gobas

Goageb

B4

8

KARAS

Groot Karas Berg

Huns Mountains

Aroab

Plateau

Ai-Ais

Ai-Ais
Hot Springs
and Fish River
Canyon Park

Karasburg

Kokerboom

B4

Warmbad

Or

Richtersveld
National
Park

Pella

Pofadder

Steinkopf

NAMAQUALAND

Nababeep

238

Springbok

Kleinsee

Namaqua
National Park

Kamieskroon

N7

1

Caries

MAP 9

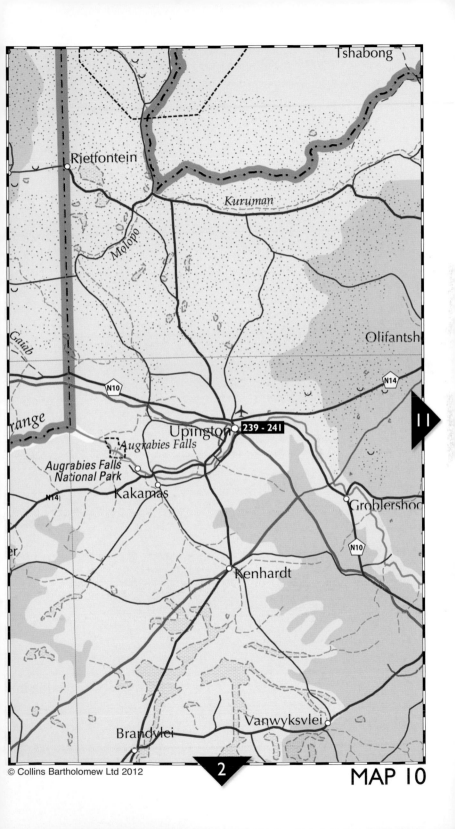

Tshabong

Rietfontein

Kuruman

Molopo

Olifantsh

Gatab

N10

N14

range

Upington 239 - 241

Augrabies Falls

Augrabies Falls
National Park

Kakamas

Groblershoo

N14

N10

Kenhardt

Vanwyksvlei

Brandvlei

1

2

© Collins Bartholomew Ltd 2012

MAP 10

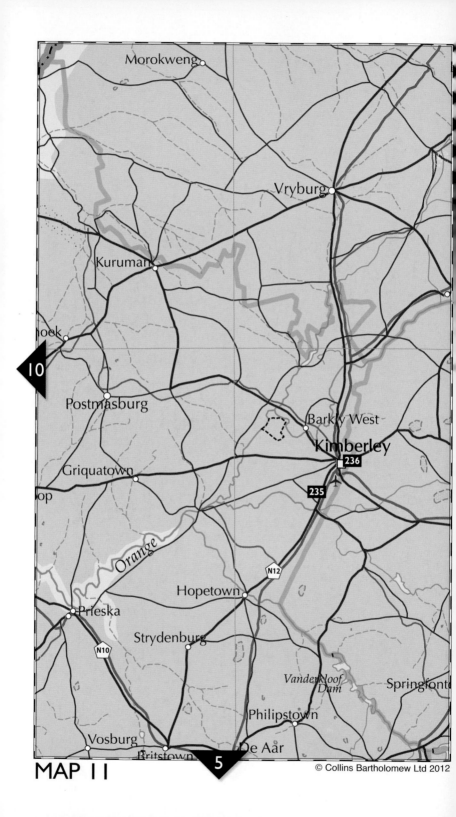

MAP 11

© Collins Bartholomew Ltd 2012

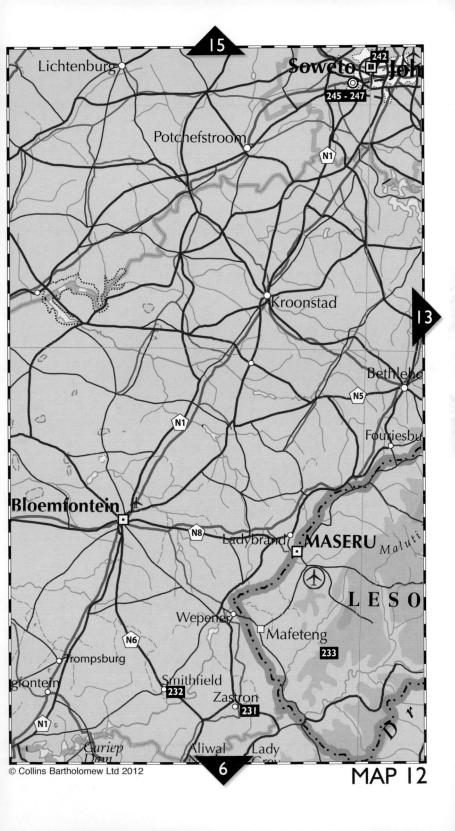

MAP 13

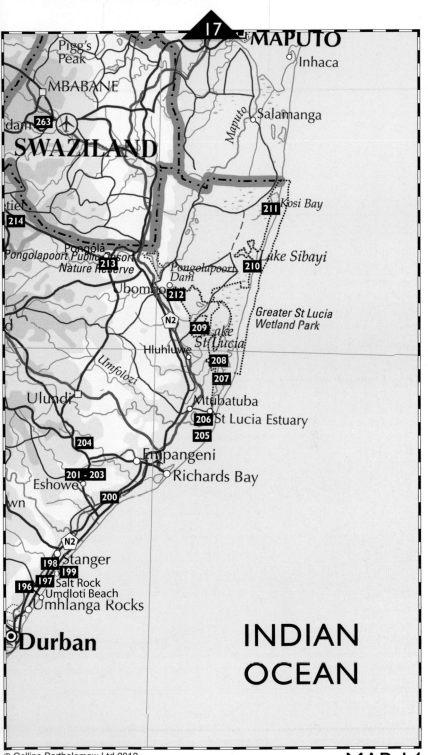

MAPUTO

Inhaca

Pigg's
Peak

MBABANE

Maputo

Salamanga

263

SWAZILAND

Kosi Bay

211

tier

214

Lake Sibayi

210

Pongola
Pongolapoort Public Resort
Nature Reserve

213

Pongolapoort
Dam

Ubombo

212

N2

209

Greater St Lucia
Wetland Park

Lake
St Lucia

Hluhluwe

208

207

Umfolozi

Ulundi

Mtubatuba

206 St Lucia Estuary

205

204

Empangeni

201 - 203

Richards Bay

Eshowe

200

wn

N2

198 Stanger

199

197 Salt Rock

196

Umdloti Beach

Umhlanga Rocks

Durban

INDIAN

OCEAN

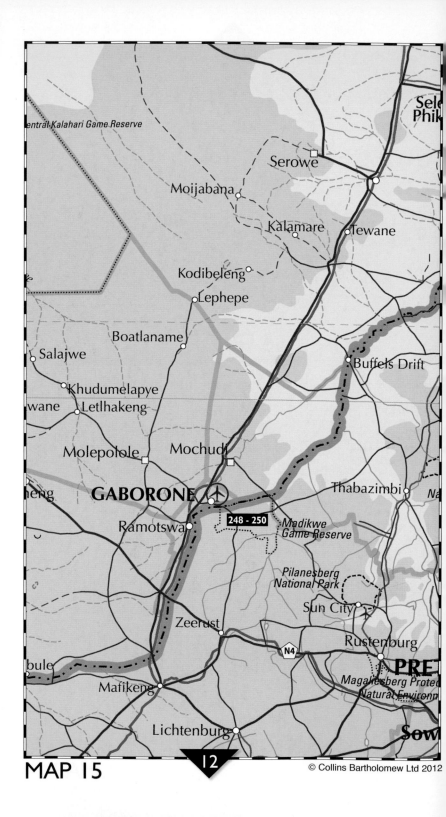

Central-Kalahari Game Reserve

Sele
Phik

Serowe

Moijabana

Kalamare
Tewane

Kodibeleng

Lephepe

Boatlaname

Salajwe
Buffels Drift

Khudumelapye
wane Letlhakeng

Molepolole
Mochudi

heng
GABORONE
Thabazimbi
Na

Ramotswa
248 - 250
Madikwe
Game Reserve

Pilanesberg
National Park

Sun City

Zeerust
Rustenburg

N4

bule
PRE

Mafikeng
Magaliesberg Protec
Natural Environn

Lichtenburg
Sow

MAP 15

12

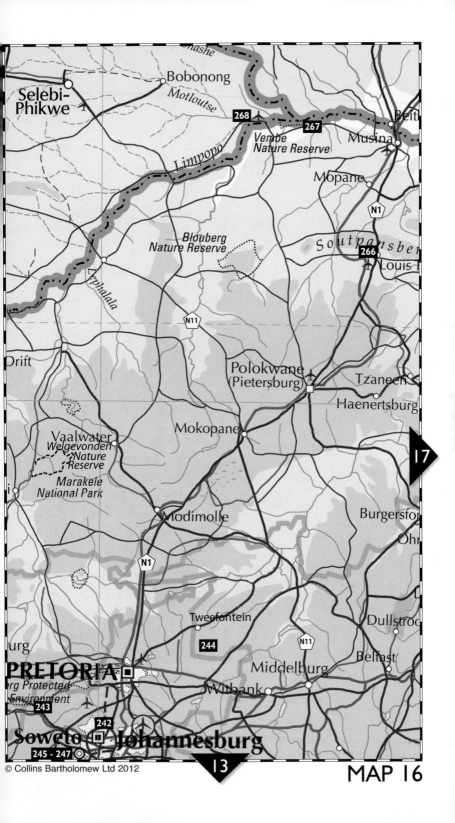

MAP 16

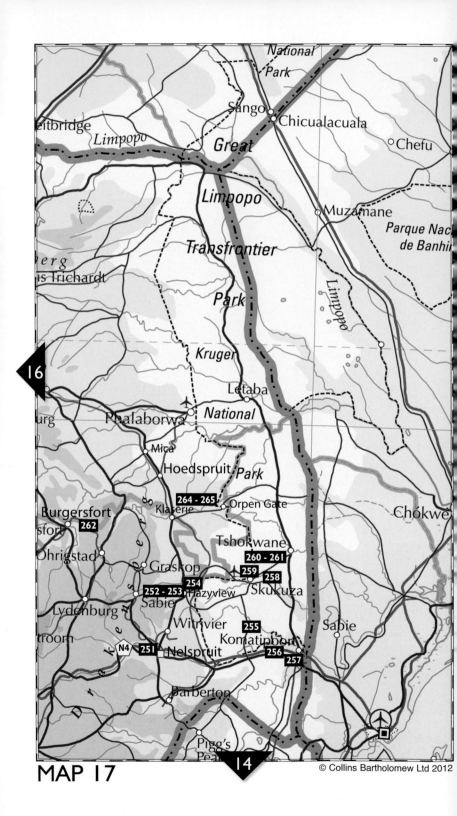

MAP 17

© Collins Bartholomew Ltd 2012

Western Cape

Albatross House

Leon and Sandy Strydom
37 Victory Way, Simon's Kloof, Simon's Town
Tel: 021-786-5906 Fax: 021-786-4297
Email: albatrosshouse@lantic.net Web: www.albatrosshouse.co.za
Cell: 082-363-6449

You can see the sea from every room in Albatross House. Despite this, you'll probably want to spend most of your time outside on the terraces overlooking the whole of False Bay and keeping an eye on the movement of the navy ships below. The terraces, dotted with deep wooden chairs, are the perfect spot for sundowners. Inside, décor is fresh and summery throughout with wooden panelling in the bathrooms that lends them a boathouse feel. With private sitting rooms and connectable terraces (lightly screened off if privacy is preferred) this is a perfect place to come with friends. Indeed I was quite envious of three English ladies who, as Sandy explained, had been chatting, laughing and playing (three-handed) bridge on the balcony into the early hours. A highlight of any stay is, of course, to indulge in Sandy's breakfasts out on the balcony or in the dining room if the weather insists. Each breakfast is tailored to your wishes, from a personal fruit platter and cereals to a hot breakfast of your choice. While Sandy is in the kitchen, Leon chats to guests and gives them tips on making their day more productive and enjoyable. As a member of a weekly hiking group, Leon knows the hiking trails, birds, fauna and flora well and can give good tips on where to go, during what times of year and weather. There are stunning jaunts just minutes from the house. If you'd rather soak up some history in Simon's Town take the path below the house, specially constructed by Leon and Sandy, through the fynbos and down into the village and beyond. *www.Facebook.com/Albatrosshouse*.

Rooms: 4: 1 king en-s bath; 1 queen en-s bath & sh'r, plus option of honeymoon suite; 2 twin/dbles en-s sh'r. Self-catering apartment, separate entrance, 2 sea-facing bedrooms, sitting room, full kitchen, covered balcony for 4 adults. Sleepercouch in lounge for 2 kids.
Price: B&B R440 - R650 pp sharing. Room only (i.e. no breakfast) or self-catering R380 - R575 pp sh.
Meals: Full breakfast included with B&B. Or you can choose room only or self-catering.
Directions: From Simon's Town station on L go past Admiralty House on L. Move to R lane. Turn R then immediately L up Soldiers Way. R into Arsenal, L into Cornwall. Cornwall becomes Runciman. Continue past 3-way stop, R into Simon's Kloof & follow signs.

Map Number: 3

Fort Vic

Lance Tooke
14 Victory Way, Simon's Town
Tel: 072-470-1638 UK: +44 (0)7986-557652
Email: simonstown@btinternet.com Web: www.simonstown.net

I didn't get the pleasure of meeting Lance who's based in London, but his friendly voice beaming down the phone was a reassuring start. And sure enough Fort Vic in Simon's Town, his second home, did not disappoint. The house is entirely made of wood and stone dug from the mountain it sits upon. Inside is a forest of dense wood beams, bamboo ceilings, red stone walls and open-plan wooden staircases making it feel a bit like a bush lodge. The real drawcard here, however, is the view. You don't - can't! - get much more of a sea view than this and the best place to absorb it from is the huge master bedroom upstairs, although big sliding glass doors run throughout the house. Actually there are many places to enjoy the view from: the plunge pool, the sitting room or the smart kitchen lined with yellowwood cupboards and fitted with a central island, complete with gas cooker and fancy oven. The motto here is keep it simple with cream sheets, stylish free-standing showers and soft natural furnishings like basket lamps, wicker chairs and red cushions. The black cloth hanging in the kitchen covered in badges from all over the world is testament to Lance's travelling days prior to finding his favourite destination, Fort Vic. Although this is definitely a self-catering arrangement, the house manager is available at all times to troubleshoot any problems, arrange trips or make bookings. *Whales can be viewed (July - October) from the master bedroom and the pool.*

Rooms: 1 self-catering house, 1 double room with victorian bath and shower in the room, 2 twins with showers in the rooms. Full kitchen and lounge area.
Price: R1,400 - R3,000 per day for the house, depending on season. Discounts of up to 50% for long stays.
Meals: Self-catering.
Directions: Detailed directions available on booking.

Moonglow Guest House

Gillian O'Leary
7 Bennett Close, Cairnside, Glencairn, Simon's Town
Tel: 021-786-5902 Fax: 021-786-5903
Email: seaview@moonglow.co.za Web: www.moonglow.co.za
Cell: 082-565-6568

"We've been here ten and a half years now but I still get goose-bumps every time I see the moon hanging over it," Gillian confides in me as we stare out over the smooth expanse of False Bay. I challenge you to find a better view of the bay than this one, and unsurprisingly most of the rooms at Moonglow take full advantage - even the ones that don't still get their own private seating areas round at the front. With Jess the dog staring lovingly at the succulent blueberry muffin that was supplied with my tea, I could have happily stayed for an eternity ensconced on the sofa of the bar-lounge... but an ever-enthusiastic Gillian was keen to show me more and I had a job to do. Throughout this house you'll find original artworks everywhere, including a stunning leopard print and four-foot-high figurines hewn from solid granite. If it catches Gillian's eye she's got to have it. Vibrant oil paintings add a splash of colour to creamy rooms, all drenched in sunlight from large picture windows or glass doors. Beds and tables have been individually designed, and a multitude of mohair blankets and the finest quality linens have had Gillian's hand-embroiderers busy detailing them with intricate dragonflies and bumblebees "... just so the colours match." Moonglow shines.

Rooms: 6 double rooms, all en-suite.
Price: R525 - R625 pp sharing. Singles on request.
Meals: Full breakfast included. Lots of restaurants nearby.
Directions: Map on website or directions can be emailed on booking.

Blue Yonder

Sally and Bruce Elliott

14 Hillside Rd, Fish Hoek
Tel: 021-782-0500 Fax: 021-782-0500
Email: info@blueyondercape.co.za Web: www.blueyondercape.co.za
Cell: 082-441-9589

For those of you on the self-catering trail this is a must. A three-storey house converted into flats Blue Yonder is a luxury ocean liner of a place. When Sally opened the door to an invading G(team the sun was blasting through the wall-to-wall windows. She was keen to show me arounc but I spent the first ten minutes standing out on the enormous silver-railed balcony, transfixed b the view. From all three apartments here you can watch the full arc of the sun, rising over glittering False Bay, and finally sinking behind the red-tiled roofs of the Fish Hoek bungalows below Excellent for whale-watching. Once the trance wears off (which it won't) head inside and mak the most of the stainless steel and cream kitchens, complete with all mod cons (including m personal favourite: the dishwasher). Sally grew up in this house, but after a huge conversion jo the Rhodesian teak floors are the only reminder of her family home. Now, gloriously indulger queen-sized beds look out on the bay and cool, beige armchairs are just waiting to be lounge in. Once you summon the energy for a dip in the ocean, your own private steps lead down t the beach, just a stone's throw away. My advice? Bring the whole family, light up a braai on th balcony and settle in for at least a month. *5 mins to food shops. All apartments have braais.*

Rooms: 3 self-catering apartments: Upper: 1 queen with en-suite shower & 1 twin with en-suite bath & shower; Middle: 1 queen en-s b & sh, 2 twins en-s b & sh; Lower: 1 queen en-s sh only. Serviced every week day.
Price: R240 - R450 pp sharing dependent on seasor and number of persons per unit.
Meals: In fridge on arrival: tea, coffee, milk, sugar. Full kitchen.
Directions: Head to Muizenberg from Cape Town, continue south along main road thro Fish Hoek. At roundabout at end of Fish Hoek main rd turn L towards Simon's Town. 1 km further take 1st R at lights up Hillside Rd. Blue Yonder c. 300m up on R.

Echo Terrace

Brian Dreyer and Renée Parker
3 Echo Road, Fish Hoek
Tel: 021-782-3313 Fax: 021-782-3313
Email: renee@echoterrace.co.za Web: www.echoterrace.co.za
Cell: 083-646-8348

I defy anyone not to be dazzled by Renée's verdant and plentiful garden. While I swooned at the clivia, bougainvillea and protea, Renée patiently named all the plants and chatted about how important privacy is for her guests. Which leads me to the next remarkable thing about Echo Terrace. From each apartment's private entrance and cleverly-concealed balcony, you'd never know this was a guesthouse. In fact, all five of the alabaster cottages feel like their own perfectly-contained little home; but with Renée and Brian's house next door, there's always someone from whom to glean restaurant tips or who will donate some sugar. The cottages are delightful – immaculate but not prim – and each has their own small garden and plunge pool or huge balcony. With open-plan kitchen, dining and sitting area the apartments are roomy-yet-cosy and decorated with taste and care. "We have restored some antique pieces, but have furnished with comfort and style in mind," said Renée as I inspected an ancient sewing-machine and admired the local seascapes on the walls. The windows that stretch the length of the sitting room and the dazzling white walls throughout make each apartment light and bright. At the front of the apartment you can immerse yourself in the staggering sea, harbour and mountain views and tune into the soporific roar of the waves, a treat worth experiencing with all senses fully switched on.

Rooms: 5 self-catering apartments: all 1 queen and 2 twins; 4 have 2 bathrooms all with bath and shower and 1 with 1 bathroom with bath and shower.
Price: R350 - R460 pp sharing. Singles R500 - R600.
Meals: Fully self-catered.
Directions: N2 from airport to Cape Town. Take M3 to Muizenberg. Turn off to Muizenberg and turn right at traffic lights to Muizenberg. Continue through Kalk Bay and Fish Hoek. At circle turn left and at traffic light right. Take first sharp left to Echo Road. Driveway is first on left.

The Mountain House

Miles and Carin Hartford

7 Mountain Road, Clovelly
Email: info@themountainhouse.co.za Web: www.themountainhouse.co.za
Cell: 083-455-5664

Welcome to your very own private mountain realm. You do not have to share The Mountain House with anyone, so you have total privacy and the freedom to come, go and do as you please. Miles and Carin are passionate about 'their mountain', known as Trappieskop, and have managed to clear out all the alien invaders and restore the indigenous flora. In the process much of the local fauna has returned too, much to the delight of all their nature-loving guests (such as I hope we all are!). The house is a simple organic space where everything fits and works perfectly. Clever innovations such as clerestory windows, Japanese sliding screen doors and a kitchen island on wheels ensure maximum use of both natural light and space. You have the option of taking one or two rooms depending on the make-up of your party. Both are gorgeous, uncluttered and supremely functional. Considering your surroundings, inside-outside living is a must and the jewel in the crown here is the sheltered deck. Protected from the prevailing south-easter, this outside living space is designed for use and with views over Fish Hoek Bay, the wetland below, the mountains and Clovelly golf course I can't see any reason not to take every meal, numerous drinks and extended bird-watching breaks right here. The Mountain House is exactly as its name suggests and is perfect for couples who enjoy being close to all things natural.

Rooms: 1 self-catering apartment with optional second bedroom.
Price: R600 - R1,200 per couple. Add R250 per additional adult.
Meals: Self-catering
Directions: See website for directions and a virtual tour.

Rodwell House

Robin von Holdt

Rodwell Road, St James
Tel: 021-787-9880 Fax: 021-787-9898
Email: info@rodwellhouse.co.za Web: www.rodwellhouse.co.za

This is the kind of boutique hotel that would make Gatsby weak at the knees. Whether it's the original teak panelling on the walls, the team of professionals employed to make it perfect, or the 15,000-bottle refrigerated wine cellar, owner Robin has made it his mission that everything at Rodwell should be as exclusive, stylish and luxurious as possible. From the trimmed lawns and vine-covered walkways of the front garden you can admire the classic Cape Town view of the St James tidal pool and multi-coloured beach huts out front, and the looming Kalk Bay mountains out back. Behind the façade of the house lie an intricately-tiled Moroccan courtyard with terracotta walls offering welcome shade and a tinkling fountain to get you into siesta mode. Robin used to work in finance, but as an art collector and enthusiastic fan of good food and wine, designing Rodwell has been serious fun. His extensive Masters art collection can be seen all over the house, including original pieces in all the rooms. The Cedar Tree contemporary art gallery is based at Rodwell too. Rooms have been positioned so that you can see the sea, either from your windows or private balcony. And modern, open-plan bathrooms are separated from the bedroom only by a risqué waist-high wall. But my favourite part has to be the tasting room, with a sweeping bar, whose curve is continued by lights in the floor, and whose stock of wine would rival the top restaurants of NY or London. *2 mins to coffee shops, restaurants and wine bars; 15 mins to Simon's Town and Constantia vineyards; 20 mins to Kirstenbosch Gardens. The Titanium Bistro is open for lunch and dinner.*

Rooms: 9 suites: 7 doubles with full en-suite bathrooms; 2 doubles with en-suite showers. All have balconies or gardens.
Price: R925 to R2,650 per person sharing. R950 to R2,350 singles. Whole house specials from R13,950 to R24,950 per night.
Meals: Full breakfast incl', fresh pastries baked daily. On-site bistro serves al fresco lunches & fine evening dining. 1,000-choice award-winning wine list; tastings by arrangement.
Directions: Directions on website or faxed/ emailed.

Map Number: 3

African Violet

Rob and Jenni Stewart

12 Mauritius Cresent, Capri Village, Noordhoek
Tel: 021-785-2836 Fax: 021-785-2836
Email: reservations@africanviolet.co.za Web: www.africanviolet.com
Cell: 078-175-9475

This is one of those places that will just keep surprising you. I followed the rambling driveway down the mountain slope and past the main house, in search of the accommodation, which is cunningly hidden in the untamed garden. It was a little adventure just to find the rooms. I've rarely encountered such creative use of space. Each suite is concealed in its own little horticultural hideaway with private paths and outdoors area so you really do feel like you're the only one there. African Violet is a labour of love and the hard work and passion are tangible. Rob, a timber-frame builder, has designed and built every suite himself. And I don't just mean overseeing the work… and I don't mean just bits of it either. Rob built everything from beds, kitchen cupboards, the pools and even the bar chairs. For those looking for romance (who isn't?), I'd highly recommend the Terrace Suite, tucked away in its own quiet nook, with its all-embracing deck, private rim pool and views stretching to the Atlantic Ocean and Chapman's Peak Drive. Travellers at heart, Rob and Jenny wanted to show fellow travellers their piece of South African heaven and they've done just that. Escape the bustle of the city and relish the mountain and beach on your doorstep. You might even spot the local troops – I am, of course, referring to the baboons that frequent the wild surrounds of Noordhoek!

Rooms: 5: 2 studios and 3 suites all king/twin with en-suite bathrooms.
Price: R350 - R725 pp (private pool).
Meals: Self-catering.
Directions: From Kommetjie Rd (M65) follow signs to Capri Village. Take fifth left into Grand Bahamas Drive and second right into Mauritius Crescent. African Violet is on your right.

Frogg's Leap

Jôke Glauser and Stewart McLaren

Baviaans Close, off Baviaanskloof Rd, Hout Bay
Tel: 021-790-2590 Fax: 021-790-2590
Email: info@froggsleap.co.za Web: www.froggsleap.co.za
Cell: 082-493-4403

The huge Frogg's Leap verandah, with its impressive views of the Hout Bay mountains and sea seems to be the focal point of life here. At breakfast the house springs to life with Jôke (pronounced *yokie*) and Stewart engaging in easy banter with all who emerge, and chiding guests for sitting at the long wooden table inside when the parasol-shaded tables outside are so enticing. Then, in the evening, with the sea breeze swinging the hammocks and a sundowner in your hand, it is not hard to get to grips with being lazy and on holiday. I can't remember a place where guests made themselves so at home. Jôke and Stewart used to run charter boats in the West Indies and Frogg's Leap has a breezy Caribbean feel with many open French doors and windows. Bedrooms are cool ensembles of natural materials: painted floors, seagrass matting, palms, natural stone in bathrooms, lazy wicker chairs, reed ceilings, thick cotton percale linen and old wooden furniture. Hout Bay itself is a fishing harbour enclosed by mountains and is within minutes of beaches and hiking trails with spectacular whale-watching when whales are in town. This is a place that has been consistently recommended both before and since the first edition and it is a continued pleasure to recommend it myself. *Guest phone 021-790-6260.*

Rooms: 6: 5 doubles/twins and 1 double, all with en suite bathrooms; 2 with shower, 4 with bath and shower. Plus extra single room.
Price: R350 - R495 pp sharing. Single supplement: +50%.
Meals: Full breakfast included and served until 10am. There are 20 restaurants nearby for other meals.
Directions: A map will be faxed to you on confirmation of booking.

Paddington's

Di and Don Lilford

3 Lindevista Lane, Hout Bay
Tel: 021-790-1955 Fax: 021-790-1955
Email: dlilford@telkomsa.net Web: www.paddington.co.za
Cell: 083-259-6025

Standing in Di's garden, I sighed with satisfaction, gazing across a valley and beach bathed in late-afternoon sunshine. Well away from the hustle and bustle of Cape Town proper, Hout Bay runs at a pace of its own... and Paddington's and the Lilfords are right in step. After years on their valley-floor farm, they have moved up onto the hillside accompanied by a gaggle of visiting guinea fowl (impatiently tapping on the French doors for their tea when I arrived) and their steady stream of guests. There's a relaxed feel of country living here and while the building itself may be new and square, it's full of old prints, family furniture and well-trodden rugs. Visitors have the run of the tiled ground floor, with both bedrooms just two yawns and a stagger from breakfast, tacked onto the drawing room and kitchen. One room gets the morning sun, the other the afternoon rays and both are blessed with gigantic beds. A deep and enticing claw-foot bath in the one and a power shower in the other. If you feel up to it, Don and Di (both journalists - Don is the editor of the Hout Bay Sentinel no less) will point you in the direction of the best restaurants, golf courses and the beach, while for the lethargic loungers among you there's pétanque on the graveled French courtyard or a book on the vine-covered verandah. With a Kronenbourg in hand, you could easily be in St Tropez. Oh, and there's always the dark and minimalist, heated jet-pool behind the house. Choices, choices....

Rooms: 2 king/twins, 1 with bath, 1 with shower.
Price: R400 - R450 pp sharing. Single rates on request.
Meals: Full breakfast included.
Directions: Faxed or emailed on request.

Dreamhouse

Ivanka and Luis Frasco
53 Mount Rhodes Drive, Hout Bay
Tel: 021-790-1773 Fax: 021-790-4864
Email: dreamhouse@yebo.co.za Web: www.dreamhouse.de
Cell: 082-547-7328

You cannot fail to be inspired by Dreamhouse and its mountainous harbour-view setting. The staggered garden contains many intimate leafy places that envelope both you and the landscape in the foliage. This is an artist's oasis and, if the mood takes you, Ivanka will dish out brushes, watercolours, canvas and frame so you can paint your own memories and take them home. The house and rooms reflect your host's own creative flair in colour, texture and line, with sweeping-armed suede sofas (it's always handy when your other half deals in furniture), a heavy wooden-beamed fireplace and high ceilings. The rooms are all different and named after their predominant colour, my favourite being the red luxury suite at the heart of the house where I imagined star-gazing from bed or rocking in the balcony-bound hammock for two. Hand-made mirrors, draped sarongs from Pakistan and an abundance of shells adorn the daily-different table décor. "Everything has its own story," according to Ivanka. Devoted to her guests, she applies attention to detail and impeccable yet unobtrusive service at all times. Whether it's a picnic basket you need, a cocktail at the pool lounge or directions for a sunrise walk up Little Lion's Head, she'll be there. Also trained in reiki, aromatherapy, reflexology and various massages there are a multitude of blissful experiences available at her hands. As we used to say at university (for some reason), "live the dream!"

Rooms: 11: 10 king/twin with en-suite bath/shower, 2 with en-suite kitchenette, 1 queen with en-suite shower.
Price: R450 - R900 pp sharing. Singles on request.
Meals: Full breakfast included. Dinner and light lunches on request (preferably with 24-hours notice as only fresh produce used).
Directions: Emailed or faxed on request. GPS: 34 01 05 10S - 18 20 54 90E.

The Tarragon

Mark and Julia Fleming

21 Hunters Way, Tarragona, Hout Bay
Tel: 021-791-4155 Fax: 021-791-4156
Email: info@thetarragon.com Web: www.thetarragon.com
Cell: 076-191-7755

These globe-trotting Brits have retired their backpacks and settled at the opposite, luxury end of the accommodation world. Seduced by South Africa's charm and sunshine, Mark and Julia permanently unpacked, kids and all, building a new life and some very stylish self-catering cottages on the wooded southern slopes of Hout Bay's leafy valley. When I arrived a fruitless effort to find a pen sent Mark dashing for a replacement and I was able to enjoy a purple moment inspired by the towering evergreens and the incredible stillness. A koi pond plinked occasionally with frogs or fish exploring the sun-freckled surface. Other visitors to the Flemings' subtly-crafted garden include peacocks, Egyptian geese, cormorants, butterflies and dragonflies. From the pool-side sun-loungers and braai area your eye will be drawn across the lawn and rocky peaks before sweeping, like the garden, into an area of dense wood. All units have private outdoor areas dappled by vine-wound frames. Marble-topped kitchens are fully kitted out with everything from top-of-the-range toasters to dishwashers, and laundering is available with the lady who does the daily servicing. Living areas, bedrooms and bathrooms are kept simple with clean-cut lines and contrasting tones; high-quality white linens gleam against dark leather headboards, fresh-cut sunflowers pose upon polished tables and square silver-tapped sinks rest against natural slate or travertine tiling. The Tarragon offers a finely-tuned mix of character and luxury.

Rooms: 5 fully-contained serviced self-catering units: 2 x 3-bedroom units, 1 x 2-bedroom unit and 2 x 1-bedroom units. All with full kitchen, living area and en-suite bathrooms.
Price: R800 - R2,300 per cottage per night.
Meals: Fully self-catering.
Directions: Faxed or emailed on request.

Le Marais

Patrice Boyer and Stevie Joubert

2 Harold Close, Oakhurst
Estate, Hout Bay
Tel: 021-790-9562
Fax: 086-544-5404
Email:
contact@le-marais.co.za
Web: www.le-marais.co.za
Cell: 082-817-1877

Rethink impressions you have of 18th-century Cape Dutch homes flaunting white interiors and possibly the odd frill. Two years ago, Patrice went home with drawings of just this type of property. But after serious brainstorming, Le Marais (named after a popular quarter of Paris) conforms to no such traditions. Apéritifs may still be served at six, but as you lean over the bar your reflection will now be cast in an inky granite worktop that has ousted the yellowwood table. Outside, uninterrupted views of the back of Table Mountain remain, as does a sun-drenched courtyard, enclosing an azure pool. It's within its whitewashed, tightly-thatched exterior that this building flies so mischievously and capriciously in the face of convention. A bath stands proud as an armchair in one suite's reception, a bed usurping the gallery overhead; an open shower in another suite rains onto rippled, lava-like, two-tone screed underfoot. Throughout its H-shaped plan, colour and form once thought too risqué are embraced. Five suites (Red, Rooi, Rouge, Rojo and Rood) are given various treatments, ranging from a Spanish pop art theme to the über-chic, with an ultra-modern finish. Patrice's cuisine is also peppy (bobotie, gazpacho or Spanish omelette breakfasts and variations of Babette de Rozières' specialities for dinner), but "I am not a cook", he insists, "I am a civil engineer". I recalled the precision screed I'd just seen, and the fact that he designed a 65km concrete tunnel for Lesotho. A lot of both, I thought, but I kept it under my hat.

Rooms: 5: 3 king/twins with en-suite showers or baths and showers; 1 queen with en-suite shower; 1 apartment with en-suite bath and shower (sleeps 4, with the option of self-catering).
Price: R350 - R600 pp sharing. Singles from R500.
Meals: Full breakfast included. Dinners on request with 24hrs notice: R250 for 3 courses (including wine, coffee and apéritifs).
Directions: From Hout Bay Road (M63), 3km after circle with Constantia Main Road (M41) look out for the Oakhurst Farm sign on your left. Take the left immediately before this farm, which is marked Dorman Way. Continue up this, straight over Oakhurst Avenue and into Harold Close.

Map Number: 3

Entry Number: 13

Amblewood Guest House

June and Trevor Kruger

43 Skaife St, Hout Bay
Tel: 021-790-1570 Fax: 021-790-1571
Email: info@amblewood.co.za Web: www.amblewood.co.za
Cell: 082-881-5430

On arrival I was greeted by a smiling Trevor, who promptly fixed me up with a much-needed G&T. Amid heavy beams and family antiques we chatted away until the rains came (which I'm afraid they do on occasion, even in the Cape). Guests wearing borrowed woollies and waterproofs returned, and Trevor raced out with a brolly for June. This softly-spoken duo love doing what they do. They share an eye for detail and an enthusiasm that will leave you feeling right at home. I browsed the library and admired the beach, bay and mountains from my balcony which I shared with two turtle-doves. All the rooms are individual in style with extra-length beds, en-suite bathrooms and sea and mountain views. Breakfast is served on the pool deck at a leisurely pace. On the night I stayed we headed to a steakhouse, where everybody knew the Krugers. I enjoyed my stay so much that I think they wondered whether I was doing a job at all. But I wasn't alone - as I left, wise-looking guests were extending their stay. For those on a return visit and with an interest in photography, you can now allow Trevor, an experienced photographer, to help you polish your snapping skills. He organises tours taking you to the most interesting locations as well as offering helpful tips and advice so you may remember your stay always.

Rooms: 6: all doubles with en-suite bath or shower. 1 self-contained suite. Some have air-con.
Price: Winter: R300 - R550 per person sharing per night. Summer: R400 - R640. Singles: winter rates R600 - R790; summer R650 - R990. Please visit their website for seasonal specials.
Meals: Full cooked breakfast included.
Directions: Faxed or emailed on booking. Also available on website.

Hout Bay Hideaway

Sue and Martin Collins

37 Skaife Street, Hout Bay
Tel: 021-790-8040
Email: info@houtbay-hideaway.com Web: www.houtbay-hideaway.com
Cell: 082-332-7853

The Hout Bay Hideaway, painted ivy green, literally disappears into the thick foliage of its delightfully overgrown garden. Smart meranti shutters lead you out of the rooms onto the long winding verandah that wraps around the house. Making my way along the tree-lined platform, where a jacaranda tree draped its purple flowers over the rail, I ogled at mountain, pool, garden and beach (which is only a five-minute walk down the hill). I'm sure most of the action takes place outside here, round the pool or rambling up buried garden paths to find the hammock platform. Inside, the rooms are a treat too, big, elegant and cosy with Turkish rugs decorating the floors, leather armchairs, palms in large pots, mohair blankets, giant wooden wardrobes, old trunks and original artwork, not to mention hard-working fireplaces for those less well advertised Cape Town winters. Skylight Suite is my favourite, with prime access to the outdoor Victorian bath buried in the shrubbery. Despite being rather exposed, outdoor bathing is apparently very popular. "They don't care, they're on holiday," laughed Sue and that's exactly the atmosphere she and Martin encourage – carefree and relaxed. One of the perks is breakfast in bed (or served to the room at least). "Couples love it. They're still wandering around in their dressing-gowns at midday," adds Martin. Thick fluffy gowns are provided, by the way.

Rooms: 4: 3 king/twin suites with en-suite showers and kitchenettes. 1 ground floor apartment with kitchenette, king/twin beds, bath and separate double cabin shower.
Price: R450 - R850 pp sharing (depending on season and length of stay), singles on request.
Meals: Full breakfast included, 5-10 mins walk from restaurants and the beach.
Directions: On the website and can be emailed on request, or just call.

The Kings Place

Kim and Ian King

The Kings Place, Valley Road, Hout Bay
Tel: 021-790-4000
Email: info@thekingsplace.com Web: www.thekingsplace.com
Cell: 082-773-8831

Even as I trundled down the drive I could see that Kim and Ian, with a helping hand from Mother Nature, have crafted a truly special place. Whether you're knocking up on the floodlit tennis court, somersaulting skywards on the trampoline, or simply lazing by the pool, the views over Hout Bay and the Constantiaberg remain imperturbably lovely. An ever-smiling Kim greeted me in wellies and a bodywarmer, fresh from tending to the animals (I counted dogs, horses, chickens and Chinese geese, but am sure plenty more are lurking within the eight acres). Strolling through the landscaped garden (Ian is a horticulturalist) we came to the expansive, single-storey 'Valley House', light, airy and well able to sleep Von Trapp-sized families if required. It's in the open-plan kitchen, dining and living area that the heart of the Kings Place beats. The maple and granite kitchen has chopping space for a whole troupe of cooks, and they'll all fit around the huge dining table too, strategically placed in front of the full-length, full-view windows. If you've exhausted all the activities on offer or have simply exhausted yourself, the lounge provides a sanctuary of cushioned, wicker armchairs that face a warming hearth in winter, or look out through glass doors to the pool terrace in summer. *Can sleep 2 - 20 people.*

Rooms: 2 self-contained units: 1st: 4 x double & 1 x 4-bed (2 with en-suite bath/sh, 2 separate bath & sh rooms); 2nd: 1 double with en-suite bath/sh, 1 twin with separate bath/sh & bunk beds. Units can be connected.
Price: R300 - R500.
Meals: Self-catering. Meals available on request.
Directions: Main Road into Hout Bay from Constantia. Right into Disa River Rd. Left onto Valley Rd. Go past World of Birds on the right and The Kings Place is 150m on the left after the 4-way stop.

Ambiente Guest House

Marion Baden and Peter Forsthövel

58 Hely Hutchinson Ave, Camps Bay
Tel: 021-438-4060 Fax: 086-670-5975
Email: info@ambiente-guesthouse.com
Web: www.ambiente-guesthouse.com Cell: 072-460-1953

Marion and Peter's affair with Ambiente Guest House began with a holiday. An initial joke to buy from the previous owners became a reality that ended in signatures on more than one dotted line: they not only bought the place, but also got married here. Many years later and they're still going strong. So what does Ambiente have to sustain such marital harmony? A base of sturdy functionality is hidden beneath a layer of exciting features and continual surprises. Original native masks, chairs and colour schemes are fused with a Mediterranean feel to produce an effect of African-themed modernity. Choose from beds suspended by chains or with wavy topless posts. Immerse yourself in the big luxurious bathrooms where showers are powerful, sinks are exciting (trust me, sinks can be exciting, you'll see) and baths cry out for a glass of champagne. Amidst these mirror-filled havens things aren't always what they seem. Is that an African spear disguised as a towel rail? A boulder in the shower? This place has playful passion. It has the drama of half the mountain in the breakfast room, the shock of sand beneath your feet in the loo. If that's not enough to keep you amused, the views of mountain and ocean will make you gawp, the pool and garden will refresh and the paintings, if you look long and hard enough, will make you blush.

Rooms: 4: 3 king suites, all with en-suite bath and shower; and 1 double room with en-suite bath/shower. Separate toilets in all bathrooms.
Price: R720 - R990 pp sharing (Breakfast Included)
Meals: Full breakfast included. BBQs possible by arrangement.
Directions: Take the N1 or N2 to Cape Town and follow signs to Cableway/Camps Bay. Remain on M62, Camps Bay Drive, with the 12 Apostles to your left and Camps Bay down to your right. Turn Left into Ravensteyn Ave then first right into Hely Hutchinson Ave. Ambiente is number 58.

Map Number: 3

Entry Number: 17

Boutique@10

Jennifer Smith and David Beach Mercer

10 Medburn Road, Camps Bay
Tel: 021-438-1234 Fax: 021-438-3012
Email: stay@boutique10.co.za Web: www.boutique10.co.za
Cell: 082-777-8007

From the moment I was greeted by the warm, Washington-State-cultivated accent of Beach (I was half-expecting an American Indian chief) and the effusive Jennifer, I knew Boutique@10 had to go in the guide. The crackling fire, flagstone walls and rich timber finishes bring a sense of security and warmth. Jennifer and Beach are such an interesting couple (Jennifer was runner-up in the 1982 Miss South Africa competition and Beach is a pro beach volleyball coach and was a commentator at the 1996 Olympics) that it was tough to tear myself away from the vast dining table at the hub of this cunningly-renovated, 55-year-old property. But I'm very glad that I did. The Boutique is cosy and opulent with some exquisite Balinese pieces. You're going to love this one!

Rooms: 4: all en-suite with king-size or twin bed option.
Price: R450 - R900 pp sharing. Singles plus 50%.
Meals: Full healthy breakfast included.
Directions: Take NI or N2 (from airport) into Cape Town CBD. Keep straight following signs to Table Mountain & Camps Bay. Drive up towards Table Mtn, over neck & down into Camps Bay. Take 2nd road to R, Geneva Dr, 1st L into Medburn Rd. 5th hse on R.

Ocean View House

Katrin Ludik
33 Victoria Road, Bakoven
Tel: 021-438-1982 Fax: 021-438-2287
Email: info@oceanview-house.com Web: www.oceanview-house.com

Tucked in between the Twelve Apostles mountain range and the turquoise Atlantic, Ocean View House is the perfect place to be mesmerised by humpback and southern right whales frolicking among the white horses that roll into Camps Bay (in season, of course.) There's no end to Ocean View's eccentric delights with its Russian marble and award-winning gardens. Everyone has either a balcony or a terrace with fabulous views of sea, pool deck, mountain or garden. It is a hotel, but such a personal one with huge wooden giraffes hiding behind every corner and the friendliest staff who smile and sing while they work (which is always a good sign). There's also a great pool and how many hotels run an honesty bar? To cap it all, Ocean View has its own nature reserve, a tropical garden that ushers an idyllic river from the mountains to the sea. They have placed tables and sun-loungers on the grassy river banks, a sort of exotic *Wind in the Willows* scenario with rocks, ferns, trees, tropical birds, succulents, waterfalls and butterflies. If you ever feel like leaving Ocean View, Camps Bay is a 20-minute stroll away with its string of outdoor restaurants and zesty atmosphere. It's a good place to watch trendy Capetonians at play. Tired out long before they were, I walked back to the hotel. The nightwatchman was expecting me and escorted me to my room, which was also expecting me, tomorrow's weather report by my bed.

Rooms: 17: 8 Suites; 7 Luxury Rooms & 2 Pool Deck rooms.
Price: R345 – R1,450 pp sharing. Single rates available.
Meals: Full breakfast is included and served until 10am. Light lunches and picnic hampers on request.
Directions: On the coast road a mile out of Camps Bay towards Hout Bay.

Antrim Villa

Jonas Sandstrom
12 Antrim Road, Three
Anchor Bay
Tel: 021-433-2132
Fax: 021-433-2133
Email: info@antrimvilla.com
Web: www.antrimvilla.com
Cell: 072-106-8844

It was pure pleasure to walk into Antrim Villa's cool interior after a long day on the road, and to savour the triple rewards of a bounteous welcome from the manager, Joy (by name and nature), a fresh orange juice and the comforting aroma of baking bread. Jonas arrived from Sweden in 2003, fell in love with Cape Town and promptly and enthusiastically opened his first guest-house. This was a success, more rooms were needed and so Antrim Villa was born. With Jonas's interior design background, he has taken this old English Victorian-style house and created a fresh and modern oasis in the heart of Three Anchor Bay (Green Point). With its high old metal sheet ceilings and original wood floors, harmonious colours and natural fabrics, you'll feel calm and relaxed in this tranquil, tropical-African villa. In the garden, you'll find a gorgeous, highly-enticing pool area, decked out with palm trees and sun-loungers. If you feel like going for a wander, then you really couldn't ask for a better location either. Antrim Villa is within walking distance of the sea, the new stadium, the Victoria & Alfred Waterfront and Green Point Main Road, with its abundance of trendy bars and restaurants. It is all on your doorstep. For those of you with real wanderlust who want to venture completely out of the 'neighbourhood', talk to Joy. She is a certified tour guide and knows a great deal about Cape Town and other areas. Antrim Villa really does have it all.

Rooms: 8: 7 doubles and 1 single. All with en-suite shower, 1 with en-suite bath and shower.
Price: R425 - R803 per person sharing. Singles R550 - R1,100.
Meals: Continental breakfast included. Lunch and dinner available on request.
Directions: Follow Strand Street which will turns into High Level Road. Turn right into Hill Road and then turn left into Antrim Road. Antrim Villa is on the left.

De Waterkant Cottages

Tobin Shackleford and Richard Gush

40 Napier Street, De Waterkant
Tel: 021-421-2300 Fax: 021-421-2399
Email: book@dewaterkantcottages.com
Web: www.dewaterkantcottages.com Cell: 072-457-4387

Now here is something a little bit different, the chance to have your own home (albeit only for the period of your stay), right in the centre of one of Cape Town's trendiest neighbourhoods. De Waterkant Cottages is a constantly-evolving array of brightly-painted former slave cottages (some dating from the 18th century) and more modern, but sympathetically-styled, homes in the National Preservation site that is De Waterkant Village. Each is individually owned, but all are run on a day-to-day basis by Tobin, Richard and their team. Only the best are selected, assuring you of high-quality fixtures, fittings and furnishings. All have standardised luxury linen, plates, knives, forks etc, in fact everything you could ever want or need to make your stay here a pleasure. The concept is all about choice (which, trust me, will be no easy thing). First you'll have to choose between traditional and contemporary, but then you'll need to choose your exact cottage. Tobin and Richard used to live in one – could there be a higher recommendation? This particular home has furniture made from car parts, speakers are embedded in the walls and the shower has a glass roof, allowing you to gaze up at the stars while you wash. There are too many to go through them all, but I also witnessed roof decks galore, exposed wooden floors, luxury leather sofas, private gardens, roof-top jacuzzis, rain-head showers, flat-screen TVs, real fires, amazing views, plunge pools… the list goes on. (See, I said it wouldn't be an easy choice.) *All accommodation serviced daily except public holidays. Property flowers, pre-stocked fridges and airport pick-ups available.*

Rooms: 18 fully-serviced cottages, with one, two, three & four bedrooms (queen, king & twin). All main bedrooms with en-suite bathrooms, showers and air-conditioning. Online bookings and availability.
Price: R825 - R3,000 two persons per night per cottage. Additional persons R250 - R450. Under 2s stay free.
Meals: Kitchen can be stocked on request.
Directions: See website for map and instructions.

Map Number: 3

Entry Number: 21

Cheviot Place Guest House

James and Brooke Irving

18 Cheviot Place, Green Point
Tel: 021-439-3741 Fax: 021-439-9095
Email: cheviot@netactive.co.za Web: www.cheviotplace.co.za
Cell: 082-467-3660

Cheviot Place is something fresh for the Cape Town accommodation scene. This was apparent from the moment James opened the front door, dressed in Hawaiian shirt (sunny) and trainers (trendy), Jamie Cullum (jazzy) wafting out behind him. I was just in time for sundowners. Impassioned tips for a tour of the vineyards were aptly passed on around the wine barrel. The verandah looks out over a perfect cityscape incorporating St Margaret Mary's church, the splendid new Green Point stadium and on to the glittering waters of Table Bay. And let's not forget the immediate gardens bursting with bright pink hibiscus and yesterday-today-tomorrow. There is something of the San Francisco vibe about this venerable, turn-of-the-last-century house, with its high ceilings, pillars and arches. New wooden floors, natural hemp-style rugs and black metal light fittings have been added to set off the original marble fireplaces. Cheviot Place is a contemporary home retaining the best of its Victorian heritage. James made me feel like an old friend over my Cheviot Scrambler breakfast (carefully selected by me the previous evening – I spurned the 'healthy morning' breakfast). The self-catering unit below the main house is surely the ultimate in 21st-century living, reminding me of the troglodyte homes carved out of the rocks deep in the Sahara. Apart from the bed there is no free-standing furniture: everything has been sculptured from the stone. Original? Yes. Cool? Very.

Rooms: 6: 4 queens, 2 twins/kings. All en-suite. Ask about the self-catering option.
Price: R350 - R650 pp sharing. Single rates on request.
Meals: Full breakfast is included. Picnics provided on request from R150. Braai on request from R150 - R300.
Directions: Ask when booking.

Pembroke 403

Séamus and Éilís Cryan

Pembroke 403, V&A Waterfront Marina
Email: info@pembroke403.com Web: www.pembroke403.com
Cell: +35 (0) 387-258-6016

Here's something a bit different for the Greenwood Guide, but with typically great owners. The only drawback is that you won't get to spend your holiday with Drs Séamus and Éilís, Pembroke 403 being a two-bedroom self-catering flat. Well, 'flat' is a huge understatement. It's a palace. Moreover, it's to be found in the V&A Waterfront Marina, playground to international jet-setters and the like. The delightful Irish owners (who'd have thought?) have made a huge investment here. As you'd expect, the flat is enormous with no expense spared on exquisite finishes: travertine marble tiles, a B&O fully-integrated sound-system, water-purifier, waste disposal unit, Poggenpohl kitchen units, Miele appliances and a selection of South African art that would put some of the local galleries to shame. Even the glasswork was hand-crafted. If you ever get bored of the views of Table Mountain and Signal Hill on the first big balcony, why not venture over to the second balcony for sundowners overlooking the bustling V&A harbour? Watch celebrities board their flash yachts or take an easy stroll into the V&A Waterfront where some of South Africa's finest shops and restaurants await. There are some nice walks past the harbour and along the sea as far as Camps Bay and beyond. The doctors have injected vibrant colour wherever possible, especially in the main living area, a huge space that flows from kitchen into a dining area and sitting room. Be sure to get the low-down on the snazzy lighting system – they're very rightly very proud of it!

Rooms: 228 sqm self-catering apartment with 2 en-suite bedrooms (1 king and 1 queen).
Price: R4,800 - R6,400 for the whole apartment per night. Mon - Fri house-keeping service included.
Meals: Self-catering. Private chef by prior arrangement. Hundreds of bars and restaurants in easy walking distance.
Directions: From the airport, take the N2. At the end of the motorway, turn right towards the V&A Waterfront. After 500m, at the roundabout, take the second exit towards the Cape Grace Hotel. Entrance is on the left just before the Cape Grace.

Map Number: 3

Acorn House

Bernd Schlieper and Beate Lietz
1 Montrose Avenue, Oranjezicht
Tel: 021-461-1782 Fax: 021-461-1768
Email: welcome@acornhouse.co.za Web: www.acornhouse.co.za

Bernd and Beate can barely contain the happiness they derive from Acorn House and their enthusiasm rubs off quickly on all but the stoniest of their visitors. I was a pushover. The listed building, designed by busy Sir Herbert Baker in 1904, sits on the sunny, sea-facing slopes of Table Mountain with tip-top views to Table Bay. (You can 'try before you buy' as there is a niftily-positioned webcam that uploads Acorn's views hourly to the website.) The house is typical Sir Herbert with timber colonnade and huge double-fronted verandah. There is an immaculate garden with black-slate swimming pool and a sun-lounging lawn, cleanly demarcated by agapanthus and lavender bushes. Breakfast, often served by the pool ("until the last guest comes down", i.e. you can sleep in), is a no-holds-barred display of meats, cheeses, eggs and freshly-squeezed fruit juices; "probably the second-best breakfast in Cape Town" is Beate's carefully-worded claim! I smiled my way around Acorn as I noted the personal touches such as fresh mint water (with mint from the garden) and upstairs, in your bedroom, notes of welcome or farewell, chocolates and sprigs of lavender. Wine-lovers are also well served: Bernd is pazzo for the stuff and regularly visits local vineyards to ensure that his house wines are up-to-the-moment (just for his guests' benefit, of course). Having lived in South Africa for several years now, Bernd and Beate are still awash with excitement about their surroundings; a stay in Acorn House will leave you feeling much the same.

Rooms: 9: 1 king, 3 twins and 3 queens all with en-suite bath; 1 family suite with twin; 1 private family cottage with king.
Price: R500 - R690 pp sharing. Singles R490 - R900. Family suite and private family cottage as double R1,000 - R1,380 + R320 for up to 2 kids.
Meals: Full breakfast included and served until you're ready for it. Free coffee & tea available all day. Finally at Acorn House: Nespresso!
Directions: See website or ask for fax.

Lézard Bleu Guest House

Chris and Niki Neumann
30 Upper Orange St, Oranjezicht
Tel: 021-461-4601 Fax: 021-461-4657
Email: welcome@lezardbleu.co.za Web: www.lezardbleu.co.za
Cell: 072-234-4448

It's going to be hard to book the treehouse, particularly when word gets round, but you have got to try! Surely the most wonderful bedroom in Cape Town. The trunks of two giant palm trees spear through a wooden deck at vertiginous heights and a tiny balcony is in among the topmost fronds and spikes. Lézard Bleu was a great house anyway, so this latest extravagant addition represents one huge cherry on a mouthwatering cake. Niki is an actress and Chris is a chef, although he has hung up his hat now… no, don't even ask! They are still young and humorous and the house remains sleek and modern with solid maplewood bedframes, white pure cotton, sandy shades and tones, bright splashes of local and modern art on the walls. Breakfast is the best beanfeast in Cape Town (and that's the opinion of other guest house owners). The Blue Lizard snakes pleasingly from area to area, each room with its own doors out to a patio and to the large pool, where deck loungers take it easy on a surrounding timber deck. There are real fires in winter, an honesty bar, free ADSL Internet access - mere details, but typical. Individual, creative, very comfortable, but most importantly this is somewhere really natural and friendly. *Children welcome from the age of 6 years old.*

Rooms: 7: 1 family room; 5 doubles/twins; 4 with en/s bath and shower; 1 with en/s shr; 1 tree-house double en/s bath and shower.
Price: Double: R530 - R770 pp sharing. Treehouse: R650 - R780 pp sharing. Single occupancy: R780 - R960.
Meals: Full (enormous!) breakfast included and served till 10.30am.
Directions: Ask for directions when booking.

Map Number: 3   Entry Number: 25

Redbourne Hilldrop

Jonny and Sharon Levin
12 Roseberry Avenue, Oranjezicht
Tel: 021-461-1394 Fax: 021-465-1006
Email: info@redbourne.co.za Web: www.redbourne.co.za

One of the happiest and most humorous guest houses in Cape Town, so it always seems to me. Many of Jonny and Sharon's guests refuse to stay elsewhere and gifts arrive daily from overseas... well almost. It's a small, intimate place and you are spoiled: free-standing baths, fluffy duvets, big white pillows, unflowery good taste in mirrors and wood floors, magazines, African artefacts, great showers. One room has a spiral staircase down to its bathroom. You eat breakfast at a diner-style bar stretched along a wall of pretty windows with incredible city views. Guests are treated as far as possible as friends and each time I visit I notice the easy rapport that Jonny and Sharon have generated with them – probably overnight. After a mere five minutes in their company I felt all the formality of my visit slipping away like a coat in hot weather. The wall-enclosed pool comes complete with a mini-waterfall spanning the length of it and Table Mountain looming above. From here you can see if the cable car is working and for the more adventurous you're not far from the start of one of several routes to the top. Otherwise it's an easy ride down to the city bustle, the Waterfront and the Atlantic beaches. Perfect location, great hosts, GSOH!

Rooms: 5: 3 doubles with en/s showers; 1 twin with en/s bath and shower and 1 twin family room with en/s bath and shower plus a sunroom (can fit 4/5 beds).
Price: R450 - R550 pp sharing. Singles on request.
Meals: Full breakfast included. Dinners by prior arrangement. Restaurants nearby.
Directions: On website.

MannaBay

David Ryan
1 Denholm Road, Oranjezicht
Tel: 021-461-1094 Fax: 021-469-8915
Email: res@mannabay.com Web: www.mannabay.com

"I've never seen anything quite like this", was the sole thought occupying my dazzled mind as butlers Shadrak and Simon kindly tended to my luggage. David, the bustling and convivial owner (whom you might catch about town shouldering an African grey parrot, name of Preston) certainly went to town with the interiors. Each room is wildly unique, from the imperial indulgence of the Versailles Suite to the acts of pith-helmeted derring-do, which inspired the Explorer Room. From the disco ball, to the enormous black-and-white photographic mural of Cape Town and from the Karen Miller artwork to the Ewok stools (not an official name), MannaBay is a treasure trove of eccentric paraphernalia. There's also a library rippling with African travel literature. Once I'd finished inside, it was on to the vast wooden sun-deck to catch a few rays and to take a dip in the pool which looked all too inviting, with Table Mountain towering overhead and that pure South African sunlight pinging off the water. I was in for a treat staying in the Versailles Suite. Embracing the regal splendour of the Palace of Versailles and the Ancien Régime, this is a suite that would have made Louise XIV cerise with envy (the same colour as the plush sofa). And there's space for his entourage as well. Sumptuous, deep, rich fabrics complement the royal blue-and-silver fleur-de-lis wallpaper. Time to kick back in my massive bed and watch the sun plunge beneath the cityscape into the harbour beyond!

Rooms: 7: 1 suite, 2 luxury & 4 standard rooms.
Price: R500 - R1,995 pp sharing. Ask for single rates.
Includes: free airport transfer, use of cell phone & GPS pre-loaded with local attractions/restaurants.
Meals: Full breakfast & high tea included. Wine tastings & private dinners (prior arrangement) take place in wine cellar.
Directions: N2 Cape Town. Take Exit 5 to merge onto De Waal Drive/M3 to Cape Town. As highway splits keep L & take lane marked De Waal Drive/Cable Way. Keep L. Turn L to Vredehoek/Cableway. Keep L & take far L slip lane to Gardens Centre marked Mill St. L at 2nd lights onto Buitenkant St. L into Yeoville Rd. MannaBay on 1st corner with Denholm Rd.

Bayview Guesthouse

Christine Matti
10 De Hoop Avenue, Tamboerskloof
Tel: 021-424-2033 Fax: 021-424-2705
Email: baychris@iafrica.com Web: www.baychris.com
Cell: 082-414-2052

Christine and her partner Corinne are passionate about their wine and, well, passionate about just about everything. When not buzzing around the house, Swiss-born Christine is usually out cranking up Cape Town kilometres on her racing bike or working on her annoyingly low golf handicap. She arrived in South Africa a wide-eyed whippersnapper some twenty years ago, and has never quite got around to leaving. When I arrived a few renovations were reaching completion. With Christine at the helm, this is a constantly evolving place with new works of modern art from large abstract copper sculptures to paintings of women splashed in colour. But whatever changes take place the fundamental theme of the guest house as an airy haven of healthy living thankfully remains constant. White-washed walls, floor-to-ceiling tinted windows and tiled floors make this a perfect mountain-side retreat from the city centre's summer heat. Breakfasts are an Alpine feast of German breads, selected cheeses and cold meats and guests are encouraged to help themselves to a bottomless bowl of fresh fruit. Take a dip in the pool, head off for a massage at any number of nearby wellness centres, read a book on your decking balcony and - once you've done all that - lie back on the sofa and gaze at a perfectly-framed Table Mountain through the sitting room skylight. My only disappointment? I didn't have time to stay the night. *Personal computer for guests.*

Rooms: 5: 2 queens, 1 with en-suite shower and bath, 1 with en-suite shower; 1 double with en/s shower, 1 twin with en-suite shower. 1 self-catering unit.
Price: R300 - R750 pp sharing.
Meals: Full and healthy breakfasts included.
Directions: Follow signs from the city centre to the Cableway. From Kloofnek Rd turn R into St. Michael's Rd and then third L into Varsity St. At the T-junction turn R into De Hoop Avenue and Bayview is the second on the right.

Gap Lodge

Linda and Le Roi Steenkamp

13 Newport Street, Tamboerskloof
Tel: 021-424-6564 Fax: 086-6424-674
Email: book@gaplodge.co.za Web: www.gaplodge.co.za
Cell: 082-896-8165

From its foundations to the stylish interior every inch of Gap Lodge has been primped and preened to Linda and Le Roi's exacting standards. With just three double rooms this is a small and ideal pocket of calm in the most vibrant part of the Mother City, within 5 minutes' drive of Table Mountain and within walking distance of the restaurants of Kloof and Long Streets. Each bedroom is practical and stylish with an antique hanger here and a vase of fresh lilies there, crisp white linen and towels offset by bold orange or blue bedheads. Linda's artistry decorates the earth-coloured walls with bold and beautiful paintings. After a deep sleep on "the best mattress in Cape Town" – thus spake a previous guest but I had a go too and it is indeed magically giving yet supportive! - Linda conjures up an exceptional full breakfast. Le Roi personally tailors day trips or tours for guests. Having worked as a tour guide since 2002 with his own company (Gap Tours), Le Roi is a fountain of knowledge and will whisk guests away in the house mini-bus. For anyone who has spent a morning queuing, sweating and possibly even swearing in a tourist information office, going on your own personalised tour with Le Roi is like being upgraded from the luggage hold to first class. From 'Flora, Fauna and Vino' day trips to golf tours he will take all the hassle out of holiday-making. 'Beyond the call of duty' is an unfamiliar phrase to this couple: Linda has even been known to raid her own wardrobe on behalf of those guests who forget to pack essential items of clothing!

Rooms: 3 kings with en-suite shower.
Price: R375 – R550 pp sharing. Singles R500 – R700.
Meals: Full breakfast included.
Directions: From the airport take N2 to City. Follow signs from City Centre to Cableway. Once in Kloofnek Road look out for convenience store 'Kloofnek Superette' on left. Turn left into Newport Street immediately afterwards and Gap Lodge is on the right-hand corner.

Alta Bay

Stephan and Beulah Cogels
12 Invermark Crescent, Higgovale
Tel: 021-487-8800 Fax: 086-543-2898
Email: info@altabay.com Web: www.altabay.com
Cell: 082-855-5053

Alta Bay is perched high on the last bit of Table Mountain that still has a slope and from this vantage you can watch the cable car floating up and down the daunting cliff face that towers above you. Behind the house walls, thick purple wisteria clambers everywhere as you meander about on wooden walkways, which lead you to any number of private corners. When Stephan and Beulah acquired Alta Bay it featured in our 8th edition as a high-end seven room B&B. After their first season they shut her down for the winter and transformed her into her present-day, more relaxed, large four-unit, self-catering pad. Furnishings are flash-yet-very-functional: what appears to be a walk-in closet is in fact a hidden kitchenette in the Garden Suite; a king-size extra-length bed and a range of mod cons adorn my favourite, 'The Loft', which has an afro-chic vibe. The postcard views of the harbour, Signal Hill and Lion's Head from the Bay Suite and the cool shade of the Garden Suite offer guests variety, individuality and style. The decision to go self-catering was not to offer less, but rather to encourage visitors to experience all that Cape Town has to offer. Should you choose to take a morning off, whisper a time in Beulah's ear and she will deliver your freshly-baked croissants and continental breakfast to your room; while energetic Stephan - who considers going up the mountain inside the cable car beneath his dignity – guides you through the mountain's hidden kloofs and gorges. Welcome back Alta Bay… we like the new you!

Rooms: 4: 1 king with en-suite bath and shower; 2 kings with en-suite shower; 1 queen with en-suite shower.
Price: R450 – R1200 pp sharing; singles R650 - R1,600; R400 – R750 for 3rd guest in Loft.
Meals: Self-catering. Continental breakfast on request.
Directions: See website for detailed directions.

Vrede Manor

Colin Craig and Mark Wilkes

10 Marais Road, Milnerton
Tel: 021-552-8090 Fax: 021-552-8090
Email: info@vrede-manor.com Web: www.vrede-manor.com
Cell: 072-0419-304

As sun beamed through soaring palm trees I was greeted by two bounding scotties (Bertie and Daisy) and Boris the Russian Terrier. Colin was every bit as welcoming. He and Mark have immaculately renovated Vrede Manor, former home to a mayor and a classical conductor, which perhaps explains the classical music which was wafting through this Edwardian, Cape-Dutch house from ultra-modern B&O speakers. Upstairs, day-room yellow walls with fabulous curved, deep-red, leather armchairs create a warm and intimate mood. The adjoining self-catering unit has a more modern, Greek island feel with whites, blues and a curved-stone, spiral staircase leading from the kitchen up to a designer white leather sofa in the open-plan living area. Sleek, grey, tiled bathrooms retain original Edwardian basins and are enlivened by rubber ducks and Molton Brown products. Modern accoutrements such as Sony Bravia flat screens, DVD players and iPod docking stations stand out against the high ceilings and traditional deal wood floors at Vrede Manor. I loved the thoughtfulness of the fruit bowls and even a complimentary bottle of wine. Colin is a fabulous chef and host - he served me breakfast on the verandah, a chance to admire his green-fingered handiwork in the exquisite garden. His take on egg's Benedict, home-made jams and the most delicious warm honey from their own apiary set me up perfectly for an assault on the Mother City... *Only 10 minutes to The Waterfront on the new RT Bus service, and 5 minutes walk to beach, restaurants and local amenities.*

Rooms: 3: Coates - shower en-suite, private balcony; Palm - bath & shower en-suite; Vrede Studio (self-catering) - bath with shower in bath en-s. Ask about renting entire 3-bedroom house.
Price: R450 pp sharing. Singles R550. Self-catering R350 pp sharing for the studio (sleeps 2).
Meals: Full breakfast included. Self-catering studio can have breakfast for an extra R100 pp. Central CT is 15-min drive away.
Directions: From airport take N2 to CT. Exit 9 - M5 to Milnerton. Exit 4, R27 to Milnerton. At 5th set of lights turn R into Loxton & almost immediately 1st L into Ascot Rd. Vrede Manor is big blue house on corner of Ascot & Marais. Rapid bus service runs through Milnerton to airport and central CT.

Map Number: 3

Roodenburg House

Drs Stuart and Judy Whittaker

74 Campground Rd, Rondebosch
Tel: 021-685-2933 Fax: 021-685-2862
Email: info@roodenburghouse.co.za Web: www.roodenburghouse.co.za
Cell: 082-531-4068

Currie Cup semi-final day at Newlands stadium. Not the best day to be trawling the traffic jammed area in search of guest houses and certainly a time slot to test the convivial mettle of an South African host. Drs Stuart and Judy passed the test with gracious aplomb as they proudly showed me around Roodenburg. Ideally located on the main road through Newlands/Rondebosch, Roodenburg was built in 1882 and more recently transformed from pathology laboratory into a guest-house. A first even for the Greenwood Guide. Original features remain including the ornate stained-glass windows, intricate woodwork and colourful fireplaces. The scene was intriguing – youthful cheers emanating from the TV room, as Western Province took the lead; a couple of psychologists were taking tea by the glistening pool and discussing, no doubt, non-rugby related topics, while an elderly lady took advantage of the empty upstairs lounge to complete a masterful spot of knitting. "Oh, and there's a young cricketer staying in the Paisley Suite. He's staying for the summer." Lucky him. Each room is uniquely decorated with lavish wallpapers, immaculately-upholstered armchairs, heavy curtains and lush carpets or cherry-wood floors. Bathrooms are either modern marble or classic Victorian, replete with claw-foot baths. Gorgeous personal touches abound, from the luxurious Moyo products to the enticing black ginger diffusers - symptomatic of a doctor's attention to detail. Roodenburg is a fantastic and generous guest-house with an excellent bedside manner!

Rooms: 5: 2 extra-length kings with en-suite bath and shower; 2 extra-length queens with en-suite bath and shower; 1 extra-length twin with en-s shower.
Price: R600 - R1,150 pp sharing.
Meals: Full breakfast included. Dinners R130 on request.
Directions: From the airport take N2 towards city until exit M57. L at M57 & continue L passing over Durban Rd and Park Rd. At next lights on RH side you will see Roodenburg House.

Au Pear

Pam Sorel

5 Manson Road, Newlands
Tel: 021-685-1310 Fax: 021-685-1311
Email: pam@aupear.co.za Web: www.aupear.co.za
Cell: 083-226-6805

Jones was putting the finishing touches to the river stone 'braai' on the morning I arrived. The pièce de résistance on an eight-month renovation of this 100-year-old property in the peaceful and leafy suburb of Newlands. Malawi Jones is the charming manager/butler/factotum who lives on the property, while the ebullient owner Pam lives just over the road next to the very handy Forrester's Arms Pub. Chatting to her on the 'stoep' with the crickets chirruping in the proteas, I could see that Pam has put her heart and soul into this project. The attention to detail is meticulous, from the flat-screen televisions and 600-thread cotton sheets to the hand-crafted ostrich egg-shell mirrors in the modern, concrete-screed bathrooms where dainty, re-upholstered, Victorian chairs sit neatly alongside deep, claw-foot baths. Antique pieces adorn the original, pine floorboards throughout, yet Pam has somehow created the atmosphere of a rather relaxed Karoo farmhouse centered around a country kitchen. Each room has its own private entrance and each is named after trees that are flourishing under Pam's nurturing supervision – plum, pear, grape and avo. On a scorching spring day I couldn't wait to get my novel, pour myself a glass of chilled water collected from the natural spring down the road and kick back under the dappled shade of the grape vine ensconcing itself around the white columns (the grapes are delicious by the by). Au Pear is quite simply fantastic. Oh, and it's amazing value for money as well!

Rooms: 4: all with extra-length king-size beds. All en-suite with bath and shower. The whole house is available for exclusive use.
Price: R350 pp sharing. Single supplement on request.
Meals: Full, healthy breakfast can be included for extra R70 pp. Other meals by prior arrangement. Kitchen available for self-catering.
Directions: From Airport, take the N2. Left after university to Lady Anne Avenue then right into Newlands Avenue. Opposite the BP petrol station and after the Forester's Arms Pub, turn right into Manson Road.

Victoria House

Corinne Coste
16 Oak Avenue, Upper Kenilworth
Tel: 0217-6177-83/89 Fax: 0217619164
Email: vichouse@deunet.co.za Web: www.victoria-house-za.com
Cell: 084-664-0506

Corinne's warm-hearted home is 'a bit of a find', especially for those who want relaxed and comfortable with a touch of elegance. If you take the short drive out to the leafy southern suburbs not only will you have the absolute pleasure of meeting Corinne, you'll also be in a superb position to explore the whole Cape. Madame Corinne and her husband (he's a hairdresser in the city) have lived in Cape Town for 13 years and can offer travel advice for your trip in French, German and English. From the hallway original stone-tiled floors and a grand staircase (bathed in a rainbow of light from the stained-glass window) set the tone for the whole house. As does the piano, which is definitely a real instrument not some interior accessory - so if you play, don't be shy! There are five high-ceilinged bedrooms in the main house with big wooden beds and vintage bathrooms. They look out onto an immaculately-tended bush-, flower- and bird-filled garden. Two further suites, dubbed the Twin Cottage, are separate from the main house and thus ideal for those visiting Cape Town with children. The kitchen is never closed and guests are encouraged to help themselves to tea and coffee or something stronger from the honesty bar. The guest book is littered with invites to homes all over the world. I wonder if this has anything to do with the highly-acclaimed breakfast which is served here with deserved pride?

Rooms: 7: 2 kings with en-suite shower and bath, 1 queen with en-suite shower, 2 doubles with en-suite bath/shower and separate shower. 2 twins with en-suite shower.
Price: R990 - R1,250 pp per night. Singles R1300.
Meals: Full cooked breakfast and healthy Continental.
Directions: See website for detailed map

Highlands Country House

Carole Armstrong-Hooper

36 Tennant Road, Upper Kenilworth
Tel: 021-797-8810 Fax: 021-761-0017
Email: info@highlands.co.za Web: www.highlands.co.za

Highlands Country House, sitting splendidly on Wynberg Hill beneath Devil's Peak, is one of the Cape's most majestic homes. In front, a formal garden runs along avenues of fig trees down to trim lawns and flowerbeds - picked daily for fresh bouquets - and I went for a wander, ambling past a fountain and various Grecian urns before reaching one of two swimming pools. Here there is a spa where they will pamper you to within an inch of your life. Up at the house, meanwhile, all was efficient bustle, with smartly-dressed maids busily clearing away breakfast, leaving only the faint but delicious smell of bacon and eggs lingering on the terrace. I passed a magnificent, carved foot-throne in the foyer and a dining room all dressed up in starched white linen on my way to meet Carole in the library for a chat… and a delectable strawberry smoothie. She fell in love with the place when she once came here for tea, which is a special time of day at Highlands, honoured with freshly-baked cakes. Meanwhile, gourmet dinners are best served by candlelight in the conservatory. Separate from the house, large European-style rooms are elegant in neutral tones, while England prevails inside a rush-carpeted warren of staircases and wings. Styles vary subtly in traditional rooms from African flourishes, to Cupid-guarded loft rooms, to Brosely-tiled bathrooms, to shades of blue in St Leger silk curtains. Part the shutters or step onto your balcony and look onto woods, sports fields, mountains and sea... and be very content with your choice.

Rooms: 14: 6 twin/king, 3 king, 4 queen and 1 honeymoon suite with king. All are fully en-suite, with the exception of one shower en-suite.
Price: R700 - R1,720 pp sharing. Singles R1,100 - R2,750.
Meals: Full breakfast included. Delicious light lunches and a la carte dinners. Private dinner parties (in the conservatory or pool house) by arrangement.
Directions: Tennant Road is a continuation of Newlands Road, reached either by the Constantia or Rondebosch exits on the M3. See website for more detailed directions.

Dendron

Jill McMahon
21 Ou Wingerd Pad, Constantia
Tel: 021-794-6010
Email: stay@dendron.co.za Web: www.dendron.co.za
Cell: 082-296-0691

(Quite) a few years ago, Jill's late husband Shaun bought a Land Rover in Taunton (UK) and drove it here. Hardly odd when you see the place, now replete with relaxed family atmosphere, colli dogs and verdant lawns. You get all the benefits of living the South African good life by default here Green-fingered Jill genuinely loves having guests and her enthusiasm for life is evident i everything. The cottages are private in leafy, jasmine-scented gardens and have fully-equippe kitchens stocked with basics, a braai and stunning views to the mountains on the right and Fals Bay in the distance. They have terracotta or tiled floors and beds with Indian cotton throws perfect for families. All are fully serviced and have their own braais. Evening pool-side views a sunset and moonrise, helped along by wine from over-the-hedge Groot Constantia vineyard, w make you want to throw away the car keys and stay (which is exactly what Shaun did when h first clapped eyes on the place). When you are hungry, Jill will send you off there through the bac gate and across the vineyards to Simon's or Jonkershuis for dinner. Return by torch- an moonlight. Dendron (Greek for tree) is a small slice of heaven.

Rooms: 2: 1 x 2 bedroomed and 1 x 1 bedroomed
1 with bath & shower, 1 with shower only. Serviced
daily Mon - Fri.
Price: R350 - R500 pp sharing. Singles on request.
Meals: Breakfast for first morning provided.
Directions: Fax on request.

Klein Bosheuwel and Southdown

Nicki and Tim Scarborough

51a Klaassens Rd, Constantia
Tel: 021-762-2323 Fax: 088-021-762-2323
Email: kleinbosheuwel@iafrica.com Web: www.kleinbosheuwel.co.za
Cell: 083-227-0700

Who needs Kirstenbosch? Nicki has manipulated the paths and lawns of her own garden (which is pretty well an extension of the Botanical Gardens anyway - less than a minute's walk away) so that the views are not dished out in one vulgar dollop! Instead you are subtly led into them, with glimpses through mature trees (flowering gums, yellowwoods and camellias) and lush flower-beds. And finally your stroll leads you down to umbrellas on a ridge with Table Mountain and the Constantiaberg laid out magnificently before you and the sea distantly below. "Keep it plain" is Nicki's motto, so the upstairs bedrooms are simply white and all naturally endowed with garden views. The salt-water swimming pool is hidden deep in the garden and Klein Bosheuwel is the sort of place where you could just hang out for a few days. I was introduced to one English guest who had clearly no intention of going anywhere that day - the cat that got the cream! Or you can stay next-door at Southdown. With a small-scale Lost Gardens of Heligan on her hands, Nicki peeled back the jungle to find pathways, walls and, best of all, enormous stone-paved circles just in the right spot between the house and pool. Today the house is filled with surprises: zebra skins, porcupine-quill lamps, onyx lamp stands, a whole stuffed eagle, a wildebeest's head, a piano, two tortoises, deep carpets and couches, marble bathrooms and terraces off most rooms.

Rooms: 8 double rooms all en-suite. Southdown Cottage sleeps 4 (fully serviced).
Price: R745 - R830 pp sharing. Singles R1,100 - R1,240.
Meals: Full breakfast included.
Directions: Fax or website.

Kaapse Draai

Annelie Posthumus
19 Glen Avenue, Constantia
Tel: 021-794-6291 Fax: 021-794-6291
Email: info@kaapsedraaibb.co.za Web: www.kaapsedraaibb.co.za
Cell: 082-923-9869

Annelie has been charming Greenwood Guide travellers since the very first edition and should be in the running for some sort of award for B&B brilliance. Relaxed, simple and beautiful seem to be the rule here. Her daughter is an artist and their talents combine to make the house a peaceful and contemporary temple to uncluttered Cape Cod-style living. Neutral furnishings and white cottons are frisked up with floral bolsters and country checks. Sunny window-seats amid the white-washed walls and light-grey, vintage-pine floorboards make perfect reading spots. Annelie is a prolific gardener and you can walk (perhaps with her dogs) from the tropical greenery of Kaapse Draai, with its mountain stream, monster gunnera manicata leaves, huge ferns and palms, into lovely Bel-Ombre meadow and the forest next door. From there it is a three-hour walk to the Table Mountain cable station. Porcupines come into the garden at night from the mountain (they love arum lilies apparently) and there are many birds too, including the palindromic hadedah. A grand old willow tree is what you'll park your car under. Delicious breakfasts are taken outside in the sunshine whenever possible. All I can say is – go and stay. *Wine estates and Constantia shopping village nearby.*

Rooms: 3: 1 double with en-suite shower; 2 twins one with en-suite shower, one with en-suite shower and bath.
Price: R440 pp sharing. Singles R550. Between Nov 1st and March 31st there is a supplementary charge of R50 per room for 1-night stays.
Meals: Full breakfast included.
Directions: Ask for fax or email when booking.

Cape Witogie

Rosemary and Bob Child

9 Van Zyl Rd (Van Zyl Way on some GPS), Kreupelbosch (Bergvliet on
some GPS), Constantia Tel: 021-712-9935
Email: capewitogie@netactive.co.za Web: www.capestay.co.za/capewitogie
Cell: 082-537-6059 or 082-852-9084

Cape Witogie (requiring a slightly gutteral pronunciation rarely mastered by English visitors) is
situated at the foot of the Constantiaberg and is named after the tiny 'Cape White Eye' birds which
flitter between the frangipani trees, shrubs and Bob's bonsais - this small bird is as charming as
Rosemary and Bob themselves! When I visited, Rosemary was frantically packing for a trip to the
UK, but she happily (and patiently) attempted to explain how the Contantiaberg resembles a
lateral cross-section of an elephant before showing me round their red-bricked home with two
separate guest suites. Both rooms have whitewashed brick walls, terracotta tiled floors and plush
white sheets and towels. The larger unit has an airy conservatory/sitting room. Both open on to
a braai area and an impeccable garden full of ferns and firs, lavender pots, lemon trees and citrus-
smelling verbena. Hot-plates, a small oven and microwaves give ample scope for knocking up
your own meals, though Rosemary enjoys making occasional breakfasts. I'd recommend coming
with some pals and taking both rooms as a base from which to explore the Cape Town area.
From the City Bowl and beaches to Table Mountain, the botanical gardens and nearby winelands
there is just so much to do in the Cape that a full week with Bob and Rosemary flies by in the
blink of an eye. These are great people running a great-value get-away.

Rooms: 2 units: both consist of 1 twin room (1
extra single bed can be added to each if required)
with en-suite showers and small kitchens.
Price: R295 - R320 pp sharing. Self-catering. R50
pp supplement for one night booking. Single rate
R430.
Meals: Self-catering.
Directions: Emailed on booking.

Majini

Suzy Digby-Smith
4 Broadacres, Colyn Road, Constantia Hills
Tel: 021-715-0155 Fax: 021-715-0155
Email: suzyds@kingsley.co.za
Cell: 082-439-9490

'Majini' is Swahili for 'by the water' but it wasn't apparent to me why the name was appropriate until I had strolled past vivid flowerbeds to the bottom of the velvety garden. A large wooden deck awaited, laden with huge braais, one side opening to the pool and the other to a small dam and stream with views of the lesser-known Elephants' Eye Peak and Suzy's chickens and ducks squabbling in the foreground. This little farmyard neighbours a flourishing organic veg patch and Suzy's guests are encouraged to help themselves to eggs and any potatoes, passion-fruit or greenery that they like the look of. The garden offerings don't end there either – the lawn to the main house winds its way through beautifully-tended lilies and colourful daisies to a well-stocked herb garden. A self-confessed auction-addict, Kenyan-born Suzy has decorated the Pool House simply, but with great care. Touches like well-thumbed paperbacks and a beautiful kiwinet over the bed make the cottage familiar, while luxuries like a Krupps coffee-machine and computer with wifi ensure that all comfort bases are covered. Suzy easily high-jumps the hospitality bar set by most self-catering owners, happily stocking the fridge for guests, loaning her garden for small parties or braais by the boma fire where the lights in the trees glow magnificently at night. A sign in the loo reads, 'Always Give Thanks'. At Majini this is an unnecessary reminder.

Rooms: 1 double room with dressing room, shower & loo, sitting/dining rm, kitchenette. Unit alarmed, DSTV, DVD, WIFI, private braais & parking.
Price: Pool House R1,100 - R1,375.
Meals: Fully self-catering.
Directions: On the N2 from the airport, take the N3 towards Muizenberg. Exit 16 for Ladies Mile. Turn right at traffic light and take 3rd exit at roundabout. Take second left onto Soetvlei Avenue. After 0.9km left onto Colyn Road and first right into Broadacres.

White Cottage

Jane and Derrick Verster-Cohen

12 Upper Primrose Avenue, Bishopscourt
Tel: 021-762-1047 Fax: 021-762-4992
Email: info@cape-townbb.co.za Web: www.cape-townbb.co.za
Cell: 082-492-2281

As soon as I met Jane - and her bouncing canine companions - I knew that she had the Greenwood *je ne sais quoi* in abundance. Whisking me through her sprawling, beautiful, lived-in home we arrived in a wisteria-draped courtyard where two rotund cherubs splash in a central fountain and French doors open to the larger cottage. Here, rose-patterned bedspreads and large blue-and-white porcelain pieces betoken Jane and Derrick's European tastes and passion for antiques. Huge modern showers and a small kitchenette show an appreciation for modernity in its rightful place, but the joy here is really in the used and beloved. Pretty with sweet peas in a vase, the upstairs cottage (I can't bring myself to call it a 'unit') is atticky with sloping ceilings. With its double and single beds, sitting area, walk-in wardrobe and huge bathroom (with free-standing bath) it's cheerful and roomy. Before Jane and I sat to a three-course breakfast feast, served from the family silver and prepared by grinning Phyllius (described by Jane as "the best thing about White Cottage"), we took a turn around the garden, busy with bougainvillea and butterflies. After energetic conversations about beehives and wormeries, I propped myself up against a well-positioned tree, to soak up the colours, smells and feels of this hideaway. Security is excellent as White Cottage is next to the British Consulate.

Rooms: 3: 2 spacious suites with en-suite bathrooms; 1 suite with 2 bedrooms and 2 bathrooms. Extra beds can be provided. All suites have kitchenettes.
Price: R375 - R425 pp sharing. Singles R500 - R600.
Meals: Full breakfast included.
Directions: From airport take the N2 to Cape Town then M3 to Muizenburg. After the 4th traffic light follow sign to Bishopscourt - Upper Torquay Ave. Cross over highway in Torquay. First left into Forest Ave. Over Hillwood. Left into Upper Primrose, house is last on left with big green gate.

Darling Lodge

Mathe Hettasch and Suzie Venter

22 Pastorie Street, Darling
Tel: 022-492-3062
Fax: 022-492-3665
Email: info@darlinglodge.co.za
Web: www.darlinglodge.co.za
Cell: 083-656-6670

Mathe, who is specifically a European (she's says she has lived in too many places to hail from just one country), came here by chance in 2004 and instantly fell in love with the house. This emotion is manifest even at the front door, where a thick wired heart hangs around the knocker. The main house, whose oak floors were originally laid in 1832, is flooded with life and colour by an abundance of flowers brought down from Mathe's husband's protea farm in nearby Hopefield. All the bedrooms are rich in light and colour too, with inviting canopies hanging over the beds and crisp white linens lying on top of them. Each room is named after a different local artist, whose work adorns the walls and is, by the bye, for sale. I would personally opt for Nicolas Maritz with its deep Victorian clawfoot bath. But it was the garden, lovingly looked after by Suzy, that finally stole the laurels, with its ancient pepper trees, fountain spraying water over blossoming roses and mass of lavender. I could think of nothing better than sitting under a tree with Carly - the adorable Westie cross (named after Carly Simon of course). Perhaps with a glass of wine in hand from one of the five nearby vineyards while digging into a good book or simply watching the industrious weaver birds build their nests. My stay was rounded off with a delicious breakfast extravaganza - fruits, cereals, freshly-baked muffins and a seriously good omelette. A darling lodge indeed. *Book early during the Voorkamerfest, Wildflower Show in September and Music Experience in February.*

Rooms: 6: 2 queens, one with en-suite bath, 1 with en-suite bath and separate shower; 1 king with en-suite shower; 2 twin/doubles, one with en-suite shower and one with en-suite bath.
Price: R400 - R450 pp sharing. Singles on request.
Meals: Full breakfast included. Supper on request.
Directions: In centre of Darling, next to the information office. Detailed directions can be sent on booking.

Kersefontein

Julian Melck
between Hopefield and Velddrif, Hopefield
Tel: 022-783-0850 Fax: 022-783-0850
Email: info@kersefontein.co.za Web: www.kersefontein.co.za
Cell: 083-454-1025

Nothing has changed at Kersefontein since the last edition. Julian's convivial dinner parties are still a reason to book in on their own. And Julian himself remains a Renaissance man, described on his business card as 'Farmer, Pig-killer, Aviator and Advocate of the High Court of S.A.'. He farms cows, sheep and horses on the surrounding fields and wild boar appear deliciously at dinner. He also hires and pilots a six-seater plane and a flight round the Cape or along the coast is a must. He modestly leaves out his virtuosity as a pianist and organist and some of us trooped off one Sunday morning, braving a 40-minute sermon in Afrikaans, to hear him play toccatas by Bach, Giguot and Widor at the local church. When not eating, riding or flying, guests lounge on the pontoon, swim in the river or read books from Kersefontein's many libraries. Or they use the house as a base to visit the coast or the Swartland wineries, which are really taking off. The homestead is seventh generation and the rooms either Victorian or African in temperament, with antiques handed down by previous Melcks. It's certainly worth splashing out on the luxury suite, in a separate barn next to a breakfast room clad in a stunning array of framed, pressed wildflowers from the nearby fields. You are fed like a king, but treated as a friend and I am always recommending people to go here.

Rooms: 6: 2 doubles, 2 twins, 1 separate two bedroom cottage, 1 new suite with double bed, lounge, en-suite shower & bath.
Price: R495 - R595 pp sharing. Suite: R895 pp sharing. No single supplements. Aircraft hire prices depend on the trip.
Meals: Full breakfast included. Dinners by arrangement: R240 – R260 excluding wine.
Directions: From Cape Town take N7 off N1. Bypass Malmesbury, 5km later turn left towards Hopefield. After 50km bypass Hopefield, turn right signed Velddrif. After 16km farm signed on right just before grain silos. Cross bridge and gates on the left.

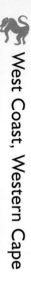

Oystercatcher's Haven at Paternoster

Sandy and Wayne Attrill

48 Sonkwasweg, Paternoster
Tel: 022-752-2193 Fax: 022-752-2192
Email: info@oystercatchershaven.com Web: www.oystercatchershaven.com
Cell: 082-414-6705 or 083-267-7051

Sandy and Wayne, ex film and advertising people, do things in style and their guest house is a knock-out! The Cape Dutch house sits on the fringes of the Cape Columbine Nature Reserve, a spectacular, fynbos-covered, hand-shaped headland, bearing its lighthouse aloft like a nine million-watt jewel. All along the coast and a mere 40 metres in front of the house knobbly fingers of grey and black granite merge into the sea and around the rocks there are secret white sandy coves where the dolphins come throughout the year. It is quite simply beautiful and I can assure you that the Oystercatcher is a haven by anyone's standards. Heave yourself out of that plunge pool, off the rocks and away from the view (available from your bed) and head inside the house. The interior, with its white walls, untreated timbers and reed-and-pole ceilings, is intentionally blank-yet-rustic to showcase some exquisite pieces, such as a four-foot-high Angolan drum, some Malinese sinaba paintings (you'll have to come and see them if you don't know what they are), Persian rugs, art-deco couches, courtyards…. Just about everything is a hook for an eager eye. Beds and bedrooms too are bliss - trust me, I'm a professional. Although they do not do dinner any more (there is no need with so many good eateries in Paternoster) they do offer fresh-out-of-the-bay crayfish dinners in season on demand.

Rooms: 3: 1 king suite with en-suite shower; 1 queen with en-suite bath and shower; 1 twin with en-suite showers. All rooms have their own private entrances and outdoor areas.
Price: From R750 - R1200 pp sharing.
Meals: Full breakfast included.
Directions: From Cape Town take the N1 and then the R27 north following signs to Vredenburg. Follow signs straight through Vredenburg to Paternoster (15km). At crossroads turn left and travel a full 1km towards the Columbine Reserve. Turn right into Sonkwas Rd. It is No.48.

Paternoster Dunes Boutique Guest House & Spa

Gavin Sproule and Deon Van Rooyen

18 Sonkwas Street, Paternoster
Tel: 022-752-2217 Fax: 022-752-2214
Email: reservations@paternosterdunes.co.za
Web: www.paternosterdunes.co.za Cell: 083-560-5600

Located right on the beach, it's not hard to see why locals referred to Paternoster Dunes as 'lovely'. I was met by Gavin and escorted past the open-air courtyard with its tempting pool and daybed and shown to my room (named Vanilla). Gavin and Deon worked in interior design for ten years before swapping the big smoke for the salt breeze. If Vanilla was anything to go by – open-plan, huge bath with its own sea-facing window, equally huge stone-floored shower and king-size bed with plump pillows and Egyptian cotton - they were surely at the top of their game. But the best treat of all was my verandah, accessed through French doors. The ocean is less than ten yards away between grassy dunes and it was here that I decided to settle down and finish off my book of the moment. Clapping the covers together an hour later, I took my satisfaction up to the communal bar/lounge, with its panoramic ocean views, for a sundowner. The design throughout the house never jars and always excites. The walls are adorned with original artwork, from contemporary pastoral scenes to palette nudes and the leather armchairs in the lounge could have been found in a London gentleman's club. My egg and pastrami soufflé at breakfast was clear proof of fine cooking (dinners are also available). But by that time you would hardly expect anything less. More 'wow!' than 'lovely'! *Gift shop on-site offering jewellery, candle-holders und, of course, the latest Greenwood Guide.*

Rooms: 6: king/queen/twins with en-suite shower and/or bath.
Price: R600 - R950 pp sharing. Singles on request.
Meals: Including breakfast. Light lunch and dinner on request.
Directions: From Cape Town take the N1 and then the R27 north following signs to Vredenburg to Paternoster (15km). At crossroads turn left then travel a full 1 km to the Columbine Reserve. Turn right into Sonkwas Street. It is No.18.

Abalone House

Stef Venter and Johan Jansen-Van Vuuren

Abalone House, 3 Kriedoring Street, Paternoster
Tel: 022-752-2044 Fax: 086-215-1839
Email: info@abalonehouse.co.za Web: www.abalonehouse.co.za
Cell: 073-844-7722

When owners Stef and Johan returned to Limpopo they kindly left their treasure trove of a home to the Paternoster guest-house scene. I entered Abalone to the tinkling of wind chimes and was immediately welcomed in very friendly fashion by manager Lindsay before being shown past the bonsai-surrounded courtyard pool to my elegant abode for the night. A private patio, high-backed armchairs, elaborate dressing table and hand-carved bedside lamps set the opulent tone for the rest of the guesthouse. In the entrance hall rich rugs lie on stone floors and gold scales rest on a grand piano opposite vibrant Tretchikoff prints. Around the corner you'll discover the Africa Bar where drums are reinvented as coffee tables between wicker thrones and lavish lampshades. The Saffron Restaurant is also an exuberant affair with pieces of silver on antique furniture and jewels draped from candelabras glowing in the orange light. I had entered a veritable Aladdin's cave! And my genie (Darren the head chef) conjured up a string of sensational dishes including pea soup with pork belly, fresh crayfish and a devilish chocolate *délice* with cumin caramel sorbet. The following morning I had time for a peek at the roof terrace where five elegant beach-house-style bedrooms surround the sun deck (don't miss the salty-aired Jacuzzi with sea and sky views), before a gourmet breakfast in the Orchid Room. As I spied Christmas and Easter, Abalone's resident ducks, foraging in the colourful garden, I thought to myself: these ducks don't know how lucky they are to live in such swanky surrounds!

Rooms: 10: 8 king/twins; 2 kings. All have en-suite bath & shower.
Price: R1,100 - R1,400 pp sharing for bed, breakfast and high tea. Single supplement.
Meals: Full breakfast and afternoon tea included. Lunch and dinner available in The Saffron Restaurant.
Directions: From Cape Town, take the R27 to Vredenburg. Turn left onto the R45. Follow the road through Vredenburg and continue straight to Paternoster. At the four way stop, turn left and follow Abalone House signs.

Oystercatcher Lodge

Luc and Sue Christen

1st Avenue, Shelley Point St, St Helena Bay
Tel: 022-742-1202 Fax: 022-742-1201
Email: info@oystercatcherlodge.co.za Web: www.oystercatcherlodge.co.za
Cell: 082-903-9668

You can't miss Oystercatcher Lodge. If you do, you'll end up in the sea. It's set right on the tip of Shelley Point, overlooking the full curve of Britannia Bay with its flocks of cormorants, pods of passing dolphins and wallowing whales (in season). Luc (smiley and Swiss) and Sue (home-grown, but equally smiley) are both from the hotel trade. After years deep in the Mpumalanga bushveld, they decided they needed a change of air and came here. Quite a change. Here on the West Coast the sea air has a salty freshness unlike anywhere else, the sun shines brilliantly on arcing white beaches and the crunching waves are a bottomless blue. A special spot indeed where the Christens' newly-built guest house juts out towards the ocean like the prow of a ship, a large pointy pool in its bows. Each of the six rooms, painted in calming sandy colours, looks across grassy dunes and beach to the sea. Breakfast feasts are served in the dining room and, if you're lucky, Luc might summon some whales for you to view by blowing on his 'kelperoo' (a whale horn made out of seaweed!) as you munch on the Christens' 'special Swiss recipe' bread. A short stroll away is their latest venture, a set of stunningly modern self-catering apartments, custom-designed so that you gaze out to sea from whichever bed you happen to be lazing in. Simple, uncluttered, each with a full kitchen, lounge with TV and terrace, the rooms share a large pool and are as princely as the original lodge itself. A super spot and super people.

Rooms: 11: 6 rooms in guesthouse: 4 kings, 2 twins, all with en-suite shower and/or bath; 5 self-catering units: 1 studio, 1 honeymoon apartment, 3 x 2-bed apartments. All serviced daily.
Price: Guesthouse: R460 - R700 pp sharing. Self-catering: R700 - R2,000 per unit per night.
Meals: Full breakfast included in guesthouse rate. Full kitchens in self-catering units. Restaurants nearby.
Directions: From Cape Town head north on R27 then turn L into Vredenburg. At lights go R. After 10km, L towards St. Helena Bay. Just before Stompneus Bay turn L. After 200m turn R. At the S/Point entrance sign in, then go left past Country Club. Continue until fountain. Half circle fountain, thatched cottages on L, Oystercatcher on R.

Map Number: 1

Entry Number: 47

Blues Breaker Cottage

Chantal d'Orthez
2 Witbaai Close, Sunset Beach, Britannia Bay
Tel: 076-862-9706
Email: bluesbreaker-sa@hotmail.com
Web: www.bluesbreakercottage.yolasite.com Cell: 076-862-9706

Have you ever flicked through Homes and Gardens Magazine (as I have) and thought, "ooh, ⬛ like to stay there!"… and then, "I wish I had the design flair to match that"… and then (as I hav⬛ contemplated your own shambles of a home and wept silent tears of shame? Well, here is ⬛ opportunity. Blues Breaker Cottage featured in February's 2011 edition and you can book in an live the dream for as long as you want! Every flawless inch is as seductive in the flesh, so to spea⬛ as it is to read about. My solitary night amongst the lofty beams, soft-coloured hues, the luxurio⬛ linens and shea butter soaps, was beachside bliss. The polished concrete flooring, plumped-u⬛ cushions and African portraits among many other details conspire to create a subtle 'beachines⬛ to coin a word. I for one must have felt most at home here as I slept the sleep of the just for nin⬛ hours, intoxicated by the sea air. I would have slept on and on, but I remembered that Chan⬛ had seen whales basking in the morning sun the day before. Fifty short metres from my pillo an⬛ I was strolling along the sandy shores of virtually unknown (and therefore virtually private) Britann⬛ Bay before taking a lazy brunch in the sunny white-walled garden. Chantal and husband Jeren⬛ are a relaxed, stylish (did I mention Chantal's career in fashion?) and musical couple (hence t⬛ name Blues Breaker) who invite you to experience simple, luxurious beach life the way they li⬛ it. It happens to be the way I like it too.

Rooms: 2 doubles with full en-suite bathrooms.
Price: R2,000 - R2,500 for whole unit.
Meals: Self-catering, Choice of local restaurants nearby in Paternoster.
Directions: Emailed upon booking.

Feathers Inn

George and Nola Fletcher
1 Kerk Street, Piketberg
Tel: 022-913-3651
Email: feathersinn@mweb.co.za Web: www.feathersinn.co.za
Cell: 082-760-3464

Climbing Kerk Street towards Piquet Mountain I spied Piketberg's landmark gothic church and opposite, the town's imposing Victorian Inn. I felt as though I had entered a bygone era where traveller's horses would have been tethered to Feathers Inn's ornate iron columns that support its wrap-around balconies above. Instead, I discovered Nola and George, innovative owners and restorers of this 100-year-old guesthouse. Nola has turned her eye for interiors to authentically refurbishing each suite in the style of a different nationality. For example, The Mandarin Duck boasts Chinese furniture, wall-mounted bamboo hats and dim sum steamers, while the Gallic Rooster is a palatial Provençal-style two-bedroom *appartement* with rustic French kitchen. All have access to the vast balconies, either overlooking the street or courtyard and gardens, which have been lovingly landscaped by the Fletchers. Wandering through transplanted olive and lemon trees you'll discover the pool, jacuzzi, sheltered braai and bar offering views across the valley to snow-capped mountains in winter. Back at the courtyard, the old laundry is now home to Archers Restaurant, where George, who was trained by a Michelin-starred chef in Simon's Town, holds sway. I loved the chef's table that sits adjacent to the kitchen in a quasi-Victorian grocery store. On the menu you're likely to find fresh ingredients aplenty and, according to George, "the finest steak and kingklip in the area". It's another feather in the cap for this first-class inn. *Also in the building there is Flutterbuy, selling antiques and other curiosities.*

Rooms: 7 units: 4 one bedroom & 3 x 2-bedroom units, all with en-suite bathrooms and fully-fitted kitchen. B&B option available.
Price: R1,150 - R2,225 per unit. R825 per couple for B&B.
Meals: Fat Catz deli is open during the day and Archers restaurant is available for a la carte, set menus and private functions.
Directions: From Cape Town take N7 to Piketberg. At large circle L into town & take 2nd L exist indicating Kerk. Follow to top. Feathers Inn is on corner of Hoog & Kerk St.

Map Number: 1

Entry Number: 49

Waterfall Farm

Helen & David Untiedt

R303 6km from Citrusdal
Tel: 021-790-0972 Fax: 021-790-0972
Email: stay@perfecthideaways.co.za Web: www.perfecthideaways.co.za
Cell: 082-775-7797

Wow! It's hard to write about Waterfall Farm without eulogising over a certain natural feature. In fact, my first instruction upon arrival was, "you cannot leave without seeing the waterfall!" Lucki I didn't. Henry, resident expert on the farm's fauna and flora and a very genial guide, showed m the way. How I longed to shower in the white water cascading over sculpted cliffs, swim in th fresh-water mountain rock pools and picnic on surrounding white sandy beaches. Away from th natural wonder the farm provides fantastic walks, breathtaking views across the Cederber Mountains with their rich fynbos and spring flowers in season and enough naartjies to keep yc in vitamin C for months. For those lucky enough to stay, the main house has a rambling lived-feel and includes a large pine dining table, well-used sofas around an open fire and table tennis the games room. Outside, cricket-pitch-sized lawns are bordered by protea beds, oak and gur trees. But it's the thatched boma that really caught my eye. Here bookworms and siesta lover will usurp the day beds and night-time revellers will light fires, cook and make merry under fair lights. For smaller groups the converted stables cottage offers an intimate living area by the countr fire and outdoor seating among vines and lavender on the stoep. In both houses fine white line and fresh-cut roses freshen up the bedrooms. Finally, for convenience, there is a dam pool on th lawn… but whatever you do, don't leave without seeing that waterfall! *The house is a no-smokir zone.*

Rooms: Farmhouse: 4: 3 doubles (2 with en-s sh); room with double and twin beds; 1 extra bathroom. Humble Cottage: 3: 2 doubles; 1 room with 3 singles; bathroom with separate loo & outdoor sh. Weaver's Nest: 1 double and 1 twin shared bathroom.
Price: Farmhouse: from R2,000 per night; Honey Cottage: from R1,500 per night; Weaver's Nest: R800 - R1,200 per night. Specials available.
Meals: Self-catering.
Directions: Directions provided on booking.

Petersfield Mountain Cottages

Hedley Peter

Petersfield Guest Farm, Citrusdal
Tel: 022-921-3316 Fax: 022-921-3316
Email: info@petersfieldfarm.co.za Web: www.petersfieldfarm.co.za
Cell: 083-626-5145

Hedley is an instantly likeable and funny host and Petersfield, his family farm (citrus and rooibos tea), ranges over the back of the mountain behind the main house, forming a huge private wilderness reserve. De Kom, an idyllic, simple-but-stylish stone cottage perched high in sandstone mountains will appeal to your inner romantic. This charming, electricity-free cottage is lit by hurricane lamps and flares with gas for the stove, fridge and hot water. Its private plunge pool with river stones at the bottom overlooks this secret valley. And what a setting, guarded to the front by a citrus orchard, to the rear by craggy sandstone and looking deep and far from the stoep down the mountain. There is a secluded farm dam nearby (300 metres) to swim in or picnic by while watching nesting eagles. Or, 2km away, there is (electrified) Dassieklip Cottage, a sweet wooden mountain cabin secreted in its own kloof and reached down an avenue of oaks. Then there's Die Veepos, a luxurious addition to the Petersfield stable. Built in the 'sandveld' style, the high bamboo-reed ceilings and cretestone walls will keep the house at perfect temperature and there is also an open-air bush bathroom looking out across the Cederberg mountains. Hedley's latest cottage, solar-powered Stonehaven, is specifically built for romantic couples and sleeps only two guests in splendid mountain luxury. It has an extra secluded bath in the bush. Bring your own food, although breakfast materials for you to cook can be provided. Wood is supplied at no extra charge and pets are also welcome.

Rooms: 4 cottages: two with 2 bedrooms; one with 3 bedrooms, one open suite with outdoor shower. All the cottages have their own plunge pools.
Price: From R700/night/cottage for 2 people - R1000/weekend/cottage for 6 people.
Meals: Self-catering, but breakfast materials provided in the fridge by prior arrangement.
Directions: From Cape Town 4km after Citrusdal on your left on the N7 travelling towards Clanwilliam. Opposite the Caltex garage.

Mount Ceder

Wian and Francile Lambrechts & Rachelle Marriott-Dodingto
Grootrivier Farm, Cederberg, Koue Bokkeveld
Tel: 023-317-0848 Fax: 086-580-9343
Email: mountceder@lando.co.za Web: www.mountceder.co.za

Do not lose confidence as you rumble along the gravel roads that lead through the Kou Bokkeveld Nature Conservancy to this secluded valley - it's always a couple more turns. Finall you will arrive in the southern entrance of the Cederberg, dry sandstone mountains rising a around you in impressive dimensions – aim to get there at sunset for full-on effect. You will b given the key to your new home and drive off along a kilometre or so of sandy track to one c three fantastic rustic stone cottages. The river flows past the reeds and rock right by the cottage clear, deep and wide all year round. You can swim and lie around drying on flat rocks. Birds lov it here too. I imagine sitting out on that stoep, on those wooden chairs, looking at that view, bee or wine in hand… a piece of heaven, as they say. You can either self-cater or you can eat at th Old Millhouse restaurant back at the lodge. There are a few other cottages nearer the lodge which are fine, but you must ask for the stone cottages, which are in a league of their own. / pristine slice of unspoiled nature, cherished by a very knowledgeable Marais family who will hel with Bushman rock art, horse-riding and fauna and flora. Do not reach for your red pen by th way… that is how you spell ceder (in Afrikaans) and that is how you spell Jaen! *Serious hiking possible from here. Daughter Rachelle will happily take you horse-riding.*

Rooms: 3 river cottages with 3 bedrooms each.
Price: R1,825 - R2,885 per cottage per night self-catering (cottage sleeps 6). Prices valid until 31st Jan 2013. After that check website.
Meals: Restaurant with meals on request: breakfast R60, 3-course set menu dinner R140 (not including wine).
Directions: From Ceres follow signs to Prince Alfred's Hamlet/Op-die-Berg, up Gydo Pass past Op-die-Berg. First right signed Cederberge - follow tar fo 17km then continue on gravel road for another 34km into a green valley.

Oudrif

Bill and Jeanine Mitchell
PO Box 409, Clanwilliam
Tel: 027-482-2397
Email: oudrif@telkomsa.net Web: www.oudrif.co.za

Fifty kilometres of fabulous sandstone formations, dams and flower-covered passes lead you deep into the Cederberg Mountains and eventually to Oudrif, the perfect hideaway-getaway on the banks of the clear, clean, cool Doring River. I was met by my hosts Bill and Jeanine, who provided me with iced tea, before escorting me to my environmentally-friendly lodge where walls and roofs are straw bales and power is solar and views spectacular. Bill and Jeanine met whilst Jeanine was working as a goatherd (absolutely true) and their shared passion for wildlife is palpable. Together they're a veritable encyclopaedia of life in the wild from eco building to bird rescues to taming their half-Siamese, half-wild pet cat Barry and bottle-feeding their pet sheep Bo. My room was light-filled, with sofas to snooze on, but it was a hot day, so I donned my trunks and ran to the river for a dip. The main house is the meeting point, library and supper room and I was quickly introduced to the other guests. Oudrif holds ten at full capacity, with a rare atmosphere whereby guests know they are sharing a unique experience, so evenings around the communal table can be very entertaining. After a laughter-filled evening and too much home-made bread (both Bill and Jeanine are master bakers), I headed off to bed. Well, in fact… eschewing the comforts of a lovely king-size double bed, I actually decided to sleep outside under an amazing starlit sky. This is a truly special spot. *Guided excursions also included.*

Rooms: 5: all twin/double with en-suite shower.
Price: R750 pp sharing, including all meals and drinks.
Meals: 3 meals a day and all drinks (wine, beer, soft drinks) included.
Directions: Enquire on booking.

Klein Boschkloof Chalets

Eleanore Colyn
Boskloof Road, Clanwilliam
Tel: 027-482-2441 Fax: 027-482-2441
Email: valentine@mylan.co.za Web: www.kleinboschkloof.co.za

What a delightful arrival! Firstly the strong scent of Eleanore's roses, then the walk along a cool green avenue of orange groves to three 250-year-old Cape Dutch farm buildings. Eleanore showed me around Die Stal (The Stable), Die Ou Huis (The Old House) and Waenhuis (Wagon Shed); each conversion sympathetically designed by her husband and resident-architect, Gilbert "He's passionate about braaing", confesses Eleanore, as I inspect the cooking facility in the lounge fireplace of Die Stal. Half-metre-thick clay brick walls, hand-made Batavian clay floor tiles and air-conditioning help to keep the chalets chilled on the steamiest of Clanwilliam days. Ceilings and furniture are a collection of ceder, pine, yellowwood and embuia woods, while leather sofas and old rugs enhance the homely vibe. Outside, each has its own stoep with seating under ancient vines and lawns possessing bountiful braais (of course!). Guests should help themselves to seasonal local produce (table grapes, oranges, figs and pecan nuts) on the trees and year-round preserves (grape chutney, plum jam and local rooibos tea) in the well-equipped kitchens. My guided tour ends at the farm dam pool, where brick terrace and loungers attract sun-worshippers while surrounding weeping boer-bean trees and giant strelizias draw in the sunbirds. "Sometimes the guests are swimming until eleven at night!", exclaims Eleanore. And with the opportunity for endless gazing at sunsets on Cederberg Mountains and starlit skies who could blame them?

Rooms: 3 chalets: Die Stal: 1 room with double & single beds (en-s bath & sh); sleeper couch & extra single. Waenhuis: 2 rooms: double & twin (both en-s bath & sh). Ou Huis: 1 room: 3 singles (en-s bath & sh); sleeper couch.
Price: R650 - R750 per chalet per night for 2 people. Additional R100 per extra guest.
Meals: Continental breakfast delivered to chalet on request (R50 per person). Dinner on request for first night only (R100 per person).
Directions: Take N7 from CT to Clanwilliam. R towards Clanwilliam (R364). In Clanwilliam go past Shell Service Station & cross Jan Dissels River. R at Boskloof sign 200m after river. Continue 9km. K.B. is on R.

Enjo Nature Farm

Andrea and Moritz Conrad
Biedouw Valley, Clanwilliam
Tel: 027-482-2869 Fax: 086-535-1634
Email: rocks@soulcountry.info Web: www.soulcountry.info

Descending into the Biedouw Valley is the New World of South Africa's scenic symphonies: crashing mountains, sandstone cliffs, a vast plain of tawny yellow shot through with a river of green – not to mention spring's blanket of flowers. It's steering-wheel-gripping stuff. Moritz, a pilot (more on that later) and Andrea, a nurse, swooped into the valley from Munich five years ago and have so far conjured up three self-catering cottages, 350 sheep, a few hectares of olives and two happy little children. The white-washed thatched cottages are buried down by the river, set privately apart from one another. Inside, find simple beds with Andrea's hand-sewn bedcovers (German-style, two single duvets on a double bed), rough concrete shower rooms, kitchenettes. Older children scamper up hand-built ladders to beds on a mezzanine. Outside, a few wandering horses, the river, stone-built braais. Take note: accommodation is basic. But the setting is supreme and the Conrads are wonderful, generous hosts. If the weather's right Moritz can take you for a flip around the Cederberg in a four-seater plane; or you can wallow in the river, swim in the farm pool, relax in the hot tub, hike up through the valley, view rock art along the Sevilla Trail, even order a pair of hand-made leather shoes in Wuppertal. Bring children, dogs, meat for the braai, and do ask Andrea to cook for you at least one night. Simple, natural, beautiful, and great value - I just loved it.

Rooms: 3: 2 chalets with queen & 2 singles on mezzanine; 1 cabin with double bed & single on mezzanine. All have fireplaces, kitchenette (cabin has outside kitchen), stone braai area & en-suite shower.
Price: Chalets: R225 pp sharing (extra adults R50, children R25). Cabin: R175 pp sharing, (extra adults R50, children R25).
Meals: Self-catering facilities & braais in all units. Breakfast (R65) & dinner (R85) on prior request. Basic supplies avail' to buy.
Directions: From Clanwilliam, take newly-tarred R364 towards Calvinia. After 40km, turn R, signed Wuppertal Biedouw Valley, onto gravel rd. Over Hoek se Berg Pass into Biedouw Valley. Turn L into Biedouw Valley & continue 11km thro' 2 farm gates.

Map Number: 1

Entry Number: 55

Villa Tarentaal

Graham and Brandi Hunter
Tulbagh
Tel: 023-230-0868
Email: grahamjhb@gmail.com Web: www.villatarentaal.com
Cell: 074-194-8202

Graham is Mike and Christine's son and, having drunk his fill of life as a highway patrolman in America (abandon any Hollywood stereotypes, Graham is charming!), he and his wife Brandi (also charming) returned home to take over the family business - and to start a family of their own. Baby was on a break from meet-and-greet duty, but I was affectionately greeted by Max and Rocky, the Villa Tarentaal dogs, and instantly reassured of the ongoing wonderful hospitality here. People come for the privacy - each of the three cosy self-contained cottages offers a private lounge, kitchenette and sheltered braai patio - but stay, I imagine, to try each and every breakfast option which Graham delivers to your cottage each morning. The French toast is sinful... but delicious! Fans of Mike and Christine needn't worry. Christine is still on hand to offer her therapeutic massages (make sure to book in advance) and Mike, known locally as the 'Man of the Mountain', will pop in to enchant you with his passion for the pristine garden: wisteria and grapevines spider up the mustard-coloured house; roses provide an orgy of colour; and the lawn is so well-kept it would make the green-keepers of Augusta, well... green with envy. Guests are not the only ones flocking here; you'll witness an abundance of bird life including the eponymous tarentaal (Afrikaans for guinea fowl), Egyptian geese, fish eagle and blue crane. The cottages weren't named after this trio of winged beauties for nothing!

Rooms: 3 cottages: Blue Crane: 2 singles & 1 king in separate rooms, en-s sh'r & bath. Fish Eagle: 1 king, en-s sh'r. Egyptian Goose: 1 queen, en-s shower. All have aircon, fireplace, ipod docking stations & full DSTV.
Price: R450 - R495 pp sharing B&B. R425 pp sharing self-catering. Single supplement plus R100.
Meals: Full breakfast included served in the privacy of your own cottage or on private verandah.
Directions: N1 from Cape Town to exit 47 Wellington/Franschhoek/Klapmuts turn-off, left onto R44 via Wellington. Follow for approx 1 hour to Tulbagh. Straight through town, 1.2km on left.

Oudekloof Guest House

Louise and Bernardt Kruger

Wavern Street, Tulbagh
Fax: 023-230-1925
Email: reservations@oudekloofwineestate.co.za
Web: www.oudekloofwineestate.com Cell: 072-705-2333

Standing on the verandah of Oudekloof, glass of wine in hand, I surveyed all that lay before me: swimming pool, lawns, vines, the entire Tulbagh valley and the Witzenberg mountain range. Such scenery impressed Pieter Potter, who was first to arrive over the Obiqua Mountains (directly behind Oudekloof) 350 years ago. Louise insisted that I follow in his footsteps and guided me up the ancient wagon route to the Voortrekker Monument, original Dutch signalling cannon and, at the top, views all the way to Table Mountain. Meanwhile, Barnardt, a viticulturist by day, was browning tjops and wors on the braai. It wasn't long before we were tucking into our Afrikaans fare around the grand dining table of this refined Cape Dutch guesthouse. Upstairs, a games room and substantial roof terrace between the thatch, separate two generous bedrooms. Both are decked out with antique wooden furniture on screed floors and Persian rugs. My bathroom was the size of a small house with raised spa bath in one corner and a family-sized shower. There are two further bedrooms of similar proportions downstairs (note the garden shower in Blanc). The central living area is focused around a capacious fireplace and French doors leading to aforementioned stoep and those views. With local wine- and chocolate-tasting, hiking and plenty of history to offer, this corner of the Winelands is well worth exploring. The Kruger family are delightful hosts and will ensure that, while at Oudekloof, you are looked after in a manner appropriate to a venerable wine estate.

Rooms: 4: 2 king (1 en-s spa bath & shower, 1 en-s Victorian bath & outdoor shower); 2 queen (1 en-s spa bath & shower, 1 en-s shower).
Price: From R450 pp sharing. Singles from R600. Free for kids under 10 (mattress in room). Whole house/self-catering R4,000 per night.
Meals: Full breakfast included. Meals on request (extra charge).
Directions: From CT take N1 towards Paarl. L onto R44. Follow signs to Wellington & Ceres. Take R46 signed Tulbagh. Drive thro Tulbagh & L at 1st stop sign after Spar. After 2km L & drive thro Montpellier's white gates. Follow 5km to Oudekloof.

Map Number: 4

Entry Number: 57

Bartholomeus Klip Farmhouse

Lesley Gillett
Elandsberg Farm, Hermon
Tel: 022-448-1087 Fax: 086-604-4321
Email: info@bartholomeusklip.com Web: www.bartholomeusklip.com
Cell: 082-829-4131

Heavenly scenery cossets this Victorian homestead in its lush gardens and stands of oak and olive. The wall of the Elandsberg Mountains rises up from the game reserve, reflected in the dammed lake by the house. Guests enjoy a leisurely breakfast in the smart conservatory dining room before heading out for an excursion onto the wheat and sheep farm. You are also taken on late-afternoon game drives to see the zebra, a variety of Cape antelope, buffalo, quaggas (a fascinating experiment to reintroduce an extinct variety of zebra), eagles, flocks of blue crane... and the largest world population of the tiny, endangered geometric tortoises. But just to be out in such nature! The spring flowers are spectacular and there are more than 850 species of plant recorded on the property. Back at the homestead you can cool down in the curious, round, raised reservoir pool, sit in chairs on the stoep, wander down to the boathouse with a drink; or, if you have more energy, bike off into the reserve or go on guided walks in the mountains. Staff are very friendly, food is exceptional and a reason to stay on its own (and all included in the price). I recommend splashing out on at least two nights. A great place indeed and very popular so book ahead of yourself if possible. *Closed July - August and Christmas.*

Rooms: 7: 2 dbles & 3 twins, all with bath & shower. 2 self-catering cottages: Wild Olive Hse sleeps 8 with 3 dbles & bunk beds; Garden Cottage sleeps 2 with double bedroom, bathroom and small sitting room.
Price: R1,513 - R2,445 pp sharing. Singles + 20%. Wild Olive House R1,472 - R1,775 pp. Garden Cottage, R1,198-R1,330 pp for self-catering cottage. Rates include all meals and game drives. 0 - 3 are free, 4 - 15 half price in cottage.
Meals: Coffee & rusks, brunch, high tea, snacks & sundowners & 3-course dinner incl' in room rate.
Directions: From CT take N1 towards Paarl. Exit 47, left at stop. Continue along road turning L onto R44 signed Ceres. Follow for 30km. Past R46 junction signed Hermon, take next R signed Bo-Hermon. Gravel road for 6km. Bartholomeus Klip signed to L - 5km.

De Langenhof Guest House

Mike & Gail Walters

18 Lang Street, Riebeek West
Tel: 022-461-2188 Fax: 086-575-7070
Email: info@langenhof.co.za Web: www.langenhof.co.za
Cell: 084-255-4109

With a warm sun setting behind the Kasteelberg Mountain, it was with considerable pleasure that I sauntered through the five gardens (Rose, Mediterranean, Aloe, Kirstenbosch and Herb) of De Langenhof ending up by the lap pool. Resisting temptation to dive in, I joined my hosts (and cats Pasha and Minkee) for a glass of the local tipple on the stoep. Mike and Gail relocated all of one hour from Cape Town to enjoy the splendid scenery, food and wine of the Riebeek Valley. Gail is involved in promoting local tourism, which was extremely handy when it came to choosing from a plethora of recommended restaurants for dinner that evening. However, if you don't fancy exploring, Mike is a dab hand in the kitchen as I discovered while savouring my cooked breakfast including grilled brinjals. Both Mike and Gail are well suited to the guesthouse game, possessing an easy manner and a fine collection of furniture. The teak-floored guest lounge, dominated by its chimney and fireplace, is full of prime pieces from grandfather clock to Dutch brass log chest. I stayed in one of two garden rooms, swathed in soft creams and pinks with decadent double shower, Victorian bath and rose-patterned curtains opening onto a honeysuckle-laden verandah and koi pond. The four verandah rooms are equally stylish with their earthy beige and olive walls and 'distressed' country furniture. All rooms offer their guests the highly acclaimed Allesverloren vintage port and Lindt chocolates. Sound like a treat? Well…it is.

Rooms: 6: 4 verandah rooms: 1 double with en-s sh & bath; 2 double with en-s sh; 1 twin with en-s sh; 2 garden rooms: both queen with en-sh & bath.
Price: Verandah rooms: R440 - R460 pp sharing. Singles R505. Garden rooms: R545 - R570 pp sharing. Singles R610.
Meals: Full breakfast included. Dinners on request R100 - R150 for 2 courses and a glass of wine.
Directions: Take N7 north from Cape Town. Exit 1st Malmesbury off-ramp onto R46 to Riebeek Kasteel & Ceres. L onto R311 & drive thro' RK. De Langenhof signed on L just before leaving Riebeek West. 3rd property on R after turning off R311.

Arum Lily Log Cabins

Mandy & Koos Moller

R46 between Tulbagh and Ceres, Wolseley
Tel: 023-2311-421 Fax: 023-2311-421
Email: moller@breede.co.za Web: www.arumlilycottage.co.za
Cell: 082-923-6430

Plato the weimaraner bounded ahead along the farm track, past pear trees and bougainvillea, eager to beat us to our destination, Arum Lily's three luxury pine log cabins overlooking the bucolic farm dam and Mostershoek Mountain. His enthusiasm was understandable. Each of the chalets is handsomely constructed and romantically decked out with spaansriet ceilings, candles, hurricane lamps and giant baths lapping up halcyon views. Much of the furniture (from kitchen counters to bathroom units) is hand-crafted from old jarrah-wood railway sleepers. Wood-burning stoves and air-conditioning units cater for climatic extremes, but surely you'll spend most of your days in the great outdoors. There are mountains to hike in, wine estates to tipple in, Mandy and Koos' fruit orchards to explore in and your own dam to fish and kayak in. You'll return to your cabin's wooden deck (overlooking the water, naturally) for sundowners, braai and to kick back by the boma fire. For those too relaxed/lazy to cook, Mandy will even deliver traditional potjie meals and breakfast baskets to your stoep, as you get to wallow in your private outdoor jacuzzi while treasuring the surrounding nature: weaver birds weave in the blue gums, geese rear their goslings on the dam and swallows return every year. Surely you can't get a higher recommendation than that! *Arum Lily is 90 minutes from Cape Town.*

Rooms: 3 log cabins: Inlukwe: 1 queen (shower over bath); Intebe: 1 king/twin & 1 queen (shared sh & corner bath); Aaronskelk: 1 king/twin (en-s sh), 1 queen (en-s bath & sh) & 1 sleeper-couch.
Price: From R400 pp sharing. Singles on request. Enquire about mid-week specials.
Meals: Breakfast baskets on request (extra cost). Traditional Afrikaans meals and braai packs can be delivered on request (extra cost).
Directions: Take the R46 from Tulbagh towards Ceres bypassing the two turn-offs to Wolseley. After 3km the black security gate with green Arum Lily Cottage sign is on your right.

Oude Wellington Estate

Rolf Schumacher

Bainskloof Pass Rd, Wellington
Tel: 021-873-2262 Fax: 088021-873-4639
Email: info@kapwein.com Web: www.kapwein.com

There seems to be so much to catch the eye even as you rumble along the 800-metre paved and cobbled road to Oude Wellington: vineyards on both sides, ostentatious peacocks, geese and hadedas, pet ostriches peering over a fence. And that afternoon four pregnant alpacas that had just arrived all the way from Australia were to be added to the menagerie. Rolf is clearly the hospitable type (how else could ostriches find a home on a winery?). It took him two years to restore the whole estate to its former glory as a wine-grape farm. Four rustic double rooms are in the original farmhouse (built in 1790) with high, thatched ceilings, low pole beams, whitewashed walls and yet underfloor heating and air-con; the other two are in the more modern main building (well, 1836!), along with the homely farm kitchen with old-fashioned pots, pans and irons, billiard room and bar, and a terrace overlooking the vineyards, where breakfast is served in the summer. There is a partly-shaded pool off to the side of the main house, a brandy still in the barn, and handily on the premises is a restaurant popular with the locals (always a good sign). Guests are also invited to watch wine-making taking place at the right time of year. "I farm and dine and love company," says Rolf in his brochure!

Rooms: 8: all kings/ twins with en-suite Victorian baths. Self-catering option available.
Price: R480 - R550 pp sharing. Single R600.
Meals: Full breakfast included. Restaurant on premises, open seven days a week.
Directions: From Wellington follow Church Street (Kerkstraat), which becomes Bainskloof Rd (R301/3). 2.5km out of Wellington on right-hand side follow brown signs to Oude Wellington.

Kleinfontein

Tim and Caroline Holdcroft
Wellington
Tel: 021-864-1202 Fax: 021-864-1202
Email: kleinfon@iafrica.com Web: www.kleinfontein.com
Cell: 072-108-5895

An evening leg-stretch with Tim proved the perfect antidote to a long and stressful day on the road. Guided by a German alsatian, an almost-labrador and an incredibly energetic fluffy white thing we strolled past Jersey cows, through a shaded stream and between rows of sunlit vines. Kleinfontein is just an hour from Cape Town at the foot of the Bainskloof Pass and the Holdcrofts are delightful hosts. And this truly is home hosting at its finest; they'll eat and drink with you, show you their farm and even have you out there clipping the vines or feeding the horses if you show willing (and riding them, too, if you're saddle-hardened). In fact there's enough to keep you busy here for days, from hiking in surrounding mountains and cellar tours galore, to the leisurely delights of a good book beneath magnificent oak trees, or a wallow in the pool in Caroline's fabulous garden. She is of Kenyan stock and Tim's British, but they spent years in Africa and over a superb supper we washed down tales of the continent with home-grown cabernet sauvignon. Like me you'll stay in a roomy, restored wing of the thatched Cape Dutch farmhouse with poplar beams and reed ceilings. Like me you'll sleep like a baby. And, like me, you'll wake to breakfast on the verandah with fresh butter and milk, newly-laid eggs and honey straight from the beehive. Sound idyllic? Well, it is.

Rooms: 2 suites, both with sitting room and en-suite bath and shower.
Price: R1,400 - R 1,700 pp sharing. Single supplement + 20%. Includes all meals, all drinks and laundry.
Meals: Breakfast, tea/coffee tray, picnic lunch and 4-course dinner included in price.
Directions: Directions are down dirt roads so map can be emailed or faxed.

The Gate House at Nabygelegen Private Cellar

James McKenzie

Bovlei Division Road, Nabygelegen, Wellington
Tel: 021-873-7534 Fax: 021-873-7534
Email: marketing@nabygelegen.co.za Web: www.nabygelegen.co.za
Cell: 084-261-7961

The previous owners of the farm named this place in reference to 'in-laws' who lived 'close by' (Nabygelegen means 'close by'). When James returned to South Africa from working in London many of his friends came to visit. He needed somewhere 'close by' to put them, so he built his friends The Gate House. Nice! There's not a blown-up mattress or hastily-thrown-together sofa-bed in sight. James's mates got luxury, their own two-bedroom palace. And now you do too. No palace is complete without king-sized beds, en-suite shower-rooms and a secluded pool. From each bedroom double doors lead onto a private terrace. So if you're staying with friends or family you need only see them in the kitchen. Having said that, you might even lose them in there! It's whopping… a grand kitchen-diner-lounge rolled into one, with gigantic windows for walls. Doors lead out to the gardens, pool and braai area. The kitchen area has a sociable island work surface and a large range designed for communal cooking. I imagine there have been some hilarious meals held around that huge dining table. The Bovlei Valley (which is as pretty as it sounds) has a budding community of restaurants, wine cellars, vineyards and miles and miles of mountain bike track. It's 100m to James' private wine cellar and if you stay here you'll have mate's rates for wine tasting too.

Rooms: 1 luxury self-catering cottage: 2 kings with en-suite shower. Large open-plan kitchen-diner, private pool and gardens.
Price: R1,950 - R2,600 per night, for the whole cottage and includes complimentary wine tasting.
Meals: Assisted catering on request.
Directions: Emailed on request.

Bovlei Valley Retreat

Lee and Abbi Wallis
Bovlei Road, Wellington
Tel: 021-864-1504 Fax: 021-864-1504
Email: info@bvr.co.za Web: www.bvr.co.za

Arriving at Bovlei Valley to the sound of a beautiful aria and the waft of baking lavender cookie drifting in from Abbi's kitchen, I settled onto a squishy sofa near the large fireplace. Abbi did degree in hospitality and it shows. Her open-plan kitchen is part of the impressive-yet-cosy mai room, with high ceilings, sofas and a dining area and she does all her home-cooking there whil chatting to guests. Next door is a comfy TV room with DVD library and every board game eve thought up for rainy days. But when the sun shines it will be hard to leave the pool, whose depth are constantly filled with fresh water from the lips of a rather fetching bearded stone head Panoramic mountain views and a plump, well-stocked honesty fridge under the verandah cate for every poolside whim. The whole place is a working guava, grape and lavender farm, with i own boutique winery, Dunstone, where guest involvement is encouraged. If wine-making is you thing… pick, foot-stomp, bottle and taste to your heart's content! The highlight of the recently renovated stable rooms is the Lavender Suite with a luxurious four-poster and a view over you've guessed it – waving fields of lavender. Guava Cottage has its own mini-vineyard and stoe and lies in front of – wait for it – the guava plantation. A granite-topped kitchen with dishwashe and generous range mean you can really self-cater in style… that is, if you can stand a night awa from Abbi's food. The cottage even has its own solar panel-heated pool, garden and braai area

Rooms: 6: 5 in converted stables: 2 (king/twin), en-s bath & shower; 3 (queen) en-s shower over bath. Also 1 self catering cottage with 1 double (en-s bathroom) & 1 twin (shower room).
Price: Stable suites: R450 - R750 pp sharing, singles R680 - R960. Guava Cottage: R500 pp based on 2 sharing. R375 pp based on 4 sharing. Add breakfast R8(pp. Extra bed in room, R100 - R150.
Meals: Full English breakfast with home-made bread; afternoon tea, fresh-baked cakes & complimentary wine tasting incl'. Dinner & light lunches with prior booking.
Directions: See website for detailed directions or a map can be faxed/emailed.

Belair

Janet Plumbly
Suid Agter-Paarl Rd, Paarl
Tel: 021-863-1504
Fax: 021-863-1602
Email: info@belair.co.za
Web: www.belair.co.za
Cell: 082-572-7062

A straight 300-metre drive up two narrow strips of weathered red brick, past roaming gangs of guinea-fowl and rows of vines, takes you to Belair, a beautiful guest house on its own farm beneath the round dome of Paarl Mountain. The view from the doorstep (and the garden and pool) across the valley towards Franschhoek and the Groot Drakenstein is spectacular… and it is rather lovely inside too. Steps lead up from a large threshing-circle style driveway into the hallway and open sitting room, which mixes antique furniture with comfy sofas and bookshelves bursting with swashbucklers. Behind is the bright breakfast conservatory, which looks onto a rose-filled garden. Janet's light but stylish touch is in evidence everywhere at Belair, from the terraced gardens to the bedrooms themselves, each with its own distinct character. All the rooms are wonderful, but the two new luxury suites, complete with fireplaces, open-plan baths and deep Flokati rugs, are sumptuous! The honeymoon suite has a deck overhanging the rose garden with a double daybed on it, while the other suite has a patio area with a swing couch. From the house, it's a short walk up to the dam where birdlife abounds among the reeds (look out for buzzards when it all goes quiet), a great spot for a sundowner. For the more energetic, Paarl Mountain Nature Reserve is further up the hill, and there are lots of golf courses nearby. *Cape Town Waterfront is also only 35 minutes away and there are great restaurants in Paarl. Bikes for hire.*

Rooms: 6: 4 double rooms in main house; all en-s with separate bath & shower; 2 new luxury suites, downstairs sitting room, patio/deck, upstairs bedroom/bathroom. Fireplace in sitting room & bedroom/bathroom.
Price: R450 - R750 per person sharing per night, including full English breakfast. Singles R100 supplement.
Meals: Full breakfast included.
Directions: On Suid-Agter Paarl Rd off R101 (next to Fairview Wine Estate).

Palmiet Valley Estate

Frederick Uhlendorff

Palmiet Valley Estate, Sonstraal Rd, Klein Drakenstein, Paarl
Tel: 021-862-7741 Fax: 021-862-6891
Email: info@palmiet.co.za Web: www.palmiet.co.za

Frederick has scoured not just this land but several in his relentless quest for fine things. There's hardly a nut or bolt in the place that isn't antique - even the loos, showers, free-standing baths and wooden wash-stands are Victorian, not to mention the aged safes and old-school slipper bed pans (that thankfully no-one ever uses!). But this is not a museum, despite the long history of the farm - Palmiet was one of the first to be established outside Cape Town in 1692. Guests come here for the luxury and the romance of the vineyards, guava fields and mountains that stretch out and up from the old farm. One four-poster bed is positioned so that you can wake up and watch the sun rise over the mountains without moving your head. The beautiful, clipped gardens are interwoven with cobbled paths and peppered with numerous dreamy spots to be peaceful. Herbs are harvested and transformed into fresh herbal teas or added to shady lunches by the pool. 'Sundowner' here means a glass of champagne on a raised astro-turf terrace - under which stands a collection of shiny 1950s Mercedes, which you can hire for a drive around the Winelands. In summer, candlelit dinners are held under the oaks and are as sumptuous as everything else, with top chefs employed to cook exclusively for residents. With so much character and reflection upon old-fashioned values, it's no wonder this place is a hot-spot for weddings. But you don't need to be married or coupled to enjoy it as I, a happy singleton, discovered.

Rooms: 14: 1 Honeymoon, 4 Luxury & 1 Presidential Suite, 4 standard tw/doubles, all en-s bath or shower; 2 junior (double beds) en-s sh'r; 2 family cottages w' kitchenette (not fully s/c) en-s b/sh'r.
Price: R610 - 1,900 pp sharing. Single rooms from R1,037. Specials available in low season (stay for 3 nights, pay for 2).
Meals: Full breakfast included. Lunches on request. 3-course set dinner R290 pp.
Directions: Heading away from Cape Town on the N1 take exit 62a (Sonstraal Road), turn first left, straight over 2 crossroads. Palmiet Valley is on left. Airport Transfer R575.

Entry Number: 66

Map Number:

Ridgeback House

Vanessa and Vernon Cole

Langverwacht Farm, Nr. Paarl
Tel: 021-869-8988 Fax: 021-869-8708
Email: guesthouse@ridgeback.co.za Web: www.ridgebackhouse.co.za
Cell: 072-500-7516

Though the ice-cold Coke that Vanessa – and her team of handsome young ridgebacks – greeted me with was just what the doctor ordered, it really should have been a glass of shiraz. For this is the place to come for the complete wine experience. Guests are encouraged to help in every way in the production of the gods' favourite tipple, whether it be lending a hand with the harvest or just making sure the bottle's not corked. The latter takes place in a smart tasting centre and restaurant in the hub of the farm, with a wooden balcony overlooking the dam – home to twenty-five species of wild fowl. A tour of the cellar is easily and enthusiastically arranged too, although the best place to sample the wine is indisputably the granite rock at the top of the farm, where Vanessa will lay on a boozy sundowner picnic and retire discreetly, leaving you to contemplate the sky melting to a pinky-purple over the wide, olive- and vine-filled valley. Stroll down through the vines and olive trees to your bedroom in the converted farmhouse, or to the latest addition, a sweet cottage on one side of the house, opposite an aviary of lovebirds, quails and budgies. Meals are served in the cavernous dining room, a short amble from a sitting room lit by wrought-iron chandeliers, and on summer evenings the braai will be fired up out by the pool. Vanessa is a superb hostess and Ridgeback the perfect place to ensure that the 2011-2012 vintage is a fine one. *If arriving after 6pm, arrange for gate to be kept open.*

Rooms: 5 rooms in farmhouse: 1 king, 1 double and 3 king/twins. All en-suite, 4 with baths and showers & 1 with shower.
Price: B&B R510 – R750 pp sharing. Singles R750.
Meals: Full breakfast included in guest-house rate. Lunches available either at tasting centre or at house on request.
Directions: From N1, take exit 47 onto R44 towards Wellington. After 16.5km, turn R after Windmeul Co-op. After 200m, turn R between school and church.

Eensgevonden Vineyard Cottages

Sally and Douglas McDermott

Near Brandvlei Dam, Rawsonville/Breedekloof
Tel: 023-349-1490 Fax: 023-349-1490
Email: info@eensgevonden.co.za Web: www.eensgevonden.co.za
Cell: 082-829-8923

Often by driving that tiny bit further in South Africa you find something particularly special. Like Eensgevonden. Winding through chardonnay and merlot vineyards, I discovered this beautiful national monument, the oldest Cape Dutch farmhouse in the Breede River Valley and home to Sally and Doug. Under the shady fingers of a giant oak tree, planted nearly three centuries ago under orders of Cape Governor van der Stel, we sampled their unlabelled, excellent wine. The couple (aided by a staff of four) hand-tend and harvest their grapes, honey bees and organic vegetables and will enthusiastically show you around. The farm itself is part vineyard, part natural fynbos, and among 400ha of private nature reserve lies the heavenly, secluded, crystal clear mountain rock pool. If you can wrench yourself away (I couldn't) and up one of the well-marked trails across the rugged reserve, keep one eye peeled; klipspringer, honey-badger and 100 identified birds reside here, as does a recently photographed leopard! A short skip from the farmstead leads you to three white-washed, spotlessly-clean self-catering cottages, surrounded by pebble-paved indigenous gardens. I adored Sunbird with its white linen, terracotta flooring, wood fire, vases of cut herbs and French windows revealing wide, cushioned verandah with magnificent views - sundowner nirvana. Eensgevonden is a treasured Greenwood destination, offering a wilder, more genuine wine experience than is on offer in more touristy towns like Franschhoek and Stellenbosch.

Rooms: 3 self-catering cottages: 2 with queen in one room and 2 singles in other, 1 bathroom with bath and shower, and 1 with shower only; 3rd cottage with single with queen, 1 bathroom with shower.
Price: R300 - R500 pp sharing.
Meals: Self-catering. Breakfast in basket with home-made muesli & muffins is available as extra. Braai packs provided on request. Good restaurants nearby.
Directions: Between Rawsonville & Worcester, near the Brandvlei Dam. Full directions given on enquiry.

Fraai Uitzicht 1798

Karl and Sandra Papesch

Historic Wine and Guest Farm with Restaurant, Klaas Voogds East (Oos),
Robertson/Montagu
Tel: 023-626-6156 Fax: 086-662-5265
Email: info@fraaiuitzicht.com Web: www.fraaiuitzicht.com

'Fraai Uitzicht' means 'beautiful view' in Dutch - no idle promise as it turns out. The wine and
guest farm, dating from the 1700s, is four kilometres up a gravel road in a cul-de-sac valley ringed
by vertiginous mountains. Sitting on the stoep chatting to Karl and Sandra over an excellent
espresso, I admired their tumbling water feature, which complements an existing sculpture-
dotted dam buzzing with birdlife and draws your gaze to the blanket of peach, apricot and olive
trees and vineyards all around. People come from far and wide for the award-winning a la carte
restaurant and the seven-course *dégustation* menu - perfectly matched with local wine and
including such delicacies as springbok carpaccio - is irresistible. Thankfully it's not far to the garden
suites, upon which the couple have let loose their imagination: returning guests will find new, huge
bathrooms and extra outside showers illuminated by colour-changing lights; one bed has been
sunk down to catch views of the highest mountains; another protrudes jauntily from an angled
alcove. A few newly-renovated cottages take it easy in the garden, a couple with metre-thick walls
and timber interiors; my favourite was the loft bedroom in the eaves. Make sure you take a peek
at the wine cellar - guests have first option on the (uniquely) hand-made merlot. I can't count the
number of recommendations we had pointing us here. *Restaurant closed to public June to August,
but always open for guests.*

Rooms: 9. 4 cottages, 2 with 2 bedrooms (1 queen, 1 twin), 2
with 1 bedroom (king, extra-length); 5 suites, 4 king, 1 queen, all
with air-con & en/s shower, some bath, some extra outdoor
shower.
Price: Cottages: R820 pp sharing. Suites: R530 – R680 pp
sharing. Singles on request.
Meals: Champagne breakfasts in the Fraai Uitzicht 1798
restaurant which is open for lunch & dinner on Wednesdays to
Sundays, but serves dinner every night for residents.
Directions: On R60 between Robertson & Ashton.
Approximately 5km from Ashton and 9km from Robertson, Klaas
Voogds East turn-off, 4km on gravel road, turn-off to left.

Olive Garden Country Lodge

Gina and Fernand Van Wassenhove

Klaasvoogds West, Robertson
Tel: 023-626-2028
Fax: 023-626-2028
Email:
info@olivegardencountrylodge.com
Web:
www.olivegardencountrylodge.com
Cell: 082-448-5393

Olive Garden Country Lodge, almost invisibly hidden in a dramatic sea of fynbos, is a destination for those who want to lose themselves in nature... but who don't want to compromise on luxury at the same time. This happy combination is typical of Gina and Fernand, serious back-to-nature eco-conscious conservationists, passionate about the wild things that crowd round the lodge and especially the award-winning extra virgin olive oil that they produce; but also epicurean in their tastes. If my room can be likened to a restaurant it would have a Michelin star - its open fire the oven, its beds a perfect soufflé perhaps. Why all the food analogies? Listen up, I'll only say this one hundred times – they are nothing short of magicians in the kitchen. I just would never have thought that the best sushi I would ever taste would be in a remote olive grove in the South African mountains – and made by a Belgian. Then came the meltingly tender pieces of home-reared mutton; and then more than one slice of fruit tartine. I think a few appreciative expletives may have escaped me at some point.... Good job Olive Garden has its own hiking trail, winding its way through olive groves and up the mountain that cradles the lodge. Looking back across the view my mouth made a perfect 'o' – and this time it had nothing to do with food. Gina was right, this place is a slice of heaven.

Rooms: 7: 4 queens; I family suite with 2 twins/queens & 2 bathrooms; 2 luxury honeymoon suites with king bed, jacuzzi, bath & shower.
Price: Rooms & family suite: R495 - R825 pp sharing. Honeymoon suites: R850 - RI,050 pp.
Meals: Full breakfast included. 4-course dinner RI80, not including wine. Wine & Dine Experience R325. Picnics on request.
Directions: From Robertson, drive 9km towards Ashton, then turn L to Klaasvoodgs West (gravel road). At T-junction turn R then immediately L. Olive Garden on right.

Mallowdeen Gardens

Rita and Wim van de Sande

Klaasvoodgs West, Robertson
Tel: 023-626-5788 Fax: 086-509-6764
Email: info@mallowdeen.com Web: www.mallowdeen.com

Driving down a long avenue of olive trees coiled in sunshine, I could have been in the hot heart of southern Spain. Rita and Wim, emerging from their traditional Cape Dutch farmhouse, have the greenest of visions for their little bit of joy caught in the centre of a spectacular panorama of rolling vine-clothed hills and the distant Langeberge mountains. Young olive saplings – nurtured in their greenhouse – fan out from the house, interspersed with spiky cacti and aloe, papaya trees, vivid red canna flowers, an apricot orchard, vegetable gardens... and when the infant Japanese garden matures it will surely embody the peace and privacy you find here. Three square rondavels (yes, that's correct) face each other across a portly figure-of-eight swimming pool. One is a breakfast room where you sit at neat hand-made tables and chairs (if not outside under the lapa) or, more unusually, cupped inside giant, hand-shaped thrones. The other two are thatched, cool, earthy and rather wonderful, with a full kitchen and a maze-like partition into the bathroom, where you'll find an ingenious sunken bath. Bird-lovers may prefer the more modern flat in the main house, which is close to the dam and its symphonic orchestra of birds. Faithful to their native Holland, Rita and Wim provide bicycles for guests to pedal out to the five wineries, two farm stalls and two good restaurants that lie within an easy 10km radius. You won't even need the incentive of a discount to stay two nights or more.

Rooms: 3 units: 2 cottages (king/twin with full en-suite bathrooms), 1 flat (twin/king with en-suite shower).
Price: R425 - R580 pp sharing. Highly discounted rates for longer stays.
Meals: Full breakfast included. Full self-catering facilities and braais in each unit. Excellent restaurants nearby (and a free shuttle service provided to and fro if needed).
Directions: 7km from Robertson toward Ashton. Take Klaasvoodgs West turning on the left onto dirt road. Mallowdeen Gardens is 1.5km on the right.

Orange Grove Farm

Carlos Araujo
Noree, Robertson
Tel: 023-626-644 Fax: 023-626-5387
Email: info@orangegrovefarm.co.za Web: www.orangegrovefarm.co.za
Cell: 076-718-0760

You're probably going to say "Wow!" a lot during your stay at Orange Grove. I know I did. I woul recommend one thing on the drive up to the farm: if you can wangle it, try not to be the driver. A I sat behind the steering wheel, sun beating down, right arm hanging loosely out of the wound down window, I felt my heart begin to race and my eyes widen to fit in the immense mountain olive-river-vine panorama that surrounded me. It was clear I had struck gold. Greenwood Guide gold that is. Abundant tortoises roam free and wild amongst the vines here, so don't forget to kee an eye on the road. I saw no fewer than six on my approach. There's a choice of four delightfu thatched cottages of varying sizes, all tucked into the mountainside and offering luxury, comfort an mod cons, including your very own pool. And there are thoughtful touches everywhere. Olive oi vinegar, wine and toiletries (all farm produce) are provided as well as freshly-picked proteas (i season) and other flowers, which perfume the cottages outside and in. Carlos, a Portugues diamond prospector - and a bit of a diamond himself - will bend over backwards to ensure that yo have everything you need during your stay from guided mountain hikes, farm tours, delicious picni or breakfast hampers, candlelit dinners under the southern stars… and, if you're lucky, stories s fascinating that Hollywood couldn't dream 'em up. "Are you afraid of heights?" asked Carlos, as w off-roaded 90 degrees vertically up and then down the mountains in his 4x4. My heart is still racing

Rooms: 4 self-catering cottages: Wouterspan: sleeps 6, 1 double, 1 king, 1 queen; Mosesberg: sleeps 2, 1 king; Longlands: sleeps 4, 1 dble, 1 twin/king; Delportshoop: sleeps 2, king/twin. Cottages have en-suites, private pool & own parking. (Delportshoop has access to a pool though it's not attached to cottage)
Price: R780 - R3,000 per unit per night.
Meals: Breakfast/lunch baskets on request. Chef can be arranged for dinners in cottage or mountains.
Directions: Take N1 CT to Worcester, then R60 Worcester to Robertson approx 30km. L at Rooiberg Kelder. Over railway on tar rd to Noree sign to R. T R on tar rd, cross stop sign, Vink Rivier Primary on L becomes gravel. Go straight to Orange Grove Fm.

Tierhoek Cottages

Bruce and Alison Gilson

Tierhoek Farm, Noree, Robertson
Tel: 023-626-1191 Fax: 023-626-1191
Email: gilson@barvallei.co.za Web: www.tierhoekcottages.co.za
Cell: 082-789-9205

Despite its name (tiger corner) the only big cats round here are the Cape mountain leopards. Bruce is sanguine: "losing a few sheep is a small price to pay for keeping the baboons off my peaches." However, the Gilson family has yet to sight such a predator since relinquishing Boschendal Wine Estate for their organic fruit farm fourteen years ago. Standing on the stoep of Quince Cottage I admired the blossoming Noree Valley and McGregor/Greyton Mountains beyond. A plum spot indeed! Come nightfall, I was equally mesmerised by the silence and the stars. Accommodation is in one of four farm cottages, which nicely combine rusticity with modernity: an old wood-burning stove with potje and kettle sits alongside the gas cooker for example. While braai enthusiasts face a tough choice between a Neanderthal fire pit and a 21st-century Weber! At first light, tucking into Alison's scrumptious quince jam and dried-fruit selection (help yourself and leave your money in the honesty bread bin), I observed the malachite sunbird performing a merry song and dance among agapanthus and surrounding fynbos. I contemplated the day ahead: whether to plunge into the private pool or dam, hike up the mountain or pick fresh fruit and veg (all you can eat in season). Or, back along the track, past resident donkeys Milly, Tilly and Violet, to sample the produce at Rooiberg Winery and their acclaimed Bodega de Vinho restaurant and bakery. Although, that would mean forsaking this heavenly hideaway… and I'd rather not.

Rooms: 5 cottages: 1 queen (en-s bath only); 1 queen & 1 twin (+ bunk-beds) with 2 baths & sh; 1 king (en-s bath & sh); 1 queen & 1 twin (+sofa bed) with shared bath & sh; 2 queens both en-s bath & sh, 1 twin with separate bath & sh.
Price: R600 per cottage (2 pax) - R1,800 (6 pax).
Meals: Breakfast basket (self-cook) R65 pp; dinner on request (self-cook) R100 pp.
Directions: On R60 between Robertson and Worcester take the road to Noree. Follow tar road for 6km. At stop by school continue straight onto dirt road. Go through Orange Grove Farm and take left turn to Tierhoek.

Natte Valleij

Charlene and Charles Milner

R44 between Stellenbosch and Paarl, Klapmuts
Tel: 021-875-5171
Email: milner@intekom.co.za Web: www.nattevalleij.co.za
Cell: 079-037-4860

Come and lose yourself in the depths of this wild and fecund garden - or do I mean jungle! Ancient trees such as the rare gingco (the oldest in South Africa, once thought extinct), several 200-year-old oaks and a wealth of growth besides keep the pool, 'moon gate' and handful of retired ponies secreted in their midst. Guests stay in the simple B&B room next to the main house, its verandah festooned with grandiflora, and eat breakfast in this most lovely of Cape Dutch homesteads (pictured above), built in 1775. If the weather's fine then you eat out on the patio under its cooling roof of vine. Or you can take one of the cottages lost down garden paths. Vineyard Cottage (pictured below), with direct access to the swimming pool, is the oldest building on the property, its original 1714 reed ceilings still intact, while Cellar Cottage is small, cute, rustic and perfect for couples. Charles and Charlene are charm personified, with the latest excitement in the shape of their son Alexander, a bright young thing whose wines are already topping the charts and who offers tours and tastings in the miniature cellar. Walks are in all directions up mountains and into surrounding vineyards. Or guests are welcome to enter next door's park where wildebeest, eland, springbok, bontebok, kudu, oryx and zebra (among others) can be seen. Local bird-watching tours with Charles are a speciality. *Well-positioned on the Stellenbosch and Paarl wine routes. Self-catering available in the cottages.*

Rooms: 3: 1 B&B room, double with en/s bath; 2 cottages (self-catering): Cellar Cottage sleeps 2 (plus 2 kids' beds); Vineyard Cottage sleeps 6 (3 bedrooms and 2 bathrooms).
Price: B&B R340 - R380 pp sharing. Cellar Cottage: R560 - R650 per night/whole cottage; Vineyard: R700-1,500 per night/whole cottage.
Meals: Full breakfast included in B&B and an optional extra in cottages.
Directions: From Cape Town take N1 Exit 47. Turn right onto R44. Farm 4km on left.

Entry Number: 74

Map Numbe

Lekkerwijn

Simon Pickstone-Taylor and Ross Hutchison-Taylor

Groot Drakenstein, Franschhoek Road, Franschhoek/Groot Drakenstein
Tel: 021-874-1122 Fax: 021-874-1465
Email: lekkerwijn@new.co.za Web: www.lekkerwijn.com

Lekkerwijn (pronounced Lekkervain) is a 1790s Cape Dutch homestead with a grand Edwardian extension designed by Sir Herbert Baker, complete with curling chimneys and original coal fireplaces imported from England. Simon's family have lived here lived here since the late 19th century when his great grand-father Harry Pickstone, pioneer of the fruit farming industry, bought the farm. You would probably have to pay to look round if Simon and his partner Ross didn't live in the grounds. You can tell when one family have lived in a grand house for generations - all the furniture, fittings and decoration look so at home. It positively creaks with family history. The house is now fully child-friendly, while large parts of the house have been kept completely quiet and free of them! There's a new play room and children's courtyard and rabbits, miniature goats and Transkei pigs happy to be petted and there are two family suites now. Susan has done a 'super-nanny course' and is now certified to look after people's kids, so babysitting is available in-house. My strongest impressions at Lekkerwijn are of the central courtyard with its orchid-lined gallery and cloister around an ancient pomegranate, the wood floors and yellowwood beams and the towering palms planted by Simon's great-grandfather, the informal taste of the nursery bedroom, a wonderful breakfast... and Simon & Ross, who together with their team, so caring of their guests. Simon's mother Wendy visits Lekkerwijn for returning guests.

Rooms: 6: 5 double rooms (en-suite) plus a self-catering cottage.
Price: R290 - R780 pp sharing depending on season and room. Quotes for singles on request. Minimum stays of 2 nights at weekends (Fri-Sat or Sat-Sun). Offers on occasion.
Meals: Full breakfast incl' for B&B. Breakfast can be served in courtyard rather than dining room. Other meals by prior arrangement.
Directions: On R45 at intersection with R310 from Stellenbosch (after passing Boschendal), alongside the Allée Bleue entrance walls.

Cathbert Country Inn

Peter & Tisha Cunliffe

Klapmuts/Simondium Road (Off R45), entrance on "Vrede en Lust" Wine
Estate, Simondium, Franschhoek
Tel: 021–874-1366 Fax: 021-874-3918
Email: info@cathbert.co.za Web: www.cathbert.co.za

If warm hosting, gourmet food and eye-watering natural beauty in the heart of the wineland
doesn't sound like your sort of thing then turn away now, because Cathbert Country Inn is all o
these things. Aubrey, ever the attentive host and connoisseur on local wineries, stomped cheeril
out to greet me in a pair of wellies. Now you don't have to so much as turn your head to se
fabulous views over the vineyards, farmland and the dam that so immaculately mirrors the hig
Simonsberg Mountains. I was shown down a poplar-lined lane, scattering Egyptian geese, to th
newly-converted cottage, a sweet, secluded place with a kitchen, braai and raised pool. Peter an
Tisha Cunliffe, the owners, have decorated Cathbert in sophisticated French country style
distressed wood, natural fabrics, scatter cushions placed just so and delicate shades of grey. Ha
an hour later Aubrey had swapped his wellies for a chef's hat and was ably assisting the in-hous
chef Max conjure up the gourmet creations that are one of Cathbert's major draw cards – in fac
guests generally eschew Franschhoek's offerings in favour of their local, often organic, alway
home-made culinary compositions. The best thing? That you can spend the day hiking, touring
wine-tasting, or perhaps just drinking up the peace and a local vintage by the pool... and not hav
to get in the car to find a great meal at the end of it all.

Rooms: 9: 2 luxury rooms, 4 luxury suites, 1 executive
suite, 1 x 2-bedroomed luxury suite, all with king-
size/twin beds, en-suite bath and shower, air-con. 1
luxury cottage with queen/double beds.
Price: R1,920 – R3,000 per room/unit (sleeping
between 2 – 4 people). Rates for singles & special offer
on request.
Meals: Full breakfast included in all room rates. Set
menu 3-course dinner, R275 pp (Mon to Sat). Fully-
equipped kitchen in cottage.
Directions: From CT take N1, take exit 47, R at end o
ramp, over 4-way stop, L at next rd towards
Franschhoek. Pass Backsberg Wine Estate. Just before T-
jct R into gates of Vrede en Lust Wine Estate, & follow
tar rd, following Cathbert Country Inn signs for 2.5km

Clementine Cottage

Malcolm and Jackie Buchanan

L'Avenir Farm, Green Valley Rd, Franschhoek
Tel: 021-876-3690 Fax: 021-876-3528
Email: lavenir@iafrica.com Web: www.clementinecottage.co.za

Running late with my mobile battery dead, I was touched to find Jef waiting expectantly for me just beyond the low-lying bridge that marks the entrance to L'Avenir Farm. He kindly guided me through the orchards of plums (no, not clementines) to meet Malcolm, who runs this 21-hectare, family-owned, working fruit farm. Jef, by the way, is a boerboel, as loyal to the Buchanans as Robin is to Batman – although after the birth of their daughter Sarah, Jef now has a rival for Malcolm and Jackie's affections. In retrospect, my timing was perfect: the sun was setting behind the mountains that frame the Franschhoek Valley and from the stoep of Clementine Cottage, looking out over the pool and the vineyard beyond, the sky was stained a deep red. The only sounds I could hear, as I enjoyed a most welcome cold beer with Malcolm and Jackie, were the frogs croaking contentedly in the dam that forms the centrepiece of the farm. If you find the pool too confining, a few lengths of this dam should satisfy any Tarzanesque impulses you may harbour. Being only a five-minute drive from the village (longer if the geese are crossing the road) I was able to enjoy a fine meal before returning to the biggest bed I've ever had the pleasure of sleeping in. Nicely done up in the original farm cottage style, Clementine Cottage has everything you could desire for a lazy break, from pool, braaing area and satellite TV to large, stylish en-suite bedrooms.

Rooms: I cottage: I double with en-suite bath and shower and I twin with en-suite bath and shower.
Price: 2 people sharing R600 pp per night, 3 people R550 pp, 4 people R500 pp. Minimum stay 2 nights. With regret no children 2-10 or pets.
Meals: Self-catering, but numerous restaurants nearby.
Directions: From Franschhoek Main Rd driving towards Franschhoek Monument turn R. Drive for 2km. Turn L up Green Valley Rd (Clementine Cottage signed). Turn L up 1st gravel rd (signed again). Drive over bdge onto L'Avenir, thro' orchards, pass shed on L, Cottage 150m further on R.

Plumtree Cottage

Liz and John Atkins
Excelsior Road, Franschhoek
Tel: 021-876-2244 Fax: 021-876-2398
Email: plumtree@kleindauphine.co.za Web: www.kleindauphine.co.za

The setting could not be more perfect. A sanctum of blooming plum-blossom, vineyards and oak trees spatter dappled shadows as they rock gently in the breeze, while magnificent mountains rise steeply from the Franschhoek valley. The Plumtree Cottage balcony is the perfect spot to soak up all this serenity. Having run B&Bs for many a year, Liz and John know exactly what people want and with this cottage they deliver it in spades. Entirely self-contained (it even has its own separate orchard-lined driveway), it allows you the space to do your own thing. This may be in the elegantly paved courtyard, cooling off in the invigorating plunge pool, or popping out to the restaurants and wineries in Franschhoek, itself just pip-spitting distance away. The interior is a calming refuge in blues and whites, much like the roses and lavender outside. With each room sharing the magnificent view, you won't know where to put yourself.... I'd choose the corner bath first, then settle down on the terrace to gaze at the Arab horse stud just over the fence. By now, Liz will be busy clothing the cottage's clotted-cream-coloured walls with wisteria, roses and any other creepers she has creeping around for when she runs out of space in the garden: "I just send the plants up the walls." Perfectly tranquil and delightfully quaint… a proper English-style country cottage.

Rooms: 1 queen with full en-suite. Mezzanine floor accessed by Swedish ladder (so sensibly made it's almost impossible to fall off) can sleep two children (over the age of 12).
Price: R900 per night + R100 for each additional person (2 max). Minimum booking 2 nights.
Meals: Self-catering.
Directions: Drive through Franschhoek and turn right at the monument. After 1.3km turn left into Klein Dauphine. Plum Tree Cottage on right.

Akademie Street Boutique Hotel & Guesthouses

Katherine and Arthur McWilliam Smith

5 Akademie Street, Franschhoek
Tel: 021-876-3027 Fax: 021-876-3293
Email: info@aka.co.za Web: www.aka.co.za
Cell: 082-655-5308

From the moment I arrived until my too-soon departure from this glorious patch of Franschhoek it felt like Katherine and I had met before, so easy and harmonious was my visit. Katherine's interest in life, literature and art is displayed throughout the house in every delicate and refined detail. There are two suites in the manor house; Twyfeling A and B. They are large and luxurious suites with paintings, gleaming bathrooms and underfloor heating. The parade of flowers and stepping-stones through citrus trees, fig trees and rose bushes lead to the garden cottages, which sit detached within the flower arrangements, opening out onto private stoeps, gardens and even swimming pools. Vreugde is a garden suite for two that has an alcove kitchenette and a sofa on the terrace. Oortuiging is a restored 1860s cottage that retains the old Cape style with antiques throughout. Uitsig is a stylish addition to the guesthouse, with a private balcony that looks out over the mountains. And Gelatenheid is a luxurious villa with, again, a private swimming pool and balcony. At the end of the balcony, suitably screened by treetops, is an outdoor, repro Victorian bathtub in which you can soak while gazing out at the mountain views. Inside, an expansive, open-plan studio is home for just two people (although there's space enough for a four-bed house), with high wooden ceilings and Venetian blinds… a decadent holiday home. As full as a full breakfast can be (including boerewors) is served under the vines at the homestead. Katherine and Arthur are two more reasons why you will love staying here.

Rooms: 6: 4 cottages & 2 bedroom suites:
Oortuiging: 1 king/twin & 1 single, both en/s bath &
sh'r; Vreugde, Gelatenheid and Uitsig: 1 king/twin,
en/s bath & shower. Main House: Twyfeling A and B:
1 king en/s bath & sh'r.
Price: R1,800 - R3,990 per cottage.
Meals: Full breakfast included.
Directions: From Cape Town take N1 then R45.
Akademie St is parallel to main road in Franschhoek,
two streets up the hill.

The Explorers Club, The Library & The Map Room

Jo Sinfield
18 Wilhelmina Street (Explorers), Cabrière Street (Map Room),
16a Wilhelmina Street (Library), Franschhoek
Tel: 021-876-4356 Email: bandoola@mweb.co.za
Web: www.explorersclub.co.za Cell: 072-464-1240

Jo sailed solo down Burma's Irrawaddy River and across the Andaman Sea before settling on a quiet mountain-ringed corner of Franschhoek and working magic with these three large and immensely stylish houses. Every piece of furniture is eye-arrestingly innovative. Check out The Explorers Club dining table perched on wagon wheels and its contemporary-rustic rooms dotted with safari chairs and artefacts from far-off lands; or the Map Room's spiralling staircase and lampshades created from milk pails. The journey through either house is one of discovery. I say 'journey' because this really is a traveller's paradise: tales of exploration, ancient and modern, are illustrated by Jo's extensive map collection and in expressive African scenes by celebrated photographer Horst Klemm. The hub of The Explorers Club is the open-plan living area, with state-of-the-art kitchen, indoor braai, fireplace, air-con, DVD library, mod-cons *ad infinitum*, opening out to a stunning deck-bound lap pool. So simple, so clever, so very, very comfortable. The Library, with its ingenious use of space (rooms downstairs opening out on the pools, living area upstairs with those spectacular views) showcases yet more of Jo's creativity and panache and is perfect for the more sophisticated explorer. The Map Room's highlight is the upper terrace, which wraps its arms around the sociable kitchen and lounge, the perfect place to drink in mountain views along with a glass of wine or two. The only exploring I did when I stayed was a short walk to one of Franschhoek's many great restaurants. Otherwise I stayed right where I was...

Rooms: 3 houses. Explorers Club: 4 rooms (king, queen, twin, bunk + cot), all en-s except twin. Map Room: 2 rooms (king, twin), both en-s. Library: 3 rooms (all king/twin), all en-s. S/C facilities in all.
Price: R550 - R800 pp sharing (minimum rate per cottage applies). Laundry/cleaning service on request.
Meals: Full kitchen in each house. Meals, groceries and braai packs can be delivered on prior request. Numerous restaurants nearby.
Directions: From CT, take Franschhoek Main Rd, after Post Office 1st R into Reservoir St, then 1st R into Wilhelmina, The Library and Explorers are on L. To Map Room turn L past Explorers into Daniel Hugo. Then next L into Cabriere. Map Room on LHS.

Entry Number: 80

Map Number:

The Beautiful South Guest House

Katarina and Peter Stigsson

4 Hospital St, Stellenbosch
Tel: 021-883-8171
Email: enjoy@thebeautifulsouthguesthouse.com
Web: www.thebeautifulsouthguesthouse.com

Katarina and Peter never do anything in half, or even three-quarter, measure. Hearing them chat about their hobbies was enough to make me want to lie down… or was it the sight of the sun-beds by the pool? Since flying in from Sweden they have poured endless energy and enthusiasm into making The Beautiful South the bright, modern, luxurious guesthouse that it is. On the outside, it is quaintly thatched and whitewashed, with Cape-Dutch-style gables and wooden windows. The surrounding garden with its mature trees and large pool is directly accessible from each of the bedrooms. On the inside, however, it's far from traditional. Katarina's inventive ideas in the bedrooms work a treat, such as the smooth pebbles in the bathroom and the old window-frame reborn as a table. The colours in the 'Austin Powers' room, complete with framed retro shirt and gigantic green leaf over the bed, hit you like a sensory bomb; 'Desert Rose' is full of romance, with a deep egg bath in the room; 'Sunrise' gulps in views of the Stellenbosch mountains; 'Sunset' has a terrace for… well, watching the sun set. They're up to their ears in community projects, supporting a crèche and football team in the local township, yet they still find time to seek out (and tell you about) the best spots in the area. 'Catch of the Day' appears at breakfast, the coffee is great and the staff are delightful. Hosting comes only too naturally to Katarina and Peter, which is presumably why they also run the Beautiful West guesthouse in Somerset West.

Rooms: 9: 7 doubles, 6 with en-suite bath or shower, 1 with private shower room opposite; 2 family suites with en-suite bath or shower.
Price: R320 - R650 pp sharing.
Meals: Breakfast included in rate with new 'special' every morning.
Directions: From N1 or N2 take turn-off to Stellenbosch. Entering Stellenbosch turn into Merriman St. After white pedestrian bridge 2nd L into Bosman, 1st R into Suete Weide, L into Hospital St. GPS: Longitude 18. 870177 Latitude 34. 929296

Mitre's Edge

Bernard and Lola Nicholls

R44 between Stellenbosch and Paarl, Klapmuts
Tel: 021-875-5960 Fax: 021-875-5965
Email: info@mitres-edge.co.za Web: www.mitres-edge.co.za
Cell: 082-400-1092 or 072-266-2990

The sea of welcoming dogs that flowed around my feet as I got out of the car made progress slow, but I managed to wade to the fine front door of Mitre's Edge, HQ for a small but busy vineyard. Bernard and Lola were in the middle of shipping some of their rosé to a thirsty recipient in Europe. "We're a hands-on and hand-crafted set-up here," Bernard reassured me, as he showed me the atmospheric little cellar and gleaming drawing room where they sometimes hold intimate meals and tastings. Well, the same can be said for the small self-catering cottage (breakfast included) at the top of the garden just opposite a home gym. The sunshine followed us in through the generous windows and glass door, lighting up an open-plan kitchen and living room. The main feature – a dark, wooden dining table – doubles as a pool table. Bookshelves are packed with books, art and board games and a flash of tropical colour emanates from the fish tank. The bedroom (beyond the sauna, obviously) is unfussy and comfortable, with proud mahogany furniture on a sisal carpet. Outside, the stoep (with a pizza oven the size of Naples, a braai, large table and Jacuzzi – you're welcome to invite friends round, whether it's you or Lola in charge of the food) leads on to the swimming pool, which in turn leads on to the mountains, with resilient snow glinting on their summits. I can see why Angela the Vietnamese pot-bellied pig seems so content to call this place home – I only wish I could. *Wine tours and tasting are available.*

Rooms: 1 self-catering cottage with one bedroom. queen-size bed and separate bathroom.
Price: R1,050 - R1,250 for the whole unit. R200 for the sleeper-couch.
Meals: Full breakfast included. Other/special meals by arrangement.
Directions: See website. Detailed directions can be emailed upon request.

Plumbago Cottage

Nathalie Ammann
Auberge Rozendal Winefarm, Omega Street, Stellenbosch
Tel: 021-887-5612 Fax: 086-612-90-46
Email: info@plumbagocottage.co.za Web: www.plumbagocottage.co.za
Cell: 083-261-9119

If cottages attended parties (and Stellenbosch was the venue), Plumbago would be the beautiful wallflower that stands on the periphery, calm and serene, unaffected by the attention-seeking masses and uninterested in following the crowd. The cottage itself sits on a small farm, Rozendal, which is found on the outer Stellenbosch boundary. It is farmed on organic and bio-dynamic principles and produces award-winning vinegar (delicious on freshly-picked salad and asparagus from the farm veggie patch). Steps, lined with blooming plant pots, lead up to the front door which opens straight into the fully-equipped, slate-tiled kitchen... wine and vinegar included in the price. The large sitting room is blessed with unthinkably lofty ceilings and I wondered how those three oriental lanterns ever got up there. There's a well-stocked open fire, fragrant flowers in abundance throughout the cottage and Natalie's insect thesis (from her natural sciences degree) hangs proudly on the west wall. Beyond the double doors there's a secluded garden, rural pastures and the neighbouring Simonsberg Mountains, which can also be seen from the double bed in the master bedroom... as can the sunrise if you wake that early. Rozendal Farm - and therefore Plumbago Cottage – is ideally positioned. Turn right out of Omega Drive and within moments the delights of Stellenbosch can be explored: bookshops, craft markets, restaurants, pubs, cafés and delis. If you turn left you'll soon be winding your way through the wooded ravines of the Jonkershoek Valley. After a day out and about you can head home to farmyard tweets and snorts, some meditation, a distant view of Table Mountain... perhaps a sauna?

Rooms: 2: 1 double and 1 twin. Separate double shower & separate toilet. With kitchen, lounge, sauna and private gardens.
Price: 2 people sharing R450 pp; 3 people R350 pp; 4 people R300 pp. Singles on request.
Meals: Breakfast at lodge optional.
Directions: From CT airport, take N2 for Somerset-West. Exit 33 to Stellenbosch. At junction turn R. After train station L slide into Adam Tas Rd, then 2nd lights R into Merriman Ave. Thro 3 sets of lights, over roundabout, 2km L into Omega St, Rozendal at end.

Map Number: 4

Entry Number: 83

WedgeView Country House & Spa

Dave & Anouk Bakker
Bonniemile, Vlottenburg, Stellenbosch
Tel: 021-881-3525 Fax: 021-881-3539
Email: info@wedgeview.co.za Web: www.wedgeview.co.za
Cell: 079-526-8093

I was sitting on a rose-wrapped, vineyard-facing stoep, inhaling the Stellenbosch dusk and generally savouring a purple moment with a glass of Zonneweelde chardonnay, when I received a welcome visit from Anouk and three tiny barefoot children intent on handing me a wriggling brown ball of hair. After much cooing over the ridgeback pup, Anouk wheeled her sprites away through multi-coloured gardens to bed next door, leaving me with Dave, a former fine food importer and Holland cricket captain, now a family man and luxury Winelands guest house proprietor. We were joined at the al fresco dining table by other WedgeView guests (as is the friendly tradition here) and we all tucked into some expertly-crafted menu of squid ink risotto, gemsbok fillet and delicate strawberry blancmange. Dave - who brought his clan here in 2007 - told me things weren't always so decadent and chilled out. Life heated up when a fire devastated WedgeView before 2010's World Cup, but Dave, the eternal optimist, took this as a sign to do some renovating. So aromatic thatched roofs were re-twigged; bathrooms received deep tubs and showers big enough to do cartwheels in; the second pool beside the high-ceilinged, deluxe family room got a grassy patio. Happily, the fire spared the spa cottage, which was (so still is) divine; I fell asleep as soon as Yolandi's magical hands touched me. Dave's new dream is to add four hectares of cricket pitch and kids' play area to his already paradisiacal one. Just you try and stop him.

Rooms: 13: 5 Deluxe & 5 Superior Rooms; 1 Honeymoon Suite with adjoining door to Deluxe Rm to form Family Suite (sleeps 4 adults or 2 adults & max 3 kids); Exec' Honeymoon Suite; Garden Family Suite (sleeps 4).
Price: R550 - R1,095 pp sharing. Executive Honeymoon Suite: R1,995 – R2,795; Garden Family Suite (sleeps 4): R1,995 – R2,795; Family unit R2,750 - R4,195 for whole unit.
Meals: Full breakfast included. Lunch, picnic baskets and 3-course gourmet dinners available on request.
Directions: On N2 towards Somerset West take R300 towards Kuilsriver. R onto M12 (Polkadraai Rd) towards Stellenbosch. Go thro 5 lights & take WedgeView & Nassau turning L onto Bonniemile. L into WedgeView Drive.

Camberley Cottage

John and Gael Nel

Camberley Wine Estate, Helshoogte Pass, Stellenbosch
Tel: 021-885-1176 Fax: 021-885-1822
Email: john@camberley.co.za Web: www.camberley.co.za
Cell: 082-690-4975

Gazing down the splendid Franschhoek Valley, all chequered with fruit farms and vineyards, Camberley occupies the kind of spot we all dream of making our own. This is exactly what Johnny and Gael did 14 years ago when they bought this former fruit farm. Heaps of pips and barrels of grape juice later, Camberley is now a small family-run vineyard producing some of the Cape's best reds and Johnny a highly-acclaimed wine-maker well-used to plum accolades (such as the Double Veritas award) being lobbed his way. An immensely likeable lot, the Nels are more than happy for you to pull up your sleeves and get busy in the picking and barrelling processes. The cottage itself sits in the thick of the vines, which screech to a halt at the rose-filled garden's edge. Although recently built, its rather sophisticated country air feels authentically matured, the floor-to-ceiling sash windows and Oregon pine floors taken from a former Cape Dutch-style bank in town. Although it has a very well-equipped kitchen and dining area, you can arrange for breakfast to appear magically on your patio table in the morning, and there are several top restaurants literally minutes from home. This low-key, homely winery is the perfect point from which to explore the Winelands and Johnny helpfully has listed all his favourite places for you. Festooned with bubbles, the plunge pool makes a fantastic sunset spot for when you're well and truly corked.

Rooms: 1 king/twin, en-suite shower and bath
Price: R1,000 per night.
Meals: Full breakfast on request R100.
Directions: From Cape Town, take N2 and turn off at Baden Powell Dr/R310 to Stellenbosch. Continue on R310 through town onto Helshoogte Pass. About 8 mins out of Stellenbosch, Camberley is signed on right, opposite Le Pommier restaurant.

Jacana Guest Farm

Dave and Sheila Scott
Jacana Guest Farm, Annandale Road, Stellenbosch
Tel: 021-881-3142 Fax: 021-881-3142
Email: info@jacanafarm.co.za Web: www.jacanafarm.co.za
Cell: 082-805-3790

Dave and Sheila moved to Jacana Guest Farm to escape the driving wind in Gordon's Bay. Th Helderberg Mountains, which encircle the farm, provide a very effective - and aesthetical, pleasing - natural windbreak. I wonder if that was a conscious factor when they decided to u sticks to the sticks ten years ago? The farm (whose ambit includes ample room for seven dogs an aviary, ducks, chickens and some resident owls) has been lovingly transformed into somethin rather special. And with three of South Africa's best restaurants close by this is now a bit of a secre hot-spot! There are five cottages, three of them thatched: Birdsong, Treetops and Vines. The surround one of two pools and look out onto the vineyards. Only Birdsong doesn't have its ow sitting area, but all the suites have more than enough room to swing a cat or several, if that's th way you like to measure things. You could even swing a couple in Treetops' monstrous shower Owl's is something a little different. It's a separate unit, which sits across the lake and views th farm from the opposite vantage, at the base of the surrounding hills. A full breakfast is served b Rita in the gazebo or alfresco if you'd prefer. A place that supplies you with freshly-squeeze orange juice and luminous cup cakes at 9.30 am on a Thursday morning clearly anticipates th needs of its guests!

Rooms: 5. 2 kings en-s shower, lounge & kitchenette, 1 king en-s bath & shower, family cottage with 2 rooms, 1 king & 1 twin (suitable for kids under 12) lounge & kitchenette. 1 queen en-s shower.
Price: R600 - R800 pp sharing. Singles on request.
Meals: Full continental and cooked breakfast included. Different breakfast everyday on a 4 day rotation. Guest have use of braai facilities.
Directions: See website for detailed directions and map.

Longfield

Pieter and Nini Bairnsfather Cloete

Eikendal Rd, off R44, Somerset West/Stellenbosch
Tel: 021-855-4224
Email: ninicloete@iafrica.com Web: www.longfield.co.za
Cell: 082-365-7554

Perched on the foothills of the dramatic Helderberg mountains, Longfield occupies a truly sensational vantage that drifts across the Winelands and over to the very tip of False Bay at Cape Point. Dreamy by day and by night (when Cape Town's lights put on their glitzy show), there are three cottages from which to enjoy the view. All are fresh, breezy and decorated in a relaxed country-house style and many of the furnishings are rare, early-Cape family heirlooms. This is luxury self-catering. Comfy beds are made up with the highest-quality, hand-embroidered linen and there are spoiling lotions in the pretty bathrooms and coffee-table books on SA wine, flora and fauna etc, and African *objets d'art* in the cosy living areas with a wood-burner for good measure. Each has its private patio or lawn and fridges and cupboards are re-stocked each day with breakfast materials for you to help yourself to. You'll probably want to disappear into your own world here, but Nini and Pieter, who live on the mountain with you, are the nicest people you could wish to meet. Formerly wine-farmers themselves, they can arrange exclusive garden and wine tours and will happily point you in the right direction for good restaurants and golf courses, all invariably within easy striking distance. But it's quite possible you won't want to go anywhere, what with the almond and olive trees (they also bottle their own olives and press their own oil) and the immense pool in the rolling hills of their garden. This is a wonderfully secluded spot, serene and calm and ideally placed for many of the Cape's attractions.

Rooms: 3 cottages: 2 with twin beds, 1 with king-size bed, all with bath and separate shower.
Price: R450 - R790 pp sharing. Single supplement by arrangement.
Meals: Continental breakfast on request.
Directions: From CT take N2 past the airport, take exit 43 Broadway Bvd. Left at lights. From the next lights 6.3km exactly, then right into Eikendal Rd. Follow up gravel road, jink left onto tarmac and follow to top and Longfield House.

Blaauwheim Guest House

Johan and Jo-Anne Blaauw
22 Bakkerskloof Road, Jonkershoogte, Somerset West
Tel: 021-855-0243 Fax: 021-855-0243
Email: blaauwheim@telkomsa.net Web: www.blaauwheim.co.za

Make no mistake: *this* is the place to experience genuine Afrikaans hospitality. After a military career and time in Kenya as defence attaché, Johan retired with Jo-Anne to the tranquillity of Somerset West having gained much experience in entertaining, a reputation for home-made boerewors and an African Grey parrot. Over a glass of Muscatel, with the indoor braai emanating delicious aromas behind me, I surveyed the place at leisure... and found it refined, generous and thoroughly magnificent. Every single artwork is original South African. Furniture is custom-made from blackwood and beautifully upholstered. The garden is an anthology of yellowwood trees, clivias, cycads so rare they're micro-chipped, with railway sleepers leading to dreamy hidden corners. Behind the house, a solar-heated plunge pool, huge braai and breakfast table. Did I say breakfast? Expect a Boer breakfast, not a puny full English version. The same goes for dinner if you request it – perhaps eland fillet, or apricot-basted snoek with grape jam. Sunlight streams into the two large suites, Chardonnay and Pinotage, the latter swathed in blood-red furnishings, the former in softer blue and gold. Both are utterly luxurious with bespoke velvet couches, the best crystal glasses, gas and electric oven, a dishwasher behind smart mahogany cupboards, gleaming bathrooms with slinky sinks, vast beds... and even the Princess (as in "... and the Pea") could sleep soundly under silk duvets. This couple won't do half measures: the place is top-notch with all the trimmings.

Rooms: 3: 2 luxury suites with super-king, extra-length or twin beds, en-s bath & shower, lounge with guest toilet & fully-equipped kitchen; 1 dble/twin with en-s bath & sh'r, private patio & braai.
Price: R650 - R750 pp for 2 sharing. Singles R950 - R1,100.
Meals: Self-catering in both suites. Full breakfast R85. Other meals & braais by arrangement (Sth African cooking).
Directions: From CT, N2 to Somerset West, exit 43 onto R44 towards Stellenbosch. Pass Lord Charles Hotel, continue on R44 up hill. 500m past bridge, L to Heldervue & Helderberg Village. At T-jct, L into Bakkerskloof Rd. Blaauwheim 3rd house on L. GPS: S 34,03,05, E 18,49,35

Seringa House

Peter and Lydia Hauspie

8 Leylands Lane, Somerset West
Tel: 021-855-2394 Fax: 021-855-2394
Email: seringahouse@gmail.com
Cell: 083-409-2722

The fact that Seringa House is perched on the slopes of Helderberg mountain overlooking Gordon's Bay and the Hottentots Holland would usually be enough on its own to attract a steady flow of guests. But the picturesque setting plays second fiddle to Seringa's most valuable asset... its hosts. Peter (an accomplished architect) and Lydia (a geologist recently returned from a Congo gold exploration adventure!) came on holiday to South Africa and within weeks they were building a home here. Drawing inspiration from their extensive travels in Africa's remotest corners and from their passion for sustainable building techniques, first they built a home, then a family (twin girls), and finally, 15 years later, on their adjoining plot, Seringa House. No two rooms are the same and the twins have given them names like Tinga Tinga, Tulip, Sunset or Sahara reflecting their individual feel. Each bathroom is a unique discovery of mosaics, pebbles or recycled tiles. Speaking of recycled, your bath and shower water is processed through a grey-water system and used to irrigate the gardens. Peter's ability to incorporate sustainable design sees skylights, solar geysers, airflow showers and many other initiatives included to reduce their/your impact on the environment. Whether you book the downstairs apartment or the more conventional double en-suite options, flexibility is key as you can self-cater using the entertainer's dream kitchen full of mod cons; or request a B&B arrangement; or even go DBB and allow Peter to wave his magic spatula and prove he is as much a maestro in the kitchen as he is behind his drawing board.

Rooms: 6: 1 apartment with 1 double with en-suite shower and 1 queen and single with en-suite shower; 1 king; 2 queens, 1 double; 2 twins, all with en-suite bath and shower.
Price: R450 - R650 pp sharing.
Meals: Self-catering. Meals on request.
Directions: From Cape Town take Broadway R44 exit off N2, head towards Stellenbosch & turn R at 1st lights, L at next lights into Helderberg College Rd, cross 3 stop streets, after 3rd stop take 2nd R, then 1st L, then 1st R into Leylands Lane.

The Vintner's Loft

André and Rhona Liebenberg
Romond Vineyards, Klein Helderberg Road, Somerset West
Tel: 021-855-4566 Fax: 012-855-0428
Email: accommodation@romond.co.za Web: www.romondvineyards.co.za
Cell: 082-445-8838

Gargoyles are watching me. Crouched on reddening wine barrels, they follow as André leads me through his rustic wine cellar, under gothic chandeliers, into a theatrical tasting-room resembling the Crystal Maze's Medieval Zone. Faint orchestral melodies mingle with crackling fire, the aural mélange completed by the de-corking of Romond's Cabernet Franc Rebus. Phew, a screw-top would really have spoiled the effect. "Those," says André, indicating the goblin props in his soothing, witty timbre, "are my other hat." Where primary and secondary headgear (winemaker and film director) collide, André's third hat (guesthouse proprietor) is born. Above the warehouse, up terracotta steps, is the loft, a wide, open, exposed-brick apartment brimming with tokens, trinkets and treasures narrating André and his wife Rhona's traveller days. Nepalese bedspreads adorn a robust, elbow-high master bed, itself constructed from old cellar doors; red silk Indian curtains hang to blackwood floors partially hidden by colourful chunky rugs; heavy antique trunks brim with games to keep little people happy in the absence of telly. I long to lie among the rubber ducks in the claw-footed bedroom bath, to explore Romond's bookshelves in the open-plan living space, to rustle up a rustic feast in the industrial kitchen before a game of pétanque on the court outside. Truthfully? I want to dangle a hosepipe through the internal window into a barrel, bags the inviting rocking chair and watch the vines dancing outside my door.

Rooms: 1 loft apartment: 1 king with full en-suite, 1 double with separate bathroom.
Price: R1,800 for entire loft, max 4 pax.
Meals: Self-catering, but if you're lucky you may find a few "yummy things" in the fridge when you arrive...
Directions: From Cape Town take N2 towards Somerset West. Turn off at exit 43 and left onto R44 at lights. Look for Romond sign, 4km from Lord Charles Hotel. Turn into Klein Helderberg Road and follow signs through vineyards.

Tanagra Wine and Guest Farm

Robert and Anette Rosenbach
Robertson Road, McGregor
Tel: 023-625-1780 Fax: 023-625-1847
Email: tanagra@tanagra-wines.co.za Web: www.tanagra-wines.co.za
Cell: 076-112-5490

On arrival at Tanagra I was met by Robert and Anette… and Jupp, their charismatic dog, who is bound to steal your heart. The first thing that caught my eye is the giant wild fig tree. Not only is it a natural air-conditioner, creating shade and a cool breeze in the burning summer months, but it also provides the name of the farm. Tanagra echoes the Khoisan word for 'shady place'. Robert and Anette have done an incredible job since moving here from Germany in 2009. Not only are they producing their own wine (the Heavenly Chaos is a must… and I don't mean unfermented grape juice!), but Robert also brought with him a German potstill resembling something of a spaceship. I couldn't wait to try the Lemon Eau de Vie, which is infused with the fruits from a tree in their garden. The surroundings are magnificent and since the property adjoins Vrolijkheid Nature Reserve (direct access from the farm) and is 'cushioned' between the Riviersonderend and the Langeberge mountain ranges, guests are spoilt for choice with walks, bird-watching or, in my case, a great view for sundowners. There are four country cottages dotted about for guaranteed privacy. But if you really want to get away from it all, stay in Hill Cottage. Just a short drive away through the vineyards, it boasts spectacular views of Tanagra and the McGregor Valley and even has its own plunge pool. As we sat in the warm evening tasting all the different Tanagra grappas, I'm told that in summer Robert and Anette host outdoor movie evenings where guest and locals are invited to sit under the wild fig tree and enjoy!

Rooms: 5: 1 queen en-s bath & shower; 2 king en-s shower; 1 king en-s bath & sh'r; 1 king/twin sh'r only. All cottages have fully-equipped kitchenettes & are let on either self-catering or B&B basis.
Price: R275 - R350 pp for self-catering; R425 - R450 for B&B.
Meals: Full breakfast included for B&B guests. 5 mins' drive to McGregor with good restaurants; 1 country restaurant in walking distance.
Directions: Follow R60 to Robertson. In Robertson R at main junction (La Verne Wine Boutique on R corner), direction McGregor. Continue for 14km. Tanagra on R. No gravel road driving required.

Map Number: 4

Rouxwil Country House

Thys and O'nel Roux

Caledon
Tel: 028-215-8922 Fax: 0866-153-230
Email: rouxwil@intekom.co.za Web: www.rouxwil.co.za
Cell: 082-575-6612

Rouxwil is perfectly positioned in the middle of nowhere. I say 'perfectly' because nowhere happens to be in the middle of everywhere. You couldn't wish for a better base from which to explore the region, with Hermanus, the Winelands, Greyton and Cape Agulhas all less than an hour away. The farmhouse is always buzzing with its farm kitchen, lounge with open fireplace and outside braai area. This is where Thys holds sway, whether grilling oryx sirloins over open coal or dispensing encyclopaedic advice on the surrounding towns' best-kept secrets (his is a brain worth picking). Since the closest restaurant is thirty kilometres away, it is an added blessing that food is one of O'nel's great talents. She likes her guests to taste traditional recipes, but regularly throws a wild-card onto her menu… springbok shanks, for example. And, having voted Rouxwil 'South Africa's best farm accommodation in 2010 and 2011' her guests seem to approve. The rooms are certainly not what you would expect on a wheat and sheep farm. No rusted old plumbing or creaking termite-eaten floorboards here. Rather slate tiles, stainless-steel power showers and plenty of king-size comfort. Sliding doors open onto gardens of cycads, roses and lavender, zebras, antelope and blue cranes. Come to think of it, with a pool to cool off in, farm tours and a river raft for sundowners, why would you want to leave Rouxwil at all? But apart from the views, food, river and wildlife, what makes this place an essential GG entry are the two charming people at the helm.

Rooms: 4: all doubles with en-suite bath and shower.
Price: R550 - R650 pp sharing. Free farm tour for those staying 2 nights or more.
Meals: Full breakfast included. Dinner R195.
Directions: From Cape Town take N2, and 8km beyond Botriver on N2, take left turn on to the Villiersdorp R43. After 14km turn right off to Greyton and Helderstroom. Follow road for 1km, Rouxwil Country House signposted.

Beaumont Wine Estate

Jayne and Ariane Beaumont
Compagnes Drift Farm, Bot River
Tel: 028-284-9194 (office), 028-284-9370 (home) Fax: 028-284-9733
Email: info@beaumont.co.za Web: www.beaumont.co.za
Cell: 083-9906-319

Jayne's guests stay in the charming buildings of an 18th-century former mill house and wagon shed, today snug with wood-burning heaters, but left as far as comfortably possible as they were, with original fireplaces in kitchens and hand-hewn, yellowwood beamed ceilings. Outside, you can sit around an old mill stone and admire the antediluvian water wheel (which along with the mill has recently been renovated and is now working as it once used to) while the willow-shaded jetty on the farm lake offers one of the Western Cape's prettiest settings for sundowners and wheatland views. While meandering through the flower-filled garden I realised that there is no real need to move from the farm, despite being only half an hour from Hermanus. While Jayne and her family busy themselves producing their annual 150,000-odd bottles of wine, you can swim in the informal swimming pool – being the lake - under the weeping willows where the weaver-birds make their nests; or you can roam about on their land – they own half a mountain! You can even put the idea of cooking on the backburner and instead arrange to have home-cooked meals delivered to you and wine-taste in the cellar flanked by an old wine press. The estate is a proud member of an exciting bio-diversity wine route which includes tours, tastings, hiking and mountain-bike trails (check out www.greenmountain.co.za). Also, to find horses and horse-riding you only have to trot down the road. The setting is beautiful - well worth spending several nights here.

Rooms: 2 self-catering cottages. Mill House has 2 bedrooms (plus 2 extra can sleep in living room); Pepper Tree has 1 double (again 2 extras possible).
Price: Low season: R300 - R450 pp sharing for 2, extra people R150 - R250 pp. High season: flat rate R900 - R1,400 per cottage.
Meals: Self-catering. Breakfast and home-cooked meals by arrangement. All meals are self-served.
Directions: From N2 take exit 92, sign-posted to Bot River. Follow signs to Bot River and Beaumont Wine Estate is signed off to the right-hand side. Map can be faxed.

Barton Villas

Peter Neill
Barton Villa, R43 Hermanus Rd, Botriver
Tel: 028-284-9283/UK +44-1489-878-673 Fax: UK +44 1489 878715;
SA 028-284-9776 Email: info@bartonvineyards.co.za
Web: www.bartonvineyards.co.za Cell: 079-622-7115

In the middle of the Kogel National Park, up a winding avenue of pine trees, I finally found three beautifully-designed Tuscan-style villas scattered across the raised valley of a working farm. As we climbed the track and stood under the arches the beam of my gaze shot straight out of the window, and spread across the vineyards and over the sprawling mountains beyond. The views are spectacular, a rolling canvas of working fields, rows of lavender and fynbos-clad mountains which wraps right around you. Built into and around the rocks the villas all have wide verandahs on which to conduct your feasts and to soak up the views. It's no secret Peter built them to stay in himself and consequently no expense has been spared. Notably the bedding, shipped straight in from The White Company because no other duvets would do! With huge sweeping lounges, open-plan kitchens, long tables, big fireplaces and an emphasis on natural materials, the villas are immaculately finished throughout. Peter has a soft spot for Persian carpets bringing colour and warmth to the airy rooms and I'm told a new one sneaks in on his every visit. With spa baths and swimming pools built into the rocks it's easy to forget this is a working farm abundant with wildlife. Don't miss the opportunity to get involved, especially with the wine grown on the farm. I imagined inviting everyone I knew to come for a week of long sunset dinners, lazy days of swimming, riding, tennis, golf, hiking and landscape painting….

Rooms: 3 villas: Heron, 3 doubles, indoor swimming pool; Blue Crane, 2 doubles, 1 twin; Plover, 3 doubles; all have en-suite bathrooms, outdoor pools, outdoor spa baths, DSTV & wifi.
Price: Peak: 15th Dec-15th Jan R4,500 per villa per night; Summer: 1st Nov-Easter (excl peak season) R3,250. Mid: Easter to 30 April and 1st-31st Oct R2,250; Green: 1st May-30th Sept R1,900.
Meals: Self-catering.
Directions: From Cape Town take N2 to Somerset West and Caledon. Follow exit 90 for Hermanus, Barton Vineyards is on R43 Botriver to Hermanus Rd 100 m after & on same side as Shell petrol station.

Barnacle B&B

Jenny Berrisford
573 Anne Rd, Pringle Bay
Tel: 028-273-8343
Email: barnacle@maxitec.co.za Web: www.barnacle.co.za
Cell: 082-925-7500

Come and explore Jenny's seaside idyll. Several natural environments collide right outside her cottage. From the deck at the back – with views all the way to Cape Point – you walk down to 'readers' corner', a private lawny enclave in the marsh reeds where narrow paths lead you to the river and beach. The sea is a hundred yards of the whitest, finest sand to your left; beyond the river, fynbos and milkwood 'forest' climb the mountain, a nature reserve. You don't have to be a kid to love this. There are otters in the river, baboons on the mountain, estuarine and fynbos birds aplenty… and Jenny is a horticultural expert in one of the world's most amazing natural gardens. Rooms are simple, rustic and country cosy, one with a Victorian slipper bath, another with a solid brass bed. The Cottage has a sitting area with its own fireplace which makes it cosy for winter breaks, while both the Cottage and The Sunshine Suite have fully-equipped kitchenettes for self-catering. The whole place is super relaxed… a hidden gem. Jenny has a canoe to take out on the river. *This area has been proclaimed a world biosphere reserve.*

Rooms: 2 units: 1 sleeping 4 with 1 double, en-suite shower, kitchen/dining area and 2 singles; and 1 sleeping 3 with 1 double, en-suite 'slipper' bath, kitchenette and one single bed.
Price: R350 - R550 pp sharing. Single and family rates negotiable.
Meals: Full breakfast included. Restaurants in Pringle Bay.
Directions: From Cape Town along N2 turn towards Gordon's Bay before Sir Lowry's Pass - follow coast road for 30km to Pringle Bay turn - follow signs down dirt roads.

Map Number: 4   Entry Number: 95

Wild Olive Guest House

Gloria and Peter Langer

227 Hangklip and Bell Rds, Pringle Bay
Tel: 028-273-8750 Fax: 028-273-8752
Email: g-langer@mweb.co.za Web: www.wild-olive.co.za
Cell: 082-442-5544

"How do you like your ostrich?" probed Peter, poking a chef's hat into the open-plan dining room where Gloria was refilling glasses and bending us double with tales of her culinary husband aerophobia and the obvious palavers which ensue when they visit his Viennese home town. Peter swapped land-locked for coastal-mountain-backdropped upon meeting South African Gloria and they opened Beachcomber restaurant in Camps Bay; he chef-ing, she front of house. In 198 they bought one of Pringle Bay's first five homes, a tiny cabin, transforming it into a spacious elegant-yet-homely guest house. But Wild Olive is no ordinary B&B. It's B&B&D for a start. dinners here are an Overberg talking point. Peter's cooking awards dangle beside pots and pan but trophies can't convey quite how tickled my taste-buds were by his red wine-poached pear, sublime follow-up to salmon teriyaki and rare ostrich fillet. Tummy happy, it was a woozy delig to slip downstairs through the shell-coloured guest lounge, past french doors leading onto th tree-lined pool, into my bright, lavender-scented, beach-blue room and wrap myself in goose down. Waking, as all guests do, to both sea and mountain was a breathtaking treat. I cooled myse with an al fresco shower on my secluded wooden terrace before breakfast, taken privately ("n everyone is a morning person") on the upstairs sun-deck. I hear Peter took early-bird guests o in the boat and it's Cape Malay prawns tonight - I wonder if there's room for a wee one?

Rooms: 3: I queen with en suite shower & 'al-fresco' shower, I with en-s shower & 'al-fresco' shr separate loo; I twin/king with optional single loft bed en-suite shower and 'al-fresco' shower.
Price: R450 - R650 pp sharing. Singles available on request.
Meals: Full breakfast included. 3-course evening dinner prepared by Peter.
Directions: From Cape Town on N2, turn towards Gordon's Bay, follow coast road for 30km to Pringle Bay turn – follow signs.

96 Beach Road

Annelie and Johan Posthumus

Kleinmond
Tel: 021-794-6291 Fax: 021-794-6291
Email: info@kaapsedraaibb.co.za Web: www.kaapsedraaibb.co.za
Cell: 082-923-9869

When the family bought "the beach house" in 1954, the milk was delivered by bike. Kleinmond still feels like a sleepy little town, but it's hardly surprising that more have fled here since. The house is but a kite-tail's length from the sea, the blue Atlantic stretching forth beyond a strip of fynbos. You can choose to watch the whales (from August to December) from two spots, the sea-side verandah or the upstairs bedroom. The latter runs from one side of the house to the other under a vaulted ceiling and ocean-side the walls stop and the glass starts, forming a small square sitting room jutting out towards the blue. Here there is a soft couch and cushioned chairs, perfect for siestas, sunsets (and of course whale-watching). Downstairs is equally adorable. It feels a bit like a Nantucket Island house: white, light, airy and adorned with simple understated beach furnishings. It is totally self-catering here, but walk a kilometre west and you'll find some untouristy cafés in the old harbour; a short drive away are white, sandy, blue-flag beaches, perfect for kids, flying kites, swimming and walking. There is a rock pool about 50 yards from the house, and apart from that all the swimming takes place at the beach and lagoon which is a 15-minute walk away. Kleinmond is near the Arabella Golf Estate, the Kogelberg Biosphere with its myriad fynbos species, the wild horses of the Bot River Estuary and Hermanus, but avoids its touristy-ness. *Closed 10th December – 10th January.*

Rooms: 1 unit with 2 rooms: 1 double with en-s shower, 1 twin with bath. Open-plan kitchen/dining/living area. Heating. Kitchen fully equipped with dishwasher & washing-machine. Serviced once a week but more often on request.
Price: R800 per day for 2 people staying; R200 per day for each additional person staying. Max 4 people.
Meals: Self-catering.
Directions: From the main road, turn down 9th Street and travel right down to Beach Road. Turn left into Beach Road. Cross 8th Street. No. 96 is the second from the corner of Beach and 7th Sts.

Schulphoek Seafront Guesthouse

Petro and Mannes van Zyl

44 Marine Drive, Guest entrance 181 Pietretief Cresent, Sandbaai, Hermanus
Tel: 028-316-2626 Fax: 028-316-2627 Email: schulphoek@hermanus.co.za
Web: www.schulphoek.co.za Cell: 083-346-0695

My heart sinks straight to the ocean floor as I wander through Schulphoek and remember I'm no spending the night. All of a sudden the verdant vegetable gardens, the daily home-made cakes fo peckish guests, the sunny salt-water pool, the sumptuous mahogany bedrooms and the deep-se squidgy sofas in the luxurious, gold-tinted guest lounge (all of which offer front-row whale spotting) seem to tease me. And then Petro utters five unforgettable words: "Stay for dinner, least?" Schulphoek suppers are events unto themselves. The full house sit at a long, oak dinin table and as an amouse-bouche, we're led into a vast wine cellar, home to some 12,000 bottle to pick our accompanying wine. Which grape complements spicy butternut soup and succule seared yellowtail, I wonder? Mannes nudges me towards a crisp Sauvignon Blanc and ensures m glass is never wanting as we chew the cud about Stony Point's penguins, France (three familie here are French) and September's Whale Festival. With regards to the food, precious litt chewing ensues: The resident chef insists food melts rather than is masticated in the mouth. Afte dinner, I yearn to sneak upstairs to Scallop (the magisterial suite occupying the entire first floor wi panoramic ocean vistas and its own telescope!) and snuggle into the gargantuan bed, or to hid under bubbles in a two-person spa bath in one of the smaller but equally decadent garden room Alas, I must leave. Goodbye, "Shell-corner". I'll be back. *Massages and treatments on request.*

Rooms: 7 suites: superior, luxury and standard, all with luxurious en-suite bathrooms. 1 family suite.
Price: R700 to R2,100 pppn incl' breakfast. Complimentary fine-dining dinner on 1st night. Single sup +50%. Discounts for longer stays & winter specials.
Meals: Professional kitchen with chef. Dinner every night: menu du jour. Lunch: on request. Cellar with 12,000 SA wines. Full breakfast included.
Directions: Take R43 towards Hermanus. At Engen petrol station before Hermanus by traffic lights (signed Sandbaai) turn right. At 2nd 'stop' turn left into 3rd Street. Continue to next stop and turn left. Marked by flags – entrance off Piet Retief Crescent.

Hermanus Lodge on the Green

Nobby and Wendy Clark
Previously known as Pebble Beach Guest House, 8 Fernkloof Dr, Hermanus
Tel: 028-313-2517 Fax: 028-313-1618 Email: info@hermanuslodge.co.za
Web: www.hermanuslodge.co.za Cell: 079-312-5588 or 082-900-7290

Golfing enthusiasts may take one look at Hermanus Lodge on the Green and assume all their Christmases have come at once! As the name suggests, it's situated on the 25th green of South Africa's 4th most popular golf course. It's no surprise that so many contented guests, golfers and non-golfers alike, congregate for evening drinks on the lodge's colonial-style, wrap-around balcony to contemplate remarkable views down the tree-lined fairway. These can be enjoyably achieved with equal smugness on colder days in the Rocky Lounge, where Nobby stokes an open fire and encourages guests to try the line-up of local wines. A lazy breakfast can be enjoyed in the downstairs dining room, which spills out onto a patio just metres from the course. Others may enjoy the sun-trapped swimming-pool surrounded by olive trees and watch para-gliders catching thermals over the mountainous Fernkloof Nature Reserve. The house, with its Zimbabwean wall hangings and sunset-slate flooring, has a subtle African flavour and is restful on both eye and spirit. The only sounds that will interrupt your peace will be the ocean, some tree frogs and if you're lucky the Cape eagle owl (apart, of course, from the satisfying clunk of a golf ball being middled). What clinched it for me? It's close enough to the whale-watching frenzy down at the village that you can join in if you want... and just far enough away that you can savour the blissful quiet if you don't.

Rooms: 6: 2 kings, 4 king/twins, 1 sofa-bed for children under 12 in family room; 4 with en-suite bath and shower, 2 with en-suite shower.
Price: R520 - R670 pp sharing. Singles R770 - R975. Children under 12 sharing with parents no charge.
Meals: Full English and continental breakfast included.
Directions: From N2 take R43 to Hermanus. Go all the way through the village and turn left at the Shell garage onto Fairview Ave. Hug the golf course and turn first right before the school. House is second after the bend.

Map Number: 4

Hartford Cottage

Gys and Wendy Hofmeyr

3, 3rd Ave, Voelklip, Hermanus
Tel: 028-314-0102
Email: gyswendyhof@telkomsa.net
Cell: 082-897-1773

If you were asked to paint a picture of your perfect country cottage, I suggest it might look a bit like Hartford; white walls, soaring chimney and a perfectly-pitched thatched roof, all enveloped by a large, tranquil, lawned garden where I challenge you to find anything out of place. As I sat under the welcoming shade of the umbrella sipping tea and thinking how delicious it would be to live here, Wendy told me - and I didn't register much surprise - that complete strangers have knocked on the door begging to stay, even though originally they only built the cottage for the family. Hiding away from the hurlyburly of Hermanus in a seaside suburb, Hartford is enviably positioned, with mountain walks five minutes in one direction, beach, sea and whales a minute or two in the opposite. Gys is a stickler for detail and a lover of wood and thatch. Door surrounds and light switches were rescued and resurrected from a condemned house in town, while an original yellowwood door hanging on huge hinges is his pride and joy. Don't think Wendy hasn't been busy too. Her eye for interior designs led to the stunning black slate fire hearth, bathroom sink surrounds and kitchen worktops. The open-plan A-frame roof makes it cool and spacious, while the whitewashed walls and an abundance of Cape antique furniture, means it retains all of its delightfully cosy cottage charm.

Rooms: 1 cottage with 1 double room with full en-suite and 1 twin bedroom with separate bathroom. Also a large attic bed/sitter with 3 beds for children. Cottage not available 20th Dec - 15th Jan.
Price: 2 people sharing whole cottage: R1,000 plus R100 an extra head (May - Aug inclusive). R1,500 plus R200 a head per extra person (Sept - April inc'). Min 2-night stay. Children under 12 free.
Meals: Cottage fully self-catering and includes breakfast provisions for your first morning.
Directions: 4km from Hermanus, direction Stanford, take 3rd exit off roundabout into 10th St (Seafront Rd), past CEM Motors & on for 300m. 3rd Ave on R, then thatched house on R.

Selkirk House

Ina Schirmeisen

29 Selkirk Street, Hermanus
Tel: 028-312-4892 Fax: 028-312-4387
Email: info@selkirkhouse.co.za Web: www.selkirkhouse.co.za
Cell: 076-587-4753

When William Selkirk landed 'that' 967kg shark onto the rocks of Hermanus in 1922, I doubt he ever dreamt his name would appear in lights that shine quite as brightly as they do at this multi-levelled mountain-side retreat. The exceptional use of space and natural surroundings through levels, landings, terraces and quiet mountain recesses is visionary, not only aesthetically but also functionally. Everything is slick, chic, minimalistic and clean, accentuated by bursts of bright fynbos flower paintings. Chrome balustrades lead you up wooden stairs to your next indulgence, whether it's your room, the pool and first living space, complete with temperature-controlled wine cellar and vent-free fireplace, or the contemporary bar room with outside deck and fireplace, or the roof-top viewing deck which provides 360° views of mountains and ocean. All suites are a spacious dream and completely automated, allowing you to control your immediate environment whether through music, climate or brightness. I think they must have had a bit of a chuckle watching me walking in and out of the various rooms, wide-eyed as a child, as lights magically switched themselves on and off. Although everything really is cutting edge, Selkirk is also welcoming and warm-spirited and you are certainly encouraged to kick off your shoes and make full use of this supa-dupa new creation. Just as I was about to leave a tortoise had made its way down the mountain and into the garden... the race is on!

Rooms: 5: 4 kings with en-suite bath and shower and 1 twin with en-suite bath and shower.
Price: Low Season: 1st May 2012 – 31st Aug 2012 R580 pp sharing & R850 single. High Season: 1st Sept 2012 – 30th Apr 2013 R850 pp sharing & R1,100 single.
Meals: Full breakfast included, lunch and dinner available on request.
Directions: From N2 take R43 into Hermanus, thru' village, pass Marine Hotel on R. After 1km at Shell Garage turn L into Fairways Ave towards mountain, turn 1st R, still Fairways Ave, next hairpin bend is start of Fernkloof Dr, then 1st L is Selkirk St.

Cliff Lodge

Gill O'Sullivan and Gideon Shapiro

6 Cliff St, De Kelders
Tel: 028-384-0983 Fax: 028-384-0228
Email: stay@clifflodge.co.za Web: www.clifflodge.co.za
Cell: 082-380-1676

This is the closest land-based whale-watching you could possibly find. I could see the whites of their eyes and the callosities on their heads. It was as though Gill and Gideon had paid them to put on a special show for me; blowing, breaching, spy-hopping, lob-tailing. I applauded delicately from the royal box. The viewing from my room and from the breakfast conservatory-balcony was don't-turn-your-eyes-away-for-a-minute magnetic. But the fun wasn't just in the looking. As soon as I walked through the door, Gideon whisked me down to the ocean for a swim through the cave (bring shoes you can swim in for the rocks) and Gill kindly booked me a whale-, sea-lion- and penguin-watching boat trip for the following morning. For the adventurous, there are also trips to view or cage-dive with great white sharks. The guest house is classy and modern and there are sea-view terraces for those rooms on the side of the house. The luxurious penthouse suite has a huge balcony and glass-fronted living room for whale-gazing in true style. On the cliff edge there is a swimming pool with loungers where you can unwind and languidly enjoy the hypnotic view. Gill, Gideon and the ever-smiling manager Nico are wonderfully hospitable hosts. They serve the best breakfast you could possibly have – exceptional loose-leaf teas, delicious barista coffee, fresh juices, a continental and hot breakfast spread. After breakfast indulge in a massage, nature reserve walks in front of the house and on a nearby flower farm, or spend the day on the unspoilt white beach a short walk from the lodge.

Rooms: 5: 1 twin/king with bath & shower; 1 twin/king with bath and outdoor shower; 1 luxury suite with king, separate living room, bath & shower; 2 twin/king with shower.
Price: R700 - R1,600 pp sharing. Single supplement +50%.
Meals: Full breakfast included.
Directions: N2, then R43 through Hermanus. Past Stanford towards Gansbaai. Turn right at first De Kelders turn-off, then right into De Villiers Rd, left into Kayser Rd and right into Cliff St.

Whalesong Lodge

Stanley and Lainy Carpenter

83 Cliff St, De Kelders
Tel: 028-384-1865
Email: stanley@whalesonglodge.co.za Web: www.whalesonglodge.co.za
Cell: 082-883-5793

"Almost forgot!" gasps Lainy, fleeing Whalesong's sun-soaked, cliff-hanging balcony for her eat-your-heart-out-Nigella kitchen. She skips back to a gaggle of performing whales, overflowing with fluffy cappuccinos and warm chocolate cookies: "wheat-free, I'm experimenting for food-intolerances". The Carpenters are foodies (and greenies) to a fault: herbs'n'veg grow behind the pool, eggs come from "a little farm up the road", cheese from local cows, and a compost worm farm ensures near zero waste. Anything not gobbled up by thousands of little wrigglers is recycled religiously. Lainy's ethical yummies are sold both here and at Stanford market and guests are welcome to loiter in the kitchen where debates range from how to sweeten sugar-free apple cake to why their home-baked croissants and home-grown grenadilla jam are so lip-smacking. Upstairs, away from the long, homely breakfast table and open-fire lounge, Whalesong is all about the water. Bright, modern, elegant rooms (cleaned with nature-friendly orange oil, naturally) and clean-line bathrooms stare out to sea while cream walls are dotted with exposed brick and images of ocean life, boats, waves, breaching whales. Photo-filled welcome packs swell with shark-diving, whale-watching and kayaking suggestions for adventurous souls, but land-lovers should ask Stanley about fynbos trails and beach walks. This is a man who gets heart palpitations if he misses his daily walk and swim so has all the insider gossip. Well, how else could he burn off Lainy's puds?

Rooms: 5: 2 twins and 2 doubles, all en-suite shower and bath. 1 suite with king and en-suite shower and spa bath
Price: R650 - R1,300 pp sharing.
Meals: Full breakfast included.
Directions: From N2 take R43 through Hermanus and Stanford. Take first right signed to De Kelders and follow down to the sea. Turn right into Cliff Street. Third house on right.

Sea Star Lodge

Ardi Hasenohrl

19 Ingang Street, De Kelders/Gansbaai, De Kelders
Tel: 028-384-0012 Fax: 086-602-4436
Email: info@seastar.co.za Web: www.seastar.co.za
Cell: 079-174-8548

Approaching Sea Star Lodge, Ardi whisked me straight onto the roof, bubbles in hand, to watch the sun set over the Atlantic. He said it would be special, but even he had to stifle chuckles as I stood gawping at the evolving hues of Walker Bay and the Fynbos Nature Reserve behind us. Darkness eventually won, but I would have happily lain under that glittering 360-degree blanket of sea stars all night had I not spied inside Sea Star's rooms en route to the rooftop and been nosy for more. Ardi is a former policeman-turned-private detective from Munich, which might explain why he is such a stickler for privacy and perfection; nothing less will do, particularly when it comes to his guests. Uber-slick, luxurious rooms are utterly mod-conified (mine boasted a fully-stocked Nespresso machine!) with blacked-out windows to stop peeping whales. Extravagant ocean panoramas made up for the fact that my Master Suite bath, though vast, was the only tub lacking a sea view, but Ardi apologised regardless by cracking open a bottle of vintage dessert wine to share on the sweeping verandah, an extension of the bright, open-plan guest living area. Joining Moulin the dog by a toasty fire, Ardi filled me in on De Kelders' clandestine pop-up restaurant Klooks At Home; on the Durban artist whose fiery Kalahari paintings dot Sea Star's walls; on his pilot pal Evan who takes guests bird's-eye whale-spotting in his four-seater plane, African Wings... I wonder if Ardi would place me under house arrest?

Rooms: 6: 5 kings with full en-suite; 1 queen with shower over bath. Rooftop suites have their own private terrace.
Price: R700 – R1,100 pp sharing. Singles +50%.
Meals: Full continental and cooked breakfast included; picnic baskets available on request. Complimentary mini-bar.
Directions: From N2 take R43 through Hermanus towards Gansbaai. Turn right at first De Kelders turn-off, then left into Hoof Weg. Take the second road on your right and turn into Ingang Street.

Klein Paradijs Country House

Susanne and Michael Fuchs
Pearly Beach, Gansbaai
Tel: 028-381-9760 Fax: 028-381-9803
Email: info@klein-paradijs.com Web: www.klein-paradijs.com

It's easy to dawdle over breakfast at Klein Paradijs. Munching crunchy home-made muesli (being Swiss, the Fuchs roll a mean honeyed oat) I was joined by an army of flapping, feathery friends who've made this expansive, colourful garden - a 140-hectare private nature reserve - their hunting ground. Susanne's chart shows 96 spottable species, but I was only quick enough to tag Cape weavers, pin-tailed whydahs and southern boubous. I'd certainly hang out here if I had wings: Klein Paradijs's ancient milkwoods are festooned with bird-feeders. Not that you need wings to enjoy this decadent pastoral paradise. For starters, there are the bedrooms. Sloping, thatched ceilings of local reed and dark wood beams smell terrific and tuck you into rustic luxury; wrought-iron beds draped in patchwork quilts are the definition of sturdy, homely elegance; soft lighting and weighty curtains ensure rooms are never anything but blissfully toasty. I prised myself away from a picturesque window (through which brightly-coloured proteas were attempting to crawl in from outside), strolled past the doughnut pool with it's grassy island centre, peeked into the earthy double guest lounge neatly stocked with antiques, nature books, African artefacts and sleepy Rhodesian Ridgebacks, and contemplated rowing the dam before dinner. It's not just birds who get a good feeding here: Michael is a trained chef so don't fill up on breakfast - save room for his superb fish bobotie. Country living has seldom been so delicious.

Rooms: 5: 2 twins and 3 doubles all with en-suite bathrooms; 2 with bath and shower, 3 with showers.
Price: R500 - R1,250 pp sharing. Special prices for longer stays.
Meals: Full breakfast included. Light meals and dinner by arrangement. The restaurant is fully licensed.
Directions: From Hermanus take the R43 through Stanford and Gansbaai. Go left at Pearly Beach crossing, then 1st left again. The house is on the right. GPS coordinates S 34° 39' 23.5" E 19° 32' 05.7"

Map Number: 4

Farm 215 Nature Retreat and Fynbos Reserve

Maarten Groos

Hartebeeskloof, Baardskeerdersbos, Near Gansbaai
Tel: 028-388-0920
Email: book@farm215.co.za Web: www.farm215.co.za
Cell: 082-097-1655

Farm 215 perches neatly among the fynbos of this private nature reserve. It's not really tha
remote, yet when I visited absolute silence prevailed, so much so that you could hear the nea
pitter-patter of Maarten's dogs following us along the boardwalks. The individual cottages, angle
to look rosy-faced into the sunset and onto sea and mountains, squat above the 35 differen
species of protea that contribute to the vast and wild garden. The conservation of the reserve her
is a constant priority. The cottages were built with sustainability in mind and this is one of very few
places in SA that are Fair Trade accredited. Testament to this is the yellow lichen, a sign of air purity
that paints the rock faces of this self-sufficient retreat. The log fire in the restaurant provides the
under-floor heating, while solar panels heat the spectacular, chlorine-free, 25m-lap pool. Maarten
is constantly improving his fynbos world and speaks with eager animation of plans in progress. The
restaurant is capacious and contemporary with two fireplaces and folding doors that open onto
wooden deck. Food is down-to-earth, simple yet delicious; all of the ingredients are fresh, organi
and either home-grown or locally-procured. The free-standing suites are luxurious, with cotton
linen and large open-plan bathrooms of wood and black slate; or you can stay in the farmhouse
rooms with their black-framed historic photographs and wide Persian rugs. With 20km of hiking
trails radiating from the door of your cottage, an astonishing number of birds and horse trails on
site, there is every opportunity to earn yourself a slice of heaven. *Children over 10 are welcome.*

Rooms: 6: 3 free-standing suites with kings, lounge
area & en-suite bath & shower; 1 ground floor suite
with private garden and 2 doubles in main house,
each with en-s bath & shower.
Price: R850 pp sharing (for rooms) and R950 pp
sharing (for the suite) in the house. Fynbos suites
R1300 pp sharing. Singles +30%. Discounts for
longer stays.
Meals: Full breakfast included. On-site restaurant for
lunch & 3-course dinner. Picnic baskets also available.
Directions: A detailed route description will be
mailed after reservation.

Rothman Manor

Andreas and Franziska Gobel
268 Voortrek St, Swellendam
Tel: 028-514-2771 Fax: 028-514-3966
Email: guesthouse@rothmanmanor.co.za Web: www.rothmanmanor.co.za

With lily-littered dam, curvaceous salt-water pool and deck-bound jacuzzi overlooking a small eco-reserve of zebras and springbok, Rothman Manor boasts grounds of park-like calibre. The original Cape Dutch house and venerable oak tree (whose shady canopy acts as a parasol for your breakfast table) both date back to 1834, yet fresh, clipped interiors (born of Andreas and Franziska's combined flair for design) shift matters decisively into the present. With pale-blue or cream-hued walls and cloud-white curtain-swept beds, heavenly rooms are earthed by wooden flooring and canvas artworks, many of which are Franziska's own. Bathrooms sport chequered tiles and African-themed titbits seem to hang suspended in cubby-holes, unique reminders of the grounds and its outdoor inhabitants. Each generous room has its own view-treated patio opening out to the garden with its hidden nooks, hammocks, benches, romantic arbours and numerous statues. Perfectly situated with easy access to numerous nature reserves, the Robertson wine valley and Bontebok National Park, Rothman Manor is its own destination and a gateway to others.

Rooms: 6: 4 kings and 2 twins, 4 with full baths, 2 with shower only.
Price: R550 - R1100 pp sharing. Singles on request.
Meals: Full breakfast included. Restaurants nearby.
Directions: Turn off N2 onto R60 (signed Swellendam West), and then turn R into Swellendam. Rothman Manor on R.

Map Number: 2

Jan Harmsgat Country House

Willie Malherbe and Xolani Mhakananzi

On the R60 between Ashton and Swellendam
Tel: 023-616-3407 Fax: 086-523-9284
Email: reservations@janharmsgat.com Web: www.janharmsgat.com
Cell: 072-279-3138

The sight of Jan Harmsgat's thatched white-gabled houses on the road between Swellendam and the Robertson wine valley is enough to warm any weary traveller's heart. Willie and his business partner Xolani had dinner at JHG and fell in love with the guest-house. When they heard it was for sale they ended up buying the whole farm! Regulars, fear not. The four rooms in the old slave quarters, plus the vast honeymoon loft above the old wine cellar, retain their rustic authenticity, complete with hefty wooden beams, shutters and original clay walls. They've also installed five new garden suites, which occupy the 19th-century Van Eeden House. The large, elegant rooms continue Jan Harmsgat's open bathroom motif, while adding yet more opulence in elaborate chandeliers, chaises-longues, oversized showers and four-poster beds. Best of all, with a chef who's been in this kitchen for 14 years, Jan Harmsgat's foodie reputation is as sound as ever. The Cape gooseberry butterfish was the perfect candlelit prelude to peppercorn beef and a devilishly gooey chocolate tart. Moreover, if you overdo it during Jan Harmsgat's oh-so-civilised evening ritual - cocktails with your hosts at the bar - you can slink back to your boudoir through your own private entrance. And to open your shutters at dawn to a citron-scented zephyr breezing over an orchard of pecan trees is blissful.

Rooms: 10: 6 luxury suites with king-size bed, en-suite bath and shower, air-con; 4 standard (2 en-suite, 2 with en-suite loo and bath in room).
Price: R650 – R950 pp sharing; luxury suites R750 – R1,080 pp sharing. Children under 12 half price. Singles on request.
Meals: Full breakfast included. Restaurant on premises open for lunch and dinner.
Directions: From N1, take Worcester exit onto R62 through Robertson and Ashton, turn right onto the R60. House on left, 21km from Ashton. From N2, take Swellendam West exit onto R60. House on right after 24km.

Bloomestate

Maarten and Carla Van der Ven

276 Voortrekker Street, Swellendam
Tel: 028-514-2984 Fax: 028-514-3822
Email: info@bloomestate.com Web: www.bloomestate.com

If it weren't for the welcoming smiles on Carla and Maarten's faces and for the giant ridgebacks bounding across the lawn, I'd have been concerned that I'd stumbled off Swellendam's main street into a photo shoot for a design magazine. This house overflows with originality and is the quintessence of modern living (I-pod stations, wireless Internet a given). The seven enormous garden rooms are identical in size and furnishings, with super-soft beds looking through French windows either to a scented lavender patch or to the pool, with its one striking blue wall perfectly framing the mountains beyond. Each room is coded by season or element, with one dashingly-coloured wall, matching cushions and a spray-painted canvas. 'Spring' is a vibrant green, 'Summer' a sun-burnt orange, the honeymooners' 'Fire' a passionate red and the brand-new, very special Red Cloud Room has gadgets galore such as diffuse floor lighting when you step out of bed. In the lounge building an LED light projects the time onto the opposite wall, and shattered glass is encased in the bar. The stoep, equipped with bespoke furniture hand-made to the couple's own designs, provides a perfect viewing platform from which to watch the sun slipping down behind the mountains – or you could book a massage in the wellness room, or skip across to the jacuzzi, which overlooks a bird-filled dam in one corner of the garden. Maarten and Carla are the most charming of hosts and the whole experience is enchanting, not least the breakfast, which is as fresh, beautifully presented and utterly delicious as the place itself.

Rooms: 7: 3 kings, 3 twins and 1 luxury room, all with en-suite bath and shower.
Price: R575 - R900 pp sharing. Singles plus 50%.
Meals: Full breakfast included. Picnic baskets, cheese platters, seasonal salads and open sandwiches available on request from R90 pp.
Directions: From Cape Town and N2 take Swellendam West exit (R60) towards Ashton. At the crossroads turn right and Bloomestate is first building on the right.

Augusta de Mist

Michel Platt and Henk Klijn

3 Human St, Swellendam
Tel: 028-514-2425
Email: info@augustademist.co.za Web: www.augustademist.co.za
Cell: 082-493-7971 (Michel) & 083-462-0969 (Henk)

Stranded in Swellendam, with no sign of torrential rains abating and far from my intended destination, I looked to the heavens. My prayers were duly answered as guardian angels, Henk and Michel, shepherded me into the alluring Augusta de Mist, a Cape Dutch National Monument (dating back to 1802) with yellowwood shutters and colonial-style verandah. Beneath the spansriet (Spanish reed) ceiling of my garden suite, Aloe, I toasted sodden toes by the open fire while supping on a complimentary muscadel. Aside from saving homeless GG inspectors, Henk and Michel are innovative hosts and master chefs as I was to discover at breakfast. Michel, a multilingual Montrealer, served up the full works complete with American-style pancake stack while Henk, of Afrikaans stock, initiated a tasting of kumquat chutney and biltong jelly with my continental cheese course! Besides these mouth-watering morsels I digested the Augusta Daily in-house news bulletin before Michel insisted on a tour of the gardens. Did I say gardens? More like indigenous wilderness! With Tucker the German shepherd as vanguard we gallivanted through prodigious foliage, past two lavish garden cottages and lavender-banked swimming pool before climbing the Augusta Valley Walk to reveal splendid sunlit views of Swellendam and a fairy tale picnic spot. "We can provide guests with blanket, hamper and a bottle of Augusta de Mist' Eau Sauvage wine", offered Michel. I only wish I could be stranded in Swellendam more often.

Rooms: 7: 3 garden cottages (2 kings & 1 queen); 2 garden suites (1 queen with 2 adjoining singles; 1 twin suite); 2 heritage accommodation (1 queen & 1 dble). All en-s & showers, most with separate oversize baths. Cot available.

Price: R500 – R930 pp sharing. Singles on request.

Meals: Full breakfast included. Set 4-course dinners at Augusta's African Kitchen on request R225. Wines specially blended.

Directions: On the N2 take the Swellendam East turnoff. Down the hill. Past Stop. Over the small bridge. Turn quick right up small hill. Left then immediate right. Press white bell.

Eenuurkop

Tersia and Jeremy Purén

PO Box 603, Swellendam
Tel: 028-514-1447
Email: info@eenuurkop.co.za Web: www.eenuurkop.co.za
Cell: 082-956-9461

Tersia issued her husband one order when he built the two cottages at Eenuurkop cattle farm: that every window's view be a living, breathing picture. Luckily, Jeremy is a cracking craftsman with a gimlet eye for detail - he designed their own house to resemble the chateaux he admired watching the Tour de France. Indeed, every Eenuurkop window frames a moving oil painting. Be it the porcupine-shaped bedside peephole (complete with porcupine shutter) at Misty Point honeymoon cottage gazing into the lush valley, or the Eenuurkop family cottage loo, whose stable door opens onto the mountains ("The men love it!"). Eenuurkop - don't let tricky pronunciation deter you, have a go! - was named after Eenuurkop Peak, the most imposing of the stunning Langeberg Mountains which envelop the farm. The peak was christened "one o'clock" by Afrikaans farmers who knew, from the sun's position over the summit, when it was lunchtime. Nowadays, lunch is up to you. Will you opt for a smoky braai on your private, flower-dappled patio? Or toss a summer salad in your terracotta kitchen? Or for lazy soup on comfy, earth-tone sofas under the Spanish reed roof on crisper days? Might you carry a picnic lunch (and swimsuit) through 110 hilly hectares to the picturesque farm dam, or hike through Marloth Nature Reserve which neighbours the property, rewarding yourself at one of Swellendam's scrumptious local eateries. A warning: dragging yourself out of these snug white cottages and away from those windows is no mean feat.

Rooms: 2 cottages: Eenuurkop: 2 doubles, 1 family room with 2 bunks, 1 full bathroom & 1 extra toilet; Misty Point: 1 double with full en-suite.
Price: Eenuurkop: R1,000 for whole cottage per night; Misty Point: R800 for whole cottage per night.
Meals: Self-catering. Self-catering food available on request.
Directions: From Swellendam, 3.4km along R60. Past cheese shop on R60, about 800 metres more, sign for Eenuurkop 1.2km along gravel track. GPS: S34 00.383 E20 24.261

De Hoop Collection

Samantha Hughes (Reservations)
The De Hoop Nature Reserve
Tel: 021-422-4522 Fax: 086-575-0405
Email: res@dehoopcollection.co.za Web: www.dehoopcollection.co.za

There are eighty-six mammal species in De Hoop Nature Reserve and, although I would hav
loved to see them all (and I did spot bontebok, eland, caracal and Cape mountain zebra), for th
clarity of my sprawling notes it was a blessing we didn't. Hidden within the Cape Nature reserv
the De Hoop Collection's accommodation is as eclectic as the wildlife. I stayed in the De Hoo
Village, a suburban-style street made up of nine whitewashed three-bedroom cottages. The tab
in the rustic kitchen was already laid when I arrived, and as I sat having supper a bontebok strolle
past eating his. My double bed - covered in white linen and crowned by a handsome headboar
- lay beneath a row of fynbos prints. Similar cottages and a few basic rondavels overlook the vle
a stunning landmark that turns golden at dusk. Houses, with larger rooms, are dotted among
the milkwood trees. Luxury lies at the other end of the vlei: a four-bedroom manor house dor
up to its former glory. Next door, the Fig Tree Restaurant serves food and drink all day, includir
an indispensible sundowner G&T. The song of some 260 species of birds was the only (!) soun

Rooms: Cottages, houses, manor houses, rondavels and camping
spots available. Ring or look at website for details.
Price: There are different accommodation types which range from
R325 – R2,045 per person. There's a minimum charge on certain
cottages.
Meals: Restaurant on-site for breakfast, lunch and dinner.
Directions: From Cape Town take N2 to Caledon. Head to
Bredasdorp on R316, and then Swellendam on R319. After about
6km turn right at De Hoop/Malgas/Infanta sign. Follow dirt road for
35km to the reserve. For De Hoop Nature Reserve turn right at
Buchu Bush sign.

Waterkloof Guesthouse

Hannes and Christine Uys

Waterkloof Farm, On R324 near Witsand
Tel: 028-722-1811 Fax: 028-722-1811
Email: info@waterkloofguesthouse.co.za
Web: www.waterkloofguesthouse.co.za Cell: 083-270-2348

Ever played chicken with an ostrich? Now's your chance. Admittedly I had the protection of a bull-barred pick-up truck but it was exciting stuff, rattling around the farm collecting still-warm eggs for the incubator and doing our best to avoid overly ruffling their fathers' feathers. Waterkloof is an ostrich farm through and through and there is nothing that Hannes (only the seventh generation of the Uys family to work this land!) doesn't know about these feisty fowl. They use the leather for bags, the eggs for breakfast, the eggshells for lampshades and the meat for supper (food is particularly good here - Christine makes sure of this). Sunk into rolling fields of barley and wheat, this is a hard-working farm but a great place to take it easy. The bathrooms have Victorian baths and separate showers, while cool, luxurious bedrooms open onto the garden and fountain. Wild fig trees shade benches built for reading on and the pool area has its own kitchen for help-yourself Sunday lunches. And if you feel like a change of scenery (and wildlife), Witsand is the place to see migrating whales. Back at the house Hannes patiently answered my babble of questions as we sank into ostrich-leather-covered armchairs and tucked into a traditional Afrikaans braai (ostrich sausages, of course) and Christine's utterly delicious and ostrich-free cheesecake. Leather goods made by Italian designers in Cape Town are sold here for a third of the price too!

Rooms: 4: 2 doubles and 1 twin all with bath and shower, 1 twin with shower.
Price: R350 - R480 pp sharing.
Meals: Full breakfast included. Traditional Afrikaans dinner on request.
Directions: From the CT and the N2 turn R onto R324 after Swellendam 32 to the farm. From Mossel Bay take R322 to Witsand. At the crossroads turn R. Farm is on the L after 17 km.

Grootvadersbosch Farm

Keith and Michele Moodie
Snelsetter, Heidelberg
Tel: 082-412-5991 Fax: 0860-067-069
Email: info@grootvadersbosch.co.za Web: www.grootvadersbosch.co.za

A yellow weaver-bird colony was busily weaving the trees into a sprawling avian housing-estate outside Michele and Keith's 18th-century farmhouse. It was difficult to know where to look next. those were definitely monkeys and not baboons that I almost ran over on the driveway - and no a zoo-keeper or game-driver in sight. The historic farmhouse is where you leave your car an where your 'working farm' adventure begins. A short drive in the bakkie via a fast-flowing rive (hence the need to leave 2-wheel drives at the house), in a pretty, lemon-tree meadow beneath the Lagenberg Mountains, there sits Snelsetter. It's a newly-renovated cottage with fou bedrooms, all en-suite and simply adorned. The lounge has an open fire and piles of wood fo every secluded self-caterer's dream. For bed and breakfasters, Michele's home-made bread jams and eggs will set you up for a day on the farm and milk is delivered straight from one of th herd. Farmer Keith and his three dogs will take you on a tour a la mountain goat (walking, drivin and mountain biking is also an option). During our morning run I observed for my own pleasur and yours: rivers and pools for swimming (and drinking), birds and buck for watching, forests an fells for exploring, pinky heathers, fynbos and protected renostorveld for painting (perhaps) an jersey cows for milking! If the farm fails to enliven you then Michele and Keith with their generou spirits, gripping tales of adventure and infectious enthusiasm surely will.

Rooms: 4. 1 double en-suite with shower, 3 twin with en-suite bath and shower.

Price: B&B and dinner R650 pp Sharing. Self caterin R300 pp sharing minimum R1,000 for whole cottage

Meals: Full breakfast and 3-course dinner included in B&B price. Picnic lunches available on request. Self-catering options available.

Directions: From Cape Town take N2. L onto R324, thro' Suurbraak (don't turn to Barrydale), alon R322 towards Heidelberg onto gravel rd (2km). Farm signed on L. From Heidelberg thro' town, then R322 onto gravel rd (ignore signs to Grootvadersbosch Nature Reserve). Farm on R 21km from Heidelberg.

De Doornkraal Historic Country House

Christopher Peppas – Chef de Cuisine

8 Lang Street, Riversdale
Tel: 028-713-3838 Fax: 028-713-3050
Email: info@dedoornkraal.com Web: www.dedoornkraal.com
Cell: 082-958-0622

If the hectic pace of today's world leaves you feeling out of breath, I would prescribe a stay at the eco-friendly De Doornkraal boutique hotel. This Cape Dutch beauty (1746) is one of the earliest buildings in Riversdale. Also found here is a 200-year-old vine, the oldest on the Garden Route and still providing grapes for the breakfast jam. Listen carefully and you can almost hear the history echoing through these walls; you can certainly see it anyway. The original yellowwood and Oregon pine floors and ceilings, blackwood furnishings and the stunning rosewood front door have all been restored to their former glory. Understatedly elegant rooms have simple, neutral-coloured upholstery so as not to upstage the beautiful woodwork throughout. Original paintings add splashes of colour, the work of a well-known artist, Johannes Meintjes, who previously lived here. They also share a fine drawing room with honesty bar, the ideal place for an after-dinner nightcap. Across the road are two comfortable and airy cottages set by a large willow-shaded pond and the syrah vineyard that rolls towards the river's bank. I sat listening happily to the fountain murmur in the tea garden, lost to the outside world. Its only reminder were hoots from the twice-daily steam-train that runs through an otherwise sleepy town. And now chef de cuisine, Christopher Peppas, heads up the De Wingerdt Restaurant. The menu is a la carte with an extensive wine list, focusing on wines of origin from Riversdale (the vineyards produce award-winning "Aant Vette", a blanc de noir). *Special dietary requirements catered for. Children are welcome.*

Rooms: 15: Meintjes Hse (2 queen/1 twin, all en-s bath/sh, sharing lounge); Annex (1Q/3D/5T, all en-s bath/sh, sharing lounge); Garden Cottage. (1Q, en-s sh, private lounge); Vineyard Cottage. (1Q, en-s bath/sh, 1T en-s sh, private lounge).
Price: R377.50 – R750 pp sharing. Single supp' +50%. Cottages R420 – R 750 p.p. sharing.
Meals: Full breakfast incl'. De Wingerdt Restaurant on premises open for breakfast, lunch & dinner.
Directions: N2 from Cape Town to Riversdale, L into town at main entrance, follow signs. Turn L just before you leave town into Lang St. 100m on LHS.

Map Number: 2

Entry Number: 115

Riversong Farm

Piers Sibson

Goukou River Road, Stilbaai (Still Bay West)
Tel: 028-754-3427
Email: pierss@mweb.co.za Web: www.riversongfarm.co.za
Cell: 082-374-8274

Long after I've left South Africa, Riversong Farm will linger among my fondest memories. A winding dirt rollercoaster flecked with rocky outcrops, grinning dassies and patchwork farmland vistas runs alongside the Goukou River, coiling back towards the N2, away from the Still Bay coast. Some 12km along this track lies Piers' place, a supremely chilled-out farm (some friendly sheep here, a pic'n'mix orchard there) where nature gives you a great big hug. The child in me whooped for joy when I dropped down the hills, through the fynbos, towards the river and onto the farm. The adult in me did too... only with a little less grace. Two super-rustic log cabins sit happily side by side on a dewy, long-grass lawn, peeping through bushy reeds across the wide lolling river, the soothing scene occasionally fleetingly broken by a laughing water-skier, a swooshing rowboat, the splash of a golden retriever (or two) leaping off the jetty into the cool swimming water. It's a scene so soothing that Wilbur Smith penned a pile of novels while residing just three farms down. Piers - the epitome of a laid-back Englishman who swapped morning commute for morning kayak - built and occupies the rather more plush Kingfisher Manor just a short pitch away. But he and his golden stick-chasers vacate should your party wish to commandeer the whole affair. And with a verandah and braai that size, every day here is a party. You'd be a fool to leave South Africa without sampling this exquisite patch of river magic. *Pets welcome!*

Rooms: 3: Kingfisher Manor sleeps 8+ in 3 doubles & dormitory; Thames Chalet: 1 double & bunk and full en-suite; Orange Chalet: 1 double with en-s shower, twins with en-s loo.
Price: Thames & Orange chalets: R140 - R165 pp sharing (min R560/R650 per chalet); Kingfisher Manor: R400 – R500 pp sharing (min R2,400 – R3,000 for whole manor). Discount for booking whole farm.
Meals: Fully self-catering.
Directions: Between Riversdale & Albertinia on N2, take Stilbaai turn-off towards sea. Once in town R over bridge, then immediately R into Goukou River Road. Farm clearly named about 12km upriver.

A Farm Story Country House

Kasselman

Kasselshoop Farm, Klein Soebattersvlakte, Riversdale/Still Bay
Tel: 028-754-2430
Email: afarmstory@easycoms.co.za Web: www.afarmstory.co.za
Cell: 082-372-6418

I unscrumpled myself from my driving seat and stepped out... into timelessness. My senses (in their entirety) were suddenly transported by the sights, sounds and smells of Kasselhoop Farm. This type of sensual overload, perhaps most keenly experienced after hours of exposure to the white noise and radio of a very long drive along the N2, is something very special. In this particular moment the wind blew softly and with it the smell of freshly-turned soil was infused with a touch of ocean saltiness. From the farmyard, the melodic grunting, mooing and hooting (I later discovered there were two resident owls living here) created the perfect soundtrack to my personal Farm Story stopover... Inside the sense of timelessness persisted. Encouraged by Liesel to take a closer look at some of the detail of her interiors, I realised that nothing was quite as it seemed. A bronze basin in the bathroom was once part of the farm's geyser (hot-water tank); the vintage gown that hangs from the wall is Granny's old wedding dress; the Victorian bathtub was previously a water-trough; upon inspection the note books in the entrance were Mum's intricate jottings from early radio broadcasts. I felt like I had entered a life-sized doll's house. It is truly perfect! After a feast of a supper, by candlelight in the cosy country kitchen, I retired to my big brass bed stuffed to bursting on vino, home-made pie and cake. The next day I explored Farm Story 'present' with Kassie, who is possible the loveliest cheese-maker/farmer you could ever meet.

Rooms: 3: I king with private bath and shower, I twin with private bath and shower, I double with private bath and shower. 2 with own outside entrance.
Price: R350 pp sharing.
Meals: Full cooked farmhouse breakfast included. Picnic lunches, braai and dinners on request.
Directions: From Cape Town airport (321 km, 3.5 hours). Take N2 towards Mossel Bay, pass Riversdale onto branch-off to Stilbaai, R onto R305 direction Stilbaai & follow rd. After 9,5km R at Melkhoutkraal/Klipfontein turn, 800m turn R, small private road to A Farm Story Country House.

Botlierskop Private Game Reserve

The Neethling Family

Little Brak River
Tel: 044-696-6055 Fax: 044-696-6272
Email: info@botlierskop.co.za Web: www.botlierskop.co.za
Cell: 082-563-8226

The Garden Route is best known for its scenery and sea life, so the last thing I expected to see as I navigated the back roads was a rhino. But there it was, chewing the cud like a contented cow. Botlierskop is a private game reserve that brings the big game south. It's not as wild as its northern counterparts (the lions are in a sanctuary) but it's a magical place to stay, set in 3,000 hectares of grassy plains and forested sandstone hills. The park is open to day visitors, though they use a separate day centre. Two real highlights are Sam and Tsotsi, orphaned elephants - now proud parents - who are trained not only in giving rides, but also as actors. Did you see *Far of Place*? Or *Elephant Boy*? Trust me they were great! Morning coffee with the rhino is also a must and personally I found nibbling on live termites pleasantly minty. Overnighters are appointed their own private guide and I had Billy, an animal almanac and rock art aficionado. From the cavernous hilltop restaurant, he ushered me into a dinghy and we drifted off down the wooded Moordkuil River before showing me to my tent. More marquee than tent, each is set above the river, giving a splendid view of both the water and the hills opposite. Inside it's luxury with a capital 'L'; deep armchairs, a writing desk and a room-for-two bath accompany the mosquito-netted four-poster. One tip though: zip it closed when you leave for the swimming pool – the vervet monkeys have a penchant for coffee and cookies. Helicopter flights and spa treatments are two more reasons to visit.

Rooms: 15 Luxury, Deluxe and Executive Tented Suites. All with aircon, en-suite bath and outdoor showers; Executive has its own lounge and outdoor splash pool. A pool is available at the lodge.
Price: R2,107 - R3,112 pp shg (inc. 2 game drives, meals & drinks). Singles R3,160 - R4,668. Child (6-12) 1/2 adult rate. 2-day stay incl. free horseback ride and 3-day stay incl. free helicopter flight.
Meals: Breakfast & dinner included & lunch too if staying 2 or more nights.
Directions: From Mossel Bay and CT on N2 take Little Brak River exit (401). Heading inland turn R to Sorgfontein. Continue 4km and after causeway turn R for 4km along gravel road to Botlierskop.

Malvern Manor

Sandra and Michael Cook
Nr Fancourt, Blanco, George
Tel: 044-870-8788 Fax: 044-870-8790
Email: info@malvernmanor.co.za or malvernmanor@yahoo.co.uk
Web: www.malvernmanor.co.za Cell: 084-867-6470

If you are having any difficulty understanding why the area is called the Garden Route, well, have a trundle up Michael and Sandra's drive. Much more colourful and vibrant than anything visible from the public thoroughfares. I drove past cows and dams onto a redbrick road overflowing with thick tangles of foliage that hide Malvern from view - and all this perfectly framed by the imposing Outeniqua Mountains. Here is another English couple who fell in love with South Africa, upped sticks and bought their country idyll. They are both of farming stock, so this 21-hectare dairy farm was perfect. But despite being just a hop, skip and a jump from George, it was no easy task converting the Manor House, the keep at the heart of the farm, into a guest house. But it's all come together so nicely. My room opened onto the garden through French doors and lavish Roman-style pillars pick out the bath – the perfect place to unwind after a round of golf at one of the many local courses. For non-golfers, two dams offer blue gill and big-mouth bass fishing and there's endless scope for pre-breakfast walks... or you can sit and bird-watch in the tranquil gardens. Play your cards right on your return and Michael might don his apron and prepare his speciality 'chocaccino'. Delightful people in an enchanting setting.

Rooms: 3: 1 queen, 1 twin or king, 1 double with single bed. All have en-suite bath and shower.
Price: R600 - R750 pp sharing. Singles on request.
Meals: Full breakfast included. Restaurants nearby and deliveries can be arranged.
Directions: From N2 take George airport exit onto R404 and follow signs to Oudtshoorn for approximately 8km. After Fancourt Golfing Estate, sign to Malvern Manor on left. Follow signs.

The Garden Villa

Gabriela Schlosser
35 Plantation Rd, George
Tel: 044-874-0391 Fax: 044-874-0391
Email: gardenvilla@isat.co.za Web: www.gardenvilla.co.za
Cell: 083-384-8499

In a frenzied hub such as George, upon which every Farmer Tomas, Henk and Willie descend for monthly supplies, what you truly need is a bit of peace and... shhh!... Gabriela's Garden Villa provides precisely that. The white Cape Dutch manor house sits at the base of the Outeniqua mountains, surrounded on all sides by lovingly manicured, luminously green lawn. I felt much more country mouse than city mouse here. A stroll round the hushed haven revealed bird baths, herb gardens, hydrangeas and bougainvillea so bright they seem to be plugged into a mains socket. Tortoises (yes, two... Ernie and big Big Bertha), wild porcini mushrooms sprouting beneath the trees, cool stone furniture and pools (yes, two... a lap pool and a heated treat inside a greenhouse where hikers and golfers can soak weary limbs). Four softly furnished, pastel coloured suites can be found teeming with freshly-cut flowers inside the main house. This they share with two welcoming lounges, a handy communal kitchen and the sunny breakfast room which bubbly German Gabriela - who adores baking and, rumour has it, makes the best apricot jam in the world - uses if clouds keep her off the terracotta garden verandah. My favourite, however, was the intimate, pale blue loft room, Hortensia, peeping across garden and mountain and offering a kitchenette for couples who have no intention of leaving their toasty, pine-panelled hideaway. Just make sure you pop down for a cappuccino and a slice of Gabriela's cheesecake not to be missed!

Rooms: 5: 2 kings with full en-suite; 1 queen with en-suite shower; 1 twin with en-suite shower; 1 twin with en-suite shower and kitchenette.
Price: R550 - R795 pp sharing. Single +50%.
Meals: Full breakfast included. Restaurants nearby.
Directions: From Cape Town on N2 turn left onto R404 into George.

Porcupine Pie Boutique Lodge

John and Judy McIldowie
10 Mile Lane, Wilderness Heights
Email: john@porcupinepie.co.za Web: www.porcupinepie.co.za
Cell: 083-447-6901

You really are on top of the world here - even the air smells different at this height! Porcupine Pie, perched at the end of a winding, climbing road, has some simply breathtaking views. The Wilderness Nature Reserve and the Outeniqua Mountains unfurl before you and a wedge of stunning blue sea looks out between its foliage-fringed peaks. Bird-watchers are completely spoiled. You don't even need to leave the deck. Just whip out a pair of bino's and watch. In the time it took me to munch just one of their biscuits, I had seen an eagle and two resident jackal buzzards. I arrived on a freakishly hot winter's day (30 degrees!), so I braved a swim before warming up in a candlelit bath. And when I looked up mid-bath, there was that view again. Each bedroom unit is a stilted wooden chalet with a verandah that seems to hover in mid-air. Judy's artwork hangs on the walls including, of course, a porcupine. During the home-made supper of chicken stuffed with feta, I had to ask, why Porcupine Pie? The morning after they laid the guesthouse path, John explained, they found a small pair of porcupine prints in the wet concrete. So really the place named itself. They do all the cooking (don't miss Judy's breakfast bran muffins), including portered picnics in the river valley below. Dozing off that night with the French windows wide open, the bush-frogs ribbeted me to sleep. No understatement here, it was the best night's kip I'd had in months. Honeymooners seem to like it here too.

Rooms: 3: all kings with en-suite bath and shower.
Price: R500 - R900 pp sharing.
Meals: Full breakfast included. Two-course dinners approx R140 pp.
Directions: From George N2 to Wilderness. L into Wilderness Village, past Protea Hotel to T-jct. L up Heights Rd 3.8km. Stay on tar until T-jct marked 'Old George/Knysna Rd'. R onto gravel rd, after 1.6km R onto 'Ten Mile Lane'. Follow Porcupine signs 3.4km.

Moontide Guest Lodge

Maureen Mansfield
Southside Rd, Wilderness
Tel: 044-877-0361 Fax: 044-877-0124
Email: moontide@intekom.co.za Web: www.moontide.co.za

It's a rare pleasure for us to stay somewhere on holiday and to experience it over a period of days. And Moontide was a palpable hit with all five of us. Its position is hard to beat, right on the banks of the lagoon, its wooden decks shaded by 400-year-old milkwood trees. Here you can sit out for bountiful breakfasts or with an evening drink from your bar fridge, and watch giant kingfishers diving for fish – well, we saw one anyway. Birdlife is profuse on the lagoon. The long white-sanded Wilderness beach is only a two-minute walk from the house, but you can also take a canoe straight from Moontide up the lagoon into the Touw River and then walk along forest trails to waterfalls to swim in fresh-water rock pools. Whatever we did it was a pleasure to return, play cards in a relaxed sitting room, or read in the cool of a bedroom. I was delighted with 'Milkwood' because I'm a sucker for dozing on a futon, in a loft, under thatched eaves, with river views by my head. But I would like to return and try them all. Since we descended en masse, Maureen has built herself a tree-top sanctuary. The deck, day-bed, even the free-standing bath, look out across thatched roofs to the river. Sportingly, she's decided it's too nice to keep for herself!

Rooms: 8: Moonriver Luxury Suite (king, 2 twins, bath, sh'r); Treetops (qu, bath, outside sh'r); Milkwood (king/twins & queen upstairs, bath, sh'r); Stone Cottage (king, 2 twins, bath, sh'r); The Boathouse (d'ble, bath); Moonshadow 1 & 2 (kings, baths & sh'rs); Moondance (king, bath, sh'r).
Price: R300 - R750 pp sharing. Single +60%.
Meals: Full breakfast included.
Directions: From George on N2 ignore Wilderness turn-off. Cross Touw River bridge, first left signed Southside Rd. Moontide at the end of cul-de-sac.

The Dune Guest Lodge

Gary and Melisa Grimes

31 Die Duin, Wilderness
Tel: 044-877-0298 Fax: 044-877-0298
Email; info@thedune.co.za Web: www.thedune.co.za
Cell: 083-941-1149

Gary Grimes is both consummate host and chief breakfast-maker at The Dune and when I pulled up (carefully avoiding parking in the space marked "for my girlfriend/wife") he and Melisa had just finished feeding the hordes with a man-stopping fry-up. "Anything you can do with eggs, I do it," he tells me. I made a note to arrive a little earlier next time. By most standards, he is greedily tall, but at 6'7" he insists he was pretty average among his basketball contemporaries and after years as a pro in Switzerland he dropped the ball in favour of a dishcloth, dinner plates and the wildness of Wilderness. If you're looking for a beach-house then you couldn't get much more beachy than this. As the name suggests it's smack-bang in the dunes and, to be numerically fastidious, exactly 85 wooden steps lead down to 7.5km of pristine sandy beach stretching away to both east and west. The whole place has a wonderfully soothing, seaside feel. Walls hung with seascape oils are whitewashed or sea-blue. Driftwood sculptures surround the fireplace and bedside sofas look south through wall-to-wall windows for round-the-clock whale-watching. Best of all though, wherever you are in the building, you can hear the surf heaving, sighing, thumping and crumping against the beach.

Rooms: 5: 2 doubles, 2 twins with 3/4 beds, all with en/s bath and shower. 1 self-catering cottage.
Price: R400 – R850 pp sharing B&B. Singles +R200.
Meals: Full breakfast included.
Directions: From CT pass Wilderness on N2. Cross the Touw River and turn right into Die Duin 700m later. Take the right fork and The Dune is first on the left.

Serendipity

Phillip and Elsabé Kuypers

Freesia Avenue, Wilderness
Tel: 044-877-0433 Fax: 0866-717-992
Email: info@serendipitywilderness.com
Web: www.serendipitywilderness.com Cell: 082-4499-701

Where else can you dine in arguably the best restaurant on the Garden Route and then wande upstairs to snuggle into bed beneath goose-down duvets? This is a place whose name is breathe in quiet reverence all along the coast. Other Wilderness guesthouses flatly refuse to cater. "What the point?" they say with community pride. Brushed up crisply for dinner after a three-chapter long soak in the bath, I stepped from underfloor-heated tiles onto the shared balcony, to watc geese flighting across a sunset lagoon. Then it was an easy meander down to the guest lounge fc an apéritif, where Rudolf, husband to head-chef Lizelle (her culinary accolades, which hang in th loo, are very encouraging indeed), gave a sensuous description of a South African-inspired men combined with European haute cuisine. Agonising, I finally plumped for snoek mousse and loin c springbok, variously interspersed by an *amuse-bouche* of kudu carpaccio and delicious butternu soup. The intimate restaurant discreetly backs onto a fireplace flanked by sheer windows lookin out onto the water. For dessert I cracked into an exquisitely fruity crème brûlée, even as m waiter taught me the basics of Xhosa. Following a 3-course, crumpet-driven, meticulously prepared breakfast (even the perfectly ripe strawberries are first brushed in a light almond syrup in ebullient sunshine I found myself discussing semantics and champion deep-sea angling wit owners Elsabé and Phillip, who had originally planned to run only a guesthouse… that was befor they invited their daughter to cook.

Rooms: 4: all twin/king with en-suite shower bathrooms.
Price: R480 - R640 pp sharing. Singles +50%.
Meals: Full breakfast included. Dinner in restaurant by prior arrangement.
Directions: From N2 at Wilderness turn north at Caltex garage following George Road to T-junction in front of Protea Hotel. At T-junction turn right, travel along Waterside Road for 1.2km. Turn right into Freesia Avenue. Serendipity 4th house on right.

Wilderness Manor

Gerald Hoch and John-David (JD) Janse van Rensburg

397 Waterside Road, Wilderness
Tel: 044-877-0264 Fax: 044-877-0163
Email: info@wildernessmanor.co.za Web: www.manor.co.za

After 20+ years in the airline industry, Gerald and JD have visited most corners of the globe. Finally they have hung up their wings and decided that Wilderness is the pick of the bunch. And who can blame them - overlooking the lagoon, the glass-encased sitting room is crammed with African artefacts that have been begged, borrowed or bought: Ndebele pipes and beads, bartered-for carvings and stones from the Cradle of Mankind. An old billiard table is hiding there too, somewhere under a pile of maps. The large bedrooms have similar horn-and-hide hues, all the luxurious trappings you could wish for, and room for Indonesian chairs and chests, chocolate leather sofas, slipper baths and dark canopied beds with reading lights. Your hosts are discreet and attentive and after serving up a faultless (and greaseless) breakfast (you might even catch a glimpse of the visiting Knysna loerie lured in by his daily apple) they will give you a map and bountiful beach-bag and send you on your way to explore your surrounds. Birdlife is rampant in the area and walks in the surrounding forests are a must. It is only a five-minute stroll along lagoon-side boardwalks to the beach, village and some good restaurants.

Rooms: 4: 3 lagoon suites (2 kings and 1 king/twin with bath and shower en-suite) and 1 garden room (king/twin with shower en-suite).
Price: R400 – R675 per person sharing per night. Singles on request.
Meals: Full breakfast included.
Directions: Turn into village of Wilderness from N2 and follow road through village for approx 400 metres. At T-junction, turn right into Waterside Road and go along lagoon for 1 km. Wilderness Manor is a 3-storey house on left-hand side, 397 Waterside Road.

Map Number: 5

Entry Number: 125

Lodge on the Lake

Frank Brauer
746 North Street, Wilderness
Tel: 044-877-1097 Fax: 044-877-1097
Email: info@lodgeonthelake.co.za
Web: www.accommodation-wilderness.com Cell: 084-383-7766

Übercool has come to Wilderness. Frank used to be in film production and his eye for precision design underlies every detail in this grandly Tuscan villa, which sits resplendent on its many pillars above the lake. As I skirted the central courtyard fountain and entered beneath the portico something magic seemed to happen. The walls suddenly disappeared, the outside was inexplicably coming inside... but most mesmerising of all was the lake that had effortlessly risen without a ripple, to the rim of the pool and forged a seamless sheet of the deepest liquid blue only finally interrupted by the mountains. I suppose that's what you call German engineering. There's a Zen-like tranquillity here, a faraway sound of trickling water, which recently attracted a pair of authors; no one's sure whether they wrote anything. More than likely they discovered the delights of the in-house spa where three treatment rooms employ the mineral wealth of the sea to leave you feeling as fresh as the surf. Naturally the rooms, reached by a winding staircase, are mindful of weight, colour and proportion to the enth degree. Thick carpeting softens a solemnity of dark wooden bedsteads, cupboards and ingenious concertina doors, with a sense of playfulness creeping into striking patterns, stalactite pillars, open tubs and creative positioning of mirrors. Each has its own fabulous private balcony.

Rooms: 5: 4 doubles, 1 twin; all en-suite bath and shower.
Price: R400 - R1,000 pp sharing.
Meals: Full or continental breakfast included.
Directions: Emailed or faxed on booking.

Villa Castollini

Nan Raturat

Uitzicht, Brenton-on-Sea, Brenton, Knysna
Tel: 044-381-8200 Fax: 044-381-8239
Email: info@castollini.co.za Web: www.castollini.co.za
Cell: 083-460-2606

Here's a little piece of Italy picked up and tweezered onto 23 of the Garden Route finest hectares, a modern Tuscan villa set on top of Knysna's western head. I arrived through a grand mosaic entrance to be greeted by Nan and her friendly Bernese mountain dog cross grizzly bear... and I felt immediately reassured that I was in safe paws. Nan and her devilishly witty French husband Patrick run their guesthouse with rare affection and energy, constantly considering guests' needs. Do, however, allow Nan time to tend to her organic veggie garden. The rewards will be reaped at breakfast. Each bedroom has its own identity. Some have dressing rooms; others have sitting rooms. All are large and lead out to 180° view of Knysna town, the Outeniqua mountains and the oyster beds of the Knysna Estuary. Put aside time each day just to appreciate this view. In fact, make a point of having a drink at the pool after dark. The sparkling lights of Knysna below make this particularly atmospheric. I enjoyed the raised, open-plan, very Italian kitchen filled with tins of decadent treats, which guests are welcome to help themselves to. My favourite, though, has to be the Ferrari room. Clearly someone here is a Ferrari fanatic, hence the Ferrari-themed bar with its collection of miniatures (cars, not bottles) and Ferrari paraphernalia. Nan has personally overseen 83 weddings here, and with no neighbours, room for 16 guests... and the Ferrari room, this might be the perfect Garden Route wedding, honeymoon or other special occasion venue.

Rooms: 8: 3 king/twin with en-suite bath and shower, 2 king with en-suite bath and shower and 3 queen with en-suite shower.
Price: R500 - R1,200 pp sharing.
Meals: Full breakfast included. Dinner available on request.
Directions: From N2 take Brenton-on-Sea/Belvidere turn-off and continue for 5.2km. Villa Castollini is on the left side.

191 Nirvana

Madi Butler
191 Rheenendal Road, Rheenendal, Knysna
Tel: 044-386-0297 Fax: 086-606-0034
Email: madibutler@cyberperk.co.za Web: www.191nirvana.co.za
Cell: 084-826-2266

Who would have thought you could make a couple of self-catering cottages out of two wate
reservoirs? Evidently Madi Butler did. (First you have to empty out the water of course.) Her tw
circular, thatched properties now stand proudly on the top of the hill. The position, at the hub c
outstanding panoramic views that stretch from the end of the Outeniqua Mountains, acros
Knysna Lagoon and into the surrounding forest, was just too good to waste. You won't quit
know where to gaze first. This is one self-catering place where you can be 100 per cen
independent, yet still have the reassuring presence of a very friendly hostess just at the bottom c
the hill. On top of all the added extras you require (Madi supplies beautiful white bed linen, towel
firewood and tit bits such as organic salad), a basket of home-grown herbs and veggies (dependin
on the season) will find its way onto your doorstep each morning. The indoor fireplace double
up as a braai area which - and this is my favourite part - becomes virtually outdoors when yc
'roll up' the walls (made of canvas blinds) at the front of the cottage. What's that? Roll up the wall
I assure you it's possible. You'll just have to come and see for yourself.

Rooms: 3 self-catering units.
Price: R350 - R425 pp sharing.
Meals: Self-catering.
Directions: Heading to Knysna from George on the
N2. Before you enter Knysna turn left into
Rheenendal Road. Follow the road for 1.6km and the
entrance to 191 Nirvana is on your right.

The Bamboo Guesthouse

Jaynie Court and Gordon Turrell

7 - 9 Bolton Street, Hunters Home, Knysna
Tel: 044-384-0937 Fax: 044-384-0937
Email: info@bambooguesthouse.co.za Web: www.bambooguesthouse.co.za
Cell: 082-812-8838

I had to call three times for directions (each time cringing a little more deeply), but Jaynie finally got through to me with, "and if you don't make it this time you forgo the bottle of red under your pillow". Moments later I arrived and closed the door on the hubbub of Knysna. All around me wooden-slatted walkways divided and ordered a jungle of plants and fountains, pools and ponds. All the walkways spiral to the main house where breakfasting, lounging and evening merriment take place. Jaynie and Gordon have transformed an ordinary garden of lawns and flowerbeds into their own mini-Eden, burying fourteen spotless rooms in a relaxing garden that grabs the senses and deceives the eye. Guests and hosts alike benefit from the tranquillity, manifest in Jaynie's smile (as warm as they come) and Gordon's obvious contentment as he braais away behind the bar. But beware: from his work-station come rustic feasts to challenge the most voracious appetite, wines to lure the most disciplined off task and stories to leave the most hardened traveller incredulous. There's something of Mick ("Crocodile") Dundee about Gordon and I felt a tad pale and urban next to him. This was not helped in any way by accepting a two-hour full-body massage with an exceptional visiting masseuse. But I got over it. A night drifting to sleep on a mountain of cushy bed pillows, vaguely aware of frogs croaking one minute and birds chirping the next, made this weak urbanite feel terrific.

Rooms: 14: 2 honeymoon suites with king beds, en-suite bath/shower and wood burning fire; 2 family rooms with king bed and twin sharing, en-suite shower; 7 king/twins with en-suite showers; 3 queen with en-suite showers.
Price: R345 - R580 pp sharing. Single rates available.
Meals: Full breakfast included. Other meals by arrangement.
Directions: From N2 in Knysna (heading to Plett) turn right down George Rex Drive. After lights take 2nd left into Howard St; at the golf club house take central road signed Bolton St, continue over 2 speed bumps and you'll see no.9 on your right.

Map Number: 5

Villa Afrikana Guest Suites

Bianca Ackermann and Rossano Giunti

13 Watsonia Drive, Paradise, Knysna
Tel: 044-382-4989 Fax: 044-382-4989
Email: concierge@villaafrikana.com Web: www.villaafrikana.com
Cell: 082-940-0867

I'd barely hauled my car up the sloped driveway (and yanked on the handbrake) when smile eyed Bianca wondered if I'd like a world-famous (ok, maybe Knysna-famous) frothy coffee. We if they're as Italian as Ross and as plush as their guest house, I certainly would. Posited up Paradise - I'm not gushing, that's truly the name of their locale - Villa Afrikana could put the swai into Hilary. Bianca (whose family live down the hill) and Ross (who hails from Florence) m working on a cruise liner - he in hospitality management, she in administration - and pooled the gifts for care and design into a tightly-run guest ship. White floors stretch through cool, clean livir areas, parting for deep white sofas, zebra-skin rugs and floor-ceiling windows revealing panoram lagoon vistas. I plumped for perusing the villa library in the starboard reading snug, propped front of a porthole peeping out to the gleaming pool. Upstairs, in unfussy, roomy, balconied suite things are no less glam. Subtle African touches tug at modern Euro-minimalism: local painter N Nieuwoudt's bespoke interpretations of Knysna grace each room while every pillow sparkles wi a cheeky Ferrero Rocher (thanks Ross!). This stylish crow's nest towers over Knysna: fro Bianca's pancake-prepping kitchen we watched yachts wriggle round the lagoon, ant-peop exploring the Waterfront and a controlled fynbos fire billowing over the Heads. Releasing th handbrake and plunging my car back into reality, I knew I'd dream of Paradise that night.

Rooms: 6: 3 extra-length king with full en-suite; I queen with full en-suite; I extra-length king with shower over bath; I king/twin with shower over bat (can connect to family room & sleep 4).
Price: R850 - R1,150 pp sharing. Singles +60%.
Meals: Full breakfast included. Lunch, lunch boxes and dinner available on request R89 - R160.
Directions: From Cape Town on the N2 entering Knysna turn left into Fletcher Road at Total Garage, left at top of Fletcher Road, right into Circular Drive. Watsonia Drive is on your right at the top of Circula Drive.

Brenton Beach House

Derrick Coetzer

116 Watsonia Avenue, Brenton-On-Sea, Knysna
Fax: 086-6911-612
Email: info@brenton-beach-house.co.za
Web: www.brenton-beach-house.co.za Cell: 078-415-5246

It's 7.30am. There's a rat-a-tat-tat at my bedroom door. Hoisting back my plump white duvet, I pad across wooden floorboards, open the door and there in the sun-dappled hallway is Derrick, tracksuit-bottomed and trainer-shod, grinning from ear to elbow. We'd promised to join two German marathon-running guests jogging along Brenton's 8km of fynbos-backed beach, but now I'm hesitant. Plus, I was having a truly joyful dream about the Knysna loeries we'd spotted in the untamed pool garden the night before.... Nevertheless, run I do. After all, what a terrible waste it would be not to spend most of one's time in Brenton on that wild and superbly untouristy beach. Brenton Beach House is a place for those who like moving about in the great outdoors. Although Derrick is South African (obvious when you see that whopping braai deck), he spent the last 25 years running a cycling company in Provence. An exercise fanatic (hence all the jubilance), Derrick "speaks golf" and has nifty deals with Knysna's golfing and bike-rental companies for special guests rates. After a pedal, big, bright, neat and airy rooms with generous bathrooms and shared balconies await. Layered over two floors across two sides of a central garden, there's a jubilant camaraderie between guests as soon as Derrick's delightful housekeeper Juliette welcomes you with tea and steaming madeleines. Over a hearty post-jog breakfast, the camaraderie was such that I truly envied those Germans, eagerly asking Derrick if they could stay for two more nights as I hit the road....

Rooms: 5: 1 XI king with full en-suite & spa bath; 3 XL king/twin with full en-suite (one with 3/4 twins); 1 queen with full en-suite.
Price: R650 - R1,300 per room. Discount for singles.
Meals: Full breakfast (with Derrick's famous home-made bread) incl'. Beach lunches & dinner on request.
Directions: From Cape Town on N2 towards Knysna. Before crossing lagoon causeway bridge, turn L following sign for Brenton & Belvidere. Continue up hill into Brenton for approx. 6km. Follow signs for Brenton Beach House.

Packwood Country Estate

Vicky and Peter Gent

Fisanthoek, Nr Harkerville, Between Knysna and Plettenberg Bay
Tel: 044-532-7614 Fax: 0865-100-741
Email: packwood@xnets.co.za Web: www.packwood.co.za
Cell: 082-253-9621

"Rooney, off!" sighs Vicky, nudging her boisterous young collie off the cream sofa and out of the back door. Rooney, tumbling into 1,000 acres of pasture and vineyard, is not complaining. He bounds off to terrorise 900 dairy cattle. Cosseted between Knysna Forest and the ocean, Packwood offers a taste of country living at its best. Up here, wrapped in mountains, gazing onto the Robberg Peninsula, free-roaming Jerseys produce 5,000 litres of milk a day. But Vicky and Peter aren't a pair to rest on their laurels. 2009 heralded their crisp Maiden Vintage Sauvignon Blanc and in 2012 they will launch their first pure pink pinot bubbly. An array of Packwood produce - from the dairy, vineyard, farm and gardens - is available for your stay, including extra mature cheddar and crisp garden salads. Plump for one of three summery, self-catering cottages or treat yourself to the main country house. Ilsa, Packwood's full-time housekeeper and cook is available by special arrangement. She will cook up a storm with her infamously fiery chicken curry and very naughty chocolate mousse cake. Guests really can have it all here: short drives lead to pristine beaches, world-class golf courses, local game parks and mountain treks; whilst relaxing days on the farm can include as much or as little as you feel up to, from farm tours, bike rides and walks to pool-side bathing. A stay at Packwood means lots of cheese and wine, lazy mornings and some heavenly peace.

Rooms: 6: main house: 3 kings with full en-suite; Family Cottage: double & 2 twins, full bathroom, extra loo; Hill Cottage: 2 doubles, full en-suite, shower room; Bottlebrush Cottage: double, en-s bath.
Price: R800 per day – R3,250 per day. Long-term holiday lets negotiable. House-keeping Mon–Fri except public holidays.
Meals: Main House: breakfast/lunch/dinner available with prior arrangement. Self-catering cottages: farm produce/dinner day of arrival by request.
Directions: From Cape Town on N2, 25km from Knysna take Fisanthoek turn-off left and travel 6km of good, untarred road.

Fynbos Ridge Country House and Cottages

Liz and Brian Phillips

Plettenberg Bay
Tel: 044-532-7862 Fax: 044-532-7855
Email: info@fynbosridge.co.za Web: www.fynbosridge.co.za

Fynbos Ridge is a botanical paradise where new owners Liz and Brian have continued an eco-conscious mission to remove all invasive alien vegetation. A wide variety of indigenous trees and shrubs have been painstakingly reinstated to create a haven where Cape flora (fynbos) and fauna can flourish. There are birds here that you will only see in the fynbos. These green-fingered nature lovers will cushion your stay with super-down duvets, pure cotton sheets and a hearty breakfast in the light-filled, alfresco-esque dining room. Lucky self-caterers can choose from newly-refurbished cottages in 'gazania' yellow, 'clivia' peach or 'aristea' blue, all inspired by indigenous flowers and fully and sensitively equipped to satisfy any modernist yearnings. I, for example, particularly liked the minimalist stone baths. They can also pick their own vegetables, but please do let Brian cook for you at least once. This private nature reserve cries out to be walked in, although unfortunately I only made it as far as the ozone-purified swimming pool (no chemicals here - just a weird-sounding contraption doing its bit to keep the establishment and all guests 100% carbon neutral). Follow the natural borders and discreet signposts to this oasis amongst the fynbos to take a dip. Hidden within the depths of a private nature reserve and contemplating the meeting of the Outeniqua and Tsitsikamma mountains, you could easily spend the whole day here languishing with a book. Now where did I pack my swimming togs? *Please enquire about painting, cooking and birding holidays*

Rooms: 9: 6 rooms in the house: 4 luxury doubles, 1 superior luxury double and 1 self-catering studio, all with en-suite bath and shower; 3 self-catering cottages, all sleeping 4-5 with 1 bathroom & 1 shower-room.
Price: B&B and self-catering from R900 pp sharing. Singles on request.
Meals: Full breakfast included in B&B price or R85 for self-catering. Lunch and dinner on request.
Directions: 23km along N2 from Knysna heading towards Plettenberg Bay. Take L into 'Blue Hills Bird Farm'. Bear L where road forks to Fynbos Ridge.

Cornerway House

Dee and Robin Pelham-Reid

61 Longships Drive, Plettenberg Bay
Tel: 044-533-3190 Fax: 044-533-3195
Email: cornerwayhouse@mweb.co.za Web: www.cornerwayhouse.co.za

Robin and Dee moved from my Wiltshire school-town (as it happens) to start Cornerway House and fantastic hosts they make too. Robin will ably point you off to the beach with sundowners or to the Robberg Peninsula walk, an exhilarating experience. Meanwhile Dee can give you a different and rewarding perspective on Plett as Chairman of The Plettaid Foundation. Her dedication has set in place home-care workers in the townships. Also a safe house for abused women and children (aptly named Invicta House) and an 8-bed hospice called Trinity House. I retired to my room - wooden antiques, comfy bed and sash windows looking onto the garden – and at dawn joined Ocean Blue to spot whales, dolphins and sharks, returning to a sumptuous breakfast, courtesy of Dee, who uses what she can from the garden: herbs, of course, and strawberries too on the day I visited. Throughout the old house there are colourful, Laura Ashley-esque quirks, to wit the yellow-washed and lilac shutters of the house, the petunias bathing in a bath, a purple TV/sitting room with bright blue cushions and the pink and yellow mohair in the garden suite. The new annex has a far more contemporary feel. I left Robin and Dee among the frangipani, gardenia and orange trees as I wrenched myself away. *See owner's website to make an online booking.*

Rooms: 8: 3 rooms in the new annex (2 twins/king with en-suite shower/bath, 1 double with en-suite shower); 4 twins and 1 double; 2 with en-suite shower, 3 with en-suite shower and bath.
Price: R320 - R595. Singles +50% except high season. All rates include breakfast except for the self-catering unit option.
Meals: Full breakfast included. Self-catering options available.
Directions: From N2 heading east, turn right into Plett. Continue to the circle and go straight over. Road descends to river and crosses it. Over circle, turn right onto Longships Dr. Continue down 0.9km to Cornerway House on right.

Aquavit Guest House

Ole and Linda Olsen

8 Serica Place, Plettenberg Bay
Tel: 044-533-6686 Fax: 086-511-4293
Email: info@aquavit.co.za Web: www.aquavit.co.za
Cell: 071-256-2162

I stepped out of my car and just followed my nose, by which I mean I was lured over the threshold of Aquavit by the irresistible aroma of freshly-baked cookies! And only moments later it seemed, I was chatting away with Ole and Linda over coffee and cakes… until Ole suddenly reached for his binos. "That's pretty neat", he mumbled, pointing out some breaching whales in the bay below. I wouldn't have predicted that my first South African whale sighting would have been from such a salubrious spot! It's not just the whales. Everything about Aquavit is pretty neat, from the elevated aspect with panoramic views of Plettenberg Bay and the Tsitsikamma mountains to the whizzo, marriage-saving beds – each side can be adjusted to your perfect firmness. The architectural and interior design, meanwhile, looks destined for a coffee-table book. It's modern, but somehow still exudes warmth and homeliness. Ole and Linda have merged their Danish/American histories into this modern, multi-level home – nautical paintings reflect the couples' great passion for art and sailing that has taken them around the world. A visit to the wine cellar coaxed me out of Plett's bubbliest bathtub where a portrait of the Viking hero Holga Dansk presides. After a fabulous night's sleep between percale sheets and among carefully-collected artifacts, I awoke to a meticulously prepared breakfast (winner of my own 'Best Croissant on the Garden Route' award) and reluctantly went on my way. *Children over 12 are welcome.*

Rooms: 5: Room 1, luxury king, bath + sep' shower; Rm 2, twin + sh'r; Rm 3, queen, bath + sep sh'r; Rm 4, qu + sh'r; Rm 5, qu + sh'r. All have semi-private patios. Wine Cellar for private functions.
Price: R550 - R650 pp sharing (1st May 2012 - 15th Sept 2012); R850 - R950 pp sharing (16th Sept 2012 - 30th April 2013).
Meals: Full breakfast incl'. Picnic baskets on request.
Directions: N2 towards Plettenberg Bay, thro' traffic circle onto Marine Way toward centre of town. Thro' 2nd smaller circle (look for Aquavit sign). 1st St on R is Cutty Sark; Take Cutty Sark to 1st St on R, Serica Place. Halfway up hill on R is Aquavit no. 8.

Bosavern

Vivienne and Gerald Dreyer
38 Cutty Sark Ave, Plettenberg Bay
Tel: 044-533-1312 Fax: 044-533-0758
Email: info@bosavern.co.za Web: www.bosavern.co.za
Cell: 082-922-4721

The striking S-shaped waves of Bosavern's timbered ceiling mimic the sea and combine with minimalist white interiors and mirrors to strike a harmonious note with the blue ocean far below. Glass doors lead off the open-plan sitting room and onto the balcony where you can treat yourself on wicker chairs to a regal cliff-top view of the Robberg Peninsula and the white beaches of Plettenberg Bay. Powerful binoculars will pick out whales and schools of dolphins which are (can be!) plentiful in the clear water. The bedrooms downstairs have the same sliding doors that disappear smoothly into the wall and the sea breeze wafts in through a square gap of sky as if from a bright blue painting. The view from your room and private balcony is no less spectacular. Comfort is a priority, with goose-down duvets on enormous beds, fine cotton sheets, a welcoming bottle of Nederberg, gowns and slippers. Vivienne and Gerald are natural hosts, who provide great breakfasts and also picnic hampers for the beach or Robberg hikes, and mountain bikes and canoes for the madly active (a pool caters for loungers). They will also point you in the right direction for golf and recommend a number of restaurants within easy walking distance. Not suitable for children under 16.

Rooms: 5: 4 twins/doubles & 1 double; 3 with en-suite shower, 2 with en/s bath and shower. All rooms and bathrooms all have heated towel rails and underfloor heating.
Price: R680 - R990 pp sharing. Singles R962 - R1,782.
Meals: Full breakfast included and served from 8am - 9am.
Directions: From Knysna take N2. Right at Shell garage into Plettenberg Bay. Turn 1st right into Cutty Sark Ave. Follow road round, then turn right again into cul-de-sac. House on left.

Beacon Lodge

Al and Clo Scheffer

57 Beacon Way,
Plettenberg Bay
Tel: 044-533-2614
Fax: 086-730-4037
Email:
info@beaconlodge.co.za
Web:
www.beaconlodge.co.za

Garden Route, Western Cape

This is a small (just two rooms), personal, friendly and involving B&B – and I mean B&B in the proper sense where you share the house with your hosts. Both rooms have their own separate entrances, mind you, if you want to slip about more furtively. The patio, for breakfasts, garden bird-watching or reading, has long views out to sea and it's only a short walk to the beach and the lagoon, presumably where you will want to spend at least some of your time. To this end Al and Clo have all beach necessities at the ready – umbrellas, towels and the like. The larger of the two rooms was my favourite (and also the more expensive) with sea views through a huge window and anti-glare solar blinds. There is seagrass on floors, plenty of immaculate seaside white in walls and towels and colour is added in the form of fresh flowers. The Scheffers take the greatest care of their guests. *Fridge facilities provided. Great restaurants within walking distance. Whales and dolphins in season. Closed mid-Dec to mid-Jan and either June or July. Enquire first!*

Rooms: 2: 1 twin and 1 double, both with en-suite bathrooms with showers.
Price: R225 - R450 pp sharing. Singles on request.
Meals: Full breakfast included. There are good restaurants in town for other meals.
Directions: From Knysna take 3rd turn-off into Plett on right & from Port Elizabeth take 1st turn-off into Plett on left at Engen One Stop Garage. The house is 600 metres further on the left.

Anlin Beach House

Dermot and Fran Molloy

33 Roche Bonne Avenue, Plettenberg Bay
Tel: 044-533-3694 Fax: 044-533-3394
Email: stay@anlinbeachhouse.co.za Web: www.anlinbeachhouse.co.za

Like a moth to a lamp, the first thing I did here after dropping off my bags was head to the beach, irresistibly close (100 metres away) and tantalizing from the top-floor balcony. A run along the soft sands all the way to the Robberg Peninsula was exhilarating at sunset. Beneath cobalt blue skies I passed only seals and surfers cresting the smooth ocean rollers. The beach really does seem to slow you down as both Dermot (a wine-marketer) and Fran (a trained counsellor) will attest. As we passed the quirky outdoor shower, Fran commented that she always wanted the place to be ultra up-to-date in terms of design, but comfortable at the same time, "I don't want guests to think 'I can't sit on that'". The style is therefore contemporary, with walls and furnishings in natural colours imitating the beach, the ocean and dramatic rocky outcrops. The bedrooms have tiled floors and cream-coloured furniture drenched in light from the private patios and vast windows. Dermot's an avid collector of South African art so expect to see some interesting pieces. If you can, book the upstairs apartment. The view, which sweeps across the ocean to the Outeniqua Mountains, finally persuaded Fran to go for the house; "when a school of dolphins swam past, I knew I had to sign!" The kitchens, with their polished-cement surfaces and hi-tech gas hobs, all come well stocked with tea, coffee and other goodies. Don't forget to ask Dermot for his autograph either. He once worked as an extra on *Zulu Dawn*!

Rooms: 4: 1 upstairs apartment (potentially 2 units) with 3 beds and 2 bathrooms, both with shower only; 2 garden apartments, both sleep 3 with 1 shower bathroom each.
Price: From R450 pp to R850 pp. Singles +25%.
Meals: Self-catering but a full Continental breakfast can be served in your apartment or on your private patio.
Directions: From N2 heading east, R into Plett. Continue to circle & go straight over. Road descends to river and crosses it. Over circle, R onto Longships Dr then left into Roche Bonne Avenue, which has a brown B&B sign. Anlin Beach House is 50m on R.

Piesang Valley Lodge

John Elliott

Piesang Valley Road, Plettenberg Bay
Tel: 044-533-6283 Fax: 044-533-4477
Email: info@pvl.co.za Web: www.pvl.co.za
Cell: 072-5190-244

If ever a place resembled its owner, this is it. Unpretentious, laid-back, friendly and personal, John has bestowed these qualities on a lodge, part of which he built with his own hands using a special vertical construction technique (just nod and make understanding grunts). These are also the rooms of choice where pine and timber frame a scene of dark wood furniture, inviting beds and earthy rugs, soothed by white-washed walls and alabaster bathrooms. All open breezily onto the garden. There's a refreshing youthful energy here as well, something else you'll notice about John, who leads a tremendously healthy life. I challenge anyone to guess his correct age. When we met he had just returned from rescuing his new houseboat that had slipped its moorings. After many years in the hospitality industry, it was his dream to start his own guesthouse and where better than on family ground, whose hill-top seat looks all the way down the valley into Plett and out to the Indian Ocean. There are plenty of good restaurants in the area, but you're welcome to bring your own grub and cook lunch and dinner in the kitchen. That's if you're still hungry after a bonanza breakfast with the birds. The garden is a great place to kick back with a cold beer and enjoy a gently sloping verdant scene of lawn, bush and tree, across which playful house hounds tumble. "It's convenient and tranquil," says John. It's very good value too. *Plettenberg Bay Country Club is a couple of minutes away*

Rooms: 6 rooms: all queen doubles or twins (2 bath/shower and 4 shower en-suite).
Price: R320 - R470 pp sharing.
Meals: Full breakfast included. Guests are welcome to cook their own lunch and dinner in the kitchen.
Directions: Take Piesang Valley Road turn-off from N2 into Plettenberg Bay. 1.4km down the road the lodge is on your right-hand side.

Christiana Lodge

Christa and Philip Joubert
Aquarius Close, Solar Beach, Plettenberg Bay
Tel: 044-533-6212 Fax: 044-533-3280
Email: info@christianalodge.com Web: www.christianalodge.com
Cell: 082-337-7490

Coiled up in a cushioned reading nook at Christiana Lodge, my gaze extending out acro
shimmering wetlands dispensing the syncopated croaking of countless unseen frogs and onto th
waves crashing on Robberg Beach over the hill, I can't tell if I'm outside or in. And that is entire
the intention. This magical place, named after the grandmother's home where Christa and he
brother Philip spent school holidays, brings the African outdoors indoors, deftly and subtly. Yo
won't be burrowing your way through proteas and springbok to find your crisply-cottone
custom-made, king-sized bed or your open-plan, super-slick bathroom (complete with 'ube
spoily', enamel-coated steel baths and in-shower benches); this is a place where natura
uncluttered minimalism is dish of the day. The illusion of being right in the thick of Plettenberg Bay
bush-life is conveyed through a camouflage of warm, natural hues and an average of, let's see.
one, two, three, four, five... five windows per bedroom! And we're not talking piddly little frame
Great swathes of floor-to-ceiling glass break up soothing, sandy walls; vast portals onto the richl
textured nature reserve hang above cane armchairs; white-shuttered French doors stretch out t
wide cherry-wood and terracotta balconies. Over coffee in the tranquil, outdoor-indoor poolsid
lounge, Christa - beautifully serene since quitting a fast-paced Jo'burg job in TV production - tel
me that style is in simplicity. Christiana Lodge is the embodiment of both.

Rooms: 10: 6 extra-length kings; 3 extra-length
kings/twins; 1 family room with extra-length
king/twins plus daybed; all full en-suite.
Price: R495 – R880 pp sharing. Singles +35%
Meals: Full breakfast included, picnic baskets and 3-
course dinners available on request.
Directions: On N2, take Piesang Valley turn-off int
Plettenberg Bay. R at roundabout past Kwikspar, R
into Longships Drive, L into Griz Nez Ave, L into
Aquarius Close. Lodge is second building on left.

Tamodi Lodge and Stables

Owen and Lynne Johnston

Keerboom Heights, Plettenberg Bay
Tel: 044-534-8071 Fax: 044-534-8073
Email: owen@tamodi.co.za Web: www.tamodi.co.za
Cell: 082-551-9313

I had only one evening at Tamodi and I wasn't going to waste a minute of it by dining out at the local beachside Italian or cosying up to a log fire on one of the lodge sofas, surfing the web and watching movies on DSTV (these luxuries for available for lucky guests staying more than one night). I planned and executed my evening, though I say it myself, to perfection. So, this is what I did. I nipped down the hill to fetch my take-away supper. Whilst waiting for my seafood pasta, I was briefly distracted by spy-hopping whales and a glorious African sunset. I made my way back up the dirt road (avoiding porcupines, bushbuck and baboons) complete with a portion of tiramisu. I sampled some wines from Owen's private wine cellar and plumped for a local red. I decanted pasta and wine into appropriate crockery. I made my way out on to the deck and watched darkness descend over the forested valley and the Tsitsikamma Mountains. After dinner I listened to the sounds of the African night and observed how different the stars look in the southern hemisphere. I contemplated a midnight swim in the infinity pool, but decided instead to retreat under thatch and take a long hot soak in my suite's free-standing stone bathtub. And then I drifted off to a deep sleep until breakfast. The whole evening was an exercise in precision self-pampering. But really I would have preferred several weeks at Tamodi!

Rooms: 3: 1 standard luxury queen, en-s bath & shower; 1 standard luxury king, en-s bath & shower (can split into 2 x 3-quarter beds); 1 honeymoon suite with king 4-poster & en-s bath, indoor/outdoor shower.
Price: R620 - R975 pp sharing. Singles on request. Whole house available by arrangement.
Meals: Full cooked and continental breakfast.
Directions: From Cape Town take N2. Approx' 10km past Plettenberg Bay towards Port Elizabeth, go past 1st 2 turn-offs to Keurboomstrand and at top of hill find a Vodacom cellphone tower. Turn R at foot of tower & go 1.5 km.

Map Number: 5   Entry Number: 143

That Place

Jo and David Butler

The Crags
Tel: 044-534-8886
Email: info@thatplace.co.za Web: www.thatplace.co.za
Cell: 082-578-1939

This is "that place...," you know the one you talk about for years after you've been there. "D
you remember the time we went to South Africa and stayed in 'That Place' where we watch
the elephants wandering through their paddock across the valley, where we hazily dreamt in t
hand-crafted sauna. We braai'd and feasted for hours on the deck, the kids duck-diving a
splashing in the waters of the private pool - do you remember?" Jo and David have created
memory-building, self-catering home. And that's just what it is - a home. It's not grand
pretentious, just comfortable and happy to have you. I was shown around by a very mode
David who failed to mention that the great wooden table and chairs, the sauna and the thr
cheeky fish sculptures suspended on the wall (amongst other details) had sprung from his ov
gifted fingers. I met the dogs too, all six of them, from John Keats the Great Dane down
McGregor the feisty Jack Russell. Don't worry, these chaps live next door and won't bother y
unless you want them to. But if you want them to…! Also next door are elephants which can
seen from the house, along with monkeys and a huge variety of birds. "You named your dog af
a poet?" I asked Jo. "David did," she replied, "he's very into his poetry." Sounds like the perfe
man to me - unfortunately already taken by Jo who is equally wonderful.

Rooms: One 3-bedroom self-catering cottage let a
a whole: 1 king with en-suite bath and shower and
twins (1 ideal for children).
Price: From R750 - R1,500 per night for the whole
house.
Meals: Self-catering, but Bramon Wine Estate an
easy walk away for lunch. Dinner can be arranged t
be ready in fridge/oven for your arrival. Discuss with
Jo when you book.
Directions: Travelling in the direction of Port
Elizabeth on the N2, 20km east of Plettenberg Bay.
At The Bramon Wine Shop, turn right off the N2 ar
follow the signs to 'That Place.'

Lily Pond Country Lodge

Niels and Margret Hendriks
R102 Nature's Valley Road, The Crags
Tel: 044-534-8767 Fax: 044-534-8686
Email: info@lilypond.co.za Web: www.lilypond.co.za
Cell: 082-746-8782

From the moment I met Niels and Margret I was confident of a great stay. Whilst their lodge is a monument to mathematical modernity (straight lines and strong angles prevail), its slickness is balanced by the natural surroundings (beige and terracotta walls contrast strikingly with the greenery of Nature's Valley). Everyone benefits from the tranquility and abundant birdlife here. The lily ponds provide a lush home to a mesmerising array of flora and fauna. The frogs serenaded me with their croaky chorus as I braved a mid-winter swim in the black infinity pool. Warming up in my polished concrete bath, I soaked up the garden suite's quirky design. Think African colonial (tribal paintings, gauzy curtains and kudu-skin rugs) with every bit of stuffiness surgically removed and replaced with funky exposed brickwork, slick crete-stone floors and a bright ochre-and-white colour scheme. In summer, the lilies outside are a carpet of colour and balmy evenings are set aside for drinks and nibbles followed by a many-coursed, mouth-watering meal in the (equally angular) restaurant. Margret, a supremely good cook, has trained a marvellous Xhosa chef, Vincent, who has a flair for flavour fusions; he crosses oriental and European dishes and is fond of African bobotie wonton starters and sushi ice desserts. All the staff are friendly and, for people who "never meant to run a guest house," Niels and Margret are doing a seriously good job. *Massage treatments on request.*

Rooms: 10: 2 queens, 2 king/twins & 2 luxury suites, all en-s bath & sh'r; 3 luxury garden suites (extra-length king/tw) & 1 honeymoon suite (extra-length king/dble), all en-s bath & sh'r plus outdoor sh'r.
Price: R595 - R1,190 pp sharing (single supp' 50%).
Meals: Full breakfast included. Fusion kitchen with 4-course dinner R225 (vegetarian on request). Light lunches available.
Directions: 22km east of Plettenberg Bay and close to Nature's Valley. From CT take first exit to Nature's Valley. From Port Elizabeth take second exit Nature's Valley (14km after toll) to the left. Then follow R102 for 3km and turn right at the sign.

Map Number: 5   Entry Number: 145

Redford House

Dr Clive Noble and Colleen Noble

12 Redford Road, The Crags
Tel: 044-534-8877 Fax: 044-534-8188
Email: redfordhouse@mweb.co.za Web: www.redfordhouse.co.za
Cell: 076-907-1019

Redford House, with its ploughs, wagon-wheels, rolling hills, meandering rivers and wizene
centuries-old oak trees, seems to exist in some previous and rather idyllic age; a rural haven
be found perhaps in the pages of a Thomas Hardy novel. If I had been staying longer I wou
surely have settled down on the verandah with a copy of Country Life to absorb some of th
pure bucolic peace where only the reassuring buzz of a bee, the brief agitation of a rooster or th
distant lowing of a cow might disrupt me. Instead I took in some polo and quaffed a glass of Pimr
by the pool-house studio (Wednesday night is 'life drawing' night) before joining my hosts in th
yellowwood-beamed Old Settler's dining room to hear stories of the buffalo and elephants th
once roamed these pastures. Colleen, who is warm, gentle and caring, and has spent a lifetim
in conservancy, and Dr Clive (an orthopaedic surgeon) are a fascinating and erudite couple. The
home has become a sort of Garden Route Speaker's Corner where the Nobles host hot sou
evenings at which you might learn about the history of global warming or perha
Gondwanaland. Or you might just light a log fire and enjoy a cup of cocoa in the splendid pin
panelled drawing room before slipping off to the land of nod amid soft cotton in a cottage th
Mrs Tiggywinkle would have loved!

Rooms: 4: 2 in Noble House (king bed, en-suite
with bath and shower); 1 in the Carriage House
(queen bed, en-suite with bath and shower); Mrs
Tiggywinkle's self-catering cottage.
Price: Noble House: R600 - R700 pp sharing;
Carriage House: R400 - R500 pp sharing; Mrs
Tiggywinkle's Cottage R600 - R700 for the whole
cottage. Single supplement R50.
Meals: Full English breakfast included. Mrs
Tiggywinkle's Cottage is self-catering. Dinner with
stories by arrangement (R120 - R180). Breakfast R5
Directions: On N2, 17km east of Plettenberg Bay
turn left in to Redford Road. Coming from PE, 16km
from Toll Gate turn right in to Redford Road. 3km u
Redford Road, look out for white poles and sign on

The Fernery Lodge and Chalets

CJ Müller

Forest Ferns, Blueliliesbush,
Tsitsikamma
Tel: 042-280-3588
Fax: 041-394-5114
Email:
reservations@forestferns.co.za
Web: www.forestferns.co.za

Garden Route, Western Cape

You've heard us harping on about beautiful views before, but now I need an even stronger superlative! Cradling my welcome G&T, I watched an enormous waterfall relentlessly plummet 30 metres down a river gorge before making its way to the sea. Beyond the forest I could see all the way to the ocean. On certain clear days, whales and dolphins complete an impossibly picturesque scene here. Unsurprisingly, The Fernery focuses on their natural visual treasures, from lodge bedrooms to dining areas, jacuzzis and pools. Decks and towers offer yet more angles for kloof-gazing with sundowners. I stayed in the main lodge, the perfect place to relax (with a massage) after another leg-achingly long drive. Here you find yourself on the end of some serious pampering, with large inviting rooms leading to even larger bathrooms. Up the hill from the lodge, wooden chalets boast traditional wood-burning heaters and outdoor braais to give them a back-to-nature feel... and no TVs. But fear not, there is entertainment at hand for chalet guests, including a pub, pool, massage therapist, driving range and canopied jacuzzi overhanging the waterfall valley. And beyond these is Frans' gift to tandem couple travellers: the luxury twin self-catering chalet. Thought through to the last detail, two sleek suites branch off a central kitchen and dining area like arms off the nave of a church, while gliding walls allow each couple to retreat into plush privacy in one swift swoosh. At last travelling couples can have their cake and eat it.

Rooms: 15: 5 doubles with en-s in lodge; 6 dble/twin B&B chalets en-s bathroom; 2 self-cater chalets with dbles & twins with 1 bathroom; 2 luxury S-C twin chalets with 2 full en-s bedrooms.
Price: B&B chalets R700 - R945 pp sharing; S-C family chalets (sleep 4) R1600 - R1850 per chalet; luxury S-C twin chalets: R2880 - R3250; B&B lodge suites: R960 - R1300 pp sh. Extra for singles.
Meals: Full breakfast incl' for B&B chalets & lodge suites. 4-course dinner available for all guests, & 3-course dinner braai available for BBQs.
Directions: Take Blueliliies Bush turn-off, 4km from PE side of Storms River bridge, then continue 7.5km down a signed track from the road.

Map Number: 5

Entry Number: 147

Thabile Lodge

Len Bornman

Vergelegen Road, Between Oudtshoorn and De Rust
Tel: 044-251-6116 Fax: 044-251-6115
Email: info@thabilelodge.co.za Web: www.thabilelodge.co.za
Cell: 082-564-5295

Arriving at Thabile Lodge is like returning home after a long journey. Len, who's reformed th
110-year-old building into the welcoming house it is today, greets his guests with genuine deligh
You'll then also be welcomed by Garfield, the largest cat you'll ever meet and who Len clair
'beat anorexia', and his best friend Pepsi, the alsation. The rooms have all been lovingly designe
and built by Len. Simple and tastefully decorated each chalet has its own verandah, which is whe
you'll want to be as the sun is setting and the mountains make their way through all the autum
colours before turning dark. But the main house is where all the action happens. There's a sp
with Jacuzzi and steam room; a fantastic bar area where you can cheer on the sports team of you
choice and the beautiful, elevated verandah where I indulged in cooked-to-perfection ostri
steak and a blended red, chosen for me by Len, that went down way too easily. Before I kne
it the Boegoe Blits was out and this signalled the start of a wonderful evening with new friend
What really makes this place special is Len and his amazing staff. As I enthusiastically wave
goodbye to my new friend, I was already planning my next visit.

Rooms: 12: 10 king/twins with en-suite shower; 2
king/twins with en-suite bath and shower.
Price: R420 pp sharing per night; R540 for singles;
R340 for children under 12.
Meals: Full breakfast included. A la carte dinner
available every evening for R180.
Directions: Follow the N12 from Oudtsoorn to D
Rust for 20km. Turn left at the Vergelegen sign.
Thabile Lodge is well sign-posted on the right less
than 2km down the road.

Rolbaken Guest House and Nature Reserve

Dick and Mary Carr

Daskop Road, between Oudtshoorn and De Rust
Tel: 044-251-6191
Email: dickcarr@hilbert.co.za Web: www.rolbaken.co.za
Cell: 072-248-4830

It took Dick and Mary just half an hour to fall in love with this scenic, tranquil farm, and gazing at the blend of Kammanassie Mountains and rolling green fields you can see why. Mary grew up in deepest Africa and Dick is a conservation biologist, so most of their 500 hectares – recently designated a nature reserve – will hopefully soon see the introduction of game to go with their 103 recorded species of birds. Dick roared up to greet me on a quad bike, while Mary followed more sedately with a plate of home-baked muffins and organic strawberries – if I'd stayed for dinner, she said, I could have tucked into local organic lamb or free-range chicken. The farm's old schoolhouse, beautifully renovated and absolutely, spankingly clean, is yours to enjoy. There are huge comfy sofas to collapse on in the high-beamed lounge and three private bedrooms lightly decorated with restored antiques and pastoral pictures – although the most spectacular pastoral scene is straight out of the large windows. The kitchen has all a cook could desire (plus a shaded outdoor braai by the splash pool), but your hosts are more than happy to cook up a breakfast of freshly-laid eggs or lay on a 3-course meal. If you need to work off some energy, head up to the dam for a swim or take the kids down to say hello to the sheep, donkeys and other livestock. As I trundled off down the road to Oudtshoorn I felt as if I was waving goodbye to old friends.... See you soon, Mary and Dick.

Rooms: 1 house: 3 bedrooms (1 queen, 1 twin, 1 double & bunk), all en-s. Cot available. Pet-friendly.
Price: R350 - R400 pp sharing. Children 4 – 14 R200. Under 4 free.
Meals: Fully-equipped kitchen & large braai in house. Groceries provided on request at cost price. Full farm breakfast (R50) & 3-course evening meal (R150) by arrangement.
Directions: From Oudtshoorn, follow N12 towards De Rust. At Dysselsdorp turn R, then L after bdge. Continue 1.6km (road becomes gravel) then R onto unsigned gravel rd opposite stadium. Continue for 18.3km, past Leeublad farm. Rolbaken on L, just after cresting hill. GPS S33 40.33' E22 33.82'

Map Number: 5

Entry Number: 149

De Zeekoe Guest Farm

Paula and Pottie Potgieter

Zeekoegat Farm, R328 (road to Mossel Bay), Oudtshoorn
Tel: 044-272-6721 Fax: 044-272-8534
Email: info@dezeekoe.co.za Web: www.dezeekoe.co.za
Cell: 082-551-3019 or 082-584-9957

Right in the heart of ostrich country you'll find De Zeekoe, whose dusty plains are ringed b mountains holding back the coastal cloud. I arrived on a sultry afternoon and took refuge in th cool, tile-floored farmhouse among soft leather chairs, vibrant oil landscapes and low Oregon pir windows. Next door, a large dining room overlooking the Outeniqua Mountains and river be promised a memorable supper and the slickly luxurious main house rooms lured me in from th indigenous gardens, source of many of chef's ingredients. Beyond the saltwater pool is a wall reeds where fish eagles nest, and beyond that a river - the farm is named after the hippos ond found here - where you can quietly canoe under a reliable summer sun. The farm stretches ove 2,000 hectares, home to springbuck, ostriches, cattle and alfalfa stretching as far as the eye ca see, so borrow a bike and introduce yourself. But I lost my heart to my rustic waterfront cabin one of only four so ensure you ask for one of these early on! In a washed-blue dawn, th mountains now faintly outlined like mascara, bright birds busied about the reeds (there are 25 species to spot). I sat on the deck, its legs planted firmly in the dam, as my neighbour cast his lin So beautiful, so peaceful.... De Zeekoe completely relaxed me and I long to return. *Beau therapies, small weddings and functions available. Wild meerkat tours done on the reserve by guid Devey. All activities subject to weather conditions.*

Rooms: 20: 7 luxury, 5 superior and 3 standard rooms in and around the house, king/twin/double with air-con & en-suite bath and/or shower; 4 rustic waterfront cabins with two bedrooms, shared showers and kitchenette.
Price: Rooms R470 – R950 pp sharing.
Meals: Full breakfast included. Lunch and 4-course farm-produced dinner available at R250 pp, excludin wine. Braais and picnic baskets also available.
Directions: Head west from Oudtshoorn (towards Calitzdorp) on R62. Turn left at sign to Mossel Bay o R328. After 7km turn right on dirt road, for 2km to De Zeekoe on left.

Mooiplaas Guest House

Viljee and Hanlie Keller

Volmoed, Oudtshoorn
Tel: 044-279-4019
Fax: 044-272-0803
Email:
info@mooiplaasguesthouse.co.za
Web:
www.mooiplaasguesthouse.co.za
Cell: 082-504-7156

Klein Karoo, Western Cape

Mooiplaas is a family-run farm, dating back to the 1800s, and Viljee and Hanlie are the fourth generation of Kellers to live here. Their main focus is ostriches with some maize, alfalfa and cattle thrown into the mix too – this is a real working farm. With Hanli a self-proclaimed perfectionist, expect nothing less than luxury in the rooms. Large and airy with high ceilings, custom-made ostrich leather headboards (leather from their farm, of course) and a verandah with views overlooking the often snow-capped Swartberg Mountains, it didn't take me long to relax and unwind with a glass of Muscadel. Although one is spoilt for choice with the Swartberg in front and the Outeniqua Mountains to the left, my attention was irresistibly drawn to the baby ostrich running around the lawn. While I was bombarding Hanli with ostrich questions, Piet, her son, arrived back from school and started looking for a torch. His Friday job is to check the eggs in the incubator to see which ones have been fertilized. This I had to see. The set-up is incredible, but the best part was going to the nursery to see the new-borns. Mooiplaas is known for its delicious ostrich steaks and its ideal position on top of the hill for stargazing. With so much to see, do and learn here, it was a real shame I only had one night.

Rooms: 16: 4 superior/honeymoon suites; 8 luxury doubles (4 with self-catering options), 1 country house with 4 rooms. All rooms are en-suite with bath and shower.
Price: R421 - R860 pp/night. Singles on request.
Meals: Full breakfast included. Dinner on request. Picnic baskets also available.
Directions: From R62 take the R328 to Mossel Bay. After 8km follow sign to right. After 1.1km the farm is on your left.

Boesmanskop

Tinie Bekker
Kruisrivier, near Calitzdorp
Tel: 044-213-3365 Fax: 044-213-3365
Email: info@boesmanskop.co.za Web: www.boesmanskop.co.za

It's amazing how many times I drove Route 62 without taking the Kruisrivier turn-off between Oudtshoorn and Calitzdorp. If you do you'll discover, along with the famed red stone hills and awesome Klein Karoo scenery, Tinie Bekker's small dairy and ostrich farm tucked neatly into the Swartberg mountain. Tinie is entirely modest about the two guest rooms he built on account of a billiard table (long story), calling 'simple farm accommodation' what more arty types might describe as 'rustic chic suites'. Rustic in the sense of reed ceilings, wonky wood floors and pebble-stoned showers – and the swallows which dart in and out in the evenings – but chic with their fine white linen and cleverly restored old family furniture, like porcupine quill lampshades and a bathtub quirkily wrapped in a wine barrel. Wonderfully unkempt gardens are a kaleidoscope of colours with such novelties (in South Africa) as pansies, while the vegetable garden provides much of your evening meal. But he's modest about his green fingers... and modest, too, about his 'paint-by-numbers' cookery skills, which allowed him to conjure me up freshly-baked bread and a delicious four-course meal in the main farmhouse. Even better, Tinie's refreshingly reasonable with his rates. Early the next morning I was taken to see cows milked in the small dairy, then spent a memorable half-hour with a just-hatching baby ostrich...before tackling the only immodest thing around here, the towering Swartberg mountain with its famed helter-skelter pass.

Rooms: 2: 1 king with extra single, 1 double with 2 extra singles, both with en-suite shower and bath. Pet-friendly.
Price: R290 pp sharing for room only. Singles + R50. R540 pp for dinner, bed & breakfast.
Meals: Full breakfast R70. 4-course dinner R180 (excluding wine) by prior arrangement.
Directions: From Oudtshoorn, take R62 towards Calitzdorp for 30km, then turn R down gravel road to Kruisrivier. After 6km, turn R at T-junction, then continue for 13km. Farm on right.

Red Stone Hills

Petro and Hermanus Potgieter

Oudtshoorn
Tel: 044-213-3783 Fax: 044-213-3291
Email: redstone@pixie.co.za Web: www.redstone.co.za

The humbling sense of the passage of time pervades this 3,000-hectare veld, whose desert colours swirl with Van Gogh vibrancy. The current Potgieters are the fifth generation to farm this land (ostrich, vineyards, cattle, fruit), but that lineage is put into perspective by the red stone hills. They date to the enon-conglomerate period, formed 120 million years ago when the earth twisted and a torrent of sanguine mud-stone settled and solidified; a few million years later, bushmen hid in the hills' stone pockets and painted wildlife; and in the 1790s Karoo cottages completed the picture. It's all been authenticated by erudite visitors: botanists, geologists and a chap from Roberts who identified 210 birds here, including eagles, black stork and five varieties of kingfisher. But you'll find Hermanus and Petro plenty knowledgeable themselves. We drove out along dusty tracks leading past the schoolhouse that his father donated to the mixed community (which still congregates there), through babbling brooks to Chinese lanterns and blankets of fynbos and medicinal succulents. Hermanus will name them all. Petro says he lives in the past, whereas she's an artist facing the future. Also on offer at certain times of year are geological, botanical and fossil tours. There are many ways to enjoy the scenery, cycling, hiking, horse-riding… kids will love the morning tractor ride to feed the animals, and ostrich-obsessed Oudtshoorn is minutes away. When you're tired out, your sleepy cottage, with original Oregon pine doors and floors and farm-made furniture, awaits.

Rooms: 6 cottages: all fully self-contained with 1, 2 or 3 bedrooms and shared or en-suite bathrooms with baths and/or showers.
Price: R230 - R400 pp self-catering. Singles and special family rates on request.
Meals: Full breakfast R78, continental breakfast R55. 3-course farm dinners or semi-prepared braai packs on request.
Directions: Halfway between Calitzdorp & Oudtshoorn on R62. Head west from Oudtshoorn 28km, then Kruisrivier turn-off. Red Stone 6km down this road. Another entrance between foot of Swartberg mountain & Cango Caves via Matjiesrivier.

Map Number: 2

Entry Number: 153

The Retreat at Groenfontein

Marie and Grant Burton
Calitzdorp
Tel: 044-213-3880 Fax: 086-271-5373
Email: info@groenfontein.com Web: www.groenfontein.com

A tiny gravel road twists along the sides of one idyllic valley to another yet more secluded one, past old Cape Dutch farm buildings and jaw-dropping views, eventually arriving at the Burtons' Victorian-colonial homestead. They ran a popular wilderness lodge in Namibia before trawling southern Africa for a new Eden, and it took years to find Groenfontein. It was worth the wait. The view from the verandah, where guest meals are served around one sociable table with your hosts (and where I sampled mouthwatering smoked snoek mousse and ostrich casserole), crosses a valley and climbs the Burtons' own mountain before joining the vast Swartberg Nature Reserve, now a World Heritage Site. What with paths winding up to intimate rock pools and excellent marked mountain trails, the opportunities for merry traipsing are limitless. When it gets hot, you can swim in the river, dam or pool, or collapse inside the gloriously cool house with its original marble fireplace and pine and yellowwood flooring. Take your pick from luxury rooms set apart from the homestead with slate floors, fabulous mountain views and surreal stoep star-gazing or more traditional bedrooms in the main house – equally inviting. It really is an incredible area to explore, with kloofs, mountain wilderness, half-forgotten roads and many animals and birds to look out for. But, best of all, you come back to award-winning hospitality: delicious table d'hôte dinners, welcoming hosts and a truly relaxed household. Give yourselves two nights at least!

Rooms: 8: 4 standard rooms in main house (king/queen/twin), 4 garden rooms (king/twin). All have en-s shower &/or bath. All rooms pet-friendly.
Price: R480 - R950 pp sharing, including 3 or 4-course dinner and full breakfast. Singles on request.
Meals: Full breakfast & 3 or 4-course table d'hôte dinner (without wine) included. Fully licensed. Light lunches & picnics from R50.
Directions: From Oudtshoorn take R62 towards Calitzdorp for 30km. Turn R onto dirt road signed Kruisrivier. After 17km keep L at fork as road gets narrower and follow for 10.7km until you see a sign for The Retreat to your R. From Calitzdorp L at Groenfontein sign - 19km to house. Drive slowly.

Bosch Luys Kloof Private Nature Reserve

Gerhard and Ans Rademeyer

Seweweekspoort, Off Route 62, Between Ladismith and Calitzdorp
Tel: 023-581-5046 Fax: 023-581-5038
Email: boschkloofpnr@telkomsa.net Web: www.boschluyskloof.co.za

The drive to Bosch Luys Kloof was an adventure in itself. Meandering through the Seweweekspoort with the swirling rocks above and then crawling down the original Bosch Luys Kloof Pass, built in 1860 for the width of a single wagon, I couldn't help but wonder what was waiting for me at the end. Sheer beauty, remoteness and tranquility would sum it up! Gerard and Ans have lovingly spent over 14 years returning the 14000ha back to its original form and creating a mini-refuge for nature-loving guests to explore. With 4x4 routes, walks of varying distances and difficulties, and game drives available too, you are guaranteed that no two days will be the same. The chalets built from natural materials with traditional thatch roofs are the perfect place to unwind with baths that boast spectacular views of the veld; or an outdoor shower if you want to get even closer to nature while you wash. The outstanding team prepares all your meals and before dinner Gerard and Ans welcome you at the bar, made from old sleepers, which opens onto the pool area. With a watering-hole mere metres away, your chances of combining sundowners and game-viewing are high. This really is a special place hidden away near the Gamkapoort Dam so make sure you give yourself enough time to explore the surroundings and enjoy Gerard and Ans's wonderful hospitality.

Rooms: 10 chalets: 4 twin/king en-s bath & outdoor sh'r; 5 dble chalets, twin/king en-s bath & outdoor sh'r in main bedroom & en-s sh'r in 2nd room; guest-house: 4 rooms en-s bathrooms, large lounge, sundeck, fireplace.
Price: Dinner, Bed & Breakfast: R995 pp. Full Day: R1,295 pp. Includes ALL meals. Nature drive included with Full Day tariff.
Meals: 2-course breakfast, 2-course lunch and 3-course dinner all inclusive.
Directions: Please contact the owners for directions or visit the website.

Mymering Guest House

Dr Andy & Penny Hillock

Mymering, Dwarsrivier, Ladismith
Tel: 028-5511-548 Fax: 028-551-1313
Email: penny@mymering.com Web: www.mymering.com
Cell: 082-891-2463

You'll hear Andy's laugh rolling through Dwarsrivier valley before you reach Mymering. And I'd bet two bunches of their home-grown table grapes - destined for Fortnum's, darling - that the joke was one of Penny's naughty ones. The Hillocks relocated from Port Elizabeth when surgeon Andy decided, reluctantly, to retire. "But look at this!" he announces, surveying his sublime Cezannean kingdom after a brisk morning hike. "Stunning!" Andy co-owned the vineyard next door for aeons so the couple were frequent Ladismithers and know the area like natives. "Andy is tour guide," says Penny, showing off her shiny industrial kitchen after a wine-soaked supper of spicy butternut soup, soft salmon with minted peas, and creme brûlée, all served on zebra-print crockery. "I'm chef." Penny's glam taste is also on show in the glittering Mae West suite, one of three secluded chalets (the others being Madiba and Jacuzzi), each bedecked as their name implies. Lavender and Rosemary, two linked family chalets sharing a plunge pool where the others have their own, pay tribute to the farm's bygone days harvesting essential oils. Gravel paths through indigenous jungle unearth a thatched self-catering cottage, ideal if you want to spend a few days exploring the majestic Swartberg Pass and Seweweeks Poort, both built by Thomas Bain, Andy's demi-god. Driving through the latter, pausing by a babbling brook to sup champagne, was my most exquisitely decadent Karoo moment! This September saw the launch of their boutique Hillock wines. *Mymering is open for wine-tastings, lunch and teas every day.*

Rooms: 6: 2 king/twin with full en-suite; 2 king with full en-suite; 1 king with double shower; 1 self-catering cottage with king/twin with en-s sh'r & queen with en-s sh'r.

Price: R600 pp sharing B&B. Cottage: R1,600 per night for whole cottage.

Meals: Full breakfast included. 3-course gourmet dinner available on request. Lunch and picnic baskets on request.

Directions: On R62 between Ladismith & Barrydale. Take Laingsburg road & follow clearly-marked signs. GPS S 33 29 55.26 E 21 10 18.65

Les Hauts de Montagu Guest Lodge

Myriam and Eric Brillant
Route 62, Montagu
Tel: 023-614-2514 Fax: 023-614-3517
Email: info@leshautsdemontagu.co.za Web: www.leshautsdemontagu.co.za
Cell: 083-529-3389 (Myriam) 083-528-9250 (Eric)

If you set your sights solely on staying in Montagu itself you would completely miss this peaceful oasis, sitting contentedly on the green slopes of the Langeberg Mountains, just three kilometres further along the road. As I slunk slowly up the long driveway past the helipad (sadly the Greenwood chopper was in for a service), Les Hauts de Montagu revealed itself in all its glory. It is not difficult to see why Eric and Myriam (both Congolese by birth but with years of Parisian industry experience) instantly fell '*tête over talons*' for this place; its setting is sensational. Perched high on the hillside it enjoys expansive views of the fynbos-clad valley and their 5-hectare plantation of olives. The main Cape Dutch farmhouse dates from 1865 and it has taken two years of painstaking restoration to bring the building back to life. These days, perfectly scrumptious breakfasts of lavish fruit platters and toasted treats are served under 21 huge beams that hold up the roof. At night, returning to the lodge after taking Myriam's excellent advice on Montagu's finest supper spots, I crunched along the loose stones leading the way to my cottage. A soaring chimney encourages the fire beneath on cold winter nights, while the huge glass doors allow refreshing breezes on hot summer ones. The glorious outside shower the following morning meant washing in the full view of Montagu… I was thankful it was those three kilometres away!

Rooms: 10: 2 twin, 6 king and 2 superior, all with en-suite baths with outside showers.
Price: R550 - R850 pp sharing. Singles on request.
Meals: Full breakfast included.
Directions: From Cape Town, take N1 to Worcester, then R60 + R62 to Montagu. Pass Montagu, stay on R62 for 3km. Hauts de Montagu signed on R. Helipad and airstrip also available.

Collins House

Tessa Collins
63 Kerk St (Church St), Prince Albert
Tel: 023-541-1786 Fax: 023-541-1786
Email: collinsh@tiscali.co.za Web: www.collinshouse.co.za
Cell: 082-377-1340

Tessa and her Karoo home have been with us since the very first edition of this guide. Should she ever make a foolhardy bid for freedom, we will be doing our utmost to restrain her! This picture book Victorian townhouse sits proudly on central Kerkstraat, eye-catching among so many Cape Dutch affairs. Stepping into the grand chequered hall amid strains of Schubert proves equally striking. Tessa welcomed me in and demanded to know my poison. Her own preference is for a G'n'T mixed with interesting grown-ups to match her razor-sharp wit. Collins' heart is the sweeping kitchen-lounge where artist Tessa sits twisting her delicate wire tree sculptures (prizes for spotting them in other GG abodes), and sky-high French windows look out onto her secret garden; a wide, walled, flower-flanked lawn boasting a swimming pool of decadent dimensions, all framed with cypress trees so vertiginous I'm sure I spied them from Die Top of the Swartberg Pass. Sundowners in Tessa's clandestine owl hangout are a sublime apéritif to being booked into one of Prince Albert's fabulous eateries - all of whom know to take excellent care of you. (Nb: Tessa also cares for your ox-wagon should you, like me, wake to find it two wheels down.) Come dawn you'll be racing down from your elegant, unfussy bedroom for the PP (perfect poached), the crescendo of a breakfast concerto conducted by Tessa and sous-cheffed by "the archangel Sarah". You're holding this book because you're after something special; you've found it. *No children.*

Rooms: 3: 2 twins, 1 with en-suite bath, 1 with bath and shower; 1 double with en-suite bath.
Price: R450 - R550 pp sharing. Single supplement R100.
Meals: Full breakfast included and served till 9.30am.
Directions: On Kerkstraat in the middle of town.

Onse Rus Guesthouse

Lisa Smith and Diana Jacobsz

47 Church St, Prince Albert
Tel: 023-541-1380 Fax: 086-548-9350
Email: info@onserus.co.za Web: www.onserus.co.za
Cell: 083-629-9196

You know you're staying in a historic house when the local tour guide stops by the verandah to enthuse about its archetypal Prince Albert gable. And you know you're in good hands when tea and home-made cake appear magically on your poolside table within minutes of your arrival. Restful in name, restful in nature, the 150-year-old Cape Dutch Onse Rus is the perfect place to experience Lisa Smith's particular brand of hospitality, which involves treating guests like friends from the moment they ring the bell. She fell in love with the house ten years ago and now runs it with the help of her wonderful mother Di. The five thatched bedrooms all have private entrances, high ceilings, white walls and simple Karoo furnishings. One used to be part of the bakery, another was the printing room for a local newspaper. The house has some history! The large living room, where breakfast is served around a sociable table, is hung with photos of Lisa's other love – her horses. Outside there's a swimming pool (a thing of beauty in such a hot climate) and shaded patio for relaxing over a good book. Explore the villagey delights of Prince Albert with its tea shops, galleries and award-winning dairy, take the unspeakably dramatic drive over the swirling Swartberg pass or the gentler (yet equally stunning) Meiringspoort towards Oudtshoorn, or try olive-tasting at the nearby farms. Superb.

Rooms: 5: king/twin with private entrances, en-suite shower and/or bath; 3 have a lounge area and patio.
Price: R395 - R450 pp sharing. Singles on request.
Meals: Breakfast included. Snacks and meals for groups available on request.
Directions: On the corner of the main street (Kerk or Church St) and Bank Sts.

Karoo View Cottages

Julie & Richard Waterson

Magrieta Prinsloo Road, Prince Albert
Tel: 023-541-1929 Fax: 086-689-7000
Email: julie@karooview.co.za Web: www.karooview.co.za
Cell: 082-882-5342

They're not kidding. This vista may be the quintessential Karoo view. Poised gracefully on
koppie, Karoo View's four deluxe self-catering suites sit within two neighbouring cottages, gazi
idly over the multi-coloured rooftops and church spires of quaint Prince Albert, across rugge
sandy veld and out to the imposing Swartberg mountains. Julie and Richard have sampled C
(cook it yourself) getaways the world over in the name of research, and with Karoo View they
positive they've got it spot on. Here's a little secret: they might just be right. Each self-containe
serviced unit is a genuine delight, with vaulted reed ceilings and cool tiled floors keeping the stic
Karoo heat at bay. Chunky French doors slide open to private stoeps furnished with cushione
wicker and wooden furniture (anyone for a braai?), while hearty windows increase the sense
both space and sturdiness - there's nothing flimsy here. Each unique interior conveys Julie
adulation for Karoo colours: dusty grey sofas, aloe-green blankets, off-white walls, deep brow
fireplaces, splashes of orange, red and green. Supremely well-kitted-out kitchens have it all, ev
panini toasters! But Julie offers braai hampers and even does your shopping should you be unab
to leave the cooling 'cuddle puddle' at the bottom of the neatly-labelled indigenous garden.
course, it's up to you to pick your own veggies from the tunnel. Might I suggest a fresh rocket a
strawberry salad to go with those lamb chops?

Rooms: 4: 2 chalets, each comprising 2
private/interconnecting suites. Each sleeps max 3 in
various bed arrangements. Two with full en-suite
bathrooms, two en-suite bathrooms with showers
only.
Price: R380 - R420 pp for 2 or more sharing.
Children R250 pp sharing same suite as adult. Single
rates upon request.
Meals: Continental breakfast provided in chalet. Fu
breakfast, lunch and braai baskets can be provided.
Directions: 350m off the main street of the village

Lemoenfontein Game Lodge

Ingrid Köster
Beaufort West
Tel: 023-415-2847 Fax: 086-650-9928
Email: lemoen@mweb.co.za Web: www.lemoenfontein.co.za

Lemoenfontein, in the shadow of the Nuweveld Mountains, is one of those places where whatever your mood on arrival – and after a tiring drive down the N1, mine was ropey - a calmness envelops you like magic vapour. I was suddenly enjoying a cool drink on the vast wooden verandah, gazing over measureless miles of veld and chatting happily to Ingrid about the history of the place. It was built as a hunting lodge in 1850, then became a sanatorium for TB sufferers (the dry Karoo air was beneficial), a farm and finally (and still) a nature reserve. Everything has been done well here, no corners cut and the result is a most relaxing, hassle-free stay. Rooms are stylish and understated with top-quality fabrics and completely comfortable beds. Outside, lawns, a pool, bar and braai area and the veld are all segregated by high dry-stone walls. You *must* go on a game drive through the reserve before dinner - to look at all the buck and zebra of course, but also to be out in such scenery as the sun goes down. And one final thing: dinner when we got back was at first mouth-watering, then lip-smacking. A real South African experience. *All rooms are air-conditioned.*

Rooms: 14: 8 double all en-suite (4 bath/shower, 4 shower); 6 twin all en-suite (2 bath/shower, 4 shower).
Price: R395 – R575 pp
Meals: Full breakfast available from R75 pp. 3-course dinner from R150 pp.
Directions: From the N1, 2km north of Beaufort West. Turn onto De Jagers Pass Road at the Lemoenfontein sign. After 1.5km turn left at the white Lemoenfontein gates. Go 4km up dirt track, following signs. GPS Co-ordinates S32 18 59 E22 36 11

Map Number: 5

Entry Number: 161

Ko-Ka Tsara

Ingrid Köster
Beaufort West, Greater Karoo
Tel: 023-415-2753 Fax: 086-513-0007
Email: info@kokatsara.co.za Web: www.kokatsara.co.za

'Drive slowly. Wild animals', announced a sign as I turned into the craggy gorge below the Nuweveld Mountains. On cue, a herd of wildebeest emerged from the crunchy-dry undergrowth to inspect the stranger. Seemingly satisfied, they allowed me to continue into the heart of the 30,000 acres of Karoo veld, where stone-and-thatch A-frame chalets are dotted camp-style around a dung-strewn lawn – evidence of zebra and buck coming to graze the night before. Even my tracking skills were up to that diagnosis. Sliding glass doors open into the stone floored chalets and a rustic wooden ladder leads up to the kids' galleried sleeping area. Although each chalet has a fully-fitted kitchen with all your basic essentials such as milk, salt, pepper, sugar etc, and a private braai and camp-fire area, guests are often found in the star-lit boma discussing their days adventures while the pojtie, braai and bar area are in full swing to fulfill their guests culinary needs. As well as being a nirvana for bird-watchers (over 195 species have been spotted and offering wonderful hikes to refreshing river pools, for the more adventurous there is the hair looking mountain pass which will take you to the top of the expansive plateau and across to the Gamka Dam. A truly breathtaking experience, Ko-ka Tsara really is a camp for lovers of the great outdoors.

Rooms: 7 chalets, three-quarter or super-king plus singles in the gallery.
Price: R650 - R1,050 per chalet per night.
Meals: Self-catering but can cater for groups larger than 6. Braai packs, salad, bread and wood all available.
Directions: On the N1, 1km north of Beaufort West, take the R381. After 7km you'll see Ko-Ka Tsara on the right.

Eastern Cape

Oyster Bay Lodge

Hans and Liesbeth Verstrate-Griffioen

in between Tsitsikamma & St Francis Bay, Oyster Bay
Tel: 042-297-0150 Fax: 042-297-0150
Email: info@oysterbaylodge.com Web: www.oysterbaylodge.com
Cell: 082-700-0553

Here's yet another film-set masquerading as a B&B… this one is for the beach scenes! Hans and Liesbeth have the very envy-inducing run of three and a half kilometres of pristine beach to themselves, the fine white sand of the dunes as pure as it is wind-driven (but for the odd vervet monkey footprint). As well as offering rollercoaster 4x4 dune safaris, Oyster Bay Lodge has eighteen horses, catering for every skill level, which roam free on the 235 hectare nature reserve. The first time I visited there simply wasn't time for a beach ride, so I dreamt hard for two weeks and managed to dream it into reality, returning to experience for real the wind in my hair, salt air in my face and sun shining down… amazing. But there's more: Hans and Liesbeth have made hiking trails from the sand dunes through the fynbos where you'll have a chance to see some of the 140 species of bird. I could hear them, but didn't quite catch a glimpse. Your stay is very personable and relaxing with use of the swimming pool and self-catering facilities if you choose. Otherwise, the restaurant menu looks to be a treat, often with a fresh catch of the day. Come here for the empty beach, the horses and walks along an unspoilt coastline, the mountain bike and the picnics at tables set upon the dunes overlooking the ocean. *Day-tours can be taken to nearby Tsitsikamma Nature Reserve and Baviaanskloof.*

Rooms: 14: 4 Luxury Chalets, 10 Comfortable Rooms (2 family; Honeymoon Suite: 2 rooms/4 beds). All extra-long kings, en-s bath & separate shower. Chalets: lounge, kitchenette, fire, verandah. All units bar 1 with sea view.
Price: All pp sharing. Luxury Chalets R1,040 B&B; Comfortable Rooms R720 B&B. Specials for stays of 3 nights or more. Ask re single & extra person rates/packages
Meals: Full breakfast included. Lunches and dune picnics available through out the day. 5-course evening dinner at extra cost unless packaged deal.
Directions: From Cape Town on N2 turn off at exit number 632 Palmietvlei & follow signs to Oyster Bay Lodge. From Port Elizabeth take exit to Humansdorp & then follow signs to Oyster Bay Lodge.

Cottage on the Hill Guest House

Anne and Rob Eaglesham

63 Assissi Drive, St Francis Bay
Tel: 042-294-0761
Email: cottageonthehill@telkomsa.net Web: www.cottageonthehill.co.za
Cell: 076-563-5662

Cottage on the Hill has been awarded five stars, which, paradoxically, might have been quite off-putting for GG. But on this occasion we would award five stars too! This is because all the luxury is fully backed up by some very warm, attentive and characterful hosting from Anne and Rob. Leading me away from their sumptuous yellowwood bar, the ever-animated Eagleshams (followed closely by their two no-less-animated dachshunds) showed me to my enormous suite, Francolin. White furniture makes for a beachy atmosphere, as does the voile drape over the bed and the exposed thatched roof. You can absorb the sea view from the black-footed Victorian bath, although I remained dry and admired it from the expansive balcony. Then below there is Mongoose Suite with its dark granite surfaces on top of white cupboards and Persian rugs on the floor and original oil paintings. The shower has a door leading to an outside bath (always a sure-fire winner with me) and braai area. A sink thoughtfully placed next to the braai meant that I could prepare the record-breaking yellow-finned tuna I'd caught earlier that day. Further round, there's a bird hide hidden by indigenous plants. And across a courtyard, past the natural rock swimming pool and some metal heron sculptures, is Guinea-fowl Cottage with its mahogany bed and cane furniture. I long to return and eat my breakfast among the lavender and aloes. If you're wondering if I really did catch that fish, you'll have to go to Cottage on the Hill and find out for yourself....

Rooms: 2 suites and 1 bedroom in the cottage: 2 king/twins, 1 queen; All with en-suite bath and shower (bath outside in Mongoose).
Price: Guinea-fowl Cottage: R450 – R850 pp sharing. Mongoose and Francolin: R600 – R1,250 pp sharing. Single rates on request.
Meals: Full breakfast and afternoon tea included.
Directions: From N2, take St. Francis Bay/Humansdorp exist. Follow sign to St. Francis Bay onto R330. Go over roundabout, past the golf course and drive for approx. 600m. First road turn left into Homestead Rd. Turn right onto Assissi - Cottage on the Hill is no. 63.

Thunzi Bush Lodge

Mark and Trenwyth Pledger

Maitland Road, Maitlands, Port Elizabeth
Tel: 041-372-2082 Fax: 086-5030-698
Email: info@thunzi.co.za Web: www.thunzibushlodge.co.za
Cell: 072-597-4810

Ex-engineer Mark has been building treehouses since he was three (well, as soon as he could co ordinate his hands with any intricacy) and Thunzi's flawlessly-planned and -finished chalets are standing proof of his skill. Many personal touches are integrated within; baths wrapped in wooden decking, sinks stationed on sealed, sniffle-free sneeze-wood (strangely enough, a beautiful wood that makes you sneeze when you work with it); and a medley of wholesome games and entertainments. The completely private cabins, linked only by gravel walkways, peep timidly through indigenous forest onto the De Stades River Wetlands where an abundance of birds have been listed. Over 352 wacky-named species flock to this eco-diverse area where coastal forest, thicket and wetlands meet (try narina trogon, African rail, Knysna loerie and the often-heard but spotted, red-chested and flufftails for size). Take a night walk through the forest and you'll be greeted by a hypnotic symphony of nocturnal sounds and even a few wandering antelope. By day relaxation comes easy (the spa packages sound blissful), but should you want a little more activity simply pop down the road to Maitland's impressive duned beach, the most isolated and untouched Port Elizabeth has to offer. Here you can hike, snorkel, whale-watch or sand-board (oh yes - the dunes really are that big). Personally a lamp-lit dinner beneath the star-lined silhouette of canopy would be enough, but I suppose one really should work up an appetite first.

Rooms: 4 chalets: 2 twin/king B&Bs, both with en-suite bath & shower; 1 family B&B with 1 queen & 1 twin room with en-suite bath and shower. 1 self-catering unit with 1 queen & 1 twin room.
Price: B&B: R595 - R895 pp sharing. 40% supplement for singles. Self-catering chalet: R995 - R2,250.
Meals: Full breakfast incl' for B&B units. Gourmet picnics, light lunches & dinners (R100 - R265) on request; extra R165 for private open-air dining.
Directions: Take the exit marked Seaview from the N2. Thunzi Bush Lodge is signed after exit. More detailed directions can be emailed on request. GPS co-ordinates: S 33° 58' 43,6" E 25° 19' 11,1"

Lemon Tree Lane B&B

Ray and Dee Kemp
14 Mill Park Road, Mill Park, Port Elizabeth
Tel: 041-3734-103
Email: info@lemontreelane.co.za Web: www.lemontreelane.co.za
Cell: 082-7763-339

By the time I reached the charming Ray at charming Lemon Tree Lane I was all Port Elizabethed out, in need of a cuppa, a soak and some TLC... and who would have thought that out in the leafy suburb of Millpark I would find all three... and some unassuming luxury to boot! After 17 years receiving guests Ray and Dee are past masters at putting you at your ease (and they have a wall of accolades to prove it). Lemon Tree's eight impeccable rooms are stuffed full of antiques (antiques are Dee's guilty pleasure). Three of the suites are accessed via the shady courtyard they share. All are huge with handy kitchenette, sitting area and pristine en-suite bathrooms. Each room has its own individual feel with common features in polished wooden floors, ornate mirrors, elegant drapes and fresh flowers... and many useful comforts like air-con, heaters, microwaves, honesty bars, tea- and coffee making facilities, hair-dryers, telephones, TVs and Wifi. Then there's The Villa, a recent addition, made up of two separate units, 'Villa Up' and 'Villa Down'. With Dee's love of PE's auction rooms it was perhaps a case of having to build the villa for the furniture rather than the guests, but it is an extremely comfortable resting place for both. From antiques to game parks Ray can point you in the right direction. And, according to Ray, PE is a sports enthusiast's dream and golf and cricket (both within walking distance) are popular pastimes for visitors to Lemon Tree Lane. To think that it all started with that lovely oak dresser in the breakfast room bought for R230 many years ago....

Rooms: 8: all large double rooms all with en-suite bath and shower. Additional sleeper beds for children.
Price: R595 pp sharing. Singles on request.
Meals: Full breakfast included. Dinners on request.
Directions: See website for detailed map and directions.

The Admiralty Beach House

Jo and Alan Byram

9 Admiralty Way, Summerstrand, Port Elizabeth
Tel: 041-583-1271 or 041-583-3720 Fax: 086-610-6770
Email: bookings@theadmiralty.co.za Web: www.theadmiralty.co.za
Cell: 083-555-6370

Breakfast was in full swing when I arrived at the Admiralty Beach House and among the local a
and curios on display (and for sale), as well as the intricate furnishings and ceramics (not for sale
although many have tried unsuccessfully to engage in friendly commerce with Jo!), I felt I ha
stumbled upon a very civilized, secret festival of feasting and creativity. Alan was quick to invite m
to join their other guests, once I'd had a quick whirl around the pool and garden with its mosaic
and kaleidoscopic colours. In the main house there are six modern suites, each with its ow
balcony or patio, fresh flowers, crisp white linens and bedrooms punctuated with bursts of colou
in pretty plumped-up cushions and delicate cotton quilted throws. Jo personally chose the Sout
African art that hangs on the walls, including, among much else, oil-painted lilies and local stree
scenes in bright acrylics. There are two other newly-built and very stylish suites, The Loft and
self-catering cottage, on Jo and Alan's home property, which is just a five-minute walk round th
corner. These manifest the same artistic sentiment as the main house, but with the advantage c
a little more space and privacy. Throughout Admiralty there are personal touches that togethe
make it a home. Alan and Jo call the Admiralty an evolution, an apt description for an establishmer
that started life as their home with a studio above the garage, where Jo used to teach ballet, an
has since evolved into this wonderfully luxurious guest house.

Rooms: 8: 2 double suites, 4 doubles, 1 family suite
with twin and double room and shared bathroom, 2
toilets. 1 self-catering cottage.
Price: R495 - R750 pp sharing. Children and family
rates. Child and single supplement.
Meals: Full cooked and continental breakfast. Other
meals on request. Light lunches on the patio.
Directions: See website for detailed map. GPS S 33
59. 526 E25 40. 446

Lupus Den Country House

Priscilla and Noel Walton

Addo/Sunland
Tel: 042-234-0447 Fax: 086-626-7380
Email: lupusden@srvalley.co.za Web: www.lupusden.co.za
Cell: 072-1814-750

Priscilla and Noel have not needed to learn any tricks about how to host. They are just naturally hospitable people who make you feel instantly at home and relaxed. When I arrived, lunch was waiting on the table and, with a home-made lemon drink in hand, I already felt part of the furniture. They have been living in their farmhouse for 40 years now – although the land it stands on has been in the family's hands since 1894 – and have made some adjustments to make the rooms all the more comfortable for their guests. The latest of these - three new large rooms, each with its private entrance - are in Garden Cottage. Two have outdoor showers and all have air-con. Their citrus and cattle farm is found on the friendly dirt roads between Addo and Kirkwood. And when I say friendly, I mean locals waved hello to me all the way there! The garden, surrounded by citrus groves, blooms with bougainvillaea and an abundance of other flowers and trees. The tiled swimming pool and an enormous tipuanu tree are two of the gardens' greatest assets, while vine-shaded terraces are the perfect places of repose after a rendezvous with the elephants in Addo (only 20 minutes away). When staying at Lupus Den you can be a tourist by day out in the parks and feel a local when back in the fold. A true farm B&B with home cooking – hard to beat.

Rooms: 6: Homestead: 1 twin, 1 dble, 1 twin/dble, 2 en-s bath & shower, 1 en-s sh'r; Garden Cottage: 3 doubles/twins, all en-s bathrooms, 2 outdoor shower. All rooms own entrance, patio & aircon.
Price: Homestead: R300 - R400 pp. Singles R390 - R520. Garden Cottage: R475 - R500 pp sharing. Singles R615 - R650. Children: under 5 free, reduced rate meals; 5 - 11 years half price.
Meals: Full breakfast included. Adults & kids from 12 up: light lunch R30 - R50 pp; set 3-course dinner R190 pp. Kids under 12: reduced meal rates.
Directions: From PE take R335 towards Addo. Cross railway in Addo, then L onto R336 towards Kirkwood. At Sunland R at Lupus Den B&B sign & follow signs.

Map Number: 6   Entry Number: 168

The Elephant House

Clive and Anne Read
Addo
Tel: 042-233-2462 Fax: 042-233-0393
Email: info@elephanthouse.co.za Web: www.elephanthouse.co.za
Cell: 083-799-5671

The bush telegraph gave advance notice of the many charms at Elephant House. Many tourist and other guest house owners had urged us to visit with a sincerity you could not ignore. It's stunning house, the brainchild of one night's sleepless pondering by Anne who mapped the whole thing out in her head – a small, lawned courtyard surrounded on three sides by thatched and shady verandahs. The house is, in a sense, inside out. The drawing room leads to a dining room outside on the verandah (with antiques and Persian rugs). All the bedrooms open onto the verandah too and dinner (advertised with an African gong) is served there on silver and crystal. Elegant evening meals are lit to stunning effect with lampshades made of Tuareg bowls. Lawns, indigenous trees and the racehorse stud (Clive used to run one in Natal) surround the house, though the gallopers were recently relocated to another paddock, jsut 1km away. The Elephant House bedrooms are luxurious affairs with antique furniture, carpets, thick duvets and deep beds, the Internet room is handy, as is the morning tea or coffee that's brought to your bed, if so desired. The Family Suite, which is separated from the main house, retains the same charm but is just a little cosier. The Elephant House also runs open-vehicle game drives in Addo, a few minutes away, morning and afternoon. *A seasonal on-site masseuse available for inside or outside treatments (Mon - Fri, Oct - May).*

Rooms: 8 rooms in the house; all king/twins with en suite bath and shower and one family room that sleeps 5.
Price: R660 - R1,450 pp sharing.
Meals: Full breakfast included in Elephant House and Stable Cottages. Lunch & dinner provided. Three-course dinners R250. Or a la carte at Wine Bar & Café (near the Stables).
Directions: From P.E. R335 through Addo 5km on the road towards the park - you will see a sign off to your left for The Elephant House.

Hopefield Country House

Kobus Buys and Gerhard Maritz

Off the R336, between Kirkwood and Addo, Sundays River Valley, Addo
Tel: 042-234-0333 Fax: 086-566-0152
Email: info@hopefield.co.za Web: www.hopefield.co.za

My mother, a conductor-pianist, would go absolutely bananas over Hopefield. Kobus actually has to pause and count when I ask how many pianos they have about the house (five… he thinks) and the soothing strains of chamber music, opera and choral melodies linger in the orange-blossom-sweet air of this 15-hectare citrus farm. Known throughout Addo as The Music Boys, Kobus and Gerhard did time in Gauteng's fast-paced record industry before repairing to Kobus's family home (along with their doting miniature schnauzers Horatio and Ophelia) to do what they love best: playing music, gardening and entertaining. And though the Beethoven busts, baby grands and roses named after composers (go on, give Edward Elgar and Benjamin Britten a sniff) will excite any musos among you, there's plenty here for everyone. Sun-worshippers may lounge in the rose-packed garden (52 varieties, to be precise), safe in the knowledge that Kobus is "happy to carry G 'n' T's to the pool on a regular basis"; disciples of design will adore one-off furniture pieces, unique bathtubs, private verandahs, the elegant Jack Vettriano prints dotted around one room, the chess-themed artwork of another; gastronomes mustn't miss orchard-fresh orange juice at breakfast or the gourmet dinners. Let's just say, you won't be getting a spatula of lasagne and a bag of chips, and Gerhard makes the best creme brûlée this side of the Mediterranean. Hopefield is a truly vibrant place to stay. And not just if you happen to be my Mum.

Rooms: 7: 3 king/twins with full en-suite bathroom; 1 king with full en-suite; 1 queen with en-suite bath; 1 queen with en-suite shower over bath; 1 king with en-suite shower.
Price: R445 - R645 pp sharing. Singles rates on request.
Meals: Full breakfast included. Packed lunches and set 3-course dinner available on request.
Directions: Signed from the R336 between Kirkwood and Addo. More detailed directions can be emailed.

RiverBend Lodge

Stefanie Marais
Off Zuurberg Road, Addo Elephant National Park, Addo
Tel: 042-233-8000 Fax: 042-233-8028
Email: reservations@riverbendlodge.co.za Web: www.riverbendlodge.co.za
Cell: 082-292-4120

Within one hot hour of PE airport I was sipping a nectareously refreshing lemonade, squeeze from one of eight variants of citrus plantations at RiverBend. Within another hour I'd moved o to vetkoek (a traditional 'doughnut' bread prepared with gourmet ingredients - irresistible! followed by a fanned power kip and a reviving speed-dip in the pool. And now six of us, new acquainted, were out spotting on a game drive – the sun, scent and space of the bush alread working their magic, dissipating the rest of the world into the dust clouds behind us. I've been t Addo already and I've also been lucky enough to experience several other game drives up an down the country, but in this 400-odd-minute taster of the Nyathi section of the park - to whic this lodge enjoys private access - I felt I could have been freshly landed from Heathrow. Unde our super-approachable ranger Chris (who's spent 11 years guiding in the bush), we learne anything from how the leopard tortoise is the only member of its family able to swim, to the caus for the genetic recession of female elephants' tusks in this area. We also fell into a trance at th beauty of a herd of 50+ ellies crossing grasslands under our noses. As Stef explained, folks dor come here for 'big five kills', nor is Addo comparable to Kruger or Botswana. This park knows i draw-cards and RiverBend specializes in providing guests with an effortless, enchanting an affecting experience to take away with them. It is also very luxurious!

Rooms: 8: 4 luxury family rooms; 3 executive rooms with outdoor showers & verandahs; 1 honeymoon suit with verandah, outdoor shower & plunge pool. An exclusive-use villa sleeps up to 6.
Price: R3,600 - R3,850 pppn sharing. Kids (3-11 yrs) R1,800pn. Luxury/fully-serviced 3-bed private villa for 4 people sharing: R17,000 pn, extra adults R3,600 pn, extra child R1,800 pn. Winter specials & incentives for stays of 4 nights or more. No single supplements.
Meals: A la carte brunch, high tea and a la carte dinner all included in the rates. Traditional African-themed evening, numbers permitting.
Directions: Allow a good hour from PE. See owner's website for detailed directions.

Idwala Game Lodge

Ernst and Alida Du Toit

Adjacent to Lalibela Game Reserve,Sidbury (40km from Grahamstown)
Tel: 046-622-2163 Fax: 046-622-9282
Email: enquiries@idwalalodge.com Web: www.idwalalodge.com
Cell: 083-277-7235

I was very excited when I first discovered Idwala. This was not just because of their introductory cocktail, complete with sunken pebble (in case you're wondering, it's because Idwala means 'rock'), but because this was a real family-run lodge, as luxurious as all its corporate competitors. Mother and daughter team Claudine and Alida have created their own unique take on bush lodge décor, hand-picking every detail of the rooms, right down to the rock soap dish. Carefully-chosen pieces of local art and craft adorn the walls. Animals made from wire paper and beads are lit from beneath, wardrobe knobs are shaped like tortoises' backs, and a beautifully gnarled knobwood tree branch wound its way to the top of my thatched ceiling. The glass doors in each room slide all the way back, so you can be completely open to the unfenced wilds beyond, and the shower has a glass wall out onto the bush. But you needn't worry about privacy. Every room is surrounded by greenery and reached by its own cliff-side walkway. The only creatures sneaking a peak through the curtains will be of the distinctly wild variety. And to get really close to them, Idwala's magnificent game drives are worth every minute of the early wake-up. Airport transfers are available as well as star-gazing with trained ranger using on-site telescope. *The lodge can also be rented out exclusively. Ask Alida for details.*

Rooms: 4: all can be double or twin with en-suite showers.
Price: R1,950 - R3,850 pp sharing. 50% supplement for singles.
Meals: All meals, local drinks and game drives are included.
Directions: Take the N2 from Port Elizabeth towards Grahamstown. Exit at the Sidbury/Kwantu/Bayete/Fagles Crag turn-off. Look out for the Idwala Lodge turn-off (to the right) 7km further down the gravel road.

Woodbury Lodge

Jennifer, Giles, Richard and Cathy Gush
Amakhala Game Reserve
Tel: 046-636-2750 Fax: 086-694-6895
Email: centralres@amakahala.co.za Web: www.amakahala.co.za

I'm more accustomed to being welcomed by barking dogs than by a giraffe nonchalantly chewing on the treetops. And was that an elephant doing its best to blend into the undergrowth? With Jennifer's eagle eye, more and more animals became apparent in the shimmering distance and I'd hardly left the N2. Don't worry, though, you'd never know it. The stone-and-thatch building huddle against rocky hills and the rooms (reached via steps dug into the hillside) are hidden from each other by aloes and wild vegetation. The yellow walls of my simple room were dotted sparingly with local art, though the window offered the most striking sight – a 'dazzle' of zebra gently following the curves of the river while a raptor rode the thermal currents above. I knew I could never forget Amakahala. And all of this from my bed, whose crisp white linen promised a sound night's sleep later on. Heading back down to the deck outside the dining room, I feasted on the high tea with a ferocity that worried a fellow guest, impelling him to warn me against ruining my supper – how kind, but how mistaken, he was. After the game drive and drinks by the outside fire that had been lit in our absence, all three courses of supper were hungrily dispatched on the long dining table with Richard (Jennifer's cousin-in-law), our genial host. With the glowing embers of the fire slowly dimming before going out altogether, we made our way to bed. My new friend looked aghast when I expressed how much I was looking forward to breakfast.

Rooms: 6: all with twin/kings and en-suite baths and showers. Two of these can be family rooms.
Price: R2,480 - R3,180 pp sharing. 30% single supplement. Prices include meals, selected beverages and 2 safari activities.
Meals: Full breakfast, high tea and dinner included. Drinks also included.
Directions: 80km from Port Elizabeth on the N2 towards Grahamstown. Turn right at Woodbury Lodge sign.

Fort D'Acre Reserve

Mel and Rory Gailey
Fish River Mouth, Port Alfred
Tel: 040-676-1091 Fax: 040-676-1095
Email: info@fortdacre.com Web: www.fortdacre.com
Cell: 082-092-3035

When the sun's gone down, you're running late and, whether you admit it or not, you are ever so slightly lost, some sort of a signal is much appreciated. On cue, the Fish River Lighthouse that stands in the middle of the reserve lit up the night sky like a beacon to guide me in (or so I like to think). The lodge, where guests stay, is not actually a fort but a mammoth thatched affair, entered via heavy, sliding glass doors from a pretty redbrick garden path. It's immediately obvious that this was a lodge designed for hunters: the rustically tiled floor is strewn with animal skins and the local taxidermist has not been idle. Even the great central hearth is framed by elephant tusks. A galleried landing overlooks the communal lounge, where a cavernous leather sofa almost prevented me from making it to bed that night. The next morning I was able to see the Fort D'Acre Reserve in all its glory. Opening the curtains in the bay windows that dominated my bedroom, I looked beyond the milling herd of zebra to the Great Fish River stretching out below me towards the Indian Ocean and the reserve's private stretch of beach. I enjoyed my breakfast on the sun-drenched terrace, but the open-walled, thatched, outside bar could be equally appealing. Down on the beach is a new lapa from where whales can be watched, sundowners drunk and romantic picnics consumed.

Rooms: 4: 3 doubles and 1 twin, all with en-suite showers.
Price: R595 - R795 pp sharing. Whole lodge available for self-catering (sleeps 8, plus a kid's room): R3,750 - R4,000 per day, minimum 3 nights. Game drives an optional extra.
Meals: Full breakfast included (B&B). A selection of restaurants nearby.
Directions: On R72 20km from Port Alfred towards East London. First turning to right after Great Fish Point Lighthouse.

The Beach House

Janine Handley
80 West Beach Drive, Port Alfred
Tel: 046-624-1920 Fax: 086-219-4763
Email: info@thebeachhouseportalfred.co.za
Web: www.thebeachhouseportalfred.co.za Cell: 082-662-5720

If you fancy a luxurious getaway in the sun, where the pace of life is… very… slow, and whe you can stare all day long at the beach from your doorstep, then head immediately for the Bea House at Port Alfred. "We love holidays and like to see others kick off their shoes too!" says Janir With this in mind, she and her husband moved here a few years ago - from not-too-dista Bathurst - to reap the benefits of the sea air and an utterly chilled pace of life. As I strode from o open verandah to another, their admirably simple life plan kept resonating in my head. All rooms have sunny balconies and a pair of white, wooden 'sun-thrones' (four of these are se facing, so whale-watching is a very real possibility); sliding glass doors allow uninterrupted viev out, even from the soft depths of your plumped-up bed, and all have wireless connections a satellite TV. Downstairs, more spongy sofas and bright, open spaces feature in an L-shaped sitti room, which sweeps in to a breakfast hall and out on to a shaded porch, eventually meeting t generous deck surround of a cobalt-blue pool. Guests soothed by a sleep facilitated by the sour of sea are encouraged to take their time over breakfast. The most important meal of the day oft rolls effortlessly into brunch as guests embrace taking it down a gear. Janine has thought everything and, to top it all, has a wonderfully relaxed hostess, Mary-Anne, who will greet y with a smile on arrival. *Children 12+ welcome. Blue flag beach 400m away.*

Rooms: 6: 1 king/twin and 2 queens with en/s showers; 2 king/twins and 1 queen with en/s baths and showers. All have balconies with seating.
Price: R710 to R900 per person sharing. Single rates on request.
Meals: Full breakfast included.
Directions: On N2 from PE towards East London turn right up Wesley Hill before the Kowie River. At seafront T junction turn right to West Beach Drive and continue over bumps passing Kellys Beach and Shelley Beach on your lef #80 is to the right on the corner of Curlew Crescent.

Loerie Hide

Sue Rainer

2b Sheerness Road, Bonnie Doom, East London
Tel: 043-735-3206 Fax: 043-735-3302
Email: info@loeriehide.co.za Web: www.loeriehide.co.za
Cell: 082-458-9825

Sue seems to be hiding more than just loeries in her backyard! You would never have guessed that there could be such a garden in the middle of East London. For behind the urban façade lies a densely-forested river valley. The garden plunges down to the Nahoon River and steep paths pick their way down through jungly vegetation full of trees that come straight from Tolkien… dragon trees, num-nums, river euphorbia, sneezewood and quar to name but a few. Guests sleep in, around and above the branches in five stylish and very different suites. You could opt for a traditional thatched rondavel or the Safari Room; the Colonial Room is rustic and cosy with a brass bed and antique-style bath. And now Sue's most modern and luxurious suites have been tastefully added to the mix. With the glass doors rolled back, you can glory in a bird's-eye view through the treetops without moving from your gigantic bed. Breakfast is served in the dining room or on a wooden deck attached to the main house, where bougainvillea spills over the balcony. One of the newly-checked-in guests reversed my car out of the drive way with practised ease, his mastery proof of many previous stays. Having been welcomed, fed, watered and generally swept up by the Loerie Hide family, I understood why so many of Sue's guests stay nowhere else.

Rooms: 5: 3 king with bath and shower, 1 queen with bath and shower. 1 queen with shower.
Price: R350 - R425 pp sharing.
Meals: Full breakfast included. Local restaurants nearby as well as take-away service.
Directions: Once on Beach Rd, take 3rd turning to L just before shops. This is Schultz Rd, becomes Sheerness Rd. 200m down on L as road dips & bends to R, No. 2B. See website for detailed directions. GPS: S 32 58.941' E 27 55.656'.

Crawford's Beach Lodge and Cabins

Mark, Ian and Lyn Crawford

Chintsa East
Tel: 043-738-5000 Fax: 043-738-5001
Email: crawfords@iafrica.com Web: www.crawfordsbeachlodge.com

I'd heard guests dine well here, so I arrived cunningly early, just in time for lunch. The hearty dining room buffet did not disappoint… and the sea view was spectacular: two humpbacks explosively breaching in the distance. A beach walkway ushered me forth for a postprandial closer look. N deep solitary footprints seemed to be the only sign of human life for kilometres in all direction Plenty of marine life though! Right before me a pod of dolphins were surfing in the breakers ar just beyond I could see the whales' huge propeller-shaped tails raise in salute before submergir once again. This natural idyll harmonises well with the naturalness of Crawford's itself, a lodge wi chalet-style accommodation, perfect for families. The design can be attributed to Ian, while th interiors and décors are a credit to Lyn. Natural materials - wood, thatch, pine, bamboo, clay very effectively set off the bright kilims, super-comfortable beds and studded leather sofas. As fe things to do, boredom is just not on the menu here. The pool, horse-riding, tennis cour playground, guided hikes, spa treatments and games room will get the blood up and the muscl working. Plus there's big five Inkwenkwezi Game Park only 7km away, boat-based whale watching and even wave jumping for those that have an urge. But should you wish to simp unwind, consider the lounge, my favourite room, with its stacks of hardcover photography boo and the telescope for studying the animated ocean life through the A-framed window. Essential there's something for everyone. This is a worthy wild coast gem.

Rooms: 30 lodge rooms, all kings and en-suite shower, some with bath; 2 self-catering 3-bedroom cottages, all kings/twins with en-suite bathrooms.
Price: Lodge rooms: R450 - R1,150 pp sharing. Sel catering cottages: R1,000 - R5,000 per night. Enquir about singles, children's and packaged rates.
Meals: Guest Lodge. Full board inclusive. Lunch buffet R120; dinner: R150 - R195; braai: R175.
Directions: Head North on N2 from East London for about 28km, turn right at Schafi Road/Chintsa turn-off. Drive about 7km to Chintsa East and follow Crawfords signs from there.

Kob Inn Beach Resort

Daan van Zyl
Willowvale Area, Wild Coast, Qhorha Mouth
Tel: 047-499-0011 Fax: 086-523-9354
Email: info@kobinn.co.za Web: www.kobinn.co.za
Cell: 083-452-0876

This is not called the Wild Coast for nothing. Barely thirty exhilarating metres from my chalet, waves pounded the rocks in huge swells and rips that have been the demise of many a stricken vessel. Xhosa chieftains have traditionally owned this unspoilt land, which, leased to the Kob Inn, ensures a close relationship with local communities. You may even recognise in your bedroom mural one of the village scenes that you pass on the 32km drive from the highway to get here… including wandering cattle, so go slowly. Soon after arriving I was guided through a labyrinth of thatch, firstly to the earthy comfort of my room… and then to a bar whose deck juts out like a prow. Sunday night was braai night and, having heaped my plate, I joined a Durban couple that come every year because they love the lack of commercialism. Waking from the sleep equivalent of the Mariana Trench, I took breakfast to the sound of laughter from a group of elderly travellers who epitomised the prevailing informal atmosphere. The Kob Inn staff are passionately keen and were only too happy to guide me to one of their favourite places, the mouth of the Jujura River. Honeymooners will love the privacy of deserted lagoons, but with so much to do on and off the water (kayaking, boating, quad-biking, games room, etc), this is a brilliant place for families and children will be exceptionally well looked after.

Rooms: 45 rooms: 28 doubles (twin/king), 15 family and 2 honeymoon suites, 1 cottage. All en-suite bathrooms, mostly with bath and shower.
Price: R650 - R950 pp sharing. Full board. Certain activities extra. Children's rates: 1 year old 10%. 2 years old 20%. 3 years old 30% etc. 10 years old and above full rate. Pensioners special available.
Meals: All included. Lunch and dinner set menus. Saturday-night seafood buffet. Sunday-night braai.
Directions: Turn off N2 at Dutywa follow the tar road for 30km to Willowvale (signposted) It's 32km from the highway along a dirt road to Kob Inn, which is signposted all the way. Make sure to branch right after 12km.

Map Number: 7

Umngazi River Bungalows & Spa

Michele and Graham Walker

Umngazi River Mouth, Wild Coast, Port St Johns
Tel: 047-564-1115/6/7 Fax: 047-564-1210
Email: stay@umngazi.co.za Web: www.umngazi.co.za
Cell: 082-321-5841

The wild coast may be South Africa's most spectacular and yet least touristy region with its rock coastline, indigenous forests, secluded coves and many river mouths. And all this is on your doorstep at Umngazi, a lively family holiday resort where the only time you will spend indoors will be to sleep and eat. The relaxed and informal lodge is on the banks of the Umngazi Estuary so you can choose between swimming in the pool, the river or the sea, fishing off rocks or boats, and walking in the forests. Bird-watching cruises are also organised for sunset. Ferries transport guests over to the beach from a river jetty. Meanwhile, back at home you will be missing out on tennis, snooker and table tennis. I guarantee that a week here, however lazy you are, will see the colour back in your cheeks and a bit of muscle on the arms and legs. And your sense of time will go haywire. Children are well catered for with trampoline, fort, sandpit and designated dining room. You have a choice of sea-, river- or garden-front cottages, four honeymoon suites with spa baths and double outside showers, and the new Ntabeni (two luxury open-plan palapa suites with panoramic views across the estuary, a buggy service, in-house pampering and canapés served at 5pm). You can fly in from Durban at 500 feet above sea level along the coastline, a great start to a holiday. *The spa offers (among other things) the signature four-hand Pondo massage and an Umoya couples treatment (one for the romantics!) while you look out on 180-degree views of the Indian Ocean.*

Rooms: 69 bungalows: 67 twin or double on request, all have en/s bathrooms, most with baths & outdoor showers; 2 luxury king suites, in-house spa treatments, canapes & golf buggy service.
Price: Bungalows: R815 – R1,240 pppn sharing fully–inclusive 3 meals. Luxury Suites R1,470 - R1,765 pp sharing. Fly-in package R9,620 – R15,395 pp for flight, 7 nights, all meals & transfers from Port St Johns.
Meals: All included.
Directions: From south, Umngazi lies 90km due east of Umtata (Mthatha). From north, via Flagstaff & Lusikisiki to Port St Johns on tarred road. Also transfer service from Umtata (Mthatha) & private flight service between Durban & Port St Johns.

Woodcliffe Farm and Cottage

Phyll Sephton-Borrowdale
Woodcliffe Farm, Maclear
Tel: 045-932-1550 Fax: 045-932-1550 / 088-045-932-1550
Email: info@woodcliffecavetrails.co.za Web: www.woodcliffecavetrails.co.za
Cell: 082-9251-030

A few hours' drive along the road less travelled you will eventually come to Woodcliffe Farm and Cottage, a farmhouse idyll smack bang in the middle of one of South Africa most staggering secret locations. After 23 years in business farmer Phyll has finally decided to let the cat out of the bag and take guests. The farm itself is a successful beef farm and herds of cattle rotate their way around the pastures and meadows. Guests can swim in the river or ramble around the lower fells and caves (Phyll is a qualified guide and is brimming with historical facts and figures about the area that won't fail to astonish). More experienced walkers can head up (up, up) into the majesty of the Eastern Cape's higher Drakensberg. Maps, routes and overnight stays on the mountains can be arranged too. Tread carefully as some of Africa's rarest and most beautiful species of fauna and flora are found here. Guests already in on the secret visit repeatedly, to indulge in Phyll's inspiring tales, genuine hospitality and lovingly-prepared grub, and because Woodcliffe Cottage is a far-flung outpost on the doorstep of the greatest of the great outdoors. You don't come to Woodcliffe Cottage for the luxury; the rooms are rustic, the kitchen is well equipped, the water is hot and the wood-burner works hard. But if you are looking for somewhere wild and exciting that hardly anyone yet knows about and where you will be wonderfully well looked after, luxury will not matter. Woodcliffe is just what we are always looking for!

Rooms: Cottage. 2 x twin and 1 x double; shared bathroom with shower and bath.
Price: Self-catering cottage: R570 per night (2 people sharing), 3 or more people R260 pp. B&B: R400 pp sharing. DB&B, R570 pp sharing. Singles on request.
Meals: B&B, fresh farmhouse breakfast including cooked breakfast. Or packed brunch for earlier risers. Dinner, meal of day - home-cooked seasonal meals. Lunches, packed lunches on request.
Directions: Woodcliffe signed from Maclear. Follow exit out of town for "Rhodes via Naude's Nek" for 14km, L at Woodcliffe Cave Trails signboard & travel for 7km. GPS:30° 59.671' S 28° 10.985' E.

Cavers Country Guest House

Kenneth and Rozanne Ross

R63, Bedford
Tel: 046-685-0619 Fax: 086-545-8517
Email: info@cavers.co.za Web: www.cavers.co.za
Cell: 082-579-1807

I can't be the first to call Cavers an oasis, but it is irresistible. There in the distance a stand of t
oaks shimmers unconvincingly in the haze. And then suddenly you are among well-watered ar
mature gardens, an Eden of lawns and vivid flowers. The fine stone, ivy-encased farmhouse wa
built in 1840 and has been in Ken's family for four generations (now exclusively for guests). Th
bedrooms, with wooden floorboards, high ceilings and voluptuously draped windows, are refine
and elegant. From one of the upstairs rooms I got an impression of living in the trees with a
hadeda nesting at eye level and yellow orioles twittering and fluttering about. Two grand upstai
rooms with pressed-metal ceilings have balconies overlooking the profusion of flowers below
The thatched cottage also has long views over the lawns and up to the Winterberg Mountain
Rozanne is a maestro in the kitchen, cooking with fresh produce from the farm and th
surrounding area and all her meals are mouth-watering feasts. The memory of that salmo
cheesecake is even now a Pavlovian trigger that gets the mouth watering. There is a clay tenn
court, hiking on rolling land inhabited with plains game, riding, cricket on the magnificent groun
nearby; swimming is in the pool or a big round reservoir; and DSTV is on hand, should 'you
team' be playing.

Rooms: 5: 4 rooms in the manor house: all
king/twins, 2 en-suite shower, 1 bath, 1 shr & bath;
cottage has 1 twin & 1 double sharing bath & showe
Price: R450 - R600 pp sharing.
Meals: Full breakfast included. Dinner and light
lunches on request.
Directions: 8km from Bedford on the R63 towards
Adelaide, turn left at the sign and follow the dirt road
for 8km.

Entry Number: 181

Map Number:

Die Tuishuise

Sandra Antrobus
Market St, Cradock
Tel: 048-881-1322 Fax: 048-881-5388
Email: info@tuishuise.co.za Web: www.tuishuise.co.za

Unique accommodation indeed! Sandra has a raptor's eye for historic detail, laced with an antique-dealer's nose and the heart of an interior designer - unparalleled in my experience of South Africa. There are 31 houses along Market Street, all antiquely furnished to reflect different styles, eras and professions. The houses were once lived in by bank managers, teachers, wagon makers etc, and you step into their 19th-century shoes when you stay - although the bathrooms, perhaps, retain a little more modernity. Each house is an antique shop in its own right, but modern comforts include fans, heaters and fireplaces. I was lucky enough to visit them all and it is no exaggeration to say I was struck dumb - reason enough for Sandra to have gone to the effort (some might feel). The hotel, a Victorian manor at the end of the street, has a further 19 rooms similarly done out in the style of the time and sherry is served in the drawing room before buffet dinners (my Karoo lamb was delicious). Sandra and her daughter Lisa are dedicated to presenting South African history in a way you can touch and feel. They do cultural performances epitomising the Xhosa and Afrikaner cultures - ask in advance. *Closed 24th & 25th December. Karoo Spa and Wellness Studio offers treatments.*

Rooms: 25 restored 19th-century houses, each rented out as one 'unit'. There is also a hotel.
Price: R330 - R800 pp sharing B&B.
Meals: Breakfast included (unless you choose to self-cater) and served 7 - 9am. Traditional dinners served between 7pm and 9pm.
Directions: From PE take N10. When you arrive in Cradock at 3-way stop turn left into Voortrekker St. Die Tuishuise is 4th block on left. Reception is at Victoria Manor.

Wheatlands

Diana, Arthur, Kirsten and David Short

Route R75, Graaff-Reinet
Tel: 049-891-0422/4 Fax: 049-891-0422
Email: wheatlands@wam.co.za Web: www.wheatlands.co.za
Cell: 076-377-4026 or 072-251-9022

Welcome to Wheatlands, where if you're looking for flat-screens, iPod docks and high-speed wi
you're in the wrong place. Wheatlands is for those who want antique, country-farm luxury an
can't spell the word 'mod-con'. Built in 1912 on the profits of ostrich feathers (a so-called 'feathe
palace'), don't expect a humble farmhouse; I found a gigantic manor mingling Cape Dutch an
Edwardian styles, a façade dominated by three extravagant gables and a lovely white-pillared rea
verandah opening onto a green lake of lush lawn where heritage roses sprout like weeds. Hau
your wagon into the huge sandy courtyard (to the strains of the goat chorus) and grace the long
cool, wood-panelled grand hall. It's a lofty pleasure after the desert heat of the Karoo and a
appropriate home for Wheatlands' antique furniture and Persian rugs. Elsewhere, the brigh
homely lounge, replete with cushioned windowsills, houses the grand piano. Corridors are line
with first editions, there's a snug for reading, and high-ceilinged guest bedrooms are not converte
outhouses but an integral, lived-in part of the home. Wonderful wanders can be had in th
sprawling back gardens and the Shorts are astoundingly nice people, brimful of the hostly art
Kirsten and Diana cook decadent dinners, eaten at one large oak table, while David and Arthu
are serious wool and mohair farmers. And cricketers. They even have their own ground. C
course, it's Aimee and Emma, David and Kirsten's tiny tots who really rule the manor.... Enjoy.

Rooms: 3 units: 1 king/twin with en-suite bath and
shower. 1 twin with en-suite bath and shower. And 3
twin rooms with 2 shared bathrooms. Self catering
option on request for whole house.
Price: Dinner bed and breakfast: R500 - R600 pp
sharing.
Meals: Full breakfast and dinner included (Karoo
lamb a speciality).
Directions: 42km on the R75 south of Graaff-
Reinet, Wheatlands turn-off to the left, 8km up a
gravel road.

Abbotsbury

Sue Scott

Graaff-Reinet
Tel: 049-840-0201 Fax: 049-840-0201
Email: info@abbotsbury.co.za Web: www.abbotsbury.co.za
Cell: 072-486-8904

A three-kilometre drive on a dirt track takes you up into the land that time forgot, a small, perfectly-formed valley that Sue calls home. She is there to greet you in her improbably lush and well-tended garden, which seems immune to the Karoo sun's forbidding glare. An ingenious old water furrow running down from the dam must take some of the credit for this, although a fence has also been added to protect the garden's aloes and roses from midnight-feasting kudus… of which there are plenty, despite the privations. You can relax under the trees in the tranquil gardens or hike up the valley in search of the ten species of antelope and other Karoo wildlife on the farm. Back at base, guests either stay in a lovely old cottage, circa 1880; or a twin-bedded suite attached to Sue's own, even older house; or the luxury garden suite with its sweeping views of the garden and wild valley in the distance. None lack for character, with polished yellowwood floors, restored old furniture and photographic prints and artwork on the walls. Sue takes your supper orders when you book so as to have a fresh farm supply at the ready (springbok and Karoo lamb are specialities) and you are served in your own private dining room with solid silver cutlery, bone china and service bell! Breakfasts are also a royal affair. *Nearby: the sculpture garden of the Owl House, historic Graaff-Reinet and the awe-inspiring views of the Valley of Desolation.*

Rooms: 3 units: 1 cottage with twin en-suite shower & King with separate bath; 1 cottage, king & en-s shower; 1 twin/king suite, en-s bath & shower. All have private lounge/dining room.
Price: R430 - R495 pp sharing B&B.
Meals: Full breakfast included. Dinner available on request: R135. Meals are served privately to each cottage.
Directions: 27km north of Graaff-Reinet on N9, turn left onto 3km farm track to Abbotsbury.

The Stone Cottage

Michèle & Graham Hobson

Ebenezer Farm, Route 75, Graaff-Reinet
Tel: 049-8910-416 Fax: 049-8910-416
Email: info@thestonecottage.co.za Web: www.thestonecottage.co.za
Cell: 082-901-8309

I can hardly see The Stone Cottage for the butterflies. A thousand wings flit between lavender, African daisy and sunny aloe flower, all vying for the best spot outside The Stone Cottage, South Africa's family-friendliest farm-stay. It took a mighty spring clean to enable stays at Ebenezer Farm, explains lovely Michèle, piling my eager plate with roast farm chicken. "My husband Graham is the sixth generation of Hobson to work Ebenezer but the cottage was a farm store for years." Two years of sprucing and one (almost) butterfly-proof stable door later, The Stone Cottage was born; darling, shuttered den of warm, earthy tones, piled with furry rugs, Karoo-themed books and games, heaven for families fleeing city stress for wholesome farm fun. The cosy kitchen is armed for battle (stock up pre-arrival, no car likes tackling a 28km dirt road twice in one day!), but Michèle hates rumbling tummies and loves spoiling people since sons Leith and Stuart (whose Picasso-inspired artworks dot the cottage walls) started boarding school. She'll happily feed you, spicing things up daily. "A big guy who looked like he'd eat quite a hectic breakfast stayed, so I threw a lamb chop in with his full English," she reveals, apologising for not having made me her signature kudu pie. After lunch, Josh the collie leads us through the gardens to vast sheep and angora goat pastures, past the pool, tree-house, tennis court and mammoth jungle gym (surely I'm not too old for monkey bars?) down to the forest where real monkeys play. The Stone Cottage is a rustic Karoo paradise.

Rooms: 1: sleeps up to 7 adults & 1 child; 1 double bedroom, 2 twins & sleeper couch in family room, shared bathroom with shower; separate bedroom with en-s bathroom sleeps 3.
Price: Self-catering R300 – R350 pp sharing. B&B R350 – R400. Dinner, bed & breakfast R470 – R520. Kids under 3 no charge, 3-12 half-price.
Meals: Breakfast, lunch, picnic baskets and country dinner available on request.
Directions: From Graaff-Reinet 42km south on R75. Take 'Wheatlands' turn-off, then 28km on good gravel rd. From Somerset East go 47km on R63 to Pearston. As leave Pearston L onto R337 after little bridge. 27.5km on good gravel rd to Stone Cottage on R.

Andries Stockenström Guest House

Rose & Gordon Wright

100 Cradock Street,
Graaff-Reinet
Tel: 049-892-4575
Fax: 086-669-1421
Email: info@asghouse.co.za
Web: www.asghouse.co.za
Cell: 083-599-9302

Eastern Cape

Attention all foodies! If the kitchen is the heart of a home, few places have more heart than Andries Stockenström (ASG), where you'll eat fiercely well and, accordingly, sleep like royalty too. ASG has always been synonymous with fine dining, but Gordon and Rose, ditching city strife in PE, have introduced a much more laissez-faire style to proceedings. For starters, non-guests are welcome. "Life's too short for bad food and bad wine," grins Gordon, whose chef's whites are speckled with kudu biltong soup (hunted and biltonged himself), Karoo lamb with peas (picked, shelled and to a large extent eaten by two small sons that morning) and rum parfait. The high-ceilinged, antique-filled rooms of the 1819 manor house, meanwhile, shimmer with Rose's oil paintings. Rose only discovered her ability with a canvas on returning to Graaff-Reinet, the town where both she and Gordon, a wonderfully fun couple, went to school. ("Rose wasn't keen on kissing me back then," he winks.) Rose has magic hands: not only a reflexologist - foot-fondling is on offer - and decorator of ASG's elegant-yet-homely suites, but also a mean lemon curd maker. In the name of research, I sampled it (by the mugful) at breakfast, alongside home-made salami (on separate plates, I'm not a monster) and sous-chef Maureen's eggs, winner of a Best Omelette in South Africa competition. In summer, you'll eat in the white-columned courtyard beneath magenta bougainvillaea vines; appropriately sublime surroundings for perfectly sublime feasts.

Rooms: 7: all king/twins, 3 full en-suite, 4 shower only.
Price: R650 - R745 pp sharing. Singles +R250 pp.
Meals: Full breakfast incl'. Lunch on request. 4-course gourmet Karoo dinner available for R295 (subject to change). Bookings vital.
Directions: Travelling north on the N9 through Graaff-Reinet, turn left onto Somerset St, then second left onto Cradock St.

Map Number: 5   Entry Number: 186

Cypress Cottages

Hillary Palmé

76 Donkin St, Graaff-Reinet
Tel: 049-892-3965 Fax: 0866-840-166
Email: info@cypresscottage.co.za Web: www.cypresscottage.co.za
Cell: 083-456-1795

After a hot and particularly bothersome drive to this historic Karoo town, it came as a huge relief to step wearily through Cypress Cottage's heavy wooden doors and immerse myself in the quiet coolness lurking within. Minutes later, cold beer in hand and propped up on a stoep with a magnificent mountain view, my recent hardships evaporated into the heat-hazed sky. Both cottages are of the beautiful early 1800s Cape Dutch variety and are understatedly decorated with a highly developed taste for the natural and comfortable. Thus, the bedrooms display high reed ceilings, solid pine and slate floors, antique chests, fresh flowers and free-standing baths. Fresh and perfectly wholesome breakfasts are laid up on the terraces - free-range eggs from the house chickens, succulent figs, peaches, prunes and apricots straight from the orchard. You can escape the heat by splashing in the bore-hole-fed reservoir that has been converted into a swimming pool. Across the sleepy street, a familiar smell wafted over from the other cottage, where guests were merrily braaiing under the shade of its vine-covered pergola. The main garden is an extraordinary feat of will and clever engineering - desert has been transformed into an oasis of lush vegetation despite the difficulties of brackish water. Historic Graaff-Reinet is worth at least a two-day stopover in my opinion.

Rooms: 2 cottages with 6 rooms: 4 doubles and 2 twins. All with en-suite bathrooms, air-con and heating.
Price: R350 - R550 pp sharing. Singles on request.
Meals: Full breakfast included. Self-catering possible.
Directions: From south enter town and pass police academy on L and go over bridge. Two filling stations on L - take road between them (West St). Follow to very end, turn R into Donkin St, guest house first on L. From north: R at T-jct (Caledon St). 4th Left is Donkin St. House last on R.

KwaZulu Natal

Willowdale Lodge and Truffle Farm

Max Bastard

Willowdale Lodge, Willowdale Farm, District Road D60, Kokstad
Tel: 039-727-3870 Fax: 039-727-4437
Email: info@willowdalelodge.co.za Web: willowdalelodge.co.za
Cell: 083-688-5817

There is no better way to round off a day admiring the spectacular scenery of the Souther Drakensberg than with some true East Griqualand hospitality at Willowdale. This country lodg has been a thriving home for three generations of the Bastard family, as testified by photos in th bar depicting prize-winning livestock farmers, a Springbok rugby international, a war veteran an even the origin of old mother Hubbard! I was welcomed by a family of Jack Russels... and Doll who busily stoked the fires before doling out a hearty repast of pea and ham soup, followed b rack of lamb on sweet potato purée and rounded off with a chocolate and strawberry mille feuilles. After my fine meal, I retreated through the wood-panelled, heirloom-endowed loung and over Oregon pine floors to my quaint Trout Room for a ball-and-claw bath soaking befor turning in under the watchful eye of a wall-mounted fish. Breakfast was served outside frenc doors on the sunlit stoep. Freshly-baked croissants and farm eggs complemented views throug the rose arch to prodigious vegetable gardens, orchards and hilly farmland beyond. "You need t make your own entertainment in the country," enthused Max as he divulged plans for a hiking tra up to a cairn-top 'vulture restaurant', a historical Kokstad gallery, a sausage smokery and a farr resorvoir swimming pool. Brimming with history and originality, Willowdale is a treat of a lodge You might want to use it as a stop-over but, like me, you'll wish you booked in for longer. *Fly fishing and horse-riding available with prior arrangement.*

Rooms: 10: 1 Honeymoon Suite with lounge, en-s bath & shower; 2 king/twin en-s bath & shower; 2 twin: 1 en-s bath & shower; 1 en-s bath only, 5 rooms outside main house with en-s sh'r.
Price: R450 pp sharing. Singles R700. Honeymoon Suite price on request.
Meals: Full breakfast included. 3-course dinner extra Light lunches provided by prior arrangement.
Directions: From Kokstad take the N2 towards Por Shepstone/Durban. 12km from Kokstad, Willowdale Lodge is signposted on the right hand side. (2.5 hour from Durban & 5 hours from East London).

Sunbirds

Liz and Jonathan Shaw

No. 54 (Lot 643) Outlook Road, Southbroom
Tel: 039-316-8202 Fax: 086-687-1991
Email: stay@sunbirds.co.za Web: www.sunbirds.co.za
Cell: 072-993-7902

Never one to resist temptation, when Jonathan insisted that I try a Sunbirds speciality breakfast I was happy to oblige. I assumed the position on the terrace overlooking the swimming pool, then palms and bush, and finally the distant ocean horizon. Today's 'mere starter' was honeyed papaya with a swirl of fresh yoghurt on the side. My galvanised tastebuds, like baby birds, craved for more and were answered commendably with a cooked breakfast, and Liz's home-made almond and cranberry slices. In sympathy perhaps, the architect has created an effortlessly light interior. With the shutters thrown open, the outside floods in along white tiles and into an open-plan merging of living room, dining area, terrace and bar. The bedrooms, both in the house and in the cottage that overlooks a sub-tropical garden, have everything you'll need. Perhaps Liz and Jonathan's eye for detail developed during their lives in England as breeders and trainers of champion gundogs. Closer inspection of the little particulars give this away: a dalmatian doorstop, comedy canine figures at the bar, photographs of their prize spinone (not to mention the picture of a visiting Acadamy Award winning actress enjoying a cocktail with the Shaws at the honesty bar). If you're a golfer, the fifth hole is almost within putting distance, along with two good restaurants and the beach, all within a 3-minute walk - easy. And who's the actress? Her initials are J.C. Otherwise, sorry, you'll have to go and see for yourself.

Rooms: 4 rooms: twin/king (all en-suite 2 with bath and shower, 2 with shower only).
Price: From R575 upwards, pp sharing (singles +R100). Seasonal specials available.
Meals: Full breakfast included.
Directions: Driving along the R61 take the Southbroom South exit and after 400m turn right into Outlook Road. Sunbirds is 2.2km on the right-hand side.

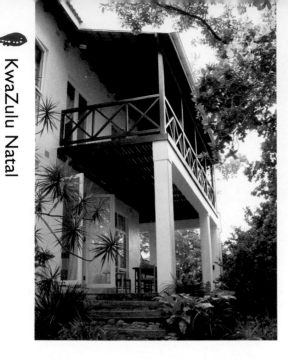

Plumbago

Mick and Libby Goodall
546 St Ives Ave, Leisure Bay
Tel: 039-319-2665
Fax: 086-689-3993
Email:
info@plumbagokzn.co.za
Web:
www.plumbagokzn.co.za
Cell: 082-561-6993

I think the coast of KwaZulu Natal gets better and better the further south you head and Leisu Bay is testament to that. It's just stunning and, buried in the banana plantations between bush an beach, is easily missed by those hammering along the N2 to more on-the-beaten-tra destinations. Plumbago itself is on the crest of a hill on sandy St Ives Avenue (just off Torqu Avenue, naturally), a gentle stroll from the sea. It's an airy double-storey home, hidden from neighbours by the thick foliage of Libby's indigenous garden, indigenous that is "except ti rosemary and the lemon tree for G&Ts," she admits. The birds are amazing and hop around rig under your nose, and while they chattered in the trees, we chattered (over lunch) at a lor central dining table made from an old jetty post. Downstairs the house is open-plan with lar windows, high ceilings and soft, blue walls – the perfect antidote to sizzling summer days. Upsta a wrap-around verandah keeps the main bedroom equally cool and if you do get over-heate you can just jump in the outside shower. There are endless sea- or land-based activities to ke you busy in the area, but with a beautiful beach on hand, well, I'd be just as happy focusing some serious R&R.

Rooms: 3: two kings with bath and shower, one king/twin with bath and an outside shower.
Price: From R410 pp sharing. Single supplement +R100.
Meals: Full breakfast included. Dinner on request.
Directions: Follow N2 and R61 south from Durba towards Port Edward. About 5km north of town tak the Torquay Ave/Leisure Bay turn off. Follow Torqua Ave to the crest of hill and turn L into St Ives Ave. Plumbago is 100 yards down on the R.

Yengele Paradise

Anna Jordan
68 Effingham Parade, Trafalgar
Tel: 071-422-0773 Fax: 039-313-0641
Email: info@yengeleparadise.co.za Web: www.yengeleparadise.co.za
Cell: 073-022-3329

Yengele is Zulu for spotted genet, a pretty cat-like creature which, along with a wide diversity of other wildlife, populates the forest bordering this property… so keep your eyes peeled when traipsing along the leaf-canopied walkway to the beach. The marine reserve waves roar ferociously here. The brave can snorkel the 90 million (give or take one or two)-year-old fossil beds at low tide, but blue-flagged Trafalgar Beach is only a scenic 25-minute stroll away for gentler swims. Significantly closer to home flows the Black Lake, a sleek, little-known horseshoe of flat water, as mysterious as its name suggests. The people who held it sacred many many years ago told the story that the stars originated from the lake. The house has been impressively reinvented with retro character and plenty of creature comfort. The autumn-coloured exterior is contrasted with bright interiors and family heirloom décor: Middle Eastern kilims, a red Victorian sofa, Zulu head-wear, a 1960's Xhosa skirt dyed in red river mud. The bathrooms are small, but bedrooms very homely. I longed to lie out on the substantial deck, sundowner in hand, gawping down at luscious indigenous gardens and an infinite Indian Ocean. The self-catering kitchen is ideal, although Anna specialises in vegan dishes, so give her a nod in that direction and expect something out of the ordinary. You should expect the extraordinary at Yengele anyway. *Children 14 years and up welcome.*

Rooms: Beach house. One couple/group at a time. 2/3 rooms. Singles on request: 2 bedrooms both with en-suite bathrooms, 1 with shower and bath, 1 shower only. 3rd bedroom unit can be added for groups of more than 4.
Price: B&B R510 - R540 pp sharing. Self-catering R320 - R360 pp sharing. Singles on request.
Meals: B&B includes continental breakfast. Home-cooked vegan meals by prior arrangement.
Directions: From Durban take N2 south. Halfway between Margate & Port Edward take Trafalgar exit. Continue c. 2 km to 2nd stop sign, turn R into Cunningham Ave. After 200m at T-jct turn R into Effingham Parade. No. 68 is at end of cul-de-sac.

Map Number: 7   Entry Number: 191

Gwahumbe Reserve Game & Spa

Neil and Raye Hampson
D368, Mid Illovo
Tel: 031-781-1082 Fax: 031-781-1083
Email: info@gwahumbe.co.za Web: www.gwahumbe.co.za
Cell: 082-347-6536

Barely half an hour into my stay at Gwahumbe and I was lying face down in the land of nod. M blissful 40 winks had been induced by the Thai-trained, knot-relieving hands of Sthe in the tranq surrounds of the spa at Gwahumbe. Alas, no time for a hydro bath (I know, it's a tough life as GG inspector!) as Liza escorted my rejuvenated body to the Serengeti room, where we crosse the rug-laden wood floor, past my cushion-strewn bed and out onto the verandah to view giraffe reclining cross-legged in the valley below. It appeared that I wasn't the only one enjoying relaxing bushveld experience. Later at the lodge, zebra and kudu heads eavesdropped on pr dinner drinks in the Crown and Eagle bar before a four-course fireside feast (tiger prawns followe by pork on crumbled putu with sesame seeds) in the Lapa Boma restaurant. I learnt that Micha and Lisa have been in the business for years managing a big-five lodge to bring big-five servic (without the prices) to the family-friendly Gwahumbe. Early the next morning we descended int the Gwahumbe Valley to discover herds of wildebeest, hippos and assorted antelope before mug of rooibos by the waterfall (also perfect for sundowners, braais and swimming). Wheth you choose to self-cater, self-drive (4x4s only), mountain-bike or simply let the Gwahumbe tea spoil you rotten, Gwahumbe offers something for everyone at great value for money.

Rooms: 9: 3 king/twin (en-s bath & shower); 2 twin/king (en-suite shower with full disabled facilities); 2 s/c cottages (sleep 4 with en-s sh); 2 s/c cottages (sleep 6 with en-s baths & sh); Mzigi Bush Camp (sleeps 10).
Price: R815 pp sharing for dinner, bed and breakfast. Singles on request. Self-catered units range from R800 to R2,750 a night. Ask about light lunches.
Meals: DB&B as above. For self-caterers breakfast is available for R70, 4-course dinner for R165. Light lunches between R30 - R95.
Directions: From Durban, on N3 towards Pietermaritzburg take Camperdown off-ramp (exit 57). L to R603 & on towards Umbumbulu. After 22km R to Mid Illov After 12km, 300m thro' Mid Illovo, then L (Ismont Rd). After 1.2 km L onto D368 (gravel rd). Follow signs to Gwahumbe

Lindsay Loft

Caroline and Pepi Jankovich

26 Lindsay Avenue, Morningside, Durban
Tel: 031-207-1634 Fax: 031-208-3227
Email: caroline@lindsayloft.co.za Web: www.lindsayloft.co.za
Cell: 083-490-0963

If your loft is anything like mine it's a dark and dusty dumping ground for old junk. Caroline's loft, I can enviously assure you, is NOTHING like mine. It's enormous. Walls are whitewashed and go up forever, floors are tiled to keep it cool in summer and there's a lengthy, decked verandah, of which more later. Actually no, I can't wait. The verandah is great, accessed from both the living- and bedrooms it peaks through the trees and across the city from its hill-top look-out. The stunning view stretches right up through the Umgeni Valley and gorge, which transforms into a starry, bright-lit cityscape by night. Back inside, the bedroom is cavernous and calming with (besides a bed of course) caramel armchairs and a beautiful old writing desk. The living area too is dotted with mahogany antiques and separated from the kitchen by a breakfast bar. For the chef, there's all the cooking kit you need and Caroline will supply the essentials to get you started. This is a great base from which to explore KZN. The Drakensberg mountains are a few hours inland, the game reserves a short drive up the coast and there are excellent beaches and golf courses.

Rooms: 1 double/king with en-suite combined bath and shower with optional spare single bed for extra family member in adjoining room. Air-conditioned. DSTV.
Price: R500 pp sharing. R950 singles.
Meals: Starter supplies and a health breakfast provided on arrival. Otherwise, fully self-catering.
Directions: From King Shaka Airport N2 to Durban. Take ramp L onto M27 Umdloti. L to Umdloti. R at M4 Umhlanga till pass stadium on R. Next R onto M17w Berea (Sandile Thusi Rd). Up hill becomes Springfield Rd. At lights before top of hill R into Essenwood /Stephen Dlamini Rd. At yield sign into Montpelier Rd. 100m ahead Lindsay Avenue.

Abalone Place

Sue and Donald Geddie

336 Cato Road, Glenwood, Durban
Tel: 031-205-6035 Fax: 0866-716-483
Email: info@abaloneplace.co.za Web: www.abaloneplace.co.za
Cell: 072-602-5052

"We wanted to create a serene and tranquil space", Sue explained, as she showed me past th
near-century-old frangipani tree, up Indian-red steps, through a grand porch bedecked with ur
of ornamental aloes and into immaculate Abalone Place. It took three years for Sue and Dona
to refurbish to their impeccably high standards and to hand-pick furniture, lights and bathroo
accoutrements from Durban's auction houses and antique shops. Every unique candelabrum
chandelier and retro light-shade is mounted on Donald's bespoke escutcheons. Stained-gla
French doors, wall panelling and circular bay windows were also styled in Donald's worksho
There is so much to admire, from the pristine 1960's kitchen units and teak and Oregon staircas
to the individual elegance of the six capacious suites. My personal favourites feature a giraffe-size
mahogany four-poster bed, antique bureau and couch, a frond-caressed balcony with city ar
harbourscape views and an original black-and-white-tiled 1920's bathroom. Every room has i
own distinctive tea set and even the bottles of water are chic. I accepted Sue's offer of Earl Gre
under the verandah of purple-flowering petria, where guests can enjoy breakfast ar
complimentary sundowners among meticulously-planted indigenous gardens and tropical birdli
from the nearby Pigeon Valley Nature Reserve. If you're seeking originality, tranquillity and r
small measure of luxury then Abalone is the place for you.

Rooms: 4 full suites: 1 king/twin with bath & shower,
1 queen with bath & shower, 2 queens with bath, all
have own sitting rooms; 1 double with shower; 1
bachelor flat with king/twin & shower. All 6 have en-
suite bathrooms & private balcony/garden.
Price: R700 - R900 pp sharing. Singles R900 - R1100
Meals: Full breakfast included. Lunch and dinner on
request. Self-catering option also available in 1 suite.
Directions: From King Shaka airport, N2 to Durban.
Before city, take 2nd M13 fly-off to Mazizi Kunene Rd
(at Tollgate Bdge). R at lights over Tollgate bdge. Thro
2 lights, past Entabeni hospital & St. Henry's school or
R, over hill, L at bottom into Mazizi Kunene Rd. 1st L
into Cato Rd. 1st house on L after Ellis Brown Ave.

The Grange Guest House

Annelie and Mutari Wada

1 Monteith Place, Durban North
Tel: 031-563-6826 Fax: 031-563-0072
Email: agrange@iafrica.com Web: www.thegrange.co.za
Cell: 072-324-1834

As I walked into the Grange I got that tingly excited feeling that GG researchers experience when they find somewhere particularly special! High ceilings create a feeling of vastness and you can't stop your eyes from wandering about the walls, which are adorned in exciting colours. The bewitching art around the house is from all parts of the African continent - my personal favourite was commissioned in Nigeria. And then, of course, there are your hosts. Mutari, who is Nigerian, met Annelie in her homeland of Australia. Never one to say no to a challenge, Annelie moved back to Nigeria with Mutari for 13 years before they decided on a new adventure in South Africa. You can chat to them for hours, which I did over a delectable steak from their local butcher, followed by a family favourite dish of warm strawberries with a dash of vodka. Listening to stories from their amazing life, it's clear that the inspiration for their home stems from their sense of adventure and passion for life. The Grange has been lovingly renovated into a very modern space, keeping in touch with the building's heritage in original wooden floors, but all the bathrooms, beds etc are super-luxurious. No expense has been spared. You'll be spoilt for choice with each room personally decorated – again, my favourite is the Indaba Tree room. With its own astroturf roof terrace overlooking the city, this is definitely the spot for sundowners.

Rooms: 6: 2 family rooms (1 full bathroom; 1 shower over bath); 2 queens (1 full bathroom; 1 shower); 2 king/twins, both with full bathrooms.
Price: R800 - R1,400 per room. Single R650 - R750.
Meals: Full breakfast included. Dinner and lunch available on request.
Directions: Drive north up Kenneth Kaunda (stadium on your left) and cross over the Umgeni River. Turn left into Norfolk up the hill. Cross over Grosvenor into Monteith. The Grange is the first property on your left.

Fairlight Beach House

Bruce and Michele Deeb

1 Margaret Bacon Avenue,
(Corner South Beach Rd),
Umdloti Beach
Tel: 031-568-1835
Fax: 0866-128-658
Email: bdeeb@mweb.co.za
Web: www.fairlight.co.za

I got my first taste of Fairlight's laid-back hospitality as soon as I arrived. It was another hot KZN day and Denise bustled me off for a joyous dip in the sea just across the road – "We can talk later". And we did. This newly-refreshed 'inspector' was soon sipping a fresh grenadilla juice by the pool and tucking into some of Maria's legendary scones. The garden behind the house is dominated by a large milkwood, a favourite hang-out for local vervet monkeys and a great place to shelter from the sun, although there are also sun-loungers around the swimming pool. The front of the house has a wooden deck running all along it, from where you can watch the surfers - six of the rooms open onto it. Dolphins love the surf too, and if you're lucky you can swim with them. Bruce can lend you a boogie-board. Inside, it is effectively a family home and luxury guest house rolled into one – plenty of light and air as befits a beach house, family snaps on the wall and a warm, welcoming vibe to it. Rays of positive energy emanate from Michele and Bruce and from their very charming managers, Jaquie and Rhona. Soak it up, then go forth and fish, surf or swim with a big smile on your face. Ten miles of heaven, a.k.a. Umdloti Beach, are but 40 paces from the house while the Mount Moreland roost site for migrating swallows (Sept - April) is just ten minutes by car. *King Shaka International Airport is 8km from Fairlight and Durban 25 minutes drive. World-class golf courses nearby and great restaurants within easy walking distance.*

Rooms: 9: 6 with en-suite bath and shower, 3 with just shower. All are fully air-conditioned and have sea views.
Price: R495 - R800 per person per night sharing. Singles on request.
Meals: Full breakfast included. Limited self-catering facilities available.
Directions: N2 exit to Umdloti. Follow down to roundabout. Keep right past Total garage and Fairlight is 500 metres along South Beach Rd. GPS S29O 40' 31.74" E31O 06' 53.98"

Comfort House

Ray Leitch

27 Dolphin Crescent, North Coast, Shaka's Rock
Tel: 032-525-5575 Fax: 032-525-8775
Email: comfort@iafrica.com Web: www.comforthouse.co.za
Cell: 082-556-9795

"I'm afraid I'm going to be a terrible host and ask you to get yourself a drink", was how Ray introduced herself to me. Within seconds I was drink in hand, utterly at ease and ready to get to know my terrible new host. As a former advocate and prosecutor for some years in the Cape, there's not much on the streets Ray hasn't seen or heard before ("everything you can possibly imagine… and also what you can't!"). She's certainly straight-talking, but also very down-to-earth, and in tandem with her manageress and niece, Debbie, who exudes calm, they have imbued Comfort House with an anything-goes, everybody's-family kind of a feel. This is a home and there's no attempt to conceal it. A Red Bear surfboard leans on a depiction of The Annunciation by the front door; family collages adorn the landing; greetings arrive in handfuls from the golden retriever and spaniel (with eyelashes longer than I believed possible). Even the four rooms are named after Ray's children (who fled the nest some time ago): Sarah, Jessica, Nicholas and Alexander. Yet none of this is overbearing. It's just what the label says: Comfort House. Each room opens on to a large communal balcony, so that guests fall into conversation and sun-loungers with equal ease, while taking in the turquoise pool below and the deep blue sea beyond. Honeymooners, of course, get the extra-special candle-lit treatment, and I admired the gorgeous dark-wood sleigh bed and intimate Jacuzzi on the private verandah… almost worth getting married for!

Rooms: 4: 2 kings, 1 queen and 1 twin, all with en-suite baths and showers.
Price: R350 - R550 pp sharing. Single supplement R100.
Meals: Full breakfast included. Dinner on request at about R100 for 3 courses.
Directions: From Durban take N2 north until off ramp 212 to Shaka's Rock Road. Turn towards the sea and continue 3.5km to a T junction. Turn left into Ocean Drive and then 2nd left in to Dolphin Crescent.

Seaforth Farm

Trevor and Sharneen Thompson
Exit 214 off N2, Foxhill, Salt Rock, Umhlali
Tel: 032-525-5217 Fax: 032-525-4495
Email: info@seaforth.co.za Web: www.seaforth.co.za
Cell: 082-770-8376

Seaforth Farm is a full-blown treat of a guest house. Trevor and Sharneen have many interest talents and motivations and Seaforth is a constant source of stimulation. Sharneen is a wate colourist and has also won medals for flower-arranging, so the house blooms with extravagar displays and paintings. Trevor is both an official tour guide and a skilled craftsman and much of th furniture has been made in his workshop (his latest piece, a huge lychee-wood bed) – and it highly accomplished work. The garden is lush and wild and envelops everything at Seaforth i tropical colour. The produce from the organic garden will always make its way to the breakfa table, with a variety of fruit and veg wide enough to stock a greengrocer's! Trevor's latest pastim is bee-keeping and after polishing off several slices of wild coastal honey cake I was duly show around the apiary. In fact the entire working farm is a hive of activity. The cattle is now pure Ngu (the painted cattle of Africa), chickens run among the pawpaw and sweet and soursops trees an then there's the dam with its abundant bird life. Trevor is coaxing it in with a cunning plantation o pond weed, lilies and islets. The guest house provides large, well-equipped bedrooms, a pool an thatched summerhouse with dam- and sea-view for heavenly breakfasts and candle-lit curr evenings. Finally, the staff have a stake in the success of their venture. A pioneering guest hous indeed…. *Zulu spoken.*

Rooms: 4: 1 family suite with 2 bedrooms, each wit en/s shower; 2 doubles and 1 twin with en/s shower and bath.
Price: R380 - R560 pp sharing. Family suite from R290 pp (min R1,020). First child free.
Meals: Full breakfast included.
Directions: From Durban take the N2 north. Exit 214 east off the N2 signed Salt Rock. Go 200m and take the 1st right into Old Fort Road, then 1st left int Seaforth Ave - the house is at the end.

Nalson's View

Wendy and Kelvin Nalson
10 Fairway Drive, Salt Rock
Tel: 032-525-5726 Fax: 032-525-5726
Email: nalsonsview@3i.co.za Web: www.nalsonsview.com
Cell: 083-303-1533

After a long, long (long, long) day on the road I finally emerged from my car at Nalson's, wild-eyed and mud-besmattered. I couldn't have pitched up anywhere more perfect. Kelvin and Wendy welcomed me as if I had been living there for years. This was my room, these my beers and friends… I owned the place didn't I? A fantastic shower washed off the mud (don't ask) and I was invited to dinner. I couldn't tell who were guests, who were family friends, such is the open-house air of friendship here, and the meal was out of this world. Kelvin and Wendy have an oyster and mussel licence (guests can go with them and pick their own) and these were by FAR the best I've had in SA. Nalson's is one of those places where guests stop over for one night and have to be prised out of the place days later. Breakfast was sensational (both local baker and butcher are true servants of the community!) and, joy oh joy, freshly-squeezed fruit juice. Guests who make the correct decision to stay more than one night will get involved in the sea activities – dolphin- and whale-watching on boats, fishing, bird-watching and the ten kilometres of beautiful Christmas Bay Beach. There's plenty to do on dry land too, including golf galore, walking-distance restaurants and the Sibaya casino 10 minutes down the road. With Durban's new King Shaka Airport just 20 minutes away, Nalson's View is a worthwhile first or last stop on any KZN adventure. *Ask about kids.*

Rooms: 4: 2 doubles, 1 family and 1 double/twin; 3 with en-suite shower, 1 with en-suite bath and shower.
Price: R450 pp sharing. Singles on request.
Meals: Full breakfast included and served when you want it. Dinners by prior arrangement. Price depends on what you have.
Directions: From Durban take N2 north. Take exit 214 (Salt Rock/Umhlali). Right at T-junction signed to Salt Rock, follow road round to the right past Salt Rock Hotel (on your left). Fairway Drive is next right.

One On Hely

Ann Walters

1 Hely Hutchinson, Mtunzini
Tel: 035-340-2498 Fax: 035-340-2499
Email: admin@oneonhely.co.za Web: www.oneonhely.co.za
Cell: 079-509-4256

Ann describes the Walters family's relocation to Mtunzini as a 'calling'. Swapping the industri chimneys of Newcastle for the rolling Indian Ocean they have much to teach about brave following your instincts. Mtunzini is an up-and-coming town on the tourist map. Its main stre leads to the greenery of the Umlalazi Nature Reserve and on to miles and miles of virginal beac "Oh dear, it's busy", Ann remarked as we walked onto the white sands and counted five peop dotted between us and the horizon. With its burgeoning independent café and shop scen Mtunzini is a gem waiting to be discovered. Here you can fish, surf, bird-spot, wind-surf, walk ar water-ski to your heart's content – although if I were you I'd factor in some time flopping by th pool at One On Hely, which is set high above a flood of greenery. A stone's throw from tow this modern guest-house is surrounded by its own lovely garden, but from upstairs views are o over forest, reserve and sea. All the bedrooms have pristine beds and linen, while pictures shells and wild flowers in dark wood frames remind you that the sea and green of the reserve just outside your private balcony. As the Walters also own The Fat Cat in town they frequent raid their own café for prawns, calamari, fresh fish and lamb. In fact, it seems, you can dine c pretty much whatever your belly is rumbling for. Get there before everybody else does.

Rooms: 6: all kings/twins with en-suite bathrooms.
Price: R600 - R700 pp sharing. Single R850 - R950.
Meals: Full breakfast included. All other meals on request.
Directions: Take N2 from Durban exit at Mtunzini toll plaza exit. Turn right and One on Hely is 1km on your right.

Chase Guest House

Jane and Jonathan Chennells
John Ross highway off R66, Eshowe
Tel: 035-474-5491 Fax: 035-474-1311
Email: thechase@netactive.co.za Web: www.thechase.co.za
Cell: 083-265-9629

Jane and Jonathan have so much to offer their guests that you hardly have to leave the premises. But leave the premises you must! Chase is in the heart of the Zulu kingdom and what better spot to catch up on the history of King Shaka or get tangled up in the Kings' Reed Dance. The Dlinza Forest Aerial Boardwalk is another highlight. Back at the ranch, the weather-boarded house is gargantuan (Mrs Chennells senior had a penchant for large, open spaces) with long views of the farm's sugar cane plantations on overlapping mounds of distant hills. On clear days you can even see 90 degrees of sea. They also have ducks, chickens and (Nguni) cows like a proper farm should, of course. Also a pair of resident spotted eagle owls. The garden is an orgy of barely controllable tropical growth, lush and colourful (check out the tulip tree and the Indian mahogany), its trees often weighed down by parasitic ferns and creepers. Birds are equally irrepressible and there are 80 species in the garden and 280 (!) in the Eshowe area. Kids will love the walled-in swimming pool (13 metres long) where you can swim by floodlight at night too. A hammock swings from a tree, a trampoline is stretched at ground level and there is a hard tennis court. Chase Guest House is an involving, very comfortable, incredibly good-value family home, with huge amounts of space inside and out. Pack a sense of humour and a pair of binoculars. *Bikes are available for use. They also do sugar farm and banana farm tours.*

Rooms: 4: 1 king with en-suite bath; 1 twin with en-suite shower. 2 king/queen/twin self-catering garden cottages.
Price: B&B R400 - R450 pp sharing. Single rates available. Self-catering R650 - R700 per cottage.
Meals: Full breakfast included for B&B (and by arrangement only in the garden cottages). Dinners on request.
Directions: From Durban take N2 north for 1 hour. Turn off at Dokodweni off-ramp R66 to Eshowe. 20 minutes to Eshowe. Take first left signed to Eshowe, Chase is 1.8km signed on left. GPS coordinates: S 28° 54.661' E 031° 28.292'

Birds of Paradise B&B

Delise Powell

45/49 Ulundi Street, Eshowe
Tel: 035-474-7738 Fax: 086-614-6709
Email: reservations@birdsofparadise.co.za Web: www.birdsofparadise.co.za
Cell: 082-532-4627

Delises's immediately and obviously friendly alsatians were bounding about chasing butterflies on the royal palm-flanked drive when I arrived at Birds of Paradise. Delise, who greeted me and showed me round, is a warm and caring former nurse who met husband Quentin at school in Eshowe, so they know the area backwards. We strolled past the trampoline, vegetable patch and tennis court and on to the charming bedrooms with their dark, wooden headboards and, of course, avian sketches. This is a great base from which to explore the Zulu Kingdom. I went on a fascinating Zulu tour, that brought home vividly the perils that faced both the Zulus themselves and also our hobnail-booted, pith-helmeted predecessors. Later, exhausted from a day of adventure and cultural learning, I retreated to the verandah that forms part of the main house. From here I looked out onto a burgeoning garden, whose rich palette of Van Gogh-esque greens, purples and reds is borrowed from the nearby Dlinza forest. A roaring lapa fire, masterminded by Quentin, crackled around a traditional Afrikaans potjie cauldron. Cards were dealt and wine flowed. Good, old-fashioned, South African hospitality! I dozed off to the calls of the adorable bush-babies and awoke the next morning to the terrific sound of the resident trumpeter hornbill – they were probably just jealous of my croissants, piping-hot fresh coffee and full English breakfast! I was ready to take on another sunny day in the Zulu Kingdom.

Rooms: 10: 6 double/twin rooms; 2 luxury rooms; self-catering rooms. All en-suite with ceiling fans and air-conditioning.
Price: R400 - R500 pp sharing. Singles R479. Self-catering R300 pp sharing.
Meals: Full breakfast included. 3-course dinner on request (R120 pp).
Directions: From Durban take N2 north for 1 hour. Turn off at Dokodweni off ramp R66 to Eshowe for half an hour. Take second entrance to Eshowe at a set of traffic lights. Pass through next set and continue till hospital, turn right and follow four sign boards.

Thornleys Guest House

Simon Gardner and Wendy Nicholson

17 Mansel Terrace, Eshowe,
Tel: 035-474-4179 Fax: 086-715-4100
Email: thornleys@iafrica.com Web: www.thornleysguesthouse.co.za
Cell: 083-442-3884

Many think, erroneously, that Eshowe is just a small town to be used as a convenient stopover on their journey between Durban and Maputaland. This is perhaps their loss and your gain, for Eshowe is in the centre of the renowned Zululand birding route; the area sports no fewer than four different types of forest (mistbelt, dune, riverine and scarp since you ask); there are game reserves; sporting activities on offer include the Eshowe Hills Golf Club and fresh-water fishing on Lake Phobane. And now you also have Simon and Wendy, a young and enthusiastic couple, who have taken over the family home of 40 years' standing and turned it into their personal paradise. With just three rooms, all beautifully decorated, Thornleys has an intimate family feel and you're encouraged to make full use of the communal areas. The peaceful lounge, with its original wood floors, high ceilings and large windows looking onto the garden, might be the perfect spot to relax and page through birding books to identify your day's sightings – of which there will be plenty. I, however, decided to prop myself up at the bar and chat to Simon who, among other things, is a field guide, bird enthusiast and part developer in the golf course – definitely the right man to know around town. The bar doors open up onto a lush garden, which borders the Dlinza Forest, a great place to relax, swim, bird-watch or play a set of tennis on their own court. Thornleys and Eshowe are destinations in themselves. *Golf clubs for hire.*

Rooms: 3 king rooms. 1 with en-suite bath and shower, 2 with en-suite shower.
Price: R300 - R350 pp sharing. Singles R400.
Meals: Full breakfast included. Lunch and dinner available on request.
Directions: From Durban take N2 for 1 hour. Turn off at Dokodweni off-ramp R66 to Eshowe. Take 1st L signed to Eshowe. Continue & turn L at roundabout. Follow road over bridge and at bottom of hill turn L onto Mansell Terrace. 5th house on L.

Thula Thula Game Reserve

Françoise and Lawrence Anthony
D312 Heatonville, Buchanana, Ntambanana
Tel: 035-792-8322 Fax: 035-792-8324
Email: francoise@thulathula.com Web: www.thulathula.com
Cell: 082-259-9732

Fresh fruit cocktail in hand, I was whisked into a 4x4 for an afternoon game drive only to find myse staring down the trunk of Nana the elephant, matriarch and star of Lawrence's best-seller, *Th Elephant Whisperer*. Anyone who has read the book will know that Thula Thula is a special plac where Françoise and Lawrence work closely with local Zulu communities. Both owners and sta are wonderfully entertaining and passionate conservationists. Here, human and animal lives ar intimately intertwined as I discovered upon meeting Thabo and Ntombi (the not-so-small bab orphan rhinos) and a pair of snuffling warthogs in camp. Thula Thula is also home to leopard buffalo, giraffe, zebra, nyala, hyenas, crocodile, kudu, wildebeest and no fewer than 400 bir species. The tented camp with its outdoor showers, laid-back meals and luxury tents big enoug for King Shaka and his entourage is perfect for families. A couple of kilometres through the bush the lodge is equally breathtaking with cathedral-sized, African-themed rooms lavishly decked ou with four-posters, zebra rugs and huge doors leading to the stoep. Not bad for the bush! Meetin other guests around a candlelit pool I was guided into the boma, complete with mesmerizing fir ("nature's TV" whispered Françoise) and presented with a four-course extravaganza of Franco-Zul cuisine. While feasting on chicken with chilli chocolate sauce and a sensational impala pie, Lawrenc offered to remove one of my wheels so that I would be forced to stay. Temptation just mad leaving even harder.

Rooms: 16: 8 lodges all king/ twin, 2 standard with sh'r, 4 luxury & 2 royal all en-s bath & sh'r. 8 luxury tents, 6 deluxe king/twin with bath & sh'r & outside sh'r, 2 family bath & sh'r.
Price: Lodges: R1900 - R2750 pp sharing. Tents: R1500 - R1700. Full board inclusive of all game drives & bush walks. See website for special packages & gourmet safari cooking clas
Meals: Includes all meals & gourmet 4-course dinner in lodge or African braai feast in tented camp. Tent users may dine at lodge by arrangement and vice versa.
Directions: From N2 take R34 towards Empangeni. Thro Empangeni turn R towards Heatonville. Follow for 10km crossing 3 rail tracks. L at next T-jct onto dirt rd for 8km. R for 2km to Thula. 2 hrs from Durban. Map on web.

Macadamia Lodge

Lucy Williamson

1st Avenue, Monzi Golf Estate, Monzi
Tel: 035-550-4427
Email: enquiries@macadamialodge.co.za Web: www.macadamialodge.co.za
Cell: 072-424-1020

I must admit, when I saw the address was on a golf estate I did have my doubts. I'm now eating humble pie, as I could not have been more wrong. Yes there is a golf course but you won't find multiplex houses and characterless lawns dotted around. Instead, you'll be welcomed by Lucy with her infectious smile and bubbly personality and ushered into their family home where mom Pat and dad Tim will welcome you with the same enthusiasm. The apple really doesn't fall far from the tree. Lucy has been in tourism her whole life and the family moved to South Africa with the dream of their welcoming lodge in mind. The two country cottages offer comfortable, private living overlooking the golf course and are the perfect places to unwind and forget about the rest of the world. Macadamia Lodge is only 15 minutes from St Lucia but with all the activities going on around the farm you wouldn't be blamed for not wanting to leave. Pat is a dedicated yoga teacher with her own studio on the farm and is also the 'foodie' in the family. Expect delicious breakfasts and baked goods made from all their own produce. And if you fancy getting involved in farm life, Tim would love some help with shaking the trees in macadamia season. As I drove past the avo, mango and various citrus trees and through the winding pines that line their driveway, I understood why Lucy refers to home as magical Monzi.

Rooms: 2 self-catering cottages: 1 double with en-suite shower; 1 with 2 bedrooms (1 double; 1 twin) with en-suite bath and shower.
Price: Self-catering R400 pp; B&B R465 pp; Children 0-3 free and under 16s please enquire about discount.
Meals: Full breakfast included for B&B guests. Home-made meals are available. Ask about costs.
Directions: From Durban take N2 pass Richards Bay. Turn off at exit 375 and head for Mtubatuba & St Lucia R618. Drive for approx 15km and turn right onto the P397 in the direction of Monzi. Turn left into Monzi Golf Estate.

African Ambience

John and Laura Engelbrecht
124 Pelikaan Street, St Lucia
Tel: 035-590-1212 Fax: 035-590-1416
Email: lejon@digitalsky.co.za Web: www.africanambience.com
Cell: 082-372-1769

Having brushed through lush, rain-shiny jungle foliage, I finally banged on the enormous door African Ambience, which opened to reveal two large wooden elephants and a beaming Joh ready to show me round. He and Laura built and designed the place from scratch and, after livin in St Lucia for 23 years, they certainly knew what they wanted. The thatched roof is set hig above the well-proportioned rooms with their cream walls and big log furniture, all built by a loc carpenter. "Are you child-friendly?" I asked. "You'd hope so, I've got at least six of my own," laughed. There was indeed a real family feel to the house with guests and kids coming and goir and everyone chatting around coffee mugs waiting for the rain to stop. John's passion is bo chartering and if you're lucky he might have caught a fish or two to braai for your supper. Th takes place in the garden - where John keeps an impressive collection of koi carp in a series raised ponds - around a candlelit figure-of-eight-shaped pool. Inside, the maids were scurryir around in brightly-coloured African aprons while I was learning about the resident fruit bat th dropped off its mother and decided to stay on as a permanent guest. Whatever you get up to St Lucia, African Ambience provides a lively base that's bound to be eventful.

Rooms: 6: 1 honeymoon suite with king, private entrance, patio and en-suite shower & spa bath; 3 luxury king/twin rooms with sofa-bed option and en-suite shower; 2 doubles with en-suite shower; 1 family room with 1 king and 2 singles with full bathroom.

Price: R395 - R545 pp sharing. Family room R1,300 - R1,600 per night. Singles on request.

Meals: Full breakfast included. Dinners on request (speciality fish braais).

Directions: From N2 take R618 at Mtubatuba turn off, following signs to St Lucia (approx 28km). Over bridge, turn R at T-jct into McKenzie St. At next roundabout veer L into Albacore Rd & then 2nd L into Pelikaan St. African Ambience is 1st house on L.

Makakatana Bay Lodge

Hugh and Leigh-Ann Morrison

iSimangaliso Wetland Park (formerly known as Greater St Lucia Wetland Park)
Tel: 035-550-4189 Fax: 035-550-4198
Email: maklodge@iafrica.com Web: www.makakatana.co.za
Cell: 082-573-5641

Makakatana Bay Lodge is sensational and I can do little to improve on these photos, which do not lie. If only we had space for ten shots, to show you every aspect of the lodge: the gleaming wooden interiors; the bedrooms (including the wonderful honeymoon suite), connected by walkways through the forest, with their gargantuan slabs of glass and warm, earthy African colours; the pool encased in decking and raised above the grasses of the wetlands; the lake itself and the extraordinary St Lucia Estuary & lake system. Guests are taken on drives into the wetlands to search for birds (360 species), crocodiles and hippos. You can also be taken on safaris to the beach for snorkelling and swimming or out on a game drive within the iSimangaliso Wetland Park before returning to a sumptuous dinner with your hosts in the outdoor boma. Safari drives to Hluhluwe Game Reserve are also available if you have a hankering to see the Big 5. The family's old 'Crab House' is the only part of the lodge not raised above the tall grasses. This was once a storeroom for crabs caught in the lake, now a wine cellar with a giant tree growing out of its roof. Huge sliding doors throughout the lodge open onto wooden decks and the absence of railings just adds to the feeling of openness to nature. The lodge is beautifully welded to its environment. An absolute treat.

Rooms: 6: 1 honeymoon suite with extra single bed, 2 king suites, 3 twin suites; all with en-suite bath and outside shower.
Price: R3,250 pp sharing, honeymoon suite R3,450 pp sharing. Singles R3,995, children (aged 8-12) R2,050. All meals and in-house activities included. Drinks for own account.
Meals: Fully inclusive of all meals and safaris.
Directions: Take N2 north from Durban for 250km to Charter's Creek. Follow road for 15km (14km on tar) to fork. Take right fork and follow signs to Makakatana Bay Lodge (4 more km or so).

Hluhluwe River Lodge and Adventures

Gavin and Bridget Dickson

iSimangaliso Wetland Park (formerly Greater St Lucia Wetlands Park),
Hluhluwe Tel: 035-562-0246/7 Fax: 035-562-0248
Email: info@hluhluwe.co.za Web: www.hluhluwe.co.za
Cell: 083-777-3439

I was greeted by a beaming Zulu smile and a wheelbarrow taxi for my luggage before being whisked off to have an ice-cold lager and some orientation with Gavin in a bar that wouldn't be out of place in trendy Soho. After being shown my fabulous wood-and-thatch chalet, I headed straight back to the massive deck, the centrepiece of the lodge, to drink in the view across the Hluhluwe River flood plain. There's a plunge pool lost in the trees, but most will want to make full use of the all-seeing, all-knowing guides who will take you exploring in this remarkable region. For the saddle-hardened, Garth leads horseback safaris among rhino, buffalo, giraffe and antelope species. Otherwise, there are drives through the Wetland Park sandforests, or to Cape Vidal National Park, but I visited nearby Umfolozi-Hluhluwe Park. And what a trip, my first real game drive and we spotted a leopard! You can also go mountain-biking, horse-riding through False Bay Park, on canoe trips and boat cruises of the Hluhluwe River or take botanical trips and guided walks to the old fossil banks (watch out for the Lebombo wattle, one of the 10 rarest trees in SA). The focus is on the exquisite topography, the majestic birdlife and the wetland environment as a whole. Not to mention the fabulous food! I feasted on a sumptuous supper of artichoke samoosas and False Bay salmon served with a cape salsa and delicious home-made bread. Whatever you choose to get up to, this is an intimate, sociable place with knowledgeable guides making the experience personal and rewarding.

Rooms: 12: 8 twins & 2 family chalets, all with en/s shower; 2 honeymoon chalets with shower & bath.
Price: From R2,100 – R3,220 pp DBB including 1 game drive; R1,600 – R2,520 pp DBB only. Winter special (1st April '12 – 31st May '12) R1,450 – R2,310 pp DBB incl' 1 game drive; R950 – R1,610 pp DBB only. Additional activities extra.
Meals: Full breakfast, high tea and dinner included.
Directions: From the N2 take the Hluhluwe off-ramp and pass through Hluhluwe town. Take the R22 signed towards Sodwana Bay. 3.4km after crossing the railway line turn right onto D540. Follow 5km signs to lodge.

Bushwillow

Julian and Liz Simon

PO Box 525, Hluhluwe
Tel: 035-562-0473 Fax: 035-562-0250; fax to email 086-650-2810
Email: info@bushwillow.com Web: www.bushwillow.com
Cell: 083-651-6777

Game reserves can be an expensive stop-over, so for visitors on a tighter budget we've uncovered some more affordable gems that still offer great access to local highlights. Bushwillow, 'more of a passion than a business' to Julian and Liz, is one such. Set in Kuleni Game Park with 170 hectares to explore (on foot) you'll spot plenty of wildebeest, zebra, warthog and giraffe, setting the mood for the 'Big 5' at Hluhluwe-Umfolozi or the Isimangaliso Wetland Park just half an hour away. It's hidden in the sand forest and while it can be reserved for your exclusive use, here you will always find an interesting array of people with whom to spend your time. I arrived on a blisteringly hot day and, passing a greedy 'sounder' of warthogs, was only too glad when Julian shepherded me inside to the cool of the fans. The three forest-green chalets blend into the bush perfectly, cunningly positioned a stone's throw from a small water-hole so you needn't go further than the deck (or plunge pool) to spot the local wildlife. Liz informed me that early risers can regularly witness giraffe stooping at their stoep. In fact, no need to rise. Just prop up a pillow and watch from your bed! The air-conditioned bedrooms are peaceful and private with basins set in jacaranda trunks and just a few steps along the boardwalk from the sociable living area. Here granite worktops and a eucalyptus dining table support Jabu and Victoria's excellent home-cooked meals. Or, have the whole kitchen to yourselves and self-cater in style! It seems they've thought of everything.

Rooms: 3 chalets (king or twin) with bath and shower. All bedrooms have air-con.
Price: R625 - R825 pp (B&B), R795 - R995 (DB&B) for stays of 2-nights or longer: complimentary game drive. Self-catering R2,000 per night (sleeps up to 6). Ask about all-inclusive deals & long-stay discounts.
Meals: 3-course evening meals, continental or full-English breakfasts. No meals available for self-caterers.
Directions: From N2 take Hluhluwe off-ramp & pass thro' Hluhluwe town. At bottom roundabout take R22 towards Sodwana Bay. Continue 16km after crossing railway & Kuleni Game Park is on L. Bushwillow signed within reserve.

Thonga Beach Lodge

Paige and Brett Gehren

Isibindi Africa Lodges, Mabibi, Greater St Lucia Wetland Park (now known as the Isimangaliso Wetland Park) Tel: 035-474-1473 Fax: 035-474-1490
Email: res@isibindi.co.za Web: www.isibindiafrica.co.za
Cell: 079-491-4422

I had been eagerly looking forward to my visit to Thonga Beach Lodge since before I had ever left Cape Town. I knew it would be great because all the Gehrens' places are (see Isibindi Zulu Lodge, Kosi Forest Lodge and Rhino Walking Safaris) but I didn't expect it to be QUITE so beautiful! Thonga Beach is sandwiched between forested dunes and ocean, an hour's sandy drive and 4x4 trail from the nearest tar road. Huts are connected by snaking, wooden walkways and in each a huge mosquito net hangs from high rafters, separating the bed from the bathroom, a design marvel in itself. One single piece of sculpted concrete flows past glass-bowl sinks and chrome taps into an oval bath. After unpacking, I took a quick dip in the sea before being whisked out for a breath-taking sundowner on Lake Sibaya. An elegant supper followed and my perfect light fish accompanied by a soft white wine sent me to my hut for a long, much-needed sleep. Come morning, I was raring to go for a sunrise stroll. The sky was a soft pink, the surf breaking onto footprint-free sand and, looking back to the lodge, I could just make out the thatched tops of each rounded room, twelve in all, poking out through milkwood brush. This is as luxurious and romantic a destination as you'll find anywhere, but it's super-relaxed too. All staff are hugely friendly, the birding, diving, walking and wildlife are superb and – a rare bonus – it's majority community-owned so your pennies help support the local economy.

Rooms: 12: 10 twins, 2 doubles, all with bath & sh'r, air-con, mosquito nets & sea or forest view.
Price: R2,630 - R3,190 pp sharing. Includes all meals, guided snorkelling, guided walks & kayaking. Spa treatments & scuba prices available on request.
Meals: Full board.
Directions: From Durban take the N2 north to Hluhluwe and then follow signs to Kosi Bay (Kwa-Ngwanase). 30km beyond Mbazwana follow signs right to Coastal Forest Reserve. Thonga car park (and lodge pick-up point) is now located at Coastal Cashew factory, 4.7km from tar rd. For 4x4 vehicles you will have to go 32km on along sandy road.

Kosi Forest Lodge

Paige and Brett Gehren
Isibindi Africa Lodges, Kosi Bay Nature Reserve, Kosi Bay/KwaNgwanase
Tel: 035-474-1473 Fax: 035-474-1490
Email: res@isibindi.co.za Web: www.isibindiafrica.co.za
Cell: 082 -873-8874

Kosi Bay is the sort of place that novelists map out and then construct adventures in. You are picked up by a four-wheel drive, which can negotiate the sand tracks criss-crossing the region. You park up not just your car, but also the modern world you are now leaving. There is no tar and no electricity here. Instead you enter a landscape of raffia palm groves, primary sand forests, mangroves, water meadows, interconnecting lakes (yes, hippo and crocodile like it too and are regularly sighted). And then there are day trips to the sea and the mouth of the river for snorkelling, swimming and fishing in 'perfect, white sand coves with huge overhanging trees' (says the lodge brochure). The reed-thatched camp itself perfectly balances the wild (your chalet is in the middle of a boisterous forest) with the romantic (candlelit meals and outdoor baths and showers). I loved the deep stillness of the early-morning guided canoe trip and other activities include boat cruises across the lakes, turtle-tracking (seasonal), forest walks and bird safaris. I consider Kosi Forest Lodge one of the most rewarding (and therefore best-value) places I have stayed in SA. I recommend a minimum of two or three nights.

Rooms: 8: 1 family 'bush suite'; 5 twins and 2 honeymoon doubles; all with outdoor bath and shower.
Price: R1,590 - R1,690 per person per night sharing. Guided canoeing on the lakes, walks in raffia forest & sundowner excursion included.
Meals: All meals included.
Directions: From Durban take the N2 north to Hluhluwe and then follow signs to Kosi Bay (Kwa-Ngwanase). From JHB pass Pongola and turn R at sign Jozini. In Jozini thru' town, L over the dam and follow for 37km. Turn R at T-jct and follow for 67km to Kwangwanase. Pass through town to end, go to Total Garage for pick from lodge (9km).

Ghost Mountain Inn

Craig Rutherfoord
Fish Eagle Rd, Mkuze
Tel: 035-573-1025 Fax: 035-573-1359
Email: gmi@ghostmountaininn.co.za Web: www.ghostmountaininn.co.za
Cell: 082-569-0596

I'd been looking forward to visiting Ghost Mountain, if only for the name, but how my excitement increased when I pulled into the car park and saw 26 pristine vintage Bentleys warming up for day's adventure. NOT what I had expected to find deep in the heart of Zululand! This is definitel a hotel (50 rooms) and thus not a typical GG entry. But I have no doubts about its suitability for this guide. Craig, who is the very charming owner, will instantly make you feel at home. In fact, cursed myself for not organizing to stay the night after he informed me, over a particularly ric and dark shot of coffee, that there was a boat trip to watch elephants drinking at nearby Lake Jozir or a trail in Hluhluwe-Umfolozi Park on offer if I wished to join them. I didn't even have time to sample a massage in the luxurious on-site health spa. Oh unhappy hour! I did, however, get to wander through the vast gardens that look up to Ghost Mountain (with its spooky history) an admire the fantastic double-trunked sycamore fig tree that stands next to a deep and invitin swimming pool. Naturally the rooms are also top notch: flat screen TV's for sports lovers, ree lampshades that cast gentle shadows across soft white linen and a private patio looking across t the Lebombo Mountains. I cast a green eye on those beautiful Bentleys as Craig escorted me bac to my car. His phone rang and he apologetically made his excuses. A Zulu princess was expecte for lunch and arrangements had to be made. *Bikes are available for guests' use.*

Rooms: 50: 1 Suite with extra-length bed and 2 bathrooms with en/s bath/shower + an outside shower; 8 Garden Rooms, king beds with en-s bath and separate shower; 19 Executive Rooms, twins, en-s bath and sep shower; 22 Standard Rooms, en-s shower in bath.
Price: From R605 pp sharing. Singles from R865. 2- and 3-night packages from R2,060 and R3,220 pps.
Meals: Full breakfast included. Lunch and dinner a la carte or set menu from R190.
Directions: From N2 continue straight past Mkuze town to a T-junction. Turn left. After 400m the hotel will be on the right-hand side.

White Elephant Safari Lodge and Bush Camp

Heinz and Debbie Kohrs

Pongola Game Reserve South
Tel: 034-413-2489 Fax: 034-413-2499
Email: info@whiteelephant.co.za Web: www.whiteelephant.co.za
Cell: 082-945-7173

When Heinz visited the original 1920s farmstead that was to become White Elephant Lodge, he found nothing but a ruin with a giant jacaranda tree growing out of the roof and a family of warthogs scurrying beneath. A far cry indeed from the elegantly furnished lodge I found myself admiring. The lodge has been restored to recapture the colonial zeitgeist with its rattan-blinded verandah, open-plan interior, Indian-silk cushions floating over deep wooden benches, tea-sets, white-pepper flowers and sprinklers nurturing the lawn. Two railway sleepers indicate the end of the colonial garden and the start of the bush, where my luxurious tent was hiding among the trees. All aboard the 1970s jeep (apparently running on paraffin and local schnapps!) for an elephant- and rhino-packed game drive. At dusk we paused for drinks in the wilderness, among circling hyenas! A full moon, carving marble patterns across Lake Jozini, lit the way back to the safety of my tent where a steaming bath was waiting, evidently run by the bush elves. During our delicious dinner among fairy-lit trees, we were visited by a fruit bat, who fell with a gentle thud onto a pristine white tablecloth. Heinz, who is a vet, transported it on a napkin-stretcher to the lawn. It's an animal-packed adventure where you'll feel spoilt rotten. For families the laid-back Bush Camp, seven self-catering thatched chalets set among knobthorn trees with private verandahs, spectacular views and swinging hammocks, is a must and includes all the activities of the lodge.

Rooms: 2 lodges: Safari Lodge: 8 king/twin luxury safari tents with bath & outdoor shower; Bush Camp: 7 thatched chalets: 1 honeymoon king, 5 twin/kings, 1 family suite (sleeps 4) all bath & sh'r or just sh'r.
Price: Safari Lodge: R2,290 - R3,050 pp sharing. Singles R3,440 - R4,585. Full board & 2 activities. Bush Camp is self-catering & for exclusive hire: R4,000 (1-8 guests, min fee). R500 pp extra for more than 8 guests. R250 pn for children.
Meals: All meals included at Safari Lodge. Bush camp is self-catering. No beverages or food incl' in rates.
Directions: From Durban (3-4 hrs) follow N2 towards Pongola. At sign on L reading Pongola Game Reserve South, turn R into main gate.

Map Number: 14

Entry Number: 213

Dusk to Dawn

Johann and Gudrun Engelbrecht

Farm Wagendrift, Piet Retief
Tel: 017-821-0601 Fax: 086-514-0237
Email: dtd@ptr.dorea.co.za Web: www.dusktodawnbedandbreakfast.com
Cell: 083-627-6454

I'm ashamed to say that I saw neither the dusk nor the dawn on Johan and Gudrun's splend
farm. After missing sundown when my three-hour hop from Jo'burg turned into a five-hour slo
I was sorely tempted by Gudrun's description of sunrise over the distant Kommetjie-Kop see
from the balcony of my room, Egret's View. Unfortunately, my alarm clock failed me yet again
blame the four-poster bed, with its soothing white linen, not to mention the in-room telescop
which had me glued to the startlingly starry night-sky far past my bedtime. The real culprit thoug
was the seriously deep bath complete with huge candles, bright enough to light a cathedra
Luckily breakfast is served until 10... and the whole pace of Dusk to Dawn is geared toward
unwinding overnight, hence the name. It's the perfect stop-off point if you're travelling betwee
KZN and the Kruger. The braai and verandah are large enough to cater for coach loads. And
you decide not to self-cater, breakfast is a healthy spread of smoothies, juices and, of course, fres
coffee - Gudrun is a trained nutritionist. Over dinner, meanwhile, I tasted some prime Dusk
Dawn pork. All the meat and most of the veggies come from the farm. Johan will happily sho
you around. He is also an expert on the Zulu Wars and the local German community whic
settled here over a century and a half ago. Use the farm as one-night stopover if you must, but
you can spare the time stay for two. *Mini-golf and mountain biking available on site.*

Rooms: 5: Egret: 1 twin, 1x4-poster en/s bath;
Hadeda: twin en/s sh'r; Sunbirds: 4-poster en/s bath
& sh; Barbet's (self-cater): queen en-s bath & sh;
Robin's (self-cater): king en-s bath & sh, lounge.
Price: R665 pp sharing including dinner and
breakfast. Single and self-catering rates available on
request.
Meals: Full board. Barbet's/Robin's self-catering. Full
English breakfast or healthy smoothies. Picnics on
request.
Directions: Signed off the N2, 35km south-east of
Piet Retief and 65km north of Pongola.

Isandlwana Lodge

Pat Stubbs (owner)

Isandlwana
Tel: 034-271-8301/4/5 Fax: 034-271-8306
Email: lodge@isandlwana.co.za Web: www.isandlwana.co.za
Cell: 082-415-3679 or 082-789-9544

Isandlwana Lodge is the place to relive Anglo-Zulu War history and approaching through the dust I could see its namesake hill from miles away. The rocky outcrop was throwing a long shadow across the valley, just as it did on January 22nd 1879 when 25,000 Zulus attacked the British soldiers encamped on the hill's eastern slope. The story of the ensuing battle is fascinating and the lodge eats and sleeps it. Rob Gerrard, an ex-Gordon Highlander (or one of his trusty guides), leads tours that include nearby Rorke's Drift. Even the lodge itself is designed around a Zulu shield, a thatched, tapered structure that wraps around the hillside and looks across the Isandlwana battlefield. Though steeped in history, it has a refreshingly modern feel. Upstairs, the lounge and bar have leather sofas, ceiling fans and high-backed, Nguni dining chairs. All twelve rooms are downstairs off a winding, rocky corridor, with very private balconies for enjoying the incredible view. Pat has furnished the lodge in a pleasingly subtle blend of hand-printed bedspreads, copper lampshades and slate-tiled, chrome-tapped bathrooms. Having arrived here from Florida and a life of "peanuts and insurance" she has taken to hosting as a duck takes to water. Once you've waltzed through her to-do list of battlefield tours, walking trails, 300 bird species, cultural tours, horse-riding, swimming and gourmet dining, you'll have happily spent at least three nights here. *Cultural tours are now available visiting local communities.*

Rooms: 13: 5 doubles & 7 twins all with showers; separate guesthouse: 3 bedrooms, sleeps max 6.
Price: Lodge (full board) R1,690 - R1,900 pppn sharing in lodge. Single supp' R950. Guesthouse (excl meals) R2,100 per night (6 people). Ask for rates for 2 or 4. Battlefield tours: R425 (2011) - R450 (2012). Ask about other activities.
Meals: Rate includes full breakfast, lunch & 4-course dinner.
Directions: From Durban take N2 north to Eshowe then R68 thro Melmouth & Babanango. Turn L at 4-way stop in Babanango. Travel approx 45km to turn-off to Isandlwana Ldge, then another 9km on dirt rd.

Isibindi Zulu Lodge

Paige and Brett Gehren

Isibindi Africa Lodges, Rorke's Drift/Battlefields, Dundee
Tel: 035-474-1473 Fax: 035-474-1490
Email: res@isibindi.co.za Web: www.isibindiafrica.co.za
Cell: 082-896-0332

Driving up to Isibindi in the early evening, the way ahead was intermittently illuminated by spectacular thunderstorm. It seemed to be following me. Ignoring the portents, I pressed c Homerically to claim my prize, a night at the wonderful (the first line of my notes just reac 'Wow!') Isibindi Zulu Lodge. It's on a hill in the middle of a 2,000-hectare nature reserve on th Buffalo River, with six secluded chalets looking out over the bush, a modern spin on the tradition Zulu beehive hut. The best view is reserved for the pool, a great place for daytime dozing befor an afternoon game drive with lodge managers who are extremely passionate about the bush. Th game wasn't playing ball on our evening outing but we heard plenty of snuffling about in th twilight as we walked back under the stars to the lodge. For those not barmy about the bush ther are Zulu dancing evenings laid on. Personally though, the tour of the nearby Isandlwana ar Rorke's Drift battlefields are the highlight. Walking the 50 yards of Rorke's Drift, having the batt described to me as the rain fell and the local Zulu choir had their weekly rehearsal in the churc on the battlefield itself, was a highlight not just of my trip, but will remain one of the mo extraordinary experiences of my life. Nature, history and culture… Isibindi has it all.

Rooms: 6: 4 twins, 1 double, 1 honeymoon suite; a in the traditional beehive shape with en-suite bath and shower.
Price: R1,350 - R1,690 pp sharing. Singles plus 30% Price includes 3 meals & 1 game activity per day plus a Zulu Boma Evening for a 2-night stay. Battlefield tours, Zulu homestead visits & panoramic day trips optional extras.
Meals: Full board includes breakfast, lunch and dinner and all teas and coffees.
Directions: Take R33 from Dundee towards Greytown for 42km, then turn left onto dirt road at Isibindi Eco Reserve/Elandskraal sign. Follow signs to Isibindi which is 21km from main road.

Sneezewood Farm

Theunissen
Dundee/Wasbank Road (P33), Dundee
Tel: 034-212-1260 Fax: 088-03-4212-1260
Email: info@sneezewood.co.za Web: www.sneezewood.co.za
Cell: 082-611-3560

Karen, Paul and Jubejube, their loyal Jack Russell, gave me a wonderful welcome to Sneezewood! Jubejube – fondly known as PR – ushered me to my room where she quickly made herself at home. She loves to look after new arrivals and Karen often has a difficult time extracting her when the time comes. The Theunissens managed a resort in the Seychelles for three years (poor things!), before deciding to create their own perfect B&B. They have clearly poured their heart and soul into the project. There is a modern crispness to the bedrooms and bathrooms, which are neat and compact, the walls painted in soft natural tones. Each room has its own colour theme and fabrics have been chosen in traditional floral patterns and linens - you can disappear into the scatter cushions on the beds. They have included original family furniture in the B&B and another nice touch was the collection of new battlefield history books in the sitting room for guests to browse through. Sneezewood is within easy reach of most of the major battlefields and just 10km away from the 20-acre Talana Museum, devoted, unsurprisingly, to the Battle of Talana and the broader history of Dundee. Paul and Karen are natural hosts, kind and caring people, and they will make you feel like you have known them for years.

Rooms: 6 double rooms 5 en-suite with shower, 1 en-suite with bath and hand shower. 2 rooms can be made into twins by prior arrangement.
Price: Until March 2012: R950 pp sharing, R600 singles; March 2012 - March 2013: R1,045 pp sharing in king room, R995 in queen room, R660 singles.
Meals: Dinner and packed lunches are available by prior arrangement.
Directions: Enter the traffic circle on Dundee's main road (Karel Landmann Str). Exit over the railway bridge signposted "Wasbank". Travel 5km along Victoria Street to Sneezewood sign on your right.

Esiweni Lodge

Natie and Magda LeRoux

Nambiti Private Game Reserve,
Elandslaagte/Ladysmith
Tel: 036-636-9002/3
Fax: 086-546-4045
Email:
information@esiweni.co.za
Web: www.esiweni.co.za

I was greeted at my car and whisked off into the wild to join other Esiweni guests already viewing the abundance of wildlife (Nambiti is the only big five game reserve in the area), which roams th historic land. After sundowners – keeping one wary eye on the lioness across the river - v migrated lodgewards, outflanking a largish herd of wildebeest en route. This lodge manages th neat trick of providing professional hospitality and exciting game drives while also feeling like involving home. Natie and Magda are your wise and welcoming parents and the big five are yo pets! It won't be long until you're hoping to be invited back for Sunday lunch. Dinner is an intima affair (maximum ten guests) where I revelled in some hysterical 'bush' stories, asked Magda abo the 'lizards' and wrung Natie's brain for top tips on wildlife photography, an art form requiri technical skill and patience... two talents I may never possess. Esiweni is known for its outstandi location and views and next morning, with the rise of the sun, I saw why. Sitting on my priva balcony at the edge of a cliff, I looked down on the Sundays River meandering through immense valley with its waterfalls and game animals. Between my perch and the valley floor myriad of birds swooped or glided, wings glinting in the early morning sun. Or you can set yourself above these same views on the martini seat in the rim-flow swimming pool. Esiweni i real treat!

Rooms: 5: all king/twins with open bathroom and outdoor shower, 1 with outdoor bath. All chalets have their own private balconies overlooking the Sundays River.

Price: R1,950 - R2,350 pp. Singles on request. All meals and game drives included. Excluding beverage

Meals: All meals included.

Directions: Heading north up the N3 take the N1 and then the R602. After 2.3km turn R onto P555. Follow Battle of Elandslaagte signboards to Nambiti Game Reserve.

Mawelawela Game and Fishing Lodge

George and Herta Mitchell-Innes
Fodo Farm, Elandslaagte
Tel: 036-421-1860 Fax: 036-421-1019
Email: mitchellinnes@mweb.co.za Web: www.mawelawela.co.za
Cell: 083-259-6394 or 073-486-8694

George and Herta are a natural, down-to-earth couple whose veins of hospitality run deep… and staying with them is to enjoy a few days awash with incidental pleasures. Herta, a bubbly Austrian, moved out to South Africa some 37 years ago and married George, who is a beef farmer – his boerewors is delicious. He is also a keen historian and leads tours out to the site of the battle of Elandslaagte. His study is full of Anglo-Boer war prints and weighty tomes including a collection of the London Illustrated News. (Ask him to show you his father's beautiful collection of bird-eggs too.) If you stay in the main house the rooms are very comfortable and the bungalow across the jacaranda-filled garden is perfect for families or groups. A short drive away from the farm itself you'll find the thatched hunters' cottage on 1500 wild hectares set aside for game. There is a trout dam at the front into which George has built a waterfall and there's a shower and a plunge pool to one side. The cane-sided shady braai area faces dam-wards and you can watch the eland and kudu come to drink in the evenings and with the Nambiti 'big five', malaria-free conservancy just a short drive away from the lodge, you won't forget you're in animal country. Finally a toast to Herta's cooking which is wonderful! Many of the ingredients are home-grown and all is served on her collection of fine china and family silver. *Bookings essential.*

Rooms: 4: 2 twins (1 with en/s bath, 1 en/s bath & shower); 1 apartment with double, twins & single (self-catering or B&B); 1 self-catering game lodge sleeps 7.
Price: R300 - R450 pp sharing B&B. Singles on request. Self-catering R250 pppn.
Meals: All meals are in the main house. Full breakfast included. 3-course dinners (excluding wine) R100 (booking essential). Main and coffee R50.
Directions: On N11, 35km from Ladysmith, 70km from Newcastle. Also entrance on R602, 35km from Dundee towards Ladysmith. For B&B look for sign to Fodo Farm. GPS 28 22' 13.00 S 29 58' 15.00 E.

Three Trees at Spioenkop

Simon and Cheryl Blackburn

Rhenosterfontein Farm, Bergville
Tel: 036-448-1171
Email: reservations@threetreehill.co.za Web: www.threetreehill.co.za

This is the comfortable way to experience the Boer War and one of its most famous battlefield Spioenkop Hill. The lodge sits in complete isolation on an opposing hill with views that flood c across the green valley and down to the Spioenkop Nature Reserve. The chalets are little color havens where the emphasis is on simple good quality, rather than elaborate decoration. Ea overlooks the reserve and rhino, giraffe, eland, warthog, various species of buck and plentiful b life can be seen from the rooms. If you can pull yourself away from your unobserved verand there's plenty to do. Croquet over a glass of home-made lemonade, a tour of the battlefield horse-riding, exhilarating guided walks tracking rhino with guide and owner Simon… or losi yourself for hours in the lounge which is steeped in history with paintings, books and a wonder collection of artifacts. Simon and Cheryl clearly have a love of life and a deep care for t environment. This is the first Fair Trade guesthouse in Natal no less; they make their ov firelighters out of teabags; they have a wormery; a wonderful veggie garden where kids a encouraged to get dirty; and a newly-purchased solar cooker. So, whether it's relaxing at t sunset spot overlooking the Amphitheatre and Spioenkop Dam, trekking Spioenkop Mount and hearing the story of the battle, or making your way through a gauntlet of dalek-like aloes the decked pool perched precariously on the hip of the valley for a little lie down, Three Tre will surely have at least one box for you to put a big tick in!

Rooms: 7: 1 family chalet with 2 bedrooms (1 double, 1 bunk and single); 6 double chalets with er suite bath and shower.
Price: R975 - R1,950 pp including all meals and guided walks.
Meals: All meals included.
Directions: From Durban take the N3 north for 260km - take the R616 left for 19km towards Bergville. Go left onto the D564 for 8km.

Montusi Mountain Lodge

The Carte Family
Off D119, Near Alpine Heath, Bergville
Tel: 036-438-6243 Fax: 036-438-6566
Email: montusi@iafrica.com Web: www.montusi.co.za

Montusi feels a bit like a hotel, which just happens to be run by your aunt and uncle. You know… you haven't seen them for years, but no sooner have you stepped from the car than they've got your bed sorted (well, your thatched, Conran-style, country cottage complete with fireplace, selected DSTV and view!) and are fixing you a sundowner on the patio. Ant bought wattle-strangled Montusi Farm in the early 1990s. Being a man of X-ray vision, he saw through the undergrowth to a lodge perfectly positioned to catch the surrounding view, he saw fields of galloping horses and he saw lakes to fish in. So he did away with the wattles and a new Montusi emerged. Meals are superb… some examples: red wine-glazed lamb with balsamic cognac, braised butternut with tomato, onion and grilled mozzarella, milk tartlet, chocolate mousse. There are many ways to burn off the calories with limitless and fabulous Drakensberg hiking on your doorstep (we walked up stunning Tugela Gorge, but the Cartes can help with suggestions). There's also horse-riding for all levels of experience, mountain-biking (bring your own bike), swimming in the wonderful pool and fishing. And just ten minutes down the road is son-in-law Chris's Adventure Centre with high-adrenaline activities ranging from zip line to quad biking. Montusi impressed me because it's a happy, family run place with plenty of style. *Relaxation massages are offered by local ladies as part of a successful community project. Picnics at waterfalls can be arranged.*

Rooms: 14 cottages: 4 are kings with en-suite bath and another twin with en-suite shower next door. 10 are kings with shower and bath.
Price: From R1,200 pp sharing per night. Singles R1,400. Rate includes dinner and breakfast.
Meals: Full breakfast and 4-course dinner included (wine extra).
Directions: If coming from the south head north through Pietermaritzburg, Estcourt and turn L signed Northern Drakensberg. Continue for 80km thru' Winterton and Bergville on R74. Follow signs (some small) to Montusi. From the north use Harrismith and R74.

Map Number: 13

Entry Number: 221

Zingela Safaris

Mark and Linda Calverley
3 Bloukrans St, Weenen
Tel: 036-354-7005/7250 Fax: 086-650-8950
Email: zingela@futurenet.co.za Web: www.zingelasafaris.co.za
Cell: 084-746-9694

Hiking, fly-fishing, abseiling, rafting, swimming, game-viewing… perhaps I'd be better off listing th
things you can't do at Zingela. Mark and Linda are delightful and, over thirty years or so, have bu
up their home/riverside bush camp to offer everything and anything, all the more astonishing give
their location. This really is wild country. From a rendezvous in the wee village of Weenen it w
an hour's 4x4 drive (not for the faint-hearted) past isolated Zulu villages and down to the Tuge
River - worth every bump. There are five palatial reed and canvas units overlooking the river,
open to the elements. Showers are more outside than in, branches provide the towel rails an
each "room" has hefty, iron-framed beds and beautiful wooden furniture from Zanzibar. Tho
on the romance beat will love the "hitching post" with doubtless the world's largest headboar
a vast, mattress-to-canvas slab of sandstone. There's electricity and gallons of hot water b
Zingela is essentially bush living ("don't-forget-the-loo-roll-or-matches kind of country," sa
Linda). When I visited the place was alive with families (there are zillions of kids' beds in ext
dormitory tents). Some youngsters were preparing for a rafting adventure and everyone w
thoroughly enjoying the endless fresh air, filling grub and lashings of good, wholesome fun. Th
thatched self-catering camp is now open!

Rooms: 5 bush units: 3 doubles and 2 twins, all with shower (one
with a bath). Self-catering option available.
Price: R850 for leisure. R1,200 includes all game walks, abseiling,
rock-climbing & rafting. Horse-riding extra. 4x4 transfer from
Weenen: R400 per vehicle.
Meals: Full board.
Directions: Faxed or emailed on booking.

Ardmore Farm

Paul and Sue Ross

Champagne Valley, Central Drakensberg
Tel: 036-468-1314 Fax: 086-503-3453
Email: info@ardmore.co.za Web: www.ardmore.co.za

Just in time for scones and tea on the lawn, the rain clouds parted and I was able to savour the stunning views of the three highest peaks in South Africa: Mafadi (highest at 3450m), Injisuti Dome (second highest at 3410m) and the majestic Champagne Castle (third highest at 3377m). The Drakensberg National Park begins just down the road so bring your hiking boots. Ardmore is a super-relaxed, free-wheeling sort of place. Paul (who bears an uncanny resemblance to Tom Hanks) is always working on something new - a deck, a tree-house or, when I got there, he was in the process of moving his wife's prized cabbage tree. He enthusiastically showed me around the Zulu cotton-weaving factory, run by Sue with the help of the local Zulu community, and the new on-site museum celebrating the renowned pottery of the Ardmore Ceramic Art Studio, which was founded here in 1985. Sociable and delicious dinners, eaten by lantern light in the yellowwood dining room, draw on the farm's organic produce - eggs from happy, roaming chickens and fruit, vegetables and herbs from a pesticide-free garden. There is masses to do at Ardmore: hike to waterfalls and mountain peaks; watch the rare bald ibis that makes its home here; fish, canoe, mountain-bike or, if you're lucky, catch the Drakensberg Boys' Choir. There are many rock art sites in the area too. The small, thatched rondavels complete with fireplaces are sweet and cosy. Ardmore has a few rough edges, but it's very sociable, great fun... and really good value too.

Rooms: 9: 6 cottages and 3 rondavels: 2 cottages with 2 en-s bedrooms with queen 4-posters; 4 cottages with 1 queen 4-poster, 1 double/twin & 1 twin; 2 en-s. Rondavels all queen; all with shower & sep' bath. All units have fireplaces and own spa-bath/Jacuzzi.
Price: R465 - R645 pp sharing. DBB.
Meals: Full breakfast and 4-course dinner with wine included.
Directions: From the N3 take the R74 to Winterton and go south along the R600 towards the Central Drakensberg for 18km. You'll see a sign on your left, 5km up partly dirt road for Ardmore.

Sewula Gorge Lodge

Graham and Santie McIntosh & Jacquie Geldart
Off R103, 18km from Estcourt
Tel: 036-352-2485 Fax: 036-352-2868
Email: info@sewula.co.za Web: www.sewula.co.za
Cell: 082-824-0329

The pictures do not exaggerate. This glorious thatched lodge lives beside a rocky-river gorge fille with cascading waterfalls (the main one is 20 metres high) and swimming pools. As soon as arrived I realized I had made a significant mistake. I had not organized to stay the night at Sewu and had missed my opportunity to swim under the waterfall looking at the stars. A group botanists and ornithologists were far wiser and subsequently had a field day on this nation heritage site. The emphasis is on relaxation and seclusion and only one party stays at a time. Sta live away from the lodge and there is absolutely no-one about except you, a very rare treat (eve by GG standards). For this far-too-low-really price, you can pretend you own this truly heaven place. It is self-catering, but with any domestic hardship extracted. For here not only does natur spoil you, but the staff do too, by washing up, servicing the rooms and lighting the log fires. Und the thatched pitch of the main lodge roof are the kitchen, bush-chic sunken sitting room, a gia fireplace, an oversized chess set and much wildly original carpentry and functional sculptur Similarly lovely are the cottages, which have sleeping lofts for children and face the falls. You ca walk to an iron-age settlement, battle memorials and great fishing spots. Jacquie is a stellar ho and constantly thoughtful. 100% (as the locals say)! *The rock art sites and white-water rafting a within an hour's drive.*

Rooms: 4 cottages (max 8 adults & 10 children): 3 have en-s shower, 2 of which have outdoor shower too; 1 cottage has en-s shower and bath. One booking at a time.
Price: R450 pp per night self catering (min 2 people). 20% discount for groups with 6 adults or more. Children are half price.
Meals: Restaurants are nearby (within 10km).
Directions: Exit 143 on N3 from Durban to Mooi River. Take R103 to Estcourt, 20.3km from off-ramp, take right turn onto dirt road to Malanspruit and follow signs to Sewula Gorge Camp.

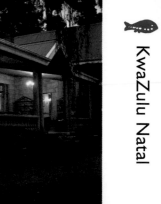

Hartford House

Mick and Cheryl Goss

Hartford House, Mooi River
Tel: 033-263-2713 Fax: 033-263-2818
Email: info@hartford.co.za Web: www.hartford.co.za

The Gosses, owners of Hartford House, humbly refer to themselves as "custodians of one of Africa's most treasured legacies". General Botha assumed command of the Boer forces here in 1899 and it was also home to the family of Sir Frederick Moor, the last prime minister of the Colony of Natal. The deputy prime minister, Colonel Richards, established the world-renowned Summerhill Stud on the property, which today hosts stallions for the rulers of Dubai. Aside from all this history, the Gosses also rightly revel in the beauty of this spectacular place… and so will you. Spread across seemingly endless landscaped gardens, the fourteen rooms have been decorated with dark wood antiques from India and West Africa. Scraping my jaw off the floor, I surveyed the four lakeside suites which are nothing short of spectacular. I was especially taken with the aptly-named "Siyabonga" ("thank you" in Zulu) with its twin egg baths and private pool. The beaded chair, the wooden cow heads on the wall and the building materials are all locally sourced. An emperor-sized round bed dominates the Inkanyesi Suite, while "Nhlanhla" ("good luck") combines Burmese antiques with bold green and rich red furnishings and a bright copper bath glints in the bathroom. Made entirely out of hay bales, this amazing example of sustainable luxury accommodation is so close to the dam it is practically floating. Oh, and by the way, the restaurant I dined in (after my Swedish massage) was the South African House and Leisure restaurant of the year. Just go.

Rooms: 15: 4 lakeside suites all king with bath and wet room; 4 garden/ pool suites all with bath and shower; 3 standard kings with bath and shower and 3 twins with bath and shower.
Price: R840 – R1,555 pp. Wellness Centre offers a variety of treatments.
Meals: Full 3 course breakfast included. A la carte lunch and 5 course set dinner. Restaurant in Eat Out top 10.
Directions: Please refer to website.

Stocklands Farm

Eve Mazery
4 Shafton Rd, Howick
Tel: 033-330-5160 Fax: 086-685-5657
Email: stocklands@iafrica.com Web: www.stocklandsfarm.co.za
Cell: 082-975-2298

The warm welcome that I received as I tumbled out of my car, late and weary, is undoubtec typical of Stocklands. Eve and Roland are natural hosts, thoughtful and funny, and they have put lot of love and plenty of style into the wonderful old house. The argument goes that half measur are not really in keeping with Stocklands and you can see their point. With a kaleidoscope colours, Eve's spectacular garden, a mix of English country and indigenous, is in bloom all ye round. The walls of the original 1850s Voortrekker Cottage are over 50 centimetres thick and th belhambra tree at the front of the house is no-less-than enormous. Birds come in droves – the love Roland's indigenous trees, "a small forest", and bank upon bank of stunning flowers. I love the fuchsia tree myself (it flowers in January). Down near the tennis court there is a wonder pond and many guests like to savour a slow, hot afternoon in the thick shade on a blanket he after a picnic. The four rooms, like the cottages, are meticulously decorated in individual theme all with a cosy, English-cottage feel about them. Eve has found hand-embroidered linen an original works by local artists to decorate. Oh, and if you want to know more about local histor ask Eve – she's writing a book on the subject. Choose from a range of breakfasts including Th Sunshine Breakfast and the Stocklands Smoothie. All cooked breakfasts are made with loca sourced free range eggs. Game can be viewed right next door. *French spoken.*

Rooms: 7: 2 suites & 2 bedrooms: one of each with en-suite bath & 1 of each with en-s shower. Also 3 cottages: with 3 bedrooms & 2 bathrooms; 2 with 1 bedroom & shower en-suite.

Price: R365 - R380 pp sharing. Singles on request. Self-catering R320 per person per night. Extra breakfasts on request @ R90 per person.

Meals: Full breakfast incl' or self-cater in cottages.

Directions: From Jo'burg take N3 to Durban. Take first exit to Howick signed Howick/Tweedie. At Stop sign L to Howick. Through lights to bottom of hill, L to Karkloof. 100m R into Shafton Rd. Stocklands is 1km. From Durban take N3 to Jo'burg. Take 3rd Howick turn-off as above. S 29° 28' 44.04" E 30° 14' 25.08".

Inversanda Farm Cottages

Tom and Lucinda Bate

Howick
Tel: 082-772-1621 Fax: 086-650-5622
Email: info@inversanda.co.za Web: www.inversanda.co.za
Cell: 082-781-3875

It's true that GG owners are a welcoming bunch, but the Bates go far beyond the call of duty. Actually, I don't think they see it as a duty at all. In fact, I know they don't! Hemmed in by mountains and a meander of the Mgeni River, the farm is in a world of its own, but in easy reach of the major routes. All four Bates (plus assorted hounds) are utterly charming and you're encouraged to participate in their farm and life as much or as little as you like. Talk about a welcome! We were hardly out of the car before we had a greedy calf and a bottle of milk in hand. Half an hour later we were bringing the horses in for feeding. Then just time for a bobble over the fields looking at pregnant cows before a delicious and greatly entertaining dinner with the family. Tom and Lucinda are serious horse-lovers, breeding and schooling polo ponies. Polo players are more than welcome for a weekend knock-about on the makeshift riverside pitch. Otherwise you can fish, walk or swim pretty much anywhere you want. If you've got a 4x4, you're encouraged to hit the trail that will take you to a fantastic waterfall and leave you with breathtaking views of the Midmar Dam and Dargle Valley. The farmhouse itself (1800s) goes on forever and guests have the choice of their own wing, a pot-planted patio with stunning views across the valley, good-sized bedrooms and a basic kitchen; or a brand-new cottage which also has a large verandah with a commanding view over the valley and two large bedrooms. But even if you had to lie on a bed of spikes, I'd still recommend Inversanda! This is a place that allows you to unburden yourself of the tourist mantle and truly feel part of what's going on.

Rooms: 1 self-catering wing with 1 double room & 1 twin room, shared bath & shower; 1 cottage with 1 double & 1 family room that sleeps 4. Both have en-suite bathrooms, 1 with shower & 1 with bath & shower.
Price: From R300 pp self-catering.
Meals: Meals available on request.
Directions: Faxed or emailed on booking.

Penwarn Country Lodge

Peter and Barbara Dommett

Bushmen's Nek Road, Southern Drakensberg, Underberg
Tel: 033-701-1368
Email: info@penwarn.com Web: www.penwarn.com
Cell: 082-773-9923 / 076-790-2419

Negotiating my way past an inquisitive eland, I was ushered straight to the bar by Peter and Barbara, a couple who care passionately about the countryside and its conservation. And now they have taken up the reins at Penwarn alongside their neighbouring dairy farm and stud. All very good news for us! The lodge boasts dark-beamed sitting rooms and bedrooms so large they make you want to run amok. Reclining on a deep leather divan in 'Nimrod' (dedicated to a much-loved otter) I goggled at a lake caressed by willows and supervised by cranes. Dinner was a buffet extravaganza. Venison pie went down a treat after my afternoon horse ride with Mondi (they call him Mondi Roberts, the Zulu horse-whisperer). The horse-back game rides are a must, through breathtaking landscapes past droves of zebras, springbok, wildebeest and hartebeest and up to the Bushmen cave figures painted a millennium ago. A couple of GG devotees insisted I visit them at the separate Mthini Lodge. From its stellar position above the dam, overlooking foothills grazed by antelope, we watched the sun set behind the mountains beyond. The sense of space is liberating, the ideal spot to escape and enjoy the gentle pursuits of fishing, paddling, a tour of the draft horse stud (8 different breeds!), flower walks in season and excellent bird-watching at the 'Vulture Restaurant'. A magical place. *Penwarn is part of the Waterford Estate with access to 3500ha, 50 fishing dams and a World Heritage site.*

Rooms: 14: 4 doubles and 3 suites at Indabushe Lodge; 4 suites at Mthini Lodge. All en-s bath and/or sh. 3 s/c cottages: The Manor House (sleeps 10); Kudu (6); Log Cabin (4).
Price: R800 - R1,170 pp sharing DBB. R250 - R400 pp for self-catering cottages. Kids under 10 half-price. Singles +50%. See website for list of activities.
Meals: Full breakfast, 4-course buffet dinner & afternoon tea included. Self-catering in cottages, but meals available in lodge.
Directions: Take Exit 99 off N3 to Underberg & Howick South. 110km west on R617, thro' Boston & Bulwer. 5km thro Underberg direction Kokstad/Swartberg, R onto Bushmansnek Rd (dirt). After 16km L to Penwarn (drive 4km on dirt).

Free State

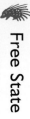

The View

Ryk and Bea and Sasha Becker

20 Bell Street, Harrismith Tel: 058-623-0961 Fax: 058-623-0961
Email: rmbecker@internext.co.za
Web: www.harrismithaccommodation.co.za
Cell: 082-775-7381 (Bea); 082-921-3624 (Ryk)

How better to while away a sticky afternoon than by nesting in a rocking chair behind teak pilla
on a shady verandah, overlooking a lush garden, slowly draining a pot of tea? Bea and Ryk hav
found a magic formula simply by being themselves at home! The actual view of the title is no
interrupted by an abundance of verdure, but I for one was glad of the green shade and th
peaceful sounds of twittering birds hidden among the branches. Inside, a portrait of Bea's bi
bearded great-grandfather, President of the Free State (deceased, of course), overlooks the soc
epicentre of this family home. The lounge, complete with creaking wooden floorboards, vibra
rugs and daringly bright sofas, sweeps through folded-back doors into the dining room where th
heavy table awaits those staying in for dinner. And I thoroughly recommend you are among ther
You would travel a long way to find a better meal and you'll miss out on Ryk spilling the beans o
what to do in this area where he grew up. Before heading up to my goose-feathered bed for m
best night's sleep in years, no visit to The View would be complete without being introduced
the rest of the family: two springer and three cocker spaniels. *Son-in-law Simon can arrange sto
gazing visits to his farm and battlefield tours through local historian and Boer War expert, Leon.*

Rooms: 2: 1 double with en-suite shower; 1 twin with en-suite
bath & shower over bath.
Price: R450 - R500 pp sharing. Singles R460.
Meals: Full breakfast included. Dinners on request from R165 p
Directions: From Jo'burg side into Warden Street (main street)
go around church. 7 blocks from church turn R into Bell Street.
From Durban & Bloem, on entering Harrismith turn away from
Spur/Engen garage into King Street. Turn L into Warden Street at
1st stop-street. Bell Street is about 10 blocks from here on L.

Franshoek Mountain Lodge

Andrew and Christine Jaeger

Franshoek Farm, Ficksburg/Fouriesburg
Tel: 051-933-2828 Fax: 051-933-2828
Email: lodge@franshoek.co.za Web: www.franshoek.co.za
Cell: 072-128-7356

It's amazing what you can see and what you can hear when you're half way up a 70-year-old cherry tree. I wasn't scrumping, honest! Christine and Andrew were showing me their cherry orchard and insisted that I pick myself a punnet. I quickly obliged. And as the sun set over the sandstone mountains the local ladies started drumming and singing loudly. I hesitate to call them scarecrows but that is what they were actually doing… scaring off crows (a novel way to protect the crop from those cherry-loving birds). I seemed to be having one of those Greenwood Guide moments… my very own African cherry festival (and not the one this area is famous for). Back at the lodge, a pretty thatched house with views of fields, mountains and gardens from every window, the big oak table had been set (dinner and breakfast is a communal affair here), wine had been poured, fire lit and dinner was ready to be served in wholesome country portions… delightful! Post-dinner I wandered back to my peaceful suite with its two bedrooms, a shared blue-tiled bathroom and my own free-standing vintage bathtub. Delight morphed seamlessly into sleep. The next morning, as the resident turtle doves cooed me along to breakfast, I imagined myself living in this gorgeous and remote valley too. I'd learn to play polo (there are two fields here), I'd keep fit with runs in the Witteberge Mountains and swim circular laps of the circular pool. I'd ride to town in the donkey cart and unwind in the thatched Lesotho steam hut. Like Andrew, I too, "just love this place".

Rooms: 6 suites, 3 doubles with en-suite bathroom, 3 doubles each with own separate bathroom and additional bedroom.
Price: R440 pp sharing B&B. Singles on request. R580 pp sharing dinner, bed and breakfast.
Meals: Light lunches on request.
Directions: Signed off R26 betw' Fouriesburg & Ficksburg. 23km south of Fouriesburg on R26, take S385 on R (10km of dirt rd) or 8km north of Ficksburg on R26 take S384 on L (12km on dirt rd).

Die Ou Stal

Piet and Zenobia Labuchagné
38 George Street, Zastron
Tel: 051-673-1268 Fax: 051-673-1268
Email: dieoustal@tiscali.co.za
Cell: 082-416-7832

In a place like Zastron, it's vital to find yourself a guide to show you the unknown gems that lur around every corner and to recount the astonishing tales of yesteryear. Look no further than Pie His enthusiasm for the geology and pre-history of Africa is infectious. After the whistle-stop tou of intriguing local rock formations, spiced up with ancient bushman legends, I'll never look at a c face in the same way again. Had I stayed longer, I'd have been begging him to take me on a da trip to nearby Lesotho, but alas I had to leave even before one of Zen's delicious suppers bobotie or chicken pie. At least I had time to sit on the stoep outside the converted stables th are now the guest rooms and watch a lightning storm hammer away at the Lesotho mountain – a majestic sight indeed. The bedrooms are simple, cosy affairs with whitewashed walls an doors that open into a small kitchen. Breakfast, however, is served at the large dining table in th main house, atop wooden floorboards and next to a fridge surely dating from before fridges wer invented (also wood): this intriguing feature is now a drinks cabinet. In a town that's won awarc for its friendliness (driving around with Piet, the whole town and his uncle Joe came out to giv us a wave), Zen is champion of champions.

Rooms: 2: 1 double with en-suite bath and shower; 1 twin with en-suite shower.
Price: R300 - R400 pp sharing.
Meals: Full breakfast included. Dinner on request: R150 pp.
Directions: From N6 turn onto R26 and follow signs to Zastror In town, turn right opposite the corner of the church into Mathee Street, then take third left into Berg Strat and see signs.

Artists' Colony B&B

Robert and Susan Jewell
3 Church Street, Smithfield
Tel: 051-683-1138 Fax: 051-683-1138
Email: colony@global.co.za Web: www.artistscolony.co.za

For service to weary travellers like me, Robert and Susan deserve knighthoods. After a long trip through the Free State mountains, I reached the serene 'oasis' of Smithfield and spotted, with relief, the calming yellow-and-white walls of the Artists' Colony peeping out from behind verdant greenery, heralding the end of my day's journey. Along with the welcoming tea Susan slipped into my hand, the house's high yellowwood ceilings and wooden floors were as soothing balms to my hotness and bother. The original settlers knew all the tricks to keeping a Karoo-style house cool. Three of the rooms are across the wide road behind a rich curtain of roses, lilies and irises in a building declared a national monument. Each has its own little quirk, whether the maroons and greens of the Birdcage Room, or the East African hair salon advert for all manner of (slightly outdated) haircuts in the Barber Shop room. The original Oregon floorboards creak as you walk on them and the door frames have their own shape! But don't worry – tie rods hold the sun-baked bricks firmly together. All this is part of the delightful charm of Artists' Colony - true 1848 heritage accommodation transformed into a real gem by the wonderfully hospitable and aptly-named Jewells - and I fell instantly in love with it. Being almost exactly in the centre of South Africa, close to the N1 and on the Friendly N6, you will undoubtedly have passed by on some trip or another. Next time don't pass by, drop in. This is a special place to stay.

Rooms: 4: 2 queens, with en-suite bath and shower; 2 twins with en-suite bath and shower. All rooms have aircon, fridges, fans and tea and coffee.
Price: R375 - R400 per person sharing. Single rate on application.
Meals: Full breakfast included.3-course dinner, available on request R90. Local restaurants nearby.
Directions: Travelling south on N1, take exit 177 at Bloemfontein onto the Friendly N6 and it is approx. 120km to Smithfield. Travelling north on N1, take exit 8 to Gariep Dam and then onto the R701 and it is approx. 115km to Smithfield. In Smithfield, turn into Church Street opposite the church.

Map Number: 12

Entry Number: 232

Lesotho

Malealea Lodge and Pony Trek Centre

Michael & Debbie Deutschmann
Malealea
Tel: 082-552-4215 Fax: 0866-481-815
Email: malealea@mweb.co.za Web: www.malealea.com
Cell: 082-552-4215

"Where are you heading?" asked the border official. "Malealea," I replied nervously. She smiled, "You'll enjoy it there." Here in the heartland of mountainous Lesotho where blanket-clad shepherds watch over their flocks, the Jones family have created a fascinating environment through a combination of their own personal warmth, native knowledge and a wealth of natural and cultural attractions. Malealea thrives on its genuine interaction with the neighbouring village and I arrived just as the choir was starting up, followed by a band playing home-made instruments with wonderful exuberance. The pony trekking centre is run entirely by the locals, who will take you on treks for up to six days (you stay in the villages you visit), and children lead you to waterfalls and rock art. Communal suppers are served canteen style - backpackers and ambassadors rub comradely shoulders – before the pub and Glenn's singing around the fire lure you away. When the generator stops, your torch guides you back to thatched rondavel or farmhouse-style accommodation. I woke to the unmistakable cries of peacocks ringing out of the early-morning mist lying low in the valleys. I loved this place. Suddenly your trip just got longer.

Rooms: 40 Basotho rondavels & farmhouse en-suite rooms, 12 doubles & 28 twins, all with shower en-suite.
Price: Rondavels R300 pp sharing, farmhouses R240 pp sharing. Single supplement 50%. Overnight horse treks R370 - R400 pp per day. Village accommodation R80 pp. Day rides from R175 pp.
Meals: Breakfast R70 pp. Lunch R80 pp. Dinner R120 pp. Four communal kitchens available.
Directions: Faxed or emailed on booking.

Northern Cape

Kuilfontein Stable Cottages

Penny and Leigh Southey

Kuilfontein Farm, Route N1, Colesberg
Tel: 051-753-1364 Fax: 051-753-0200
Email: kuil@mweb.co.za Web: www.kuilfontein.co.za
Cell: 082-552-2488

A drink is always welcome in the middle of the blazing Karoo and I was gasping when Penny poured mine in the chilled-out guest lounge. Kuilfontein has been in Leigh's family for five generations and is still a busy dairy and sheep farm. Surrounded by a vast hinterland of arid fields it's hard to believe it's only 1.2 kilometres from the N1. The white-washed Stable bedrooms are all named after racehorses, the theme continuing inside with newspaper clippings and framed shots of 'Danny Boy' or 'Equilateral' (among others) in action. French doors lead from your own verandah onto gleaming screed floors sporting locally-made furniture, as well as the odd family heirloom, while brightly-coloured walls and fine-quality linen create a homely feeling. The 'Feed Room' has been appropriately converted into a dining/breakfast room where resident chef, Maryke, produces tantalising meals from the organic produce on the farm. 'Home-grown' Karoo lamb, venison and fresh cream from the dairy are used in conjunction with cactus fruit and other Karoo specialities. Pre-dinner drinks are taken in the bar with its upside-down trough counter and a great selection of wines are available in an old feed bin. A tall wicker stool is the perfect spot to park yourself for cheerful banter, beverages and hilarity. Coffee and liqueurs are served under the spectacular starry skies. For the more energetic there is a spring-water swimming pool, boules and bird-watching. A popular stop-over point, but this farmstead is worth staying a lot longer for. *Children over 6 are welcome.*

Rooms: 8: 5 standard double bedrooms, 2 luxury double rooms and 1 family suite, all with en-suite showers.
Price: R405 – R495p.p. R90 single supplement. Children 6+ on request.
Meals: Full 'health' breakfast included. 3-course dinners: R150 - R170.
Directions: 12km south of Colesberg, 60km north of Hanover on N1. Look for Kuilfontein sign. If you are flying they have a 1300m airstrip on the property. The runway co-ordinates are as follows. Kuilfontein, S 30 49 04,86 E 024 59 37,05.

Map Number: 5

Entry Number: 234

Langberg Guest Farm

Paul & Hannelize Neethling
Beaconsfield, Kimberley
Tel: 053-832-1001 Fax: 086-601-1210
Email: getaway@langberg.co.za Web: www.langberg.co.za
Cell: 073-338-7314

After hours on the Northern Cape's driest and openest road I finally scooted up the driveway Langberg, a smooth transition from the deeply inhospitable to the deeply hospitable. Langberg something of an oasis. It took a while for my eyes to adjust from wide-screen 'drive' mode, b soon I was able to focus and attend to the details that welcomed me: wild flowers, reclaimed far equipment effectively 're-zoned' as garden sculpture, a pretty courtyard contained within th white stone walls of this historic Cape Dutch farm… and, of course, Paul and Hanneliz Langberg's delightful owners. Langberg has been in the Neethling family since 1940. Formerly horse farm it now breeds game. The stables have in their turn been transformed and today hou guests in big brass beds, vintage en-suite bathrooms… and in great comfort too. Guests a encouraged to use the farm's short hiking trail (part of the battle of Magersfontein (Boers vs Britis was fought on the farm and the hiking trail takes you to one of the Boer cannon position observe antelope and buffalo at the water trough and even go out on the afternoon game/feedi drive. As the warm evening drew in, I settled down in the courtyard to an alfresco chicken dinn and a traditional South African dessert of malva pudding. An early start meant that I would ha to eschew morning delights from the farm's kitchen, but Paul made sure I was sent on my journ with a huge packed breakfast… which was enough for lunch too!

Rooms: 11: The Stables: 4 doubles & 1 twin with en-suite bath; The Kraal: 6 self-catering/family units with en-suite shower.
Price: R150 to R420 per person sharing.
Meals: Breakfast, lunch and dinner available on request. Braai packs R95.
Directions: 22km south of Kimberley on the N12 Sign-posted. Look out for white wall on right-hand side when coming from Kimberley (left-hand side when driving towards Kimberley).

Mattanu Private Game Reserve

Jacques Kriek

Near Barkley West, Kimberley
Tel: 083-235-1993
Email: info@mattanu.com Web: www.mattanu.com

Dig deep into the wild Kalahari bushveld to discover an absolute diamond of a game reserve. Allow me to list some of the many reasons to visit: 2,300 hectares of indigenous camel thorns, black monkey thorns, raisin bushes, inhabited by 36 species of game (antelope, zebra, giraffe), watched over by fish eagles and cory bustards; a family passionate about wildlife conservation, from protecting rare roan and sable antelope to a breeding programme for disease-free buffalo; the chance to swoop down into the bush by helicopter and get hands-on with game captures and treatment; five stunningly luxurious 'tents', all champagne and chocolates, carved wooden beds, jacuzzi baths, under-floor heating and air-con (yes, it gets that hot - and that cold) (I don't think the word 'tent' quite gets across how nice these are!). Where was I?... Oh yes. Dinners (courtesy of Jacques' mother Daleen and Zimbabwean chef Lass) in the smart thatched lodge with its huge shaded verandah and two braais, with wine from the cellar downstairs. You can also dine deep in the bush, transported to and from table by helicopter. There's a swimming pool which laps around a sundowner spot; a tree-house lapa and viewing deck overlooking a water-hole. And the rest. Jacques knows this area intimately, so ask him about diamond tours, fly fishing, quad-bikes... and Kimberley's star attraction, the truly impressive Big Hole. A place to live out game-ranger fantasies – but with a reassuringly serious side.

Rooms: 5 luxury tents: double/twin with en-suite shower & jacuzzi bath.
Price: Tents: R1,490 pp sharing. Rates include breakfast, dinner and 2 game drives. Helicopter game safari/capture: R570.
Meals: Dinner and breakfast included in rate (alcohol extra). Other meals and snacks available during the day. Bush dinner (additional to helicopter safari) R250.
Directions: 58km north-west of Kimberley near Barkley-west. Call for directions. Helicopter/vehicle pick-ups possible from Kimberley airport.

Papkuilsfontein Guest Farm

Willem and Mariëtte van Wyk
Nieuwoudtville
Tel: 027-218-1246 Fax: 086-573-1246
Email: info@papkuilsfontein.com Web: www.papkuilsfontein.com

Well, this is certainly up there among the most memorable places to stay in South Africa! For starters, you stay in an old stone cottage, high up on the summit of a wild mountain plateau surrounded by rich geological rock formations, fynbos vegetation (including huge taaibos and kraaibos shrubs, wild olives, restios, sonkwas reeds) and bouncing dassies, not another human in sight and no mountains to break the golden horizon. The quality of peace and stillness defeat description. Gas-fired plumbing for baths, hurricane lamps for light - many guests have refused to return if the van Wyks install electricity (although there's a restored corrugated-iron cottage for those who can't do without). Then there's the small matter of the gorge and waterfall. Your jaw will drop 180 metres into the canyon. In winter, when the water runs, take picnics to the swimmable rock pools above the falls. Alternatively, opt for a quick plunge in the bore-hole water dam between the cottages. Spring's wild flowers are sensational here even by Namaqualand standards; the plantlife - part Cape fynbos, part Karoo succulent - a botanist's dream; steenbok, klipspringer and porcupine can be sighted hopping about if you look carefully. Alrie and her mother Petru are excellent cooks (breakfast is a string of surprises) and can set up hearty farm suppers in your cottage. It's a magically secluded retreat that few people know about and the van Wyks are lovely, helpful hosts. Stay at least two nights.

Rooms: 3 stone cottages: Rondekraal sleeps 2 (1 double) with bath & outside shower; De Hoop sleeps 4 with bath & outside shower; & Gert Boom sleeps 4 (2 more beds for kids if needed), with 2 bathrooms, each with shower only.
Price: From Aug 2012: R350 pp sharing. Minimum per cottage pn in flower season (without meals): Gert Boom R1,400, De Hoop R850 & Rondekraal R820; kids u/12 half-tariff, u/2 free.
Meals: Full breakfast R110. 3-course dinners R215, 2-course dinners R160. Self-catering facilities in cottages.
Directions: From CT take N1 then N7 to Vanrhynsdorp. Turn off onto R27 to Nieuwoudtville. Turn right into town, and straight through onto dirt road for 22km. The farm is signed to the right. GPS co-ordinates S31 33.548 E19 10.978

Entry Number: 237   Map Number:

Naries Namakwa Retreat

Julene Hamman

27km from Springbok (N7), on the way to Kleinzee (on R355),
Namakwaland Tel: 027-712-2462 (reception) or 0861-99-1118
(reservations) Fax: 086-766-3915
Email: reservations@naries.co.za Web: www.naries.co.za

27km from Springbok, Naries is set in the heart of Namaqualand, with its beautiful plains scenery, its arid mountains and its magical seasonal flower display – 600 species. Among the varied options for accommodation, the most spectacular are the three Namakwa Mountain Suites, which have been constructed on the edge of a high escarpment with an eagle's eye view of the dramatic and barren mountains that march off to the sea 70km away at Kleinzee. The architecture is in the form of a domed Nama-dwelling-styled cottage and is perfectly integrated with the round granite kopies of the area. Their exterior simplicity, however, is deceptive, for the interiors are vast and luxurious, while retaining some natural features: the almost woven texture of the walls of the cottage, for example, and the bare rocks which erupt into the space as bed-heads or in the sublime bathrooms. The old Cape Dutch manor, where dinners are served, also houses some fine bedrooms. The house is painted in plain colours, which offset the 1930s furniture perfectly. A short stroll from the manor, two new family self-catering cottages offer a Cape country style and an embarrassment of space, mountain views and braai facilities. *Naries recommends various day excursions to explore the beauty of Namakwaland: 4x4 Shipwreck Experience, Goegap Nature Reserve, Namakwa and Richtersveld National Parks. Also, make sure you book well in advance for the desert flower season! But advance booking is always essential.*

Rooms: 10: 3 Namakwa Mountain Suites with en-suite bathrooms; 5 Manor House rooms with en-suite bathrooms; 2 family self contained cottages with en-suite bath & shower, sleeps max 4.
Price: Dinner, B&B: Mountain Suites R1,075 – R1,590 pp sharing; Manor Hse R750 – R1,110 pp; Self contained family cottages: R325 – R435 pp (aged 5 - 11 R175 – R200). Ask for singles & specials.
Meals: 3-course dinner & breakfast included in rates of Namakwa Mountain Suites & Manor House.
Directions: 27km from Springbok (N7), on your way to Kleinzee on tarred road (R355).

Map Number: 9

A Riviera Garden B&B

Anneke Malan

16 Budler Street, Upington
Tel: 054-332-6554 Fax: 054-332-6554
Email: ariviera@upington.co.za Web: www.upington.co.za/ariviera
Cell: 072-447-6750

Riviera is a true slice of paradise on the banks of the impressive Orange River, a place that ha: given Anneke and her guests a lifetime of pleasure. Considering its position in Upington's ci centre, its riverside setting is particularly special. It was the garden, though, that I loved above a a lush parade of palm trees, roses and agapanthus and racing-green grass that cools even the mo overheated of travellers (as I certainly was when I visited). The lawn flows like a tributary past th pool, right to the water's edge and a secluded white bench at the end of the garden, the perfe spot to sit and contemplate the river's flowing depths. It's from here that guests hop onto a cruis boat at six o'clock for evening river trips, bobbing downstream, washing down the sunset with G&T before ambling into town for some dinner (ask Anneke to reserve one of her favouri restaurants for you). The evenings can be as hot as the days in this part of the world and you'll b glad to find the two cool air-conditioned garden rooms hidden among the greenery with the hefty beds and bags of cupboard space for longer stays. Another major draw at Riviera are th scrumptious and beautifully-presented breakfasts. Upington is a gateway to the Kalahari Dese and Namibia with vineyards and national parks and lots to keep you busy. It's a must-do stop o any tour of the unspoiled Northern Cape – especially for those who love birds, gardens ar nature. And A Riviera Garden B&B typifies all that is great and good about the region.

Rooms: 2: 1 twin with bath and shower, 1 double with extra single and bath.
Price: R350 pp sharing. Singles on request.
Meals: Full English breakfast R85. Restaurants nearb'
Directions: Follow main roads right into the centre of Upington. From Schröder St turn onto River St towards the river. This leads into Budler St and Riviera is number 16 on the right about halfway dow the street. Safe parking in garage.

A la Fugue

Jacqueline Castella
40 Jangroentjieweg, Upington
Tel: 054-338-0424 Fax: 054-338-0084
Email: a-la-fugue@mweb.co.za Web: www.lafugue-guesthouse.com
Cell: 082-789-9324

Chaud, hot, heiss! Upington was knocking on almost 40°C when I visited, so Jacqueline definitely had the right idea, meeting me at the car in a pink swimming costume and sarong. Positively melting after hours on the road I was invited to flump myself down on a plant-shaded pillow by the pool and was fed a glass of iced tea. What initially struck me about A la Fugue, as I was led along a rose-lined and plant-dotted path, was the tropical garden, absolutely dazzling in the intense sunshine. Named after great composers, each of La Fugue's bungalows has their own unique identity. Rossini and Rusticana, two quaint wooden chalets, seem to originate from the Swiss element of your host, while studio bungalow Mozart and family unit Vivaldi perhaps embody the classic French side. The two B&B rooms in the house (Chopin and Bach), soothing in golds and creams, are found along a short landing where Jacqueline's stunning model daughter beams warmly from the wall. Jacqui's gourmet dinners and breakfasts, touched with a little foreign pizazz, are served outside on one of the bright mosaic tables (your hostess has a distinct flair for mosaics and you will find examples in many unexpected places). It's a good thing that each room has its own outdoor seating area as with such a garden you won't want to sit inside. Personally I would rarely be found far from the thatched African-themed poolside lapa and loungers. *Jacqueline is fluent in French, English and German.*

Rooms: 5: 2 self-catering studios, 1 self-catering family unit, 2 B&B dble rooms All en s sh'r & own entrances.
Price: R250–R400 pp sharing for B&B. Ask about singles & self-catering prices. Breakfast-brunch for self-caterers: additional R80 pp. Extra bed R80.
Meals: Full breakfast incl' in B&B rate. For self-caterers, breakfast/brunch on request at R80 pp. Gourmet dinners on request (with 24 hrs notice), R340 pp incl' all wine & drinks.
Directions: In Upington take Schröder St towards Olifantshoek, N14, under rail bridge past Gordonia hospital. 1.7 km after hospital, R at Engen garage. L (Groenpunt Rd). From Bi-Lo (left), count 4 streets on R till Jangtroentjieweg. GPS coordinates: 28d26m25.1s E / 21d17m40.8s S

Map Number: 10

Browns Manor

Heidi Brown

N14 Olifantshoek Road, Upington
Tel: 054-338-0384 Fax: 054-338-0505
Email: heidi@brownsmanor.co.za Web: www.brownsmanor.co.za
Cell: 082-577-3749

Planted amidst the red sands of the Kalahari, Browns appears as an oasis where the palms grow tall, the lawns sprout extensively and among the many rock pools hundreds of giant koi carp cavort prodigiously. With the thermometer touching 35 degrees, I was warmly welcomed by Heidi, the eponymous owner of Brown's and embodiment of the guesthouse's cool, calming air. Meanwhile, Bonni the butler was on hand to relieve me of my luggage in exchange for an energy-reviving coke from the honesty bar. "What you see is what you get", beamed Heidi as we chatted in the shaded outdoor lounge adjacent to vine-topped verandahs and the most enticing of swimming pools overlooking the surrounding sandveld. Inside, sports fans reclined on chesterfields honing in on a rugby-field-sized flat-screen TV. I opted for a siesta in the confines of my sleek air-conditioned room where mahogany brown furniture, striped armchairs and the odd modern art canvas soothed body and soul. Once revived, I nipped into town for an Orange River sundowner cruise before returning to find Heidi's husband, Stephen, centre stage at the pool-side braai. 40 Upingtonians and one GG inspector revelled in an Afrikaans feast of boerewors and chops before sampling chef Wiliana's paradisiacal pavlova. The next morning, a stroll past a frog breeding pond, a shaded hammock, bonding lovebirds and a kids' trampoline took us to the meerkat manor. Just like Heidi's guests, these small entertaining mammals appear entirely at home in such luscious surrounds.

Rooms: 9: 3 king/twin (all en-s bath & shower); 2 queen (1 en-s bath & shower; 1 en-s shower); 3 double (all en-s shower); 1 3/4 bed (en-s shower).
Price: From R600 - R1,000 pp sharing. Singles from R700 - R1,200.
Meals: Full breakfast included. Lunch and dinner available from a la carte menu at extra cost.
Directions: From Upington, follow signs for N14 towards Olifantshoek & Johannesburg. Drive past the casino on your left and Nabu Lodge on your right. Browns Manor is on the right-hand side.

Gauteng

Melrose Place Guest Lodge

Sue Truter

12a North St, Melrose/Johannesburg
Tel: 011-442-5231 Fax: 011-880-2371
Email: info@melroseplace.co.za Web: www.melroseplace.co.za
Cell: 083-457-4021

Once ensconced behind the electric gates at Melrose you have entered an Eden-in-the-city. The verandah overlooks a large flower garden and enormous swimming pool, all shaded by trees. Eight new rooms don't crowd it at all. It is such a pleasant environment that you may find yourself shelving projected tasks for a day's lounging about. My room was a suite attached to the main house, with mounted TV, huge bed (built up with cushions and pillows), a big bathroom and double doors onto the garden. The high levels of luxury in all the rooms are not reflected in the rates. Sue is the sweetest of hostesses, quick to smiles and reacting sensitively to the mood and wishes of each guest. On the night I stayed we had a braai with an amazing array of meat dishes and salads which appeared from nowhere and Sue's team will cook dinner or, if the mood dictates, a braai for anyone who wants it. Her aim is to maximise the number of happy campers staying. This is her home after all, complete with dachshund and a talking parrot in its 50s. While guest contentment is running at 100 per cent, it's difficult to see what else she can do. *Laundry provided on request. Complimentary gym access and unlimited internet access available. Nearby Wanderers cricket ground, Melrose Arch, Rosebank and Sandton shopping/business precincts and many restaurants. Airport transfers arranged by Sue.*

Rooms: 30: 12 premium suites; 18 classic rooms. All king/twin. All en-suite. All with garden patios/balconies.
Price: R700 - R900 pp sharing. Singles R1,150 - R1,500. Airport transfers arranged by Sue.
Meals: Full breakfast included. Lunches and dinners by arrangement. Rosebank and Sandton shopping precincts and many restaurants nearby.
Directions: Ask for a map when booking. Or a map is on the web site.

Kashan Country House

Peter Curle (owner), Wilna Bekker (manager)

Portion I Farm, Steynshoop, Hekpoort
Tel: 014-576-1035
Email: reservations@kashanhouse.co.za Web: www.kashanhouse.co.za
Cell: 082-552 4876

From the Cradle of Humankind, and barely out of first gear, I followed the steep and winding track up to civilisation. And you don't get much more civilised than Kashan. A pretty thatched house sat beneath the Magaliesberg mountains with 'top-notch' views of the lush ancient valley. I had come home (not just historically!) or so I was made to feel by Wilna and the team. Within minutes my bags had been unloaded into my pristine, white, four-postered bedroom and I was gliding around in no fewer than 22 metres of infinity pool. Peter's friends thought he was 'mad' to install such a massively luxurious pool. Well I think he's a genius! I whiled away the afternoon spying on birds and monkeys through the lodge telescope, toyed with the idea of investigating the hiking trail up the mountain or having a game of croquet out on the lawn (I told you it was civilised here). But instead I opted for a sprawling chill-out on the sofa with books, movies and tea (I felt totally at home). An unforgettable sunset brought nightfall, together with a nocturnal amphibian choir, Peter, back from the city, and a three-course gourmet dinner prepared by the highly-skilled resident chef – cigar optional! Peter hand-picked the delicate yellowwood furnishings, commissioned the construction of two outside showers and insisted on high-spec mattresses to ensure his guests the best night sleep this side of the equator. It's not often you come across perfect equilibrium, but Kashan House with its luxury, relaxed hospitality, historic views and fantastic food might just have achieved it.

Rooms: 9: 4 luxury rooms with king-size extra-length beds & en-s bath & shower (2 rooms have additional outside shower); 5 standard doubles (3 en-s bath & shower, 2 en-s shower).
Price: R665 – R850 pp sharing. Singles R945 – R1,050 pp. Price includes breakfast.
Meals: 3-course dinner R220. Lunches on request
Directions: See website for detailed directions.

Abloom

Carmen Tecklenburg & Lowie Geenevasen
Klipfontein K118, Cullinan
Tel: 012-734-0555
Email: info@abloom.co.za Web: www.abloom.co.za
Cell: 076-840-2863

"All luxury spa retreats are created equal," spake George Orwell's lesser-known, better-groomed more relaxed sister. "But some luxury spa retreats are more equal than others." She was indubitab deferring to Abloom, a bush spa where relaxation and luxury combine so sublimely that I'd go ou on a lavender-oiled limb and coin a term for what happens here: reluxuriation! Carmen and Lowi - she a trained beauty therapist and pamper-me junkie, he an adman-turned-chef - designed an built Abloom with their nimble Dutch hands just outside Cullinan, the quaint, historic mining tow where, in 1905, the world's largest diamond was found. Four divine, wholly private, high-ceilinge stone-and-thatch chalets pepper 27 red-earth hectares of wild, sweet-smelling African bush. Sturc partial walls divide bedroom, lounge, kitchen and bathroom, giving each earthy abode a decaden sense of space, while chunky French windows haul in vast private outside areas, bush shower an hot plunge pool included, thanks very much. Indulgent treatments take place in-chalet, so m masseuse Sonto propped her table on my sunny stoep, pummelling the sticky drive from Jozi ou of me with Abloom's signature African wood massage. And the next morning, after the dreamie slumber imaginable, Carmen furnished my al fresco table with Lowie's exquisite nouvelle cuisine, breakfast almost too picturesque to devour, but too delicious to simply photograph (from 4 different angles). Abloom is Cullinan's second biggest diamond.

Rooms: 4 fully-serviced chalets: all with XL king, bath dble shower, outside shower, fully-equipped kitchen, fireplace, living area, outside dining area, braai & heated plunge pool.
Price: Executive Suite R1,895 or Presidential Suite R2,195 per night on a self-catering basis.
Meals: Full gourmet breakfast (R115) & 3-course gourmet dinner (R395), served in-suite, available if pre-booked.
Directions: From Pretoria take N4 east. Take Rayton/Cullinan off-ramp, L into R515/R483. Drive fc 27km, through Rayton, past Cullinan (do not turn L into Cullinan), onto dirt rd for 5km. L at Abloom sign & continue 2km to farm.

Soweto

Introduction by Ross Bowers

Lots of tourists come for the day, but if you really want to get under the skin of the South West Township, then staying over is a must. Soweto is a 50-square-mile labyrinth, so getting lost is a distinct possibility. Your tour guide can drop you off at the guest-house and arrange transport to one of the funky local restaurants where extensive wine lists sit comfortably alongside samp 'n' beans, tripe, mutton curry and other Sowetan favourites. There are, of course, many shanty dwellings and much extreme poverty, but there are also tree-lined streets, impressive houses and bustling wide main roads. As you'd expect in a place crammed with an unofficial total of over four million, there's a lot to see. Our selected trio of B&Bs are within 20 metres of each other in the heart of the Vilikazi district of Orlando West, a vibrant, culturally-rich destination. Simon really wanted me to see the Hector Pieterson Museum and I was moved to tears as the reality of the 'struggle' and extreme injustices of the past glared me straight in the eye. If time permits, get yourself to the Chris Hani Baragwanath Hospital, the largest hospital in the world, as well as the Regina Mundi Church. After a truly eye-opening day, I relaxed over an apéritif in the Rusty Bar at the trendy Soweto Hotel in Freedom Square, Kliptown. I recommend you do likewise.

There are a couple of tour guides that we heartily recommend (see below for their contact details). The gentle and genial Simon Mosikare of Soweto Guided Tours kindly picked me up from Oliver Tambo Airport and drove me straight into Soweto. We've also been with Vhupo Tours, run by David Luthaga, a friendly bear of a man with a laugh that could shake Soweto's infamous power station. "You will see all of Soweto. The good, the bad and the very ugly, nothing will be hidden," was his opening gambit. And, true to his word, David showed us Diepkloof Extension, the millionaire's row also known as Diepkloof Expensive. He then handed us over to Reginald who walked with us around the squatter camp Motsoaldi, a patchwork of corrugated iron and wooden planks that he calls home. David emphasised that wherever we were, especially in the squatter camps, the inhabitants expected us to take photos so that people worldwide could witness their living conditions. This attitude stems from pre-Apartheid days, when images from the Sowetan uprising of 1976 galvanised worldwide outcry and it put paid to any concerns that I had over voyeurism.

Vhupo Tours
David Luthaga
www.vhupo-tours.com
info@vhupo-tours.com
011-936-0411

Soweto Guided Tours
Simon Mosikare
www.sowetoguidedtours.co.za
info@sowetoguidedtours.co.za
011-985-6249
083-324-2096

For more information look out for the Soweto Township Complete Guide, published by Soweto Spaza and sold in the shop outside Nelson Mandela's former house on Vilakazi St. On the way in or out of Soweto, be sure to visit the Apartheid Museum near Gold Reef City in Ormonde.

Vhavenda Hills Bed and Breakfast

Kate Luthaga
11749 Mampuru St, Orlando West, Soweto
Tel: 011-936-4275 Fax: 086-503-0469
Email: vhavendahills@iburst.co.za Web: www.sowetobnb.co.za
Cell: 082-213-1630

Soweto born and bred, Kate lives just down the road from Nelson Mandela's old house in the Vilakazi precinct of Orlando West – one of Soweto's numerous suburbs, better known as "The Wild West" during the apartheid years. The great man himself popped round for tea after his release from Robben Island. Clean, white art deco lines make Vhavenda one of the standout properties in the neighbourhood. It is very much a family home with pictures of Kate's children around the TV and friends of various offspring popping in and out. Kate's husband David grew up in the property which they converted into a B&B over 10 years ago. He runs the burgeoning Vhupo Tours from his office in one of the back rooms. The bedrooms are comfortable with magnolia walls, baby-blue hues and multi-coloured coverlets. From 2010 they also have new beds and dazzling custom-made checkered headboards to compliment Kate's dashing decor. Ask for the palatial double room with its bath on a plinth and pair of double beds where I fell asleep to the sound of cicadas and the buzz of Johannesburg traffic in the far distance, before waking to the smell of sizzling bacon. An easy stroll to the Hector Pieterson museum, Mandela House and the superb Sakhumzi and Nambitha restaurants.

Rooms: 4: 1 king/ twin with en/s bath & shower, 1 king/ twin with en/s shower over bath and separate loo, 1 twin double beds with en/s bath and shower, 1 queen with en/s shower.
Price: R350 - R400 pp sharing. R400 - R450 singles.
Meals: Cooked breakfast, plus yoghurt and cereal included. Dinner on request at R120 - R150 pp.
Directions: Arrange a pick-up from Johannesburg, though directions are available on website.

Dakalo B&B

Dolly Hlophe

6963 Inhlwathi St, Orlando West, Soweto
Tel: 011-936-9328 Fax: 086-661-7282
Email: dakalobandb@iburst.co.za or info@dakalobedandbreakfast.co.za
Web: www.dakalobedandbreakfast.co.za Cell: 082-723-0585

The term 'township chic' was invented for Dolly's B&B. I loved the bathroom tiled with blue spotted mosaics and the rooms with their red quilts, mini-Zulu shields, strawberry table-cloth and zebra print curtains, hand-made by Dolly. Not only is she a wizard on the sewing-machine but she is also heavily involved with the local tourism association, setting a high standard with her own guesthouse. She and Kate from nearby Vhavenda were off to a hospitality seminar at one of the Southern Sun hotels on the day I arrived. Not that these ladies need any tips! With opera playing in the background and freshly-cut arum lilies on the front table, the house exudes calm. Outside guests can sit under the lapa, or admire Dolly's garden, where geraniums sprout from potjie cooking pots and pink bougainvillaea crawls up the walls. You are right in the heart of where history was made in Soweto, particularly when Dolly can count two Nobel Peace Prize winners (Desmond Tutu and Nelson Mandela) among her neighbours. She has some astonishing stories herself of 'the struggle' and is a short walk away from the fascinating Hector Pieterson Memorial and museum. Or, if you're interested in the latest chapter in this extraordinary area's history, the impressive soccer city stadium, which hosted the 2010 World Cup final, is a fifteen-minute ride on the new bright-red Rea Vaya bus service.

Rooms: 4: 3 king/twin; 1 twin. All with en/s shower.
Price: R350 - R400 pp sharing. R400 - R450 singles.
Meals: Full English breakfast. Evening meals on request for R120 - R150.
Directions: Arrange pick-up in Johannesburg.

Nthateng's B&B

Nthateng Motaung

6991 Inhlwathi St, Orlando West, Soweto
Tel: 011-936-2676 Fax: 086-600-5141
Email: info@nthateng.co.za or nthateng@iburst.co.za
Web: www.nthateng.co.za Cell: 082 335-7956

Snappily dressed in tight jeans and gold jewellery, the glamorous Nthateng happily took the time to talk to me about the history of Soweto before insisting that I accompany her to the wedding down the road between a Zulu man and a Swazi woman. "Everyone's invited," she said. Between the tribal colours and shaking dancers, Nthateng sat me down with some fried chicken and samp, washed down with a glass of sparkling ginger (apparently it wouldn't be a proper wedding without it!). Then it was back for a tour of her own place. Optical lighting illuminates the up-to-the-minute sandy-coloured rooms that boast carved wooden bedheads inlaid with red and gold mosaics. One double room also houses a vast Louis XIV-style dressing table; it's not hard to imagine Marie Antoinette perched on the ornate seat, powdering her wig and applying beauty spots. See Soweto in style – not only is Nthateng's close to the museums and restaurants, but insist that she takes you backstage on Soweto TV. It's a hub of creativity, the crew are really friendly and their studios are located just a couple of blocks up adjacent to a talented seamstress and an inspiring art school for children. With the Hector Pieterson Memorial, Nelson Mandela's house and Soccer City also within easy striking distance Nthateng attests "people must stay in Soweto for two or three nights to get the full experience". Later on, after revelling in an evening of live music and high-energy dancing at the Soweto Beer Festival I'd gladly move in for a week.

Rooms: 5: 2 queens, 1 king and 2 twins. All en/s.
Price: R350 - R400 pp sharing. R400 - R450 for singles.
Meals: Full cooked breakfast is included. Evening meals available on request for R120 - R150.
Directions: Arrange a pick-up from Johannesburg. Nthateng can also arrange airport transfers for R450 (daytime) - R550 (at night).

North-West Province

Mosetlha Bush Camp and Eco Lodge

Chris, June and Caroline Lucas
Madikwe Game Reserve
Tel: 011-444-9345
Fax: 011-444-9345
Email:
info@thebushcamp.com
Web: www.thebushcamp.com
Cell: 083-305-7809

Mosetlha puts the wild into wilderness; no doors or glass here as they would hinder the feel and dust of Africa permeating your very core; no worries either as you leave them at the gate. Facilities are basic but real; guests draw their own hot water from a donkey-boiler before proceeding to the shower. Recently the kitchen was extended and a new thatch and stone lapa has been added for guests to read, relax and compare sightings, but the authenticity remains untainted. The wooden cabins are comfortable, but used only for sleeping - you are here for the wilderness experience of the outdoors. Chris's passion for conservation and his environment shines through and is contagious (which reminds me to say that the area is malaria-free). His guests depart much the wiser, not only because of the game drives, but also (conditions permitting) because of the superb guided wilderness walks. Yes, the Madikwe Game Reserve (70,000 hectares) has the so-called 'Big Five', but a game lodge worth its salt (such as this) will fire your imagination about the whole food chain. Even the camp itself is an education - all sorts of birds, small mammals and antelopes venture in. Come for a genuine and memorable bush experience. *Children welcome from 8 years old up.*

Rooms: 8 twins sharing 3 shower/toilet complexes.
Price: All-inclusive from R1,795 per person. Gate entrance fee and drinks from the bar extra.
Meals: All meals and refreshments (tea, coffee, fruit juice) included.
Directions: Detailed written directions supplied on request or see website.

The Bush House

Sue and Gordon Morrison

Madikwe Game Reserve
Tel: 076-694-0505 Fax: 086-678-6077
Email: camp@bushhouse.co.za Web: www.bushhouse.co.za
Cell: 083-379-6912

Sue and her husband Gordon stayed here as guests in 2006 and decided they didn't want leave… so they bought the place, along with its history. The Bush House dates back to 194 when this otherwise barren bushveld afforded no more than cattle farming and citrus fru orchards. In 1987 it was bought out by the government and incorporated into what became th 75,000 hectare Madikwe Game Reserve. Operation Phoenix the relocation of 10,000 anima into the Reserve created one of the finest conservation areas in Africa, where rare species occ naturally and over 340 species of birds have been recorded. While Sue and Gordon are hand on around the lodge, out in the bush you will be guided by Coenie or Debbie, both walkir talking, driving wildlife encyclopedias and passionate photographers. The lodge retains its structu as a farm building but has been refurbished on the inside. The bedrooms come with your ov private patio. Dining is a relaxed affair, with everyone eating together and in downtime guests c explore the grounds' nature trails on foot, leaf through one of the many David Attenborou books in the lounge, indulge in some savoury or sweet nibbles for afternoon tea or hang out o lush lawns overlooking the water-hole, which regularly refreshes all of the big five (plus wild do Having practically tickled the trunk of an inquisitive elephant on the afternoon drive we returne to sundowners in the company of four rhinos and three lions quenching their evening thirst. A the magic of Madikwe!

Rooms: 6: 2 double, 4 twins/kings all with en-suite bath and shower.
Price: From R2,750 pp sharing.
Meals: All meals included plus two game drives a day.
Directions: From Pretoria take N4 to Zeerust, the R49/47 towards Madikwe. At Madikwe turn right at the Wonderboom Gate, The Bush House is signposted 1km from entrance. Federal Air Flight als flies to the reserve daily.

Jaci's Lodges

Jan and Jaci van Heteren

Molatedi, Madikwe Game Reserve
Tel: 083-700-2071 or 083-4477-929 Fax: 086-517-5780
Email: jacisreservations@madikwe.com Web: www.madikwe.com
Cell: 083-447-7929, reservations 083-700-2071

After hurtling down dusty tracks to Madikwe and negotiating a blockade of elephants I gallivanted across the swing bridge (Indiana Jones eat your heart out) to Jaci's award-winning Safari Lodge. Built on the banks of the Marico River around old leadwood trees and a giant termite mound it could hardly be more stunningly entwined with the bush. My first mission: sundowners by the dam next to Jaci's Tree Lodge (equally striking with its rosewood tree-house suites linked by raised walkways in the canopy of a tamboti forest) where rhinos stopped by for an evening slurp and brown hyenas fought over the remnants of an earlier wild dog kill. Back at the lodge head chef Matthew presented a fillet of beef fit for any carnivore (and enough julienne veg to satisfy the most voracious of herbivores), followed by a sumptuous strawberry pana cotta. No scavenging was required. A clap of thunder heralded the season's first rains and a lightning-quick transfer from boma fire to lodge dining table where families and wonderfully attentive staff mingled excitedly. I retired to my opulent thatched suite with hippo-sized stone bath and jungle shower. Awakening to the sweet smell of the dampened bush, we headed out on 'a serious game drive'. A couple of hours tracking revealed a pride of nine lions including a pair of playful cubs. Just another 'day in the life' at Jaci's.

Rooms: Safari Lodge: 8 king/twins, 2 exclusive family suites. Tree Lodge: 8 king/twins. All with outdoor "jungle" shower.
Price: From R2,995 pp sharing. Game drives, walking safaris and meals included.
Meals: All meals and game drives included.
Directions: Only 1.5 hours' drive from Sun City or a 3.5 to 4-hour drive from Johannesburg. Daily road and air transfers from JHB and Sun City. Ask for details when booking.

Map Number: 15 Entry Number: 250

Mpumalanga

Bee Eaters Farm

John and Carol Stephen
Lowveld Agricultural College Rd (D725), Friedenheim Valley, Nelspruit
Tel: 013-755-3225 Fax: 013-748-0489
Email: info@bee-eaters.co.za Web: www.bee-eaters.co.za
Cell: 083-625-7082

Driving onto the 30 hectares that John and Carol have turned into their beloved home over the past 20 years, it was clear what had prompted the name Bee Eaters. I spotted at least 15 of these gorgeous little birds busily flitting about. Then as I turned the corner it was also apparent why the birds in their turn have chosen to reside with John and Carol. Continuing up the drive I passed a veggie garden that would turn Mr McGregor spinach-green and round the next corner was a serene water feature filled with koi carp. A feeling of great peacefulness suddenly washed over me. After drinking in the panoramic views from the huge balcony of the entertaining area, I headed down to my room beneath the litchi trees. The building of each room was a real family affair. Rich, dark-wood furniture was all hand-made by their son; their daughter created floors that resemble the scorched Sahara; and even the building bricks come from their son-in-law. Bee Eaters was born when Carol and John went into the catering business. From feeding 1,000 people to an intimate dinner for two they really have done it all. Their success and popularity encouraged them to create a full venue, which then led to the B&B. Carol says that for her it's all about quality of life. This is something she clearly wants for her guests as well.

Rooms: 10: all twin/kings with double sleeper-couch and en-suite bathroom.
Price: R440 - R670 pp sharing.
Meals: Full breakfast included. Dinner and lunch available on request.
Directions: From Jo'burg turn left onto the R40/White River Road. After 6km. Turn right onto the D725 towards Lowveld Agricultural College. Continue for 5km and you will see Bee Eaters Farm sign on your left.

Plumbago Guest House

Ilara and Robbie Robertson

R40 between White River and Hazyview
Tel: 013-737-8806 Fax: 086-607-5222
Email: plumbagoguesthouse@mweb.co.za
Web: www.plumbagoguesthouse.co.za Cell: 082-954-0467

Through wrought-iron gates at the end of a bougainvillaea-lined drive I found Plumbago, as pretti as the flower that shares its name. Set on an avocado and banana farm, it sits above the plantatio watching over it and out to Kruger Park in the distance. When I arrived, 1940s jazz was swingir out from the radio, just the right aural accompaniment to the nostalgic, colonial-inspired settin. In the drawing room and bar, an eclectic collection of antiques, paintings and rugs are intersperse with vases filled with exotic flowers and extravagant palm-leaf fans that stretch up to the ceilin. The rooms have the same casual gracefulness about them with their subtle, natural tone Jacobean print curtains, mahogany beds and abundance of vased and water-coloured flower. With a large lived-in verandah, elegant pool and sauna in the beautifully-tended garden there plenty of opportunity to relax and mull over days gone by. But what really makes this place stan apart are the Robertsons themselves. On my visit, Ilara (who honed her culinary skills cooking fc diplomats) was deciding on that evening's dinner menu while Robbie was itching to go flyir before being back for waitering duty later on. A young and active bunch, they are often busyir about doing their own thing but are more than happy to share their passions with you. *20 mir to Kruger and close to Panorama Route and God's Window. Babysitting available. Activities, gam drives, beauty treatments can be arranged with help from Ilara. Small weddings can be arranged . the garden.*

Rooms: 3 garden chalets: 1 king/twin with en-s shower; 1 king with en-s shower; 1 king extra-length sleigh-bed en-s bath. All rooms air-con heating & cooling.
Price: R680 - R950 pp sharing. Singles R840. Extra beds available on request. Pets & kids by arrangement.
Meals: Full breakfast included. Lunch & dinner on request.
Directions: From Jo'burg, take N4 to Nelspruit and then on to White River. Go on R40 to Hazyview, Plumbago is signposted on right 34km out of White River and 10km before Hazyview. A comfortable 4hrs drive from Jo'burg.

Porcupine Ridge Guest House

Janet & John Wills

5 Vanaxe Estate, Hazyview Road, Sabie-Hazyview
Tel: 082-818-0277 Fax: 086-661-4006
Email: info@porcupineridge.co.za Web: www.porcupineridge.co.za
Cell: 073-611-6349

Janet and John are sitting on a gold mine. Literally. Along with nine similar, private homes, Porcupine Ridge B&B forms an old mining village built high upon Vanaxe gold mine. Don't worry, it closed years ago. The only drilling you'll hear these days is the drilling of cuckoo on eucalyptus. After 38 years in residence, the Wills may be more South African than British, but they still chose Sabie as their retirement spot from Durban because, infinitely green and smack bang in the centre of the Panorama Route, it reminded Lancashire-born Janet of the Lake District. Sitting pretty up in the skies, Porcupine Ridge's mountainous doorstep is the active nature-lover's playground. Scenic leg-stretchers sprout from all corners of the sunny yellow house. The climb to the waterfall with deep, refreshing, swimming pools is my favourite, and George and Alice, Porcupine Ridge's resident golden retrievers, may even act as your guides. Closer to home, two acres at least of this wilderness have been tamed in the form of a beautiful 50-year-old garden. Barely a lion's roar from Kruger Park or an oar's toss from Blyde River Canyon, you couldn't get bored up here. But if exhaustion sets in, John and Janet (such affable hosts that one returning guest published and gifted them a photography book of their B&B) will be back at your cosy home-from-home, ensuring your snug, comfortably kitted-out rooms are still spic'n'span, plumping sofa cushions in the laid-back lounge, pouring terrace sundowners while you take in dramatic ridge-top views, drawing up tomorrow's itinerary.... *Children over 6 by arrangement.*

Rooms: 5: 3 queens with en-s shower; 2 kings/twin with en-s shower over bath, 1 with extra bed.
Price: R430 - R530 pp sharing. Single supplement on request.
Meals: Full breakfast (featuring unique treats such as cheesy potato pancakes, sweetcorn fritters and kedgeree) incl'. Breakfast can be packed if required.
Directions: From Jo'burg take N4. Turn left onto R539 to Sabie, L at Rosehaugh T-junction, R at Lydenburg/Sabie T-junction into Sabie. Leave Sabie on R536 Hazyview Road. After 4km, R at sign for B&B. Follow gravel road up hill for 1km.

Blue Jay Lodge

Philip and Margi Nichols

645 – 647 Blue Jay Steeg/Lane/Alley, Hazyview
Tel: 013-737-7546
Email: phil@bluejaylodge.co.za Web: www.bluejaylodge.co.za
Cell: 082-575-1798

I would have been happy enough plonked in a hippo wallow on such a hot and humid day, but Blu
Jay Lodge, a cool oasis hidden among lush, indigenous trees, was so much better! And when I sa
hidden, I really mean it. The neighbours are completely blocked out by the undergrowth ar
among all the sycamore figs and fever trees I could have been in dense rainforest. I had found m
very own tropical oasis. Sensing my heat fatigue Phil showed me to my huge room (past blossomir
orchids), switched on the air-con and invited me to take a chilled drink from the mini-fridge. A ne
calmness prevailed as I lay back on the giant bed and gazed up at the high thatched roof. A sho
walk across the screed floor was my balcony, where the braai area and swimming pool are visib
beyond the leaves of an old kiaat tree whose branches reached out to me from under th
balustrades. The Nichols are wonderful hosts and I managed to wangle myself an invite to join Ph
and his family for lamb chops and boerewors. I slept particularly well that night and was only dragge
back to consciousness by the irresistible smells of a cooked breakfast with my name on it. Sitting c
the verandah, lingering over a second cup of coffee, I watched an African paradise fly-catcher duckir
and diving between the leaves. With more than 80 bird species on offer you could easily forget th
day's activity and just sit and bird-watch at the lodge. Like I did! *No children under 14. Blue Jay Lodg
is 10 minutes from Kruger Park gates. Can organise hot-air ballooning and safari drives.*

Rooms: 5: 4 king/twin with en-suite bath and shower. I self-
catering unit with king, kitchenette and en-suite bath and shower.
Price: From R695 - R795 pp sharing. R595 - R695 for self-caterin
Meals: Full breakfast included when staying on a B&B basis.
Directions: Five-minute drive from Hazyview centre. See website
for detailed directions.

Lukimbi Safari Lodge

Sally Kernick
Kruger National Park
Tel: 011-431-1120 Fax: 011-431-3597
Email: info@lukimbi.com Web: www.lukimbi.com

The giraffes and elephants that sauntered across the road to Lukimbi Lodge were in no rush. Unfortunately I was, having missed the evening game drive already, but it is impossible (and unwise) to get irate with these wonderfully leisurely beasts. And it was just as difficult to feel any stress once I arrived at luxurious Lukimbi. While sipping a home-made lemonade the only thing I could think to write was a deeply-felt "Wow." With the sun beating down as it was that day, I lounged around on the huge deck, keeping an eye out for any game down by the river and watching the monkeys fool around on the stilts supporting us. The rooms, found down a wooden walkway past the boma, are mini-lodges themselves. They all have their own viewing decks and in my case a private plunge pool. Geckos scarpered as I jumped in and while I wallowed something about my stomach must have brought to mind the hippos doing the same thing so close by. One scrumptious supper later, during which the fellow guests gloated about what I'd missed that afternoon, we retired to beds covered by opulent mosquito nets in order to rise in time for the morning drive. To have our tea-stop interrupted by the growl of a territorial leopard is a thrill I'll never forget. It was only back at the lodge, though, that the guests spotted the biggest baddest beast of them all: me, as I guzzled the breakfast laid out for us before my sad, but inevitable, departure. *There is a crèche and activities for children are organised, while luxury walking safaris are now offered to everyone else*

Rooms: 16 suites: 14 twins and 2 kings with en-suite bathrooms with indoor and outdoor showers.
Price: R3,760 – R5,850 per person sharing. Singles available on request. Includes meals, game drives and bush walks. Children 2-12 years R2,680 - R4,150.
Meals: All meals included (breakfast, lunch/high tea and 3-course dinner).
Directions: Directions available on website.

Buckler's Africa

Cheryl and OJ Venter
Ngwenya Rd, Tenbosch, Komatipoort
Tel: 083-627-1229 Fax: 086-524-7107
Email: info@bucklersafrica.co.za Web: www.bucklersafrica.co.za
Cell: 084-400-0703

Cheryl and OJ are two of the most unshakeably laid-back, jolly people I've ever had the good fortune to meet and when they gave me the official Buckler's tour I could see why: that view for starters. Plonked directly on the high southern bank of the Crocodile River, Buckler's lush lawn (and most of the beds in its thatched, chalet-style rooms) gaze out upon a vast, sloping section of the Kruger National Park: "The Kruger is our back garden," is Cheryl's well-founded boast. It's the sort of view - perfectly angled and complete with natural water-hole - about which pricy private lodges physically inside the Kruger National Park can only dream. "A family of lions lives over there," OJ nods nonchalantly, pouring me an icy cider as we scout for hippos, all wisely buried ear-deep in mud on a smoking hot November afternoon." And the eles are forever scratching their backs against the pool wall," he tuts, raising a jocular eyebrow. With each idiosyncratic, uncluttered, naturally wood-furnished dwelling arranged around the garden, pool and bush oasis, Buckler's is a half B&B, half self-catering affair. Saying that, guests of the latter often poke sheepish sleepy heads into the breezy outside dining areas when aromas of coffee and croissants sneak through those generous windows. Similarly, OJ will happily give B&Bers a hand with a braai if a day in the park works up an appetite for flame-grilled impala fillet.

Rooms: 6: 3 standard rooms with queens, twins or singles with en/s or private bathrooms with bath/shower; 3 self-catering units: 1, 2 or 3 bedroom queens, twins or singles with en-suite bathrooms, some with outside showers, all bedrooms air-conditioned.
Price: R485 per person sharing B&B (kitchenettes in all B&B rooms). R485 pp sharing in self-catering chalets (serviced daily).
Meals: Full breakfast included for B&B guests.
Directions: 11.5km outside Komatipoort. From N4 take Komatipoort turn, also signed to Crocodile Bridge Gate. Thro town on R571 & continue 6km until wide dirt road on L signed Buckler's Africa. Drive 3.5km, following signs.

Entry Number: 256   Map Number: 1

Trees Too

Sue and Martyn Steele

Komatipoort
Tel: 013-793-8262 Fax: 086-688-0177
Email: info@treestoo.com Web: www.treestoo.com

Originally from Blighty and the rains of Manchester, Martyn and Sue have adapted well to the B&B malarkey in lush, sub-tropical Komatipoort. Seven years ago, this "wildlife mad" couple wanted to be near animals and they'd be hard pressed to get much closer. A short drive from Kruger National Park, Trees Too is ideal for budgets that don't quite stretch to top-end lodges inside the park itself. Relaxed, friendly and informal, its rooms surrounding a kidney-shaped pool draped with languid palms and crawling bougainvillaea; Trees Too's atmosphere is more tropical beach than arid savannah. It's unsurprising really, when you consider that Maputo, Mozambique's capital on the Indian Ocean coast, is just one hour away. After a dusty day's game drive, grab a cool sundowner from the bar and submerge yourself in cooling water before sitting down at the friendly poolside restaurant. I found myself happily swapping game-spotting stories with other diners while tucking into topical croc pâté and kudu stew! With a storm brewing it was only a quick skip to bed - terracotta flooring, a soaring thatched roof and comfortable, air-conditioning thankfully keep things cool in the forty degree heat of summer. If you manage to tear yourself from the pool and badminton court and tire of SA's biggest game park, then your hosts have plenty of ideas up their sleeves: elephant-back safaris anyone, or perhaps even a trip to a Mozambique beach or the mountains of Swaziland?

Rooms: 8: 3 doubles, with en/s shower; 2 triple rooms with a double plus 1 single, with en/s bath and shower; 1 twin, with en/s bath/shower; 2 family rooms (one sleeping 4 and one sleeping 6, 1 with 4-poster bed), 1 with shower and 1 with bath/shower.
Price: R300 - R420 pp sharing.
Meals: Breakfast is a cold buffet with cheeses, meats and cereals, plus a full English. A range of delicious dinners available at poolside restaurant.
Directions: Take the N4 from Jo'Burg. On reaching Komatipoort, turn left at the R571 into Rissik St, go 4km through 2 stop signs then right into Gilfillan St. Take 1st R into Furley St. Trees Too is No.11 on L.

Map Number: 17

Notten's Bush Camp

The Nottens
Sabi Sand Game Reserve, Hazyview
Tel: 013-735-5105 Fax: 013-735-5970
Email: nottens@iafrica.com Web: www.nottens.com
Cell: 082-414-2711

I want my enthusiasm for this place to hijack your curiosity, my words to infiltrate your subconscious and somehow or other to get you to sleepwalk to Notten's. Few camps are family run and it's the kind of place GG loves to be affiliated with. Just ask the regulars who return here year upon year (I expect they'll be a bit miffed I'm singing its praises so publicly). Although Notten's is jealously protected by its stalwart patrons who downplay the lodge as an earthy-sounding 'bush camp', comfort is certainly not in short supply. The chalets, with their gaping doors, white linen, dark woods and private decking, sit within a shaded line of trees overlooking a pastured impala oasis. This territory is known for its game, particularly leopards and rhino. Animals can wander into camp unhindered by fences. If you are skeptical have a close look at the elongated lap pool where there's a paw-print from a visiting lion that recognised a wet-cement celebrity opportunity when it saw one. Nights are especially wonderful at Notten's. Returning from a G&T bush sundowner, I thought the distant camp looked like an AGM for lazy fireflies, an illusion created by hanging paraffin lamps. While ceiling fans rotate and showers run hot – there is minimal electricity for such necessities - the paraffin lamps encouraged we happy campers one step nearer to a state of nature. I found the Notten's 'feel' addictive; camaraderie flourished and apprehensions melted. Why don't more camps operate like this?

Rooms: 8: 2 family units with 1 king and 2 singles. 6 doubles, all with en-suite bathrooms with baths and indoor and outdoor showers.
Price: R2,950 - R3,350 pp sharing. Includes game drives, bush walks and all meals.
Meals: All included. Full breakfast, lunch, afternoon tea, bush sundowners and dinner.
Directions: From Hazyview, take R536 towards Paul Kruger Gate & Skukuza. After 37km see Notten's sign, L onto dirt road. After 7km reach Sabi Sand Reserve Shaws Gate. Entrance fee R110 per vehicle + R20 per person. Follow Notten's signs.

Idube Private Game Reserve

Sally Kernick
Sabi Sand Game Reserve
Tel: 011-431-1120 Fax: 011-431-3597
Email: info@idube.com Web: www.idube.com
Cell: 083-457-1648 (weekends)

There are few establishments where the staff seem to have as much fun working together as at Idube. Be they guides, trackers, managers or chefs, the Idube crew exude a delightful sense of goodwill to each other and to all mankind. And it's not difficult to see why. Warthogs and friendly nyalas roam through the camp, elephants pass nearby, squirrels frolic about the grass as if they've hopped straight out of a Disney movie; there is space and greenery, beauty and beast. The land was bought in 1983 by Louis and Marilyn Marais and Louis sensibly built the swimming pool before designing and constructing the rest of the camp himself. Guests sleep in chalets dotted around the sloping grounds, while the thatched seating and dining areas look out over the Sabi Sand Game Reserve. A rope bridge over the river bed takes you to a hide where you can admire the Shadulu dam and its regulars without being admired yourself. Two game drives per day plus guided walks give you the chance to see what's happening elsewhere in the reserve and tracker Titus amazed us with his ability to read bent grasses and droppings. We took time out for sundowners by a dam, accompanied by a bull elephant and a bull hippo. There was much posturing and manliness, not least from me, before a return to camp for dinner (which was excellent!) and conviviality under the stars. *A vast range of activities available - hot-air ballooning, microlighting and village tours to name a few - please ask lodge for details.*

Rooms: 12: 2 kings and 8 twins all with en/s bathrooms and both indoor and outdoor shower; 2 Makubela executive suites with mini bar, own plunge pool and area for private dining
Price: R3,220 - R4,730 pp sharing. Single supplement +35%. Includes meals, game drives and bush walks. Children 8 - 12 years: R2,680 - R4,180.
Meals: All 3 meals plus morning and evening drives and a guided walk included. Drinks and transfers extra.
Directions: 34.4km from Hazyview along R536 towards Kruger Gate. Follow signs off to the left. 19.5km along a dirt road.

Map Number: 17

Entry Number: 259

Rhino Walking Safaris - Plains Camp

Nikki and Gerrit Meyer (Managers)
Rhino Walking Safaris, Kruger National Park, Skukuza
Tel: 011-467-1886 Fax: 011-467-4758
Email: info@rws.co.za Web: www.isibindiafrica.co.za
Cell: 083-631-4956

This is where I fell for Africa: sitting outside my tent in the Kruger, sipping G&T (for the anti-malaria quinine, you understand) and watching game serenely traverse the Timbitene Plain. This is the only private lodge where you can walk in pristine wilderness - nothing short of a privilege. Here the refined, pioneer tents have dark wood furniture with brass hinges and leather straps, bathrooms with copper taps protruding from tree stumps and the largest, softest towels. During the day, you can doze on the chocolate-leather sofa or sip highball cocktails in the plunge pool. Pith helmets, surveying tools, maps and a gramophone add to the bygone feel. Walking on rhino footpaths, the trails let you soak up both the scale and detail of the bush. There's no mad rush to tick off half-glimpsed Big Five. This is all about the quality of the sightings. That said, we encountered glowering buffalo, rampant rhino, lionesses on a hunt and had a pulse-quickening showdown with a bull elephant that I'll dine out on for ages. Afterwards we sent the sun down the sky and, wrapped in rugs, headed toward gas-lamp beacons for a never-ending feast. A safari fantasy come true.

Rooms: 4: all twin-bed African-explorer style tents, each with en-suite loo, shower and overhead fan. Tree house sleep-out option also available.
Price: R3,200 – R3,390. Ask about 3-, 4- or 5-night packages and single supplement.
Meals: All meals, soft drinks, house wines and beer, safari activities (primarily walking) and optional sleep-outs included.
Directions: From the Paul Kruger Gate follow signs to Skukuza Rest Camp & Rhino Walking Safaris. Drive past Skukuza on H1-2 towards Tshokwane and Satara. Cross Sabie and Sand rivers and after second turning to Maroela Loop, turn left signed Rhino Walking Safaris. Meet at Rhino Post Safari Lodge.

Rhino Post Safari Lodge

Nikki and Gerrit Meyer (Managers)

Kruger National Park, Skukuza,
Tel: 011-467-1886 Fax: 011-467-4758
Email: info@rws.co.za Web: www.isibindiafrica.co.za
Cell: 083-631-4956

After 6 hours' drive from Jo'burg it was with a mixture of relief and anticipation that we rolled the last few kilometres through the Kruger Park to Rhino Post Safari Lodge. On arrival our bags were magically transferred to our lovely, luxurious, wood-framed chalet with its big glass windows and deck overlooking a dry river bed (or should I say animal motorway?). Although the chalets have phones and electricity, it still feels as rustic and as open to nature as is safely possible. The camp is not fenced so animals are able to walk through the lodge area (you will be escorted back and forth along the boardwalks after dark). So… first an outdoor shower, then tea up at the lodge, on a deck overlooking a frequently-used waterhole; and then straight out in search of game and adventure. Our thanks to Bernard, our guide and driver, for some wonderful experiences. I don't know if we were lucky or not, but 16 rhino on our first night didn't seem bad! We also saw two prides of lion fighting over a giraffe carcass, with scores of vultures in the trees and a large pack of hyenas watching the action for scavenging opportunities. This sunlit tableau is etched on my memory and it was a sighting to brag about that evening over fireside drinks. All the meals at Rhino Post are exceptional and it does not take long to get into the new schedule of early starts, late breakfasts, siestas, late-afternoon game drives… and finally dinner. It was a proper wrench to leave when the time came.

Rooms: 16: 2 double and 6 twin chalets. All with ensuite bathrooms, deep free-standing baths, outside showers, overhead fans, mini bar, telephone, safe and hairdryer.
Price: R2,650 - R3,190 pp sharing. Ask about 3-, 4- or 5-night packages and winter rates.
Meals: All meals and safari activities included.
Directions: From the Paul Kruger Gate follow signs to Skukuza Rest Camp & Rhino Walking Safaris. Drive past Skukuza on H1-2 towards Tshokwane and Satara. Cross Sabie and Sand rivers and after second turning to Maroela Loop, turn left signed Rhino Walking Safaris.

Map Number: 17   Entry Number: 261

Iketla Lodge

Albert and Hennielene Botha
off R555, Ohrigstad
Tel: 013-238-8900 Fax: 086-514-5288
Email: relax@iketla.com Web: www.iketla.com

'Be relaxed... be peaceful' is Iketla's poetic English translation from the local Sotho dialect. Appropriately named, as it turns out. Surrounded on all sides by hills and rocky outcrops, Albert and Hennielene greeted me in the shebeen, where the late afternoon sun was gushing through the open sides, flooding the thatched, tiled dining area. For those that don't know, a shebeen is a drinking den and it's to this magnet that guests began to flock as they returned, brimming with exhilaration, from the day's adventures. Some had been exploring the Panorama Route, others had been walking guided trails through Iketla's 540 hectares of wilderness, inspecting all creatures great and small, and learning about the impressive range of birdlife and traditional uses of indigenous plants. They regaled us with their new-found knowledge and enthusiasm, with Albert, a bushman at heart, chipping in with many jewels of profounder expertise. A faint drumbeat interrupted the banter to signal supper, though my acute senses had already picked up the aroma of something sensational in the air... ostrich strips in a sherry sauce as it turned out. At daybreak I inspected my chalet, similar in style to the main lodge with rugged stone walls, a thatched roof and a verandah outside sliding glass doors. There I read my book and rested my bones, listening to the morning wildlife bring this African wilderness alive.

Rooms: 8 chalets: 3 doubles and 4 twins, 1 honeymoon suite, all with en-suite showers and outside showers.
Price: R1,040 – R1,140 pppn. Singles R1,350 – R1,450.
Meals: Full breakfast and dinner included.
Directions: From N4 turn off at Belfast and follow R540 through Dullstroom to Lydenburg. Follow R36 through Lydenburg (also known as Mashishing) to Ohrigstad. 4km past Ohrigstad turn left onto R555. Sign to Iketla 6km further on right.

Swaziland

Wide Horizons

Rose Roques
Rosecraft Farm, Egebeni/Malkerns
Tel: +268-250-53915
Email: roseroques@googlemail.com
Cell: +268-7604-1373

Just the drive to Wide Horizons is an adventure in itself and a great way to see the beauty
Swaziland. Down the hill and through the stream, the road all of sudden turned purple. It was
though the jacaranda trees somehow knew I was coming as the purple leaf-confetti swirled aroun
my car. And the fairy tale didn't stop there. Pulling up to the gorgeous Alice in Wonderland-sty
thatched house I was convinced a crazy white rabbit was going to come running out. Thankfully
was greeted by the much saner and more tranquil Rose, who has lived on the farm for the bette
part of 38 years. As well as overseeing the farm and running the B&B, she also runs Rosecraft,
hand-weaving workshop that not only produces magnificent blankets, scarves, curtains and muc
more, but also provides much-needed employment to the local community. Guests a
encouraged to have a look around and watch the ladies working the traditional looms and spinnir
wheels. After a roam around the garden with its spring that runs through and into the natural ro
swimming pool (no chemicals here), we headed down to the ever-popular luxury tent. Sitting o
the Makungutsha Mountain and overlooking the Lebombo Mountains the panoramic views ov
this vast space make the drive worth the effort on their own. You should definitely take a walk alor
the sculpture trail. Not only is this a wonderful way to experience the natural beauty of th
landscape and those jaw-dropping views, but you can also enjoy the fruit of the labours of loc
sculptors as you go. There is nothing about Wide Horizons I would not recommend.

Rooms: 2: B&B in the house: 1 unit with 2 double
rooms, both en-suite shower. Can sleep 6 (4 adults
+ 2 kids); 1 luxury safari tent (sleeps 2), en-s
bathroom & separate kitchen for self-catering.
Price: B&B in house or tent R360 pp; self-catering i
luxury tent only R300.
Meals: Breakfast included for B&B guests. Dinner in
house extra and on request.
Directions: From Mbabne head down Malagwane
Hill. On bottom turn L onto MR103. Past
Sundowners Backpackers and take 1st R. Follow sigr
for Rosecraft. Email for more detailed directions.

Limpopo Province

Pezulu Tree House Game Lodge

Claude and Lydia Huberty

Guernsey, Hoedspruit
Tel: 015-793-2724 Fax: 015-793-2253
Email: pezlodge@mweb.co.za Web: www.pezulu.co.za
Cell: 083-294-7831

The sorry victim of a treehouse-free childhood, I was intrigued by the concept of Pezulu - eig
different reed-and-thatch constructions spread among the trees surrounding the central buildin
itself entwined around a large marula tree. They are all hidden from view behind branch and lea
Many have bits of tree growing up through the floor to provide the most natural of towel rai
chairs and loo paper holders. Most 'houses' are named after the trees in which they sit: 'Fals
Thorn' has a magnificent shower with views across Thornybush Reserve – be prepared fo
inquisitive giraffe. 'Huilboerboom' is a honeymoon suite set five metres above ground (privac
even from the giraffe); while 'Dream Tree House' is the ultimate in canopy living, luxurious
expansive with a king bed that wheels outside so you can sleep within the stars. But it's brand ne
'Mountain View', stretching a whopping seven metres up and affording panoramic eyefuls of th
Drakensberg Mountains, that is the real king of the skies. Hearty dining takes place in the bom
where I chatted to the Hubertys about their Luxembourg origins. Pezulu is situated in th
Guernsey Conservancy on the edge of the Kruger Park. There are no predators, only plain
game, so you and the buck can wander around the property in relative safety. The usual mornin
and afternoon game drives, full day Kruger trips, visits to rehabilitation centres and other activitie
are easily arranged... assuming you can be persuaded down from the trees.

Rooms: 8: 3 family units (1 double and twins) and 4
doubles (2 standard and 3 luxury), variously with
outside shower, and/or bath.
Price: R850 - R1,290 pp sharing, inclusive of all
meals. Singles R1,095. Children under 12 years:
R495. Game drives and other activities optional extra
Meals: Includes full English breakfast, high tea and 3-
course dinner in the boma.
Directions: Ask when booking.

Sunset Game Lodge

Doris Paul & Juergen Oehl

Guernsey Private Nature Reserve, Hoedspruit
Fax: 086-2752317
Email: info@sunsetgamelodge.co.za Web: www.sunsetgamelodge.co.za
Cell: 082-374-1523

The first thing I noticed as I parked my car at Sunset Game Lodge was the sign saying: 'Beware of the wild animals'. I like signs like that. They put me in a good mood. And I can honestly say that the smile didn't leave my face until the end of my stay. Doris, Juergen and Jacky greeted me with more smiles, much-needed refreshing liquids and a cold cloth for my dusty face. The lodge – well, it is more a home than a lodge – with its high ceilings, walls adorned with spectacular wildlife photography and its open-plan kitchen, lounge and dining room, is an involving sort of place, particularly around meal times when guests get together to chat. The house leads out to the pool, shaded by steepling palms, and just when I thought I had seen it all (including a beautiful boma and even a sauna) Doris insisted I hadn't yet seen the best part. And she was completely correct. Perched high on the roof is a viewpoint like no other. With bags of space, sofas, dining tables and irresistible hammocks you'll battle to tear yourself away. I didn't even try, leaping straight into a hammock, whereupon I fell into a contemplative, dreamy, silent communion with the outstretched Guernsey Nature Reserve, my fenceless garden, and watched the ball of fire set behind the Drakensberg. Not much came to mind. No need for any thinking....

Rooms: 6: 2 king both with en-suite bath and shower; 2 twin both with en-suite shower; 2 double both en-s, 1 with bath and shower and 1 shower.
Price: Until 30th September 2012: R799 pp sharing B&B, singles R895 B&B. From 1st October 2012 until 30th September 2013: R880 pp sharing B&B, singles R985 B&B.
Meals: Full breakfast included. Dinner and lunch on request.
Directions: From Nelspruit take the R40 Acornhoek. 5km pass Acornhoek turn R onto Orpen Road. After 2km take L at Gurnsey sign and go through control gate. A Further 8.6km turn R to Gurnsey Private Nature Reserve. S 24 Degrees 31.8274 E 31 Degrees 7.0414.

Map Number: 17

Entry Number: 265

Madi a Thavha Mountain Lodge

Marcelle Bosch and Aart Van Soest

Soutpansberg, Louis Trichardt
Tel: 083-342-4162 or 072-172-2830 Fax: 086-648-2924
Email: info@madiathavha.com Web: www.madiathavha.com

At Madi a Thava's dynamic lodge, with its rare and oh-so-commendably integrated approach tourism, inspirational people are doing inspirational things. Locals from the Venda and Tsong communities are proudly on the front lines, all the while being encouraged to learn new skills an business ventures. The ripples from this carry further. Marcelle and Aart have helped establis dozens of workshops within the rural villages, which you can visit to see how the pottery, bead carvings, jewellery, statues, clothes and bags are made. It's all for sale in the lodge shop, wi proceeds rolling back into the pockets of the craftspeople. The lodge has the slogan 'a colour experience' and this is underlined in the rooms. Vibrant pastel-coloured pieces enliven the whi walls, including throw rugs, locally-carved mirror frames and Venda-styled cement floors coloure with an oxide powder. You can trek off up towards the impressive cliff-faced horizon and whe you return, revive in the hourglass-shaped pool beside the clay-coloured lapa, the ideal spot fo braaiing. Although I think chef Percy's meals will probably surpass your barbecuing ability. And, you're lucky, he'll sing. His trembling bass voice will make you put down your knives and forks, while his food will make you pick them up again! Kids will have fun, baking bread, braaiing, playin music, making textiles and learning from the locals. Madi a Thava is educational, pride-promotin fun and has a heart that's definitely in the right place. *Fair Trade certified.*

Rooms: 7 units. 3 twin rooms with en-suite shower
1 wooden cottage (2 twin rooms & shared
bathroom); 1 family house (1 twin with en-suite
shower & 1 twin with en-suite bath); 2 main lodge
rooms (1 queen and 1 twin both with en-s shower).
Price: R505 pp sharing B&B; R425 pp sharing self-
catering. Singles plus R100.
Meals: Full breakfast available. Lunch, 3-course
dinners, picnic baskets or packed lunches by
arrangement.
Directions: From Polokwane, take N1 to Louis
Trichardt (Makhado). At first four way stop, turn left
R522 to Vivo. After 8.5km, turn right at Madi A Thav
sign and follow for 2.5km.

Mopane Bush Lodge

Paul and Rosemary Hatty and Claudina Fernhout

Mapungubwe, Off the R572, Musina
Tel: 083-633-0765 or 015-534-7906 Fax: 015-534-7906 or 086-610-3410
Email: mopanebushlodge@limpopo.co.za
Web: www.mopanebushlodge.co.za Cell: 083-633-0765

This is a fascinating, under-visited frontier of South Africa and both these facts make this a great destination. Hidden in 6,000 hectares of semi-desert mopane scrub, the lodge itself is an oasis where fine food (either taken in the huge, open-plan dining area or outside in the boma round a fire), a swimming pool and intimate cottage-rooms provide all the trappings of sophistication and luxury you could wish for. The game reserve has plains game only, so walking about is safe and I recommend taking the track to a waterhole to birdwatch before dinner. But during the day I loved my two visits to the Mapungubwe National Park, five minutes' down the road. First an early-morning visit to the archaeological site of South Africa's earlier version of Great Zimbabwe. This ancient civilisation took place on and around a gigantic rock in dramatic scenery interspersed with giant other-worldly baobab trees. And then a second visit took us to the lush confluence of the Limpopo and Shashe rivers and to a heavenly sundowner spot where you can look out onto Zimbabwe and Botswana. As for wildlife they have it all up here ('big five' etc), but the birdlife takes the *palme d'or*. You'll find some real rarities, including the broad-billed roller and the collared palm thrush. Another big draw at Mopane is the nearby Predator Research Facility. I have been round and round South Africa, but this area was a real find and I heartily recommend both the lodge and its environment. *Mountain bikes are available for guests to use.*

Rooms: 8 rondavels: all can be double or twin, with en-suite indoor and outdoor showers.
Price: R1,350 - R1,670 pp. R250 to R735 per person for off-site tours.
Meals: All meals and all activities on Mopane's own private nature reserve are included.
Directions: Take N1 from Joburg to Polokwane (Pietersberg). Follow signs thro town for R521 to Dendron. Travel 140km on this road to Alldays, then R to Pontdrif. Travel for 46km & turn R onto R572 to Musina & Mapungubwe. Mopane Bush Lodge is 29km along this road, just past cell phone tower on R. Map on web.

Map Number: 16

Entry Number: 267

Botswana

Tuli Safari Lodge

Wendy du Toit and Vikki Threlfall

Northern Tuli Game Reserve
Tel: +267-264-5343/4 Fax: +267-264-5344
Email: info@tulilodge.com Web: www.tulilodge.com
Cell: +27 (0) 83-77-59655

I was welcomed into Tuli Safari Lodge with a rhythmical, scuffed, stamped and harmonised *a capella* song from the staff choir, a smiley and chatty crew whose strong and obviously genuine spirit of hospitality makes it hard to stray into low spirits here. That said, it's also noticeably quiet, the peace only disturbed by birdsong and wind-rustled leaves; the whole soundtrack was thoroughly conducive to an afternoon kip I have to say! All of the rooms have good beds, newly-renovated bathrooms, dark wood frames, light walls and thatch ceilings. The large 'Guinea Fowl' suite looks out upon the lodge's green lawns where the nonchalant bush buck graze beneath the fever and rain trees. The 17,000 hectares transform seasonally here, from lush wild-flower grasslands during the rainy season, to an apocalyptic desert during the dry. I loved the isolation, especially during the safari walk. You can truly appreciate it beside the Limpopo River at the Nokalodi bush camp - no electricity here, just paraffin, gas and fire. Really active types can venture out on the four-day 'Wildguides' safari course. Or sleep in the night hides, or visit local communities, or the local orphanage - there's plenty to keep you busy. Personally, I stayed close to the bar beneath the nyala berry tree, drawn to the friendly camaraderie of the other guests. While at dinner, just after the choir gave another performance, we all agreed – this is a cultural, visual and culinary experience well worth returning to.

Rooms: 8 suites: 4 'Four Ele' suites: 2 family units with shower over bath & 2 dbles with shower en-suites; 4 'Five Ele' suites: 2 twins & 2 doubles, all en-s sh'r & bath.
Price: Dinner, bed & breakfast rates R975 - R1,985 pp sharing or rates fully inclusive of all meals & 2 guided game activities a day from R1,380 - R2,410. Self-catering bush camps (located elsewhere on the reserve) from R335, camping from R95. Ask re child, single & group rates.
Meals: All meals included at lodge. Drinks are extra.
Directions: It is safe to leave cars at Pont Drift border & arrange transfer with Tuli to save on vehicle fees. From Jo'burg, follow N1 to Polokwane, L at R521 & drive 210km to Pont Drift Border. If driving thro, follow signs after border - 8km from Pont Drift.

Map Number: 16

Entry Number: 268

Index

Index by town name

For our rural properties, we have listed the nearest town

BOTSWANA

Northern Tuli Game Reserve 268

LESOTHO

Malealea 233

SOUTH AFRICA

Addo 168-170
Amakhala Game Reserve 173
Beaufort West 161-162
Bedford 181
Bergville 220-221
Between Knysna and
    Plettenberg Bay 132
Between Ladismith and
    Calitzdorp 155
Between Oudtshoorn and
    De Rust 148-149
Bot River 93-94
Britannia Bay 48
Caledon 92
Calitzdorp 152
Calitzdorp 154

    CAPE TOWN
    Bakoven 19
    Bishopscourt 41
    Camps Bay 17-18
    Cape Town 20
    Clovelly 6
    Constantia 36-39
    Constantia Hills 40
    De Waterkant 21
    Fish Hoek 4-5
    Green Point 22
    Higgovale 30
    Hout Bay 9-16
    Kenilworth 34-35

    Milnerton 31
    Newlands 33
    Noordhoek 8
    Oranjezicht 24-27
    Rondebosch 32
    St James 7
    Simon's Town 1-3
    Tamboerskloof 28-29
    V&A Waterfront Marina 23

Champagne Valley 223
Chintsa East 177
Citrusdal 50-51
Clanwilliam 53-55
Colesberg 234
Cradock 182
Cullinan 244
Darling 42
De Kelders 102-104
De Kelders 104
Dundee 216-217
Durban 193-195
East London 176
Elandslaagte 219
Elandslaagte/Ladysmith 218
Eshowe 201-203
Estcourt 224
Ficksburg/Fouriesburg 230
Franschhoek 76-80
Franschhoek/Groot Drakenstein 75
Gansbaai 105-106
George 119-120
Graaff-Reinet 183-187
Harrismith 229
Hazyview 254
Hazyview 258
Hazyview 252
Heidelberg 114
Hekpoort 243

Hermanus	98-101		Oudtshoorn	150-151
Hermon	58		Oudtshoorn	153
Hluhluwe	208-209		Oyster Bay	163
Hoedspruit	264-265		Paarl	65
Hopefield	43		Paarl	67
Howick	226-227		Paternoster	44-46
Isandlwana	215		Piet Retief	214
iSimangaliso Wetland Park	207		Piketberg	49
iSimangaliso Wetland Park	210		Plettenberg Bay	133-143
Kimberley	235-236		Pongola	213
Klapmuts	82		Port Alfred	174-175
Klapmuts	74		Port Elizabeth	165-167
Klein Drakenstein, Paarl	66		Port St Johns	179
Kleinmond	97		Prince Albert	158-160
Knysna	127-131		Pringle Bay	95-96
Kokstad	188		Qhorha Mouth	178
Komatipoort	256-257		Rawsonville/Breedekloof	68
Kosi Bay/KwaNgwanase	211		Riebeek West	59
Koue Bokkeveld	52		Riversdale	115
Kruger National Park	255		Riversdale/Stil Bay	117
Ladismith	156		Robertson	70-73
Leisure Bay	190		Robertson/Montagu	69
Little Brak River	118		Sabi Sand Game Reserve	259
Louis Trichardt	266		Sabie-Hazyview	253
Maclear	180		Salt Rock	199
Madikwe Game Reserve	248-250		Shaka's Rock	197
McGregor	91		Sidbury	172
Melrose/Johannesburg	242		Skukuza	260-261
Mid Illovo	192		Smithfield	232
Mkuze	212		Somerset West	88-90
Montagu	157		Somerset West/Stellenbosch	87
Monzi	205		Southbroom	189
Mooi River	225		Soweto	245-247
Mtunzini	200		Springbok	238
Musina	267		St Helena Bay	47
Nelspruit	251		St Lucia	206
Nieuwoudtville	237		St. Francis Bay	164
Ntambanana	204		Stellenbosch	83-86
Ohrigstad	262		Stellenbosch	81

Still Bay	116
Swellendam	107-111
The Crags	144-146
The De Hoop Nature Reserve	112
Trafalgar	191
Tsitsikamma	147
Tulbagh	56-57
Umdloti Beach	196
Umhlali	198
Underberg	228
Upington	239-241
Weenen	222
Wellington	61-64
Wilderness	122-126
Wilderness Heights	121
Witsand	113
Wolseley	60
Zastron	231

SWAZILAND

Egebeni/Malkerns	263

Index

Index by house name

BOTSWANA

Tuli Safari Lodge	268

LESOTHO

Malealea Lodge and Pony Trek Centre	233

SOUTH AFRICA

191 Nirvana	128
96 Beach Road	97
A Farm Story Country House	117
A la Fugue	240
A Riviera Garden B&B	239
Abalone House	46
Abalone Place	194
Abbotsbury	184
Abloom	24
Acorn House	2
African Ambience	20
African Violet	
Akademie Street Boutique Hotel and Guesthouses	7
Albatross House	
Alta Bay	3
Ambiente Guest House	
Amblewood Guest House	
Andries StockenstrÜm Guest House	18
Anlin Beach House	14
Antrim Villa	2
Aquavit Guest House	13
Ardmore Farm	22
Artists Colony B&B	23
Arum Lily Log Cabins	6
Au Pear	3
Augusta de Mist	11
Barnacle B&B	9
Bartholomeus Klip Farmhouse	5
Barton Villas	9
Bayview Guesthouse	2
Beacon Lodge	13
Beaumont Wine Estate	9
Bee Eaters Farm	25
Belair	6
Birds of Paradise B&B	20
Bitou River Lodge	13
Blaauwheim Guest House	8
Bloomestate	10
Blue Jay Lodge	25
Blue Yonder	
Blues Breaker Cottage	4
Boesmanskop	15
Bosavern	13
Bosch Luys Kloof Private Nature Reserve	15
Botlierskop Private Game Reserve	11
Boutique@10	1
Bovlei Valley Retreat	6
Brenton Beach House	13
Browns Manor	24

Buckler's Africa	256
Bushwillow	209
Camberley Cottage	85
Cape Witogie	39
Cathbert Country Inn	76
Cavers Country Guest House	181
Chase Guest House	201
Cheviot Place Guest House	22
Christiana Lodge	142
Clementine Cottage	77
Cliff Lodge	102
Collins House	158
Comfort House	197
Cornerway House	134
Cottage on the Hill	
Guest House	164
Crawford's Beach Lodge	
and Cabins	177
Cypress Cottages	187
Dakalo B&B	246
Darling Lodge	42
De Doornkraal Historic	
Country House	115
De Hoop Collection	112
De Langenhof Guest House	59
De Waterkant Cottages	21
De Zeekoe Guest Farm	150
Dendron	36
Die Ou Stal	231
Die Tuishuise	182
Dreamhouse	11
Dusk to Dawn	214
Echo Terrace	5
Eensgevonden Vineyard	
Cottages	68
Eenuurkop	111
Enjo Nature Farm	55
Esiweni Lodge	218
Fairlight Beach House	196
Farm 215 Nature Retreat and	
Fynbos Reserve	106
Feathers Inn	49
Fort D'Acre Reserve	174
Fort Vic	2
Fraai Uitzicht 1798	69
Franshoek Mountain Lodge	230
Frogg's Leap	9
Fynbos Ridge Country House	
and Cottages	133
Gap Lodge	29
Ghost Mountain Inn	212
Grootvadersbosch Farm	114
Gwahumbe Reserve Game	
& Spa	192
Hartford Cottage	100
Hartford House	225
Hermanus Lodge on the Green	99
Highlands Country House	35
Hluhluwe River Lodge and	
Adventures	208
Hopefield Country House	170
Hout Bay Hideaway	15
Idube Private Game Reserve	259
Idwala Game Lodge	172
Iketla Lodge	262
Inversanda Farm Cottages	227
Isandlwana Lodge	215
Isibindi Zulu Lodge	216
Jacana Guest Farm	86
Jaci s Lodges	250
Jan Harmsgat Country House	108
Kaapse Draai	38
Karoo View Cottages	160
Kashan Country House	243
Kersefontein	43
Klein Boschkloof Chalets	54
Klein Bosheuwel and	
Southdown	37
Klein Paradijs Country House	105
Kleintonteln	62
Ko-Ka Tsara	162
Kob Inn Beach Resort	178
Kosi Forest Lodge	211
Kuilfontein Stable Cottages	234
Langberg Guest Farm	235
Le Marais	13
Lekkerwijn	75
Lemoenfontein Game Lodge	161
Lemon Tree Lane B&B	166

Les Hauts de Montagu
  Guest Lodge | 157
Lézard Bleu Guest House | 25
Lily Pond Country Lodge | 145
Lindsay Loft | 193
Lodge on the Lake | 126
Loerie Hide | 176
Longfield | 87
Lukimbi Safari Lodge | 255
Lupus Den Country House | 168
Macadamia Lodge | 205
Madi a Thavha Mountain Lodge | 266
Majini | 40
Makakatana Bay Lodge | 207
Mallowdeen Gardens | 71
Malvern Manor | 119
MannaBay | 27
Mattanu Private Game Reserve | 236
Mawelawela Game and
  Fishing Lodge | 219
Melrose Place Guest Lodge | 242
Mitre's Edge | 82
Montusi Mountain Lodge | 221
Mooiplaas Guest House | 151
Moonglow Guest House | 3
Moontide Guest Lodge | 122
Mopane Bush Lodge | 267
Mosetlha Bush Camp and
  Eco Lodge | 248
Mount Ceder | 52
Mymering Guest House | 156
Nalson s View | 199
Naries Namakwa Retreat | 238
Natte Valleij | 74
Notten's Bush Camp | 258
Nthateng's B&B | 247
Ocean View House | 19
Olive Garden Country Lodge | 70
One On Hely | 200
Onse Rus Guesthouse | 159
Orange Grove Farm | 72
Oude Wellington Estate | 61
Oudekloof Guest House | 57
Oudrif | 53

Oyster Bay Lodge | 163
Oystercatcher Lodge | 47
Oystercatcher's Haven at
  Paternoster | 44
Packwood Country Estate | 132
Paddington's | 10
Palmiet Valley Estate | 66
Papkuilsfontein Guest Farm | 237
Paternoster Dunes Boutique
  Guest House and Spa | 45
Pembroke 403 | 23
Penwarn Country Lodge | 228
Petersfield Mountain Cottages | 51
Pezulu Tree House
  Game Lodge | 264
Piesang Valley Lodge | 141
Plumbago | 190
Plumbago Cottage | 83
Plumbago Guest House | 252
Plumtree Cottage | 78
Porcupine Pie Boutique Lodge | 121
Porcupine Ridge Guest House | 253
Red Stone Hills | 153
Redbourne Hilldrop | 26
Redford House | 146
Rhino Post Safari Lodge | 261
Rhino Walking Safaris -
  Plains Camp | 260
Ridgeback House | 67
RiverBend Lodge | 171
Riversong Farm | 116
Rodwell House | 7
Rolbaken Guest House and
  Nature Reserve | 149
Roodenburg House | 32
Rothman Manor | 107
Rouxwil Country House | 92
Schulphoek Seafront
  Guesthouse | 98
Sea Star Lodge | 104
Seaforth Farm | 198
Selkirk House | 101
Serendipity | 124
Seringa House | 89

Sewula Gorge Lodge	224
Sneezewood Farm	217
Southern Cross Beach House	138
Stocklands Farm	226
Sunbirds	189
Sunset Game Lodge	265
Tamodi Lodge and Stables	143
Tanagra Wine and Guest Farm	91
Thabile Lodge	148
That Place	144
The Admiralty Beach House	167
The Bamboo Guesthouse	129
The Beach House	175
The Beautiful South	
Guest House	81
The Bush House	249
The Dune Guest Lodge	123
The Elephant House	169
The Explorers Club, The Library	
and The Map Room	80
The Fernery Lodge and Chalets	147
The Garden Villa	120
The Gate House at Nabygelegen	
Private Cellar	63
The Grange Guest House	195
The Kings Place	16
The Mountain House	6
The Retreat at Groenfontein	154
The Stone Cottage	185
The Tarragon	12
The View	229
The Vintner's Loft	90
Thonga Beach Lodge	210
Thornleys Guest House	203
Three Trees at Spioenkop	220
Thula Thula Game Reserve	204
Thunzi Bush Lodge	165
Tierhoek Cottages	73
Trees Too	257
Umngazi River Bungalows	
& Spa	179
Vhavenda Hills Bed and	
Breakfast	245
Victoria House	34
Villa Afrikana Guest Suites	130
Villa Castollini	127
Villa Tarentaal	56
Vrede Manor	31
Waterfall Farm	50
Waterkloof Guesthouse	113
WedgeView Country House	
& Spa	84
Whalesong Lodge	103
Wheatlands	183
White Cottage	41
White Elephant Safari Lodge	
and Bush Camp	213
Wild Olive Guest House	96
Wilderness Manor	125
Willowdale Lodge and	
Truffle Farm	188
Woodbury Lodge	173
Woodcliffe Farm and Cottage	180
Yengele Paradise	191
Zingela Safaris	222

SWAZILAND

Wide Horizons	263

Index of activities

Gardens
Places with lovely gardens and owners who are enthusiastic gardeners.
1, 4, 5, 6, 7, 10, 11, 12, 13, 14, 15, 16, 18, 19, 20, 22, 24, 25, 30, 31, 32, 33, 34, 35, 36, 37, 38, 39, 40, 41, 42, 46, 48, 49, 51, 52, 54, 56, 57, 59, 62, 63, 64, 65, 66, 67, 68, 69, 70, 71, 72, 74, 75, 76, 77, 78, 79, 80, 83, 84, 85, 86, 87, 88, 90, 92, 94, 96, 98, 100, 105, 106, 107, 108, 109, 110, 111, 113, 114, 115, 116, 119, 120, 122, 124, 127, 128, 129, 130, 131, 132, 133, 134, 135, 136, 137, 139, 143, 145, 146, 147, 149, 150, 152, 153, 154, 155, 156, 157, 158, 159, 160, 164, 166, 167, 168, 169, 170, 171, 172, 174, 176, 179, 180, 181, 182, 183, 184, 185, 186, 187, 188, 189, 190, 191, 192, 193, 194, 196, 197, 198, 201, 202, 203, 204, 205, 209, 212, 213, 214, 220, 221, 222, 223, 225, 226, 229, 230, 232, 233, 238, 239, 240, 241, 243, 244, 246, 249, 251, 252, 253, 254, 256, 263, 267

Rock art
Sites found either on the property or guests can be shown/guided to nearby sites.
5, 7, 49, 50, 51, 52, 53, 54, 55, 114, 116, 118, 138, 149, 153, 154, 155, 156, 159, 160, 161, 180, 182, 187, 215, 216, 221, 223, 225, 228, 229, 230, 231, 233, 237, 255, 267, 268

Culture
Township visits can be organized by owners or cultural experiences (e.g. Zulu dancing) available on site.
3, 5, 7, 8, 9, 10, 11, 12, 14, 15, 16, 20, 21, 22, 24, 25, 26, 28, 29, 30, 31, 32, 34, 36, 37, 38, 39, 40, 41, 42, 61, 62, 65, 66, 69, 72, 75, 77, 81, 83, 87, 88, 91, 100, 102, 104, 107, 108, 109, 115, 117, 118, 122, 127, 129, 130, 131, 132, 133, 134, 136, 137, 138, 140, 143, 145, 146, 147, 150, 151, 156, 159, 161, 163, 166, 167, 169, 170, 171, 172, 174, 176, 177, 179, 182, 186, 187, 189, 191, 193, 194, 195, 196, 197, 198, 200, 201, 202, 203, 204, 205, 206, 207, 208, 209, 210, 211, 212, 213, 215, 216, 218, 219, 220, 221, 222, 223, 225, 227, 228, 230, 231, 233, 239, 243, 244, 245, 246, 247, 250, 251, 252, 253, 254, 255, 257, 259, 263, 264, 265, 266, 268

Wine-maker
Wine made on the property.
61, 62, 63, 64, 67, 68, 69, 72, 74, 75, 82, 86, 90, 91, 93, 94, 132, 144, 156

Good and original cuisine
7, 11, 13, 32, 35, 45, 46, 49, 53, 58, 61, 62, 63, 64, 66, 69, 70, 72, 75, 76, 83, 84, 88, 92, 96, 98, 105, 106, 108, 110, 115, 118, 121, 122, 124, 133,

134, 145, 147, 148, 152, 155, 156, 163, 165, 168, 170, 171, 172, 179, 181, 184, 186, 188, 190, 195, 204, 207, 208, 210, 211, 213, 214, 215, 216, 218, 220, 221, 225, 229, 230, 234, 237, 238, 240, 243, 244, 250, 251, 252, 257, 258, 259, 261, 264, 266, 267

Horse-riding
Available on site.
8, 9, 10, 11, 13, 14, 20, 22, 40, 42, 43, 44, 45, 46, 47, 49, 51, 52, 54, 61, 62, 63, 67, 68, 69, 70, 75, 77, 87, 91, 93, 100, 106, 107, 108, 109, 117, 118, 121, 128, 129, 132, 139, 142, 146, 148, 150, 151, 153, 156, 163, 169, 171, 174, 177, 181, 187, 194, 195, 197, 198, 199, 200, 203, 205, 206, 207, 208, 209, 212, 215, 218, 220, 221, 222, 223, 225, 227, 228, 229, 230, 233, 241, 251, 252, 253, 254, 257, 263, 265, 268

Boat Charter
Property owns boats or can organise charters.
1, 4, 5, 7, 8, 9, 10, 11, 12, 13, 14, 15, 16, 20, 22, 23, 26, 28, 29, 31, 34, 37, 40, 41, 44, 45, 47, 68, 69, 96, 98, 99, 100, 101, 102, 104, 105, 106, 109, 117, 118, 119, 121, 124, 125, 126, 127, 128, 129, 130, 131, 132, 133, 134, 135, 136, 137, 138, 139, 140, 141, 142, 143, 145, 146, 163, 164, 165, 166, 167, 171, 173, 174, 176, 177, 179, 188, 189, 190, 191, 193, 195, 196, 197, 198, 199, 200, 205, 206, 207, 208, 209, 210, 211, 212, 213, 223, 231, 239, 240, 241, 265

Canoeing
Canoes owned or organised by the property.
3, 4, 5, 7, 8, 11, 16, 20, 22, 26, 28, 31, 43, 44, 45, 46, 49, 52, 53, 54, 58, 60, 62, 66, 67, 68, 69, 70, 72, 91, 95, 96, 98, 99, 100, 101, 102, 104, 107, 108, 109, 116, 117, 118, 119, 121, 122, 124, 125, 126, 127, 128, 129, 130, 131, 132, 133, 134, 135, 136, 137, 138, 139, 140, 141, 142, 143, 145, 146, 147, 150, 151, 155, 164, 165, 167, 173, 174, 176, 178, 179, 182, 185, 188, 189, 190, 191, 193, 196, 197, 198, 200, 205, 206, 207, 208, 209, 210, 211, 212, 213, 222, 223, 228, 230, 231, 251, 252, 253, 254, 265

Historic house
These places are historic buildings
7, 21, 24, 31, 32, 34, 35, 43, 49, 54, 57, 61, 66, 68, 69, 72, 74, 75, 79, 93, 100, 107, 108, 109, 110, 112, 114, 115, 117, 146, 150, 154, 155, 157, 159, 161, 171, 181, 182, 183, 184, 185, 186, 187, 198, 213, 223, 225, 226, 229, 231, 232, 234, 235, 238, 249

History tours
Organised here (including battlefields).
5, 8, 9, 10, 14, 16, 20, 22, 28, 29, 31, 34, 37, 38, 41, 42, 49, 62, 65, 72, 77, 79, 81, 87, 90, 115, 117, 127, 131, 150, 151, 155, 156, 167, 170, 171, 172, 179, 181, 182, 186, 187, 195, 199, 201, 203, 204, 212, 214, 215, 216, 217, 218, 219, 220, 222, 223, 224, 225, 226, 227, 228, 229, 230, 231, 234, 243, 244, 245, 246, 247, 252, 267

Self-catering option available here.
1, 2, 4, 5, 6, 8, 10, 11, 12, 13, 15, 16, 19, 21, 22, 23, 28, 30, 31, 33, 36, 37, 39, 40, 41, 43, 45, 46, 47, 48, 49, 50, 51, 52, 54, 55, 56, 57, 58, 60, 61, 63, 64, 66, 68, 71, 72, 73, 74, 75, 76, 77, 78, 80, 82, 83, 85, 86, 87, 88, 89, 90, 91, 93, 94, 95, 100, 104, 111, 112, 114, 116, 117, 120, 123, 128, 131, 132, 133, 134, 140, 141, 143, 144, 146, 147, 149, 150, 151, 153, 156, 160, 162, 163, 164, 165, 166, 167, 174, 176, 177, 180, 181, 182, 183, 185, 190, 191, 192, 193, 194, 195, 196, 201, 202, 203, 205, 209, 213, 214, 215, 219, 222, 224, 226, 227, 228, 230, 231, 233, 235, 237, 238, 240, 244, 246, 256, 263, 266, 268

Bird-watching
Owners are enthusiasts.
1, 2, 4, 5, 6, 7, 8, 10, 11, 12, 14, 16, 18, 37, 39, 40, 42, 43, 44, 45, 46, 47, 48, 49, 51, 52, 53, 54, 55, 56, 57, 58, 61, 62, 63, 64, 65, 67, 68, 69, 70, 71, 72, 73, 74, 75, 76, 77, 78, 79, 80, 82, 83, 86, 88, 90, 91, 92, 93, 94, 96, 97, 98, 99, 100, 101, 102, 105, 106, 107, 108, 109, 110, 111, 112, 113, 114, 115, 116, 117, 118, 119, 120, 121, 122, 124, 125, 126, 129, 131, 132, 133, 134, 136, 137, 138, 139, 141, 143, 145, 146, 147, 148, 149, 150, 151, 152, 153, 154, 155, 156, 157, 159, 160, 161, 162, 163, 164, 165, 166, 168, 169, 170, 171, 172, 173, 174, 178, 179, 180, 181, 184, 185, 186, 187, 188, 189, 190, 191, 192, 194, 196, 197, 198, 199, 200, 201, 202, 203, 204, 205, 206, 207, 208, 209, 210, 211, 212, 213, 214, 215, 216, 218, 219, 220, 221, 222, 223, 224, 225, 226, 227, 228, 229, 230, 232, 234, 236, 237, 239, 240, 241, 243, 244, 248, 249, 250, 251, 252, 253, 254, 255, 256, 258, 259, 260, 262, 263, 264, 265, 266, 267, 268

Whale-watching
Available from the property or from so nearby that it makes little difference.
1, 2, 3, 4, 5, 6, 7, 9, 10, 11, 14, 15, 16, 19, 44, 45, 46, 47, 48, 95, 96, 97, 98, 99, 100, 102, 103, 104, 105, 112, 123, 134, 136, 137, 138, 140, 142, 147, 163, 164, 175, 177, 178, 179, 189, 190, 191, 196, 197, 199, 200, 206, 207, 210

Beach house
5, 44, 45, 47, 48, 95, 96, 97, 98, 100, 102, 103, 104, 123, 131, 138, 140, 163, 164, 175, 177, 179, 189, 191, 196, 210

White-water rafting
Can be arranged in-house.
5, 7, 29, 53, 96, 109, 115, 130, 142, 145, 163, 182, 222, 223, 228, 251, 264, 265

Fully child-friendly
Places where children will be particularly well looked-after.
4, 7, 11, 12, 13, 16, 25, 26, 37, 40, 41, 43, 51, 55, 57, 62, 70, 74, 75, 81, 82, 84, 95, 99, 100, 108, 111, 128, 133, 144, 150, 152, 153, 154, 160, 161, 169, 171, 173, 178, 179, 185, 187, 190, 192, 195, 196, 198, 201, 202, 203, 205, 206, 212, 214, 222, 223, 224, 227, 229, 230, 231, 232, 233, 235, 236, 239, 240, 242, 249, 250, 251, 255, 266, 267, 268

Fishing
Can be arranged.
1, 8, 9, 10, 14, 16, 20, 22, 28, 37, 39, 42, 43, 45, 46, 47, 48, 49, 52, 53, 62, 68, 69, 72, 77, 87, 91, 96, 98, 100, 101, 102, 103, 109, 116, 117, 122, 127, 128, 129, 131, 133, 135, 141, 143, 154, 155, 160, 162, 165, 166, 167, 176, 179, 180, 181, 188, 190, 191, 192, 195, 197, 199, 201, 203, 205, 207, 208, 209, 212, 213, 214, 216, 218, 221, 222, 223, 224, 227, 229, 230, 239, 251, 252, 253, 257, 263, 265